MIGRANT SITES

REENCOUNTERS WITH COLONIALISM: NEW PERSPECTIVES ON THE AMERICAS

Dartmouth College Series Editors
Marysa Navarro
Donald E. Pease
Ivy Schweitzer
Silvia Spitta

For the complete list of books that are available in this series, please see www.upne.com

DALIA KANDIYOTI
Migrant Sites: America, Place, and Diaspora Literatures

JONATHAN BEECHER FIELD
Errands into the Metropolis: New England Dissidents in Revolutionary London

MICHELLE BURNHAM
Folded Selves: Colonial New England Writing in the World System

JENNIFER L. FRENCH
Nature, Neo-Colonialism, and the Spanish American Writers

DAN MOOS
Outside America: Race, Ethnicity, and the Role of the American West in National Belonging

HERSHINI BHANA YOUNG
Haunting Capital: Memory, Text, and the Black Diasporic Body

JOHN R. EPERJESI
The Imperialist Imaginary: Visions of Asia and the Pacific in American Culture

JOHN J. KUCICH
Ghostly Communion: Cross-Cultural Spiritualism in Nineteenth-Century American Literature

RUTH MAYER
Artificial Africas: Colonial Images in the Times of Globalization

IRENE RAMALHO SANTOS
Atlantic Poets: Fernando Pessoa's Turn in Anglo-American Modernism

C. L. R. JAMES
Mariners, Renegades and Castaways: The Story of Herman Melville and the World We Live In, with an introduction by Donald E. Pease

RENÉE L. BERGLAND
The National Uncanny: Indian Ghosts and American Subjects

SUSANA ROTKER
The American Chronicles of José Martí: Journalism and Modernity in Spanish America

CARLTON SMITH
Coyote Kills John Wayne: Postmodernism and Contemporary Fictions of the Transcultural Frontier

CARLA GARDINA PESTANA AND SHARON V. SALINGER
Inequality in Early America

FRANCES R. APARICIO AND SUSANA CHÁVEZ-SILVERMAN, EDS.
Tropicalizations: Transcultural Representations of Latinidad

MICHELLE BURNHAM
Captivity and Sentiment: Cultural Exchange in American Literature, 1682–1861

DALIA KANDIYOTI

MIGRANT SITES

AMERICA, PLACE, AND DIASPORA LITERATURES

DARTMOUTH COLLEGE PRESS
HANOVER, NEW HAMPSHIRE

PUBLISHED BY
UNIVERSITY PRESS OF NEW ENGLAND
HANOVER AND LONDON

Dartmouth College Press
Published by University Press of New England,
One Court Street, Lebanon, NH 03766
www.upne.com

Printed in U.S.A.
5 4 3 2 1

Library of Congress Cataloging-in-Publication Data
Kandiyoti, Dalia.
Migrant sites : America, place, and diaspora literatures / Dalia Kandiyoti.
p. cm. — (Reencounters with colonialism: new perspectives on the Americas)
Includes bibliographical references and index.
ISBN 978-1-58465-805-4 (cloth : alk. paper)
ISBN 978-1-58465-846-7 (pbk. : alk. paper)
1. American fiction—20th century—History and criticism. 2. Immigrants' writings, American—History and criticism. 3. Place (Philosophy) in literature. 4. Emigration and immigration in literature. 5. Immigrants in literature. 6. National characteristics, American, in literature. I. Title.
PS374.I48K36 2009
810.9'920691—dc22 2009016157

University Press of New England is a member of the Green Press Initiative. The paper used in this book meets their minimum requirement for recycled paper.

CONTENTS

ACKNOWLEDGMENTS

Almost all of the initial supporters of this book and many more assisted me through the long journey to the finish line. I received institutional support at the book's earliest stage from New York University's Graduate School of Arts and Science. I received support from the Professional Staff Congress—CUNY Research Award Program, release time from the College of Staten Island, and an Andrew Mellon seminar fellowship at the Humanities Center of the CUNY Graduate Center. I am grateful for all these gifts of time. Within the vast world that is CUNY, many helped me create a productive home: Dean Francisco Soto at the College of Staten Island strove to provide the conditions to facilitate scholarship and helped with resources at critical times. Janet Ng, exemplary department chair and friend, provided the spirit and support faculty need in balancing teaching and research. My colleagues in the English department and the Women's Studies and Science, Letters, and Society programs provided a collegial and supportive environment. At the Humanities Center, the participants in the Mellon seminar "Divided Loyalties" helped me reformulate the book conceptually by giving me valuable feedback on drafts that turned into the initial chapters: I am especially grateful for the comments of Alisa Salomon, Sarah Chin, Amy Chazkel, Ida Susser, Aiobheann Sweeney, and Yasmin Ramírez.

From the book's beginnings at New York University's Comparative Literature department till its end, Sylvia Molloy and Jennifer Wicke provided encouragement and counsel. I am incredibly lucky and thankful to have as teachers, role models, and friends these formidable people and scholars. Richard Sieburth patiently taught, encouraged, and supported my interests through many years with the kind of engagement, insight, and enthusiasm that is truly rare. Shari Huhndorf has read significant parts of the book, offered terrific comments, and listened me to talk (and talk and talk) about this project for a long time. I am grateful to Shari for her exceptional generosity as a friend and colleague. I also thank those others whose friendship and work nourished my personal and professional life from near and far: Sonia Bakar, Anita Gilodo, Aylin Gözübüyük, Jizel Kohen,

Helen Lee, David Leeming, Ilana Navaro, Liz Ornston, Arzu Öztürkmen, and Kerri Sakamoto.

I wrote the last stage of this book in Toronto. I thank Ato Quayson, the director of the Centre for Diaspora and Transnational Studies at the University of Toronto, for graciously hosting me as a visiting scholar at the Centre during the 2007–2008 academic year. I am grateful to Kerri Sakamoto, Kathy Wazana, Richard Fung, Tim McCaskell, Ratiba Hadj-Moussa, and Valentina Napolitano Quayson for making me feel welcome in this city. Thanks to their friendship and hospitality, Toronto, along with Istanbul and New York, is another home now.

Many thanks to reviewers at the University Press of New England for their exceptionally engaging reading of the manuscript and helpful suggestions. I also thank my editor Richard Pult, for shepherding the book so smoothly through the publication process, and Peter Fong and Ann Brash, who were very helpful and responsive during the production stage.

Robert Latham held my hand, listened, and encouraged me through many ups and downs. Patiently and caringly, he shared this journey more than anyone. I am thankful for his love, confidence, commitment, and insights (the nudging helped too). Without my mother Beki Kandiyoti's exceptional sense of humor and devoted, extensive child care, it would have been impossible for me to continue my work; I am grateful for all the labor—and all the laughs. I have grown by raising my children Alegra Kandiyoti and Shiran Kandiyoti, who always inspire me with their creativity, true beauty, and the joy that is in their very names. They made many things possible, including this book.

An early version of chapter 2 was published as "Comparative Diasporas: The Local and the Mobile in Abraham Cohen and Alberto Gerchunoff" in *Modern Fiction Studies* 44.1 (1993): 77–122.

PART I

PLACE AND DIASPORA LITERATURE

INTRODUCTION

The idea of place figures large in American identities and fictions. The fantasy of open and expansive geographies ("the West," the prairies, the deserts) and the magnetism of the metropolis (its scale, its promises, its possibilities) have informed the national imagination and works of both "classic" as well as contemporary American literature. Along with a "sense of place," immigration is another essential component in the self-definition of the United States, referred to frequently as a "nation of immigrants." Yet the stories about places that inform national identity narratives, such as "the West," or the small town, and even cities, are not examined frequently enough from the perspective of immigration and diasporization experiences. *Migrant Sites* is an exploration of the senses of place in a selection of migration and diaspora writings from roughly the past hundred years. Through the analysis of novels, novellas, and short stories by Abraham Cahan, Willa Cather, Estela Portillo Trambley, Sandra Cisneros, Piri Thomas, and Ernesto Quiñonez, *Migrant Sites* offers a transformed understanding of the relation between migration imaginaries and consciousness of place in U.S. writing: it repositions national literature as diaspora literature and highlights spatial enclosure and translocality as central to the spatialization of diaspora experiences created in fiction.

Much of the scholarship on U.S. migration and diaspora fiction has been devoted, appropriately, to issues of race, gender, sexuality, and class. *Migrant Sites* extends this work by focusing on place as another crucial category that articulates with the others in shaping migration and diaspora identities and storytelling. A sense of place figures extensively in experiences and stories of migration and diasporization even though "diaspora has often been equated with lack of space" (Fonrobert and Shemtov 3). Because of this association of diaspora and migration with an absence, scholarly and other analyses have focused on the cultural and migratory "flows" through places more than on the spatialized, territorialized experiences of diasporas. One geographer complains that in diaspora studies, space is often but a metaphor: "in many of these accounts borders are traversed, boundaries are dissolved and space is something that is overcome. Space is invoked, but often left un-interrogated" (Carter 55). Paying attention to place is not less important in diaspora and migration contexts than in others. On the contrary, because displaced subjects carry with them narratives of their originary places, stories of eviction from place often constitute the core of their cultural and literary identities. Moreover, the places of *re*settlement, whose representations articulate with representations of class, race, gender, and sexuality, also form diaspora identities, practices, and narratives.

Because the physical, political, emotional, and cultural aspects of remembered and resettled places shape narratives of migration extensively, humanities criticism needs to pay particular attention to discourses of *place-based* ethnic and diasporic identities and literatures. Similarly, the recent explosion in the study of space and place in many disciplines is extremely useful to understanding migration. Philosophers and geographers, such as Doreen Massey, Edward Soja, Henri Lefebvre, Michel De Certeau, and Michel Foucault, have provided ample arguments for the spatial situatedness of knowledge and power. These insights, which have had wide influence in the humanities and social sciences, can be fruitfully extended to the study of immigration and diaspora. In 1998 *American Literary History* featured an article that pointed to "the emergence of the new space studies," which is a reconsideration of U.S. places that are "crucial to the writing of American material and experiential histories" (Blair 550). More recently, Karen Halttunen further solidified the importance of place in her 2005 presidential address to the American Studies Association, positing that "space and place have never been more analytically important than they have recently become in the humanities and social sciences, demonstrating that globalization . . . has actually made place more important, not less" (2). Inspired by the plethora of works on diaspora fiction and theory and scholarship on the intersections of place, literature, and culture, *Migrant Sites* combines issues of spatiality to examine place in a cross-section of U.S. migration narratives to argue for the spatial underpinnings of migrant and diaspora cultural productions and to accentuate the overlapping aspects and differences among spatial histories in the United States.

One of the ways in which I point to the complexity of place is to investigate its import to the putative inverse of place: displacement, which is key to diaspora identities. The stasis and continuity associated with place and the mobility and disjunction related to displacement are dismantled in diaspora narratives. In unstable situations related in migration narratives, the struggle with and the attachment to place are no less central to literary and cultural expression than in stories of more stable contexts. The imagined and changing nature of place, underlined by geographers like Doreen Massey and others, becomes more salient through the diaspora lens. The analyses of place and displacement in this book center on a series of related issues about fictions that are wide-ranging *and* overlapping in style, genre, and ideology, including Cahan's Jewish local colorism, Cather's European-immigrant regionalism, Portillo Trambley's and Cisneros's merging of Mexican folk stories with everyday environmental and sexual politics, Piri Thomas's autobiographical realism of the East Harlem barrio, and Quiñonez's Latino noir. How do such works convey the immigrant or diaspora "sense of place" in the representation of places of dispersal and resettlement? How does this "sense of place" borrow and depart from mainstream American spatial discourses? How do the American tropes of openness (vast landscape), harmonious community (small town), power and riches (cities), and the physical facts of "American place" inform migration stories? What do the ways in which migration narratives are spatialized in theme and form tell us about U.S. literature and about the diaspora experiences in the United States?

Despite the variations in authors and contexts, I suggest, the works converge upon an identifiable "diaspora sense of place" that I am expressing in the term *migrant sites*. The diasporic sense of place in narratives of labor and colonial migrations is characterized by two conflicting inclinations. On the one hand, every text challenges the idea of openness and possibility embodied in the mainstream American sense of place through literary forms, themes, and motifs that emphasize what I shall be referring to as *enclosure*, the confinement and containment of ethnoracialized diaspora populations in bordered areas. I am using the term enclosure not as the counterpoint of "the commons," which typically refers to the historical British enclosure of public lands. Rather, enclosure here encompasses racialized spatial segregation and immobilization *and* literary modalities that "enclose"; that is, they center around discursively bordered, particularized loci, such as regionalism and urban writing. As I explain further in chapter 1, enclosure as a theme and literary strategy is one that has garnered insufficient attention in literary and cultural studies. Yet the sense of enclosure reverberates through U.S. migration literature, even though the attributes of places of migration, from border towns to urban "ghettos," and the meanings attached to such places differ in important ways. At the same time, each text I have chosen also provides a sense of American place as *translocal* by staging the circulation of boundary-crossing languages, identities, and collective memories *against the grain* of enclosure. In his response to Halttunen's address, Lawrence Buell warns us that the definition of place as "particular, finite countries locatable on a map" leads to the idea that place is primarily a "hearth-centered"—or, in the words of Edward Casey, "hestial"—site. Buell makes a brief but important comment: "every modern place is also shaped by the multiple places that the inhabitants of a particular place bring with them from a migratory or diasporic past" (18). Similarly, even the enclosed sites in diaspora literatures are imbued with reference to other places and displacements.

Migrant Sites is dedicated to illuminating the complex ways in which texts about diaspora experiences are spatialized around the enclosure of diasporas in restricted sites and literary modes (for example, the urbanist, localist, or regionalist genres) *and* the shaping of those sites by translocal imaginaries that go beyond enclosures. This tension between enclosure and translocality is expressed in my term *migrant sites*. As I explain in greater length and theoretical context in chapter 1, I use "site" to refer to the places of enclosure and containment as well as to the prevalent spatial stereotypes that circulate about bordered places, such as "urban ghetto" or "Mexican-border town." "Migrant" refers to those movements and translocalities embedded in the narrative of place—whether "ghettos," towns, or prairies—that are characterized by a constant influx of new people, languages, and cultures. Through the lens of "translocality," we can view the production of place as a crossroads of practices and memories of multiple loci and understand the complexity of place-making. The identity of a diaspora place of settlement, even one that is contained and enclosed, is created, lived, and represented through other national or non-national loci. Azade Seyhan observes of transnational narratives that they "recuperate losses incurred in migration, dislocation, translation" (4). Similarly, the narratives in this book posit an enduring (if always transforming) sense of translocality, a sense of place produced by the imagining of overlapping locales; they negate enclosure as absolute, reject enclosed places as static, and recuperate the damages of diasporic enclosure. Enclosure is the predominant theme and literary form of the diaspora narratives, then, with the representation of "migrant" or translocal consciousness and experience its constitutive counterpoint.

The works that produce the dialectic of enclosure and translocality in original and influential ways were written in two of the most significant periods of immigration and diasporic cultural production: the turn of the twentieth century and the post–civil rights era. During these periods, the numbers of immigrants reached record levels, making immigration and ethnicity burning topical issues (although, as Carmen Teresa Whalen explains [5], despite popular perception, there was no real "hiatus" between the two periods given the enormity of the Mexican and Puerto Rican migrations in the World War II and postwar eras). Along with the expansion in "foreign" population and discourses about them, these two periods witnessed a great flowering of important narratives of migration set not only in those periods but also in times of prior migrations. For example, Cahan's and Cather's works were published within about a decade of each other, but while Cahan's is set approximately, in his present day, Cather's reaches back to the mid-nineteenth century. Thomas writes during the civil rights era about a migration that dates from before the Second World War, with a background in the colonization of Puerto Rico. Hence, the stories' origins are not only in historically momentous immigrations but also in the ascendance (not the origin) of U.S. expansionism, beginning with the 1840s conquests of the West and the 1848 annexation of Mexican lands, reaching an apex in 1898, and subsequently continuing this project in the next centuries, albeit as "an empire without colonies" (see Pease). Thus, Cather's novel is one narrative of the changes following the Homestead Act, an 1862 instrument of settler colonialist expansion into the West, and Sandra Cisneros's story is infused with the conquest of northern Mexico, which precedes the act by little more than a decade. Cather's and Cisneros's texts, separated by multiple factors of time, space, cultural context, and ideology, overlap in their departure points embedded in expansion into the West and the South. There is a direct connection between Cather and Chicana authors like Cisneros: they write and rewrite the story of expansion, immigration, and diasporization, from gendered perspectives, producing vastly different effects that reflect their historical and ideological positionalities. Shifting from the heroic frontier to the colonized *frontera*, Chicana literature rewrites the immigrant story that Cather attempted to valorize in her own xenophobic, anti-immigrant times, at the expense of subsuming the story of conquest and settler colonialism. Chicana literature lays bare the colonized spatializations that lie at the expansion-immigration nexus—spatializations that are obscured (though present, as I shall show) in Cather's exclusive focus on immigrants. Relatedly, nineteenth-century continentalism, presented as a "domestic" affair carried out through "purchase," "acquisition," and "cession" rather than as conquest (see Dallal), is of a piece with the "foreign" imperial ventures of 1898. This date, two years after Cahan published his novella, is also the point of reference for the Puerto Rican diaspora narratives as the year in which the island came under U.S. dominion. Cahan's work and Puerto Rican diaspora literature are informed by the historical conjuncture of immigration and colonization; both tell stories of urban immigrant places. Cahan is more obliquely critical of Americanization than Thomas and Quiñonez and is less directly informed by the discourses of empire. Nevertheless, his spatialization of the urban migrants is influenced by the civilizational/racialist discourses facilitating the overlapping phenomena of expansion and immigration. All the works speak to the overlap between domestic and external productions of empire (see Amy Kaplan "Left Alone"; Pease; Jacobson, *Barbarian Virtues*).

Each of the authors, Cahan and Cather writing in the first period and Portillo Trambley, Cisneros, Thomas, and Quiñonez in the second, is a groundbreaking storyteller who has made unique contributions to the European immigrant, Jewish American, U.S. Puerto Rican, Chicana/o, immigrant, diaspora, localist, regionalist, and urbanist bodies of writing. Most are "firsts" in their respective literary traditions, and others have shaped new ways of seeing migration, ethnic and diasporic identities and literatures, and American place. Further, each represents a diasporic and/or literary tradition that is unique and longstanding in terms of the centrality of spatial discourses. The Jewish, Chicana/o, and Puerto Rican cultures and narratives are intensely spatialized, especially around the discourses of eviction from and conquest of place. The identities and sense of belonging in the Jewish and Latina/o texts are emphatically shaped by the various loci in which these diaspora groups are placed and those from which they are displaced. While there are many social groups that have experienced eviction and displacement, there are few other diasporic literatures about nation-crossing migration that have as large a part of their corpus concerned with representations of place and spatial discourses of belonging. Willa Cather's approach to place works differently, but she is the first to underline the intensely spatialized nature of the immigrant experience as foundational to not only diaspora memory but also the dominant American memory landscape. She "grounds" immigrant and diasporic identities by having her protagonists inherit the American land: at once erasing Native American presence and bypassing anti-immigrant xenophobia, thus helping form new mythologies of American place. Focused on urban representations (in Jewish American and U.S. Puerto Rican contexts) and on the broadly defined nonurban "West" (in the writings of Cather and feminist Chicana authors), the texts with which I engage present a strong case for the prevalence of the spatial imaginary in U.S. narratives of migration and the ethnoracialized diasporic experience. Each of the works is a particularly striking example of the centrality of enclosures to narrating diasporas. They complement one another in this book, as they not only refract enclosure through distinct narrative, generic, thematic, and ideological means but also overlap in their maintaining of the tension between enclosure and translocality.

The spatialized discourses I highlight in these works serve both to complicate our understanding of place, race, and ethnicity in U.S. literature and to present "the nation of immigrants" as an unevenly conceived formation. Diaspora literature addresses and often challenges the simplified picture evoked in "a nation of immigrants" entering and folding themselves into an "empire of liberty" in Thomas Jefferson's terms. In the nineteenth- and twentieth-century periods that inform the works discussed here, intentionally or not, the European and Jewish immigrants were able to benefit both from empire (the land and prosperity afforded by expansion and global hegemony) and from liberty (afforded by the eventual integration into the higher echelons of the racial hierarchy). Other immigrants, particularly those with experiences and collective histories of migrations that are the byproducts of empire *and* are subject to negative racialization, continue to struggle with exclusion.

My focus on spatiality draws attention to the place-based barriers, enclosures, and racial/colonial differentiations (Grosfoguel and Georas) with which newcomers and some long-standing diasporas contend.[1] The juxtaposition of multiple cultural and historical contexts destabilizes the prevailing conception of "immigrants," often presented as (and expected to be) an undifferentiated block following the same trajectory. While I argue that diaspora narratives highlight enclosure, their range testifies to the differential spatialization and integration of migrants.

Why do I refer to these works as diaspora narratives when "ethnic literature" or "immigrant fiction" are the more common labels? I use the term "diaspora" to indicate not only groups' dispersal from prior places outside the United States but also their re-gathering in the United States in the first and subsequent generations. Much recent scholarship on diaspora is instead devoted to typologies that aim to define and distinguish this kind of community. Sociologists and other scholars have rethought the long-standing definitions of diasporas, which were based primarily on the Jewish, and to some extent Armenian, experiences. They have established new criteria to understand diasporization, some of which include dispersal from an original homeland, alienation from places of settlement, idealization of the homeland and of the narrative of return, ongoing relationship with the homeland, and a consciousness of "ethnonational" group identity (Butler, Cohen, Safran, Tölölyan). "Diaspora" does not suffice to explain the colonial, nation-state, religious, ethnic, or other provenance of the particular displacement and resettlement. It is necessary to specify the context in which diasporas form or are deployed as a practice of culture, consciousness, politics, and so on. Because it is difficult and unhelpful to produce a totalizing definition, scholarship in the realm of cultural criticism and most influentially forwarded by Paul Gilroy, Stuart Hall ("Cultural" and "The Local"), James Clifford, and more recently, Brent Hayes Edwards, approach diaspora as a discursive mode rather than as a delineated social formation. For Clifford, Gilroy, and Hall, diaspora articulations are distinguished by hybridity and contingency; for Edwards, diaspora is a practice that builds on translation and reciprocity among, especially, cultural workers dispersed through many national and linguistic contexts. My own approach, based on textual, expressive materials, is closer to the perspective of diaspora as a mode of reading, specifically here of literary and cultural affinities created through displacements. Reading a literary work as a diaspora text means thinking of it as placed at the juncture where the local is translocalized through the experiences and practices of other places: we are taken outside of the nation-based literary, social, and political frame even though we cannot bypass it. Reading in the diasporic mode also makes us attend to the ways in which place figures as a dynamic and relational entity.

"Diaspora" here can refer to either the "immigrant" first arrival or the subsequent generations—all of them different experiences of the diasporization process. Because I have been struck by how central the spatialized imagination is to these narratives that concern displacement, I find that "diaspora" works better than the more common "ethnic": "diaspora" evokes translocal and transnational connectivities that "ethnic" does not in the United States. "Ethnic" presumes settlement and integration with a "difference" that does not exceed or challenge U.S. national boundaries. Further, diaspora is inseparable from the idea of place (original homeland or other loci). Diaspora, as I see it then, is evocative of both translocality and settlement and suits well the displacement narratives I have chosen to read. Let me point out that I am not championing the term or the idea of diaspora but using it to illustrate particular conjunctures of literature, place, and displacement. Diaspora does not substitute for ethnicity, race, or nationality but refers to these categories at the same time that it evokes multiple spatial connectivities. Without contextualization, however, it does not necessarily conjure all the complexities of displacement and belonging. For example, although I use diaspora to refer to the Puerto Rican and Mexican migrations, I am aware it does not express the colonial status of Puerto Rican migrants nor the roots of Mexican American history and minoritization through war and conquest. Nonetheless, diaspora is indeed a term used commonly now in scholarly, activist, and institutional contexts to describe those who identify as Puerto Ricans and Mexicans outside of Puerto Rico and Mexico, and I adopt that use despite its imperfection, acknowledging other terms such as Chicana/o or Boricua. Further, I do use "immigrant" with reference to first generation of arrival, although the term has been associated with legal status as well as with mostly European and Jewish populations eventually racialized as white—and whose experiences of integration are frequently deployed against those of people of color as a yardstick of success and integration in the "immigrant analogy" (see, for example, Omi and Winant). That use has shifted however, with the demonization of immigration with nefarious initiatives like California's Proposition 187 and the further hardening of attitudes and practices after September 11, 2001. "Immigrant" continues to be used and to be relevant for the newcomers themselves as well as used to effect in activitist and multiethnic contexts (the Immigrant Solidarity movement, "Day Without Immigrants," and so forth). "Migrant" and "migration" here encompass both supposedly "official" displacements like "immigration" as well as other kinds of movements across political boundaries.

In the texts I have chosen, where localizing aesthetic and political strategies intersect with translocal practices and ideas, places are more than settings. Conventionally, settings are containers and backdrops of the plot, symbols of characters and events, or, sometimes, characters themselves. The representation of place in diaspora fictions can assume these aspects but go beyond them. In the diaspora frame I am proposing, place is not simply an enabler of narrative but a constitutive element shaping the genre, plot, character, and cultural and racial politics of the narratives. I use the term "spatial" because there is no equivalent for expressing place-qualities, but I choose "place" over "space" to indicate the specificity and lived, experiential quality of location. Although this distinction is commonly made, I do not subscribe to the equally common assignations of value and power to the terms. The differentiations are usually based on the neutrality or emptiness of space and plenitude of place, the abstractness of space and the concreteness of place: "place" is a "space" that is filled, defined, structured, lived, stable (see Tuan). Reworking the terms in *The Practice of Everyday Life*, Michel de Certeau suggests that "place" is inertia, stability, and signification, whereas "space" is movement and "operationalization." De Certeau thereby depreciates place, effectively mapping the aged time-space dichotomy (see Soja, Kern) onto the notions of space and place. And yet, as scholars critiquing the time-space binary have argued, there is no such thing as empty and neutral space, or a unified, stable place (see Soja; Foucault "Of Other Spaces" and "Questions"). On the other side, in his commanding work *The Fate of Place: A Philosophical History*, Edward Casey suggests that "from place space is (eventually) generated" (275), turning on its head the supposition that space is anterior to place. In overemphasizing laden distinctions between place and space we risk duplicating binaries. For example, Doreen Massey has shown how the binaristic division of space and place is gendered, where place is "local, specific, concrete, descriptive" ("Geographies" 9) and is romanticized as the site of "meaningful," grounding, rooted identity (7). I abstain from championing one term over the other, preferring to understand and complicate how we view place as a lived and imagined loci that, unlike a setting, is inseparable from its so-called contents; it is dynamic and subject to change. Further, place is characterized by both abstract form subject to the control we associate with space (Harvey) and everyday concreteness and particularity (Tuan)—not necessarily one or the other.

Each body of literary works whose examples I study here has produced particular places to tell its migration and diasporization stories. I have chosen to analyze places of broad cultural significance to the particular diaspora groups, represented by entire neighbourhoods, towns, and imaginary homelands. The authors' representation of some of these places respond directly to what I am calling "sites," the spatial stereotypes about diaspora places, as I explain in chapter 1. The Jewish ghetto, the immigrant prairie, the Chicana/o-Mexican border town, and the Puerto Rican barrio are constructed in fictional works to explain and challenge the site-making apparatus that defines "ethnic place" from the unsympathetic outside and assert spatialities unique to various cultural and literary contexts. What are some of the unique ways in which diaspora spatialities function vis-à-vis more prevalent notions of place in the U.S. imaginary? Diasporic literature is often treated as a "lower-case" form of writing, not because it *always* carries subaltern status (though it frequently does), but because it questions the very capitalization necessitated by the nation-state–based organization of literature. Thus, it is important to think about the ways in which diaspora literature, in lower case, functions with relation to upper-case American Literature, specifically its spatial traditions. The writing of diaspora situates itself within U.S. literary conventions of writing the local, the region, and the city; at the same time, it repositions these spatial literary traditions beyond the U.S. geographical, linguistic, and literary boundaries.

COMPARATIVE STUDIES

Migrant Sites brings together varying bodies of writing about diasporas and is inspired by recent redirections in U.S. ethnic studies and comparative literature that are relevant to analyzing the cultural production of diasporas. Within institutions and in much scholarship, ethnic studies fields in the United States have functioned in ways parallel to "area studies" or "national literatures"; they have been separate "areas" gathered within the wider discipline. Born out of the civil rights struggles of the 1960s, ethnic studies was comparative at its inception in its emphasis on overlapping cultural and political logics through which ethnic and racial experiences have been created in the United States. Yet, even though African American, American Indian, and Asian American studies came under one umbrella early on, they in fact crossed paths less frequently than one would imagine, especially as ethnic studies became more institutionalized and the dividing lines became more fixed than had been intended. Gradually however, a comparative approach has become institutionalized across the country—despite, as Manning Marable explains in an overview of the field, the resistance of some scholars (54).

The more recent burgeoning of comparative ethnic studies witnessed in the emphasis on hiring scholars who do comparative work and in new scholarship (e.g. by Buff, Prashad, and Marta Sánchez, for just a few examples) is particularly interesting, because it is taking place at the same time as comparison as an idea and practice is being challenged, especially in the humanities. The debates within comparative literature, a field always in the throes of the agony of self-definition but now questioned more than ever, have been especially rich and plentiful. The critique of comparative literature's ongoing Eurocentricity has received substantial attention (e.g. Spivak, Chow). Moreover, comparative methods' overemphasis on tracing similarities has been criticized as obscuring differences. Relevantly for ethnic studies, comparative literature and comparative history have been critiqued for treating the compared areas as discrete and separate units thus obscuring their mutual and relational constitution. (Singh and Schmidt 7; Seigel). Although comparative studies in the humanities and social sciences, with their different historical origins and institutional situations are not simply parallel with ethnic studies, scholars affiliated with ethnic studies have also submitted comparison to scrutiny using similar critical terms. Recently, Vijay Prashad commented that comparison as a remedy for the "balkanized situation" of ethnic studies, such as, for example, investigating Dominican small business ownership along with the Korean, is limited because it elides "a relational model that sees how the construction of identities impact on each another" ("Ethnic Studies" 171). Instead of "mutual interaction," comparison often offers "static model of epistemological judgment" (172). In lieu of comparison, some scholars have offered a transnational perspective, in which the units of analysis emerge as interactive and mutually constitutive (Seigel) instead of as similar or different. Others suggest not the elimination of the comparative method but its enhancement through a transnational lens. Sharon Marcus suggests, for example, comparative literature can profit from Inderpal Grewal and Caren Kaplan's definition of transnationalism as a system of unequal exchanges and asymmetries to better observe "variations and interactions" (680). As these few examples of recent critiques show, one of the most important charges against comparative work is the occlusion of exchange and interaction, ironically, at the same time as there are more and more institutional and scholarly efforts that undertake bridge-building work within ethnic studies that emphasize mutuality *and* are defined as "comparative" work. While it seems like contradictory or a tricky enterprise, comparison can serve ethnic studies well. I will now explain my own view of comparison as it pertains to the different texts and contexts analyzed in this book.

There is no ideal or single way of resolving the problem that arises in comparative work. On the one hand, there is the danger of collapsing differences in the attempt to identify linkages among literary or cultural phenomena that have not been related frequently, usually for ideological reasons. Rey Chow discusses the questionable prevalence of parity and "peaceful coexistence" among compared objects in comparative studies and provides an apt quote from a 1993 study: "Communication, commingling, sharing were key words in this view of comparative literature, which depoliticized writing and aspired toward universal concord" (Basnett qtd. in Chow 290). Traditional comparative method, which isolates commonalities and suppresses differences, ill-serves ethnic studies, which needs to retain specificity at its core. On the other hand, one could overemphasize differences and specificity. Falling into the "balkanization" Prashad refers to risks the replication of hegemonic structures that isolate communities and cultures from one another through, for example, spatial and literary practices of enclosure, as I argue in this book. Differences are also artificially reinforced in ideologies—like multiculturalism, which privileges "the diversity of discrete cultures" and occludes "the histories of interchange and subordination" (Prashad, "Ethnic Studies" 162). Moreover, specificity can be an impossible project, given the internal differentiation of institutionalized groupings. Variation of national, racial, class, gender, and sexual origin is often the subject of ethnic studies itself: for example, work on the South Asian dimensions of Asian American studies, the "separate" status of Puerto Rico and Puerto Ricans within Latina/o studies, or feminist and queer transformations of the idea of ethnoracial communities.[2] Comparative studies of ethnicity, race, and diasporization, then, must tend to exchanges and mutuality as well as to similarities in the context of differences.

Although contact and interaction require attention, other kinds of scholarship remain crucial. The study of single-group narrative traditions is one. Further, it remains important to identify imaginings of U.S. ethnoracial and diasporic formations that do not explicitly signal inter-ethnoracial contact but are nonetheless connected, often in contrapuntal and asymmetrical ways, through their situatedness in a historically changing national context. The transnational and diasporic dimensions of ethnoracial formation and literature I point to in this book do not dispense with the national frame, even though the construct of the nation is malleable and constituted by what lies outside of it. Writings of U.S. diasporas and immigration connect, at a minimum, through the obligatory reference to dominant, albeit always shifting, U.S. national literary and political ideologies—informed by racialization and empire even as they diverge in literary and political strategy and historical context.

Comparing diasporic literatures—including those without explicit "interchange"—helps to understand the asymmetries within the grand, dominant narratives of spatiality, enclosure, ethnoracial formation. Such comparisons reveal, for example, the hierarchization of ethnicity according to national origin, or the impact of "external" imperial projects on domestic racialization. Willa Cather's and Abraham Cahan's works do not seem to constitute each other mutually via actual transaction, whether through intertextuality or the representation of interaction among the immigrant groups that are their subjects. Yet, they are created with reference to similar hegemonic as well as counterhegemonic conceptions of migration, racialism, and literary and geographic localizations like regionalism and localism. Their significant divergences lie in their framing of cultural specificity and their literary strategies in representing enclosure and translocality, which reflect the different spatializations in urban "ghettos" or in the prairie through which the projects of nation-building and expansion are realized. Similarly, Chicana/o and Puerto Rican diaspora works may or may not refer to one another, but in the post–civil rights period, they engage literary and political constructions of ethnoracialization and spatial enclosure as "Hispanics" that are sometimes coincident and at others incommensurable. As Seyhan explains, through comparisons, varying narratives can be understood in novel ways when they are "reflected through one another. The process of reflection and counterreflection also accentuates differences in historical course, critical agendas, and modes of expression" (18). Kenneth Reinhard points to possibilities for comparative study as "otherwise than comparison" through a reading in terms not of 'families' but of 'neighborhoods,' which are determined by accidental contiguity, genealogical isolation, and ethical encounter" (qtd. in Apter 785). Instead of a genealogical joining of texts, Reinhard proposes to view them as "'neighbors,' both strange and proximate" (786).

In assembling a variety of texts, I am not establishing "multiculturalist" equivalences among the literary diasporas I analyze but proposing them as literary neighbors at the nexus of localization, ethnoracialization, and displacement.

I am well aware that I am treating as neighbors texts and communities that are outside the purview of current U.S. ethnic studies by placing writings by and about people of color side by side with narratives of "white ethnics." This is not to challenge the focus of ethnic studies as an institution on people of color but to be able to think also of these diaspora cultural productions as "both strange and proximate." Despite the whitening of European and Jewish immigrants and the vastly different racialization processes people of color have experienced and continue to contend with (see Omi and Winant), I suggest that we can think about these communities and literatures as inhabiting the United States as a "diaspora space" (Brah) constituted by intersecting, contending, and segregated diasporas. Their strangeness and proximity can be fruitfully considered to reveal common as well as very different hegemonic and counterhegemonic spatialization narratives and processes in the United States. The narratives of European and Jewish immigration I examine reflect the initial period of unstable, unaffirmed whiteness and as such are closer in terms of ethnoracialization to the civil rights–era cultural productions. As Dean Franco points out in his consideration of the comparability of Jewish, African American, and Chicano literature, this is not to say that the theorization of ethnicity or strategies of resistance are parallel or even comparable between the literatures and politics of "white ethnics" and people of color (15–17). The works in part 1 and part 2 overlap in their inevitable reference to racialization as well as to the discursive practices of empire in the literary and political landscapes they emerge from in the United States, but they are also instructive in the differential treatment of such practices. In Cahan and Cather, empire and racialization haunt the texts, in which the immigrants are shown to be closing the gap between themselves and the dominant order. Although both authors also effect critiques of this order, the counterhegemonic literary and cultural strategies in the later texts I examine are much sharper and more direct, most significantly because their subjects are more consistently and adversely shaped by racism and histories of colonization. Yet, although the texts with which I engage are born of asymmetrically constructed literary, cultural, and political strategies, I suggest that they are strange neighbors in the vicinity of diasporic spatialization within the U.S. immigration-expansion nexus.

In *Migrant Sites*, then, I draw on the connective impetus of comparative studies as well as on cultural and historical specificity and difference that are axial to ethnic studies. The assemblage of texts may not be transactional in the strict sense of the word, but they are each embedded in U.S. imaginaries of immigration, place, and diasporas—even though, as diaspora texts they are also constituted by other spaces. They show up "immigration" and "place," two cornerstones of the U.S. national and literary imaginations, as processes contingent on history and the ethnoracial and literary formation in question. This study is not predicated on static literary or social categories like "genre" or "immigrants" that I trace through time and through various ethnic literatures. Although I do identify the representation of enclosure as common to all the texts, the divergences in the nature of the engagement (including in the formulation of translocality as constitutive counterpoints) highlight each case's uniqueness and the forms of rearticulation and disarticulation of hegemonic spatial ideologies and representations. The objects of comparison are not discrete: as they emerge from the immigration-expansion nexus and contend with enclosure, they resonate with and refract one another, despite their asymmetrical political and literary status.

Juxtaposing key works from different traditions shows how American literature is written with regard to many cultural contexts inside and outside of the United States. Further, noting the differences among *and* within bodies of migration narratives (whether European, Jewish, Chicano, and so forth) helps diffuse both the idea of an easily definable American Literature and of "the" immigrant or diaspora experience (which often appears in unvarying terms and images in popular culture). Not only do the works revise the endlessly repeated, triumphant scenario of the settlement experience; they also illustrate the divergences in the creation of ideas around immigration and diasporization. Despite their overlaps, for example, the two authors rewriting "European" immigrant lives, Cather and Cahan, offer significantly different experiences, histories, and languages in addition to narratives strategies and styles. Further, although the civil rights era and its aftermath are particularly rich in various kinds of diaspora writing, I chose Latina/o examples rather than others because spatialized themes and narrative strategies are more central to Puerto Rican diaspora and Chicana/o fictions than many other narratives of transnational migration. Because so much of Puerto Rican and Mexican history is shaped directly by U.S. expansionism, spatiality tends to be primary in these Latina/o literatures, no matter what their setting (mainland or elsewhere). The complexly geographical nature of U.S. migrations is central to these fictions. Chicana/o and Puerto Rican writing in the United States are exemplary cases of diaspora literature that exceed U.S. national borders through an intense, bilingual consciousness of colonization and imbricated political and literary fates of the United States and the respective homelands in the Americas. As Román de la Campa has written, "it could be said that U.S. Latinas/os provide a living challenge to the historical blueprints of American imaginaries, since their specific gaze on America often cuts through the customary North/South divide" (235). Chicana/o and Puerto Rican narratives are particularly instructive in complicating the category of the immigrant, as subjects with a history of colonization and not readily identified as archetypal immigrants, like the European and Jewish ones. The spatial stories that emerge from the geographies of colonization in barrios and borderlands mark explicitly the historical and ongoing place-based struggles against enclosure and racial hierarchization as part of a "decolonial imaginary" (Pérez); such struggles are muted or expressed indirectly in Cahan and obscured in Cather. Quite fittingly then, as I elaborate in chapters 4 and 5, Chicano and Puerto Rican diaspora literatures place their geographical imaginaries, which contest the colonization of places both in the metropole and elsewhere in the Americas, at the very center of their literary enterprise.

Again, both similarities and differences emerge in narratives about groups often considered a homogenous unit, in this case under the rubric of "Latino." To be perfectly clear, if my aim had been to represent all or even most U.S. diaspora groups' writings, I might have chosen one or more literary examples from each of several self-defined or institutionally defined groups. I chose not to do this, first of all, because I think such presumed totality, comprehensiveness, or representativeness is impossible. Moreover, my aim is to point to important texts that illustrate particularly well the imbrication of enclosure and translocality. There are certainly many other works in which place feeds the construction of diaspora imaginations, but I chose a few representative works that position enclosure as a central axis and a literary mode in the context of foreign migrations. By not analyzing texts in the African American or Native American traditions, I am not attempting to reinstitute an artificial division between the "foreign" and "domestic" subjects of empire. The plantation and the reservation are never far from sight and inform other spatialization practices from the "ghetto" to the prison complex. My analyses in several chapters, especially 3 and 5 make reference to these as the original enclosures of the civilizing and conquering process that undergird hegemonic national identity narratives. The principal aim of this book is to complicate and revise the category of those who have been perceived as "immigrants" and "immigrant literature" and to offer a spatial lens to examine those diasporas that have not been the subjects of so extensive analyses of place and spatial assignment as African Americans and Native Americans. Finally, putting together several groups of examples serves to demonstrate the quantity and quality of migration narratives and "foreign" contexts produced in the United States, so that these can be more frequently considered an integral (and not only a "particular" or marginal) aspect of U.S. culture and literature.

Migrant Sites focuses on key narratives of diasporic experiences in four chapters that thoroughly contextualize the literary and social context of the works. These are preceded by chapter 1, which presents the concepts that inform the book as well as the nexus of literary, migration, and spatial studies. In that chapter, I argue for the centrality of spatial perspectives to diaspora and immigration studies. I draw on James Clifford's insights on diasporas to argue that while mobility and homelands are crucial to diaspora identities, settlement and re-location are equally significant. In this chapter, and throughout the book, I emphasize diaspora fictions' foundations on re-location and spatial enclosure. To elucidate the nature of diaspora spatiality, I adapt ideas on place in the works of such philosophers, geographers, and cinema scholars as Doreen Massey, Michel de Certeau, Gilles Deleuze, Félix Guattari, Edward Casey, and Hamid Naficy, and propose the idea of "migrant sites" to characterize diasporic texts. I expose the literary and political operations of spatial enclosure and boundedness found prominently in texts about diaspora experiences and explain the counterforce of cultural, linguistic, and literary practices that cross the boundaries of geographic confinement. This dynamic is central to the chapters to come. Chapter 1, then, is an exposition of concepts rather than histories; nonetheless, I provide a historical context for understanding place in U.S. literature and culture and the role of expansionism and ongoing colonialities in shaping migrations and their narratives. The contextualization of literary history and diasporic/ethnic representations is specified and elaborated in the following chapters that provide close readings and broader cultural contextualizations of the fictional texts.

Chapters 2 through 5 are organized in two sections: the turn of the twentieth century and the post–civil rights era. I chose the works examined in both sections not because each one represents an entire diaspora tradition, but because they exemplify a spatialized experience of immigration and diasporization and exhibit in compelling ways the tension between containment and translocality that I define as "migrant sites." Further, the works not only thematize place but also deploy *spatialized literary genres* that are organized around enclosures, such as regionalism, local color, and urban writing.

Part II discusses works that deal with nineteenth-century immigration and were written between the end of the nineteenth century and the second decade of the twentieth century. This part addresses the intersection of migration through the spatialized literary forms of regionalism and localism, which were prevalent at this time. Cahan, a prominent man of letters, is considered the "progenitor" of contemporary Jewish American literature. The fact that he garnered mainstream attention through the use of literary localism (encouraged by the eminent William Dean Howells) and thematization of immigrant life in a contained "ghetto" makes him essential to the study of place and migration. Willa Cather's "prairie novels," two of which I analyze, informed a whole literary generation's imagination of the western settlement and landscape. Cahan and Cather are ideal to juxtapose: they both explore and question issues of assimilation in terms of the spatialization of immigrants (as simultaneous enclosure and translocality). At the same time, they differ in emphasis: gender and European civilization in diaspora (Cather) and Jewish language and ghettoization (Cahan). They both critique assimilation, treatment of immigrants, and use of civilizational discourses, which, as I explain, overlap with the project of empire. Treating different immigration experiences, these authors also complicate for us the oversimplified category of "European" or "white" prevalent in the characterization of that era's immigration and in the literature of the period.

While the post–civil rights era is particularly rich in diasporic articulations and geographies, writing from the earlier period of intense immigration also lends itself to the analysis of alternative spatiality, especially of those writing in the localist and regionalist modes like Cather and Cahan. Although they are not oppositional writers like Estela Portillo Trambley or Piri Thomas, they too create a diaspora sensibility in their representations of immigrant topographies, one that offers a partial revision to the nationalist and nativist vision of place and belonging prevalent at the time. Their treatment of enclosure and confinement refracts aspects of imperial discourse about race, civilization, and place, even as they reproduce other aspects. For example, Cather erases indigenous presence and reproduces civilizational discourses; at the same time, she diasporizes both the Europeans and the U.S. space, instead of simply folding the newcomers into a preexisting immigrant narrative that expunges their prior senses of place and belonging. Similarly, Cahan conforms to the conventions of writing the urban and the local in his period. But unlike the exemplary Theodore Dreiser, for example, Cahan locates his spatial and cultural references in ethnoracial contexts both within and beyond national borders. His transnational frame of reference partially but notably destabilizes the localist and nationalist context of its production. Unlike the later works I examine, the fictional output of Cahan and Cather is characterized by an ambiguous, part conformist, part challenging relationship to the dominant literary and social ideologies. They are rereadings of the traditional immigrant narrative that suggest the United States is not so much a "nation of immigrants" as a "diaspora space" (Brah).

Chapter 2 explores Abraham Cahan's foundational work of Jewish American writing, *Yekl: A Tale of the New York Ghetto* (1898) through a discussion of localism in late-nineteenth century writing. I analyze Cahan's representation of the ghetto as both enclosed by American social and literary forces and shaped by outside worlds and multilingual practices in the contexts of American literary localism (with reference to the work of W. D. Howells and Hamlin Garland), nativism and immigration, and Jewish culture. Cahan's entry into American letters through localist representations of culture and the enclosed place of "the Jewish ghetto" is the focus. I argue that the "fly-in-amber" effect (Raymond Williams 231) of literary localism affords the representation of Jewish place in America through conformity to established genres but also constrains it through concession to the dominant dichotomies of the civilized-uncivilized that plagued immigrants and colonial subjects in restricted spaces. At the same time, Cahan destabilizes the literary and social production of enclosure: his multilingual strategies that evoke prior places and the staging of the internal differentiation of the Jewish community undermine the image of spatially enclosed ethnic and immigrant subjects as linguistically and culturally homogenous. The past and enduring importance of New York's Lower East Side as a topos in Jewish American culture also informs the analysis.

Building on this discussion of localism and regionalism in terms of enclosure and translocality, chapter 3 moves to a locale represented in vastly different but also overlapping ways with Cahan's work. The chapter treats Cather's *My Án-*

tonia (1918) and *O Pioneers!* (1913) and the regionalist impulse, which I link to the pluralism of Cather's time by discussing how the pluralism of Horace Kallen, Randolph Bourne, and others finds spatial form in these two works. Cather brings a spatial dimension to pluralism's emphasis on cultural retention by representing her protagonists' attachment to and ownership of land as central to the story and their status as heroic immigrants. She presents the immigrants and their attachment to land in these works as marked by both civilization and primitivism. Situated in these oppositional discourses, immigrants are primarily identified with enclosed land they have adopted, even as they perpetuate European cultural traditions. Cather is the first major author to portray immigrants sympathetically as primitive inheritors of the earth and to establish frontiers and foreignness as a nexus. She acknowledges and even advocates for "the foreign" in the "regeneration" of America; yet, at the same time, she confines foreignness. She champions the female immigrant in the "open" and seemingly boundless landscape but also contains her in place and her own discrete culture in the pluralist fashion. Cather thus produces what I am calling a "civilized primitive," one whose body and whose attachment to land suffuses the frontier with primitivist vitality, racialized as differently white, while her European culture civilizes "the frontier." Cather's erasure of indigenous precedence is nevertheless haunted by her use of such civilizational discourses. Her depiction of immigrants in enclosure unwittingly connects the immigrant with the absent Native American and immigration with expansion. This chapter also examines how the gendered dimension of immigration, land, and diaspora cultural retention complicates the standard narratives of migration to America by endowing women rather than men with "pioneer" heroism and cultivation, ownership of land and place, and cultural continuity.

Part III treats Chicana and U.S. Puerto Rican spatial representations in the post-1965 period. These texts overlap with those of the earlier era in their focus on urban enclosures (Cahan, Thomas, and Quiñonez) and gender and western places (Cather, Portillo Trambley, and Cisneros); in addition they offer the common inscription of diasporization through "foreign" languages, places, cultures, and ethnonational politics. They are written at the time when both the numbers of legal/izable immigrants swell tremendously after a comparative slowdown of forty years, and the national conversation around immigration and ethnicity intensifies once again—all of which coincides with the civil rights–era emergence of narratives and politics specific to race, class, and gender identities. As examples of this period, I chose works from U.S. Puerto Rican and Chicana/o literatures, both of which witnessed tremendous growth since the 1960s. Because Puerto Rican and Chicana/o displacements were shaped directly by U.S. politics and territorial conquests and interventions, these narratives are more charged spatially than other bodies of U.S. diaspora and immigrant writing. For example, in many Chicana/o narratives, the U.S. "Southwest" appears as "Occupied Mexico"; "Mexican immigration" appears as a "return" to the original spaces of the Mexican populations, or what is known in Chicano discourses as Aztlán. As for the Puerto Rican context, Puerto Ricans from the island who migrate to the mainland are U.S. citizens; technically at "home" in the United States, they are nonetheless considered marginalized immigrants. U.S. Puerto Rican literature involves in great part a center-staging of this in-between nature of Puerto Rican diasporas. The U.S. Chicana/o and U.S. Puerto Rican literatures of place are more critical of dominant colonizing spatial practices and narratives than those considered in Part II. While, broadly speaking, the earlier literature of immigration is one primarily preoccupied with the vagaries of assimilation and the transition to Americanness, the post–civil rights literature of immigration, diasporization, and ethnoracialization tends to foreground (1) a critique of empire and its attendant social and political injustice and (2) an abiding foreignness or outsiderness rather than assimilation. As Franco also observes, this difference is not only indicative of how the fictional productions vary historically, but also of a "divide between the old and new conceptions of ethnic American identities." This divide is both along "color lines"—with the older, whitened diasporas contrasting to the diasporas of people of color—and ideological lines (15). Chicana/o and Puerto Rican literatures are additionally informed by the histories of conquest, indigenousness, and colonialism; they are therefore connected to Latin American and Third World decolonizing imaginaries and struggles. The lens of colonialism, internal and external, was particularly useful for the Mexican and Puerto Rican struggles, given that these diaspora populations are linked to the expansion and colonialism of the United States.[3]

The Chicana/o and Puerto Rican works analyzed in the final chapters highlight stories of the colonized and exploited diasporic populations in U.S. territory, with particular attention to racist spatialization. Modern coloniality, built on racist civilizational hierarchies dating to the conquest of the Americas and still effective even without formal colonialism (Quijano), is spatial, based on territorial isolation and segregation. Hence, in Chicana/o and Puerto Rican diaspora works, the spatial confinement of diasporic populations is a central as well as a generic feature in the writing of the small town, noir, or the barrio. The counterpoints of such thematic and generic enclosures are found in the representation of Chicana feminist place-narratives, the Puerto Rican island-homeland, and the utopian loci of Chicana/o folklore and pan-Latina/o coexistence. In both these final chapters, I analyze pairs of authors to underline the extensive production of diaspora identity and political discourses in this period as well as to differentiate among the many imaginative approaches to migration, cultural continuity, and localization within each of these diasporic narrative "traditions."

In chapter 4, following an overview of the centrality of spatial stories to Chicana/o politics and writing and its positioning within the wider U.S. literature, I examine the works of Estela Portillo Trambley (1975) and Sandra Cisneros

(1991), Chicana writers of different generations. Both works draw on folk and mythopolitical stories of Chicano place (including Aztlán). Portillo Trambley (the first woman writer to earn the Chicano literary prize Quinto Sol [1973]) and Cisneros (the most widely acclaimed contemporary Chicana poet and novelist) are groundbreaking writers, who have reinvented preexisting Chicana/o narratives from feminist perspectives. The production of gender identities in Cisneros overlaps with Cather's generative approach to women's particular relation to place and spatial history, but its conclusions about "American" place are rather different, given the politics and aesthetics of the borderlands. The issues of gender raised in chapter 3 are now transformed by the Mexican experience in the U.S. territory, as the spatial issues of conquest and borders are treated through the lens of the gendered experience of migration and enclosure. In Portillo Trambley's novella, the enclosure of the exploited, polluted Chicano town is contrasted to the iconic space of Aztlán. In Cisneros's short story, Mexican folklore, the 1848 war, and border-crossing are presented from a gendered point of view, in which the lived environment on both sides of the order are confining for women (especially immigrant women). Nonetheless, the geographies of imagination that women create, transforming received narratives of place and gender, make it possible both to uncover the buried history of conquest and its legacy and also to imagine exits and freedom. The confining experiences of diaspora and immigrant habitats in both works are juxtaposed with the symbolic expanse provided for by the mythical, translocal Chicano space of Aztlán and the liberating places of feminism.

Puerto Rican diaspora literature is informed by a similar yet different legacy of conquest and migration. Chapter 5 is an examination of Puerto Rican barrio (neighborhood) writing in the works of Piri Thomas and Ernesto Quiñonez. The authors are of two different generations in a postwar diaspora literature. Thomas is the first U.S. Puerto Rican writer to write a novel in English, begin a new diaspora literary tradition, and gain mainstream recognition: the work, analyzed here, is *Down These Mean Streets* (1967). More than thirty years later, Quiñonez's acclaimed rewriting of the barrio looks back to Thomas but also deploys different genres (such as noir) and engages new discourses of Puerto Rican and Latino identity and the demands of the literary marketplace. Thomas's *Down These Mean Streets* (1967) and Quiñonez's *Bodega Dreams* (2000) both taking place in East ("Spanish") Harlem, are compared and contrasted in the last chapter in terms of their production of what I call *barriocentric* narratives. Although the barrio narratives are very much local to U.S. spaces, the decolonizing project stemming from the colonial experience of Puerto Ricans is articulated in the critique of racism and the attendant enclosure and containment of fictional characters. The topos of the street, the relationship to the mainstream genres of autobiography and noir and dynamics of mobility and enclosure are examined to reveal political differences in the ownership and practices of urban place and literature. The juxtaposition of the colonized homeland and the barrio as key Puerto Rican places are also positioned as a dialectic between enclosure and translocality, a continuum between the colonized island and the diaspora barrio. Further, the reception of barriocentric literature by the mainstream is examined from a spatial point of view. To what extent the writers fulfill the expectations of mainstream readers vis-à-vis the representation of place is a question I pursue to underline the spatialized politics of writing and diasporic cultural representation. This chapter also returns to the study of Cahan to signal both enduring and vastly different issues in the writing of restricted urban space in U.S. literature of roughly the last one hundred years. In the conclusion, I reiterate the importance of attending to enclosures and translocalities and discuss U.S. literature as a "diaspora space."

The merging of diaspora studies and critical spatial studies that I undertake in this book is meant to draw attention to the production of literary geographies that may not be centered around more familiar "privileged settings" of U.S. literature (Fisher) but have far-reaching implications for U.S. ethnoracial formations and the literature of displacement. The enclosures and translocalities of the displacement narratives I analyze are at the heart of "American literature" and my understanding of them in a similar spirit to the recent calls for transnational, intersectional, or comparative American Studies (Shelley Fisher Fishkin, Radway) and ethnic studies (Hu-DeHart, Marta Sánchez).

The emphasis on spatiality and enclosures is also highly relevant to our current condition under the new globalization. We are living in a time of alarmingly vast new fences, walls, and barricades dividing political and cultural entities. We are also experiencing unprecedented movements, travels, long-distance networks and nationalisms, and circular migrations. This situation is not untenably paradoxical; as I show in this book, enclosure and movement/translocality have long coexisted in the experience and imagination of migration. Workers pouring into wealthier countries that need and invite them unofficially (and disinvite them officially through immigration and security procedures and miles-long walls and fences) find conditions of exploitation, ghettoization, and persecution that immobilize them in narrow zones of undocumented living. While some have joined circuits of migration for a lifetime of border-crossings, many are unable to leave the country of migration for years, sometimes decades, until they obtain documents. The transnational circuits continue through remittances, investments, and telecommunication, but actual undocumented bodies are often immobilized and subjected to disciplinary enclosures, from impoverished and dangerous neighborhoods to incarceration. As I explain in chapter 1, while a nonterritorial "biopolitics" based on statistics and other modes of control is characteristic of the contemporary era, spatial enclosure also continues to inform practices of place and immigration. In their introduction to a special issue of the journal *Identities*, entitled "Movement on the Margins: Mobility and Enclosures at Borders," anthropologists Hilary Cunningham and Josiah McC. Heyman provide a rare reflection on enclosure and movement as twin processes that are crucial to the making and definition of places. They argue, "As the role of states has grown in the reproduction of society and in education, health care, urban services, the environment, and political debates that surround those roles, boundaries rise in importance as a means of regulatory enclosure" (293–294). New measures against immigrants are primary examples of such enclosures as well as of mobilities. Further, while global workers try to overcome literal and metaphorical fences, risking their lives and negotiating narrow circuits that may or may not elude the state, the privileged citizens of wealthy and not-so-wealthy countries voluntarily enclose themselves in gated communities and high-security workplaces. No one avoids enclosure or surveillance; as Michael Sorkin points out, the most privileged and mobile are the ones who are most easily tracked through their credit card purchases, passport stamps, and airline reservations (8–9).

The coexistence of enclosure with translocality that I argue has been a feature of migration narratives has intensified recently. Involuntary and voluntary enclosures act contrapuntally to "global flows." Enclosures belie that we now live in a placeless world; moreover, as the geographer Ash Amin has argued, "Cultural globalism has become the everyday filter through which regional attachment or sense of place is developed. . . . The result is not necessarily a weakened sense of place, but a heterotopic sense of place that is no longer reducible to regional moorings or a territorially confined public sphere, but is made up of influences that fold together the culturally plural and the geographically proximate and distant" (37). Diaspora narratives have long taught us that the experience of any one place is always "multi-sited" and that the local, even when enclosed, is shaped by the translocal. Paying close attention to the particular forms of enclosure in different moments and sites recasts historical constructions of national identity and national literature whose mythologies insist on the openness of and access to space. Reading U.S. place through enclosures keeps us alert to the fact that the age of global flows is also the era of fences and walls and reminds us to take account of historical and ongoing immobilizations and containments of our places, interactions, and literatures.

CHAPTER I

REFORMULATING DIASPORA SPATIALITIES

Diaspora stories are about the possibilities and the impossibilities of being in place. This chapter is a consideration of the ways in which spatial discourses in U.S. literature and in critical interdisciplinary approaches inform our thinking about diasporas. Lived and imagined places play a significant role in the production of diaspora communities and literatures. In the literary production of diaspora experiences, new spatialities are created and established ones are engaged and destabilized. Place is also a source through which cultural identities and practices are constructed. Diaspora literatures about labor migrations and racialized diasporic settlements, such as the ones examined in the next chapters, stage the diasporic sense of place as a struggle with existing spatial discourses based on racialization and enclosure—what I shall call the coloniality of place. I begin by underscoring the import of place to U.S. literature to understand better how diaspora social formations and narratives negotiate with prevalent spatial practices and discourses, especially around enclosures. The exposition of the idea of migrant sites in the latter part of the chapter builds on the discussion of place in U.S. literature and diaspora spatiality. In that section, I explain how the term "migrant sites" encapsulates the the tension between the translocal (migrant) dimension of place, produced by the knowledges, languages, and memories of other places, and the enclosures of diasporas through spatial stereotypes generated by civilizational, racialist discourses (sites).

AMERICAN PLACE

While there is certainly not a single force or concept shaping American Literature, nature and place have provided a cornerstone that shaped its "national fantasies." In the formation of most national identities, land or territory is axial. As Jonathan Boyarin and Daniel Boyarin explain in their book *Powers of Diaspora*, "In the modern, territorial nation-state space is an unchanging ground of identity" (31). In the nations of the "young" Americas, geography was destiny. American nations built their identities around places constructed as available, vacant, and endless. Seen as a boon and a curse, a desert and a garden in turns, American space became a medium for the creation of some imagined communities and the locus for the near-demise of others. In the U.S. North American context, the Puritan vision of a civic society depended on a designated American space. As the political scientist David Jacobson has explained in *Place and Belonging in America*, "civic politics was also an inherently territorial phenomenon, as it involved the need to order the world, to delineate and determine God's jurisdiction territorially, and the territorial jurisdiction of his people.... People and civil polity become synonymous with 'place' and constituted, and are constituted by a 'territory'" (39), necessarily of a bounded, bordered nature. Pointing to the prevalence of references to land, gardening, and planting in Puritan writing, Jacobson argues that, contrary to the perception of Puritan denigration of the wilderness as a site exclusively associated with demons and darkness, "the land, the vegetation, and the soil were ... part of the very soul of Puritanism and its ethic, contributing to, and anticipating, a theme in American national identity and, indeed, in all national movements" (50). The territorial nature of early American morality, ethics, and politics served to justify the conquest of "nomadic" unbordered peoples, and to sow the seeds of nationhood. Thomas Jefferson's agrarian ideal itself was an instrument of national identity construction around territory, property, and individualism, which undergirded the expansion projects into the West, Louisiana, and the Northwest.

Key to the self-representation of "America" as nation, land and nature are also the basis of its putative uniqueness. The American imaginary has long constituted itself as possessing a special, exceptional relation to nature. Of course, geography has been central to the symbologies of many, if not most, nations in their formative stage and thereafter. Yet the "exceptionality" of the United States might lie in the immense discursive proliferation of "exceptionality" itself regarding the relationship between nation and nature. The perceived singularity of the United States in its relationship to nature has strong foundations in its self-image as a "frontier" settler nation. Indeed, in both of the foundational myths of "the frontier" and "the garden," land is the key component that shapes the idea of America and its uniqueness (see Dyck). While the industrial revolution in Europe was propelled by available capital and labor, the United States, which lacked both, relied on its vast natural resources (that is, the exploitation thereof for raw materials) to spur development and eventual prosperity. A "substitution of natural resources for capital" took place as one scholar wrote (qtd. in Schivelbusch 92). Making land accessible and available by any means necessary was the national project of modernization. What launched the U.S. industrial revolution was not manufacturing (as it was in England), but pursuits related to nature: agriculture and the railway system, both of them subduing, cutting through the wilderness, transforming it into profit and property (Schivelbusch 89–92).[1] The attempt to mask the struggles of race, colonialism, and capital with the triumphant ideology around wilderness and bountiful nature and the discourse of the "intimate and constant relation with nature" positioned as "exceptional" (de Sousa Santos 2) succeeded. The abstraction of "nature" and "land" from actual soil and territory and its signification as "culture" is found in untold conceptualizations of American identity. For the French immigrant farmer Hector St. John de Crèvecoeur and historian Frederick Jackson Turner alike, it is land (whether as frontier or garden) that has forged an exceptional (or superior) "American" identity *ex nihilo*. The particularity of the land itself, and of course, its indigenous inhabitants, is largely evacuated; it is its sheer abundance and "availability"[2] that shapes national character.[3]

Scholars researching the later, nineteenth-century geographical imagination and empire such as Martin Bruckner, Susan Schulten, and others have shown that the construction of a "special relationship" with American place was part and parcel of the projects of conquest. One observer reacting to English criticism of American imperialism claimed in 1828 that Americans had "vastly more geographical feeling than the European," and added, "this and that corner of the continent must be *bought* (or conquered if it cannot be bought)" (qtd. in Brückner 239, emphasis in original). The said attachment to place and varieties of determinism that located human identity as well as human progress in geography (see Schulten) served to justify empire as well as Americanness; national identity and conquest have been inextricably linked through the "special relationship" to place. As Howard Mumford Jones observed, along with "the scramble for real estate" and individual property, the unfolding of Americanness had much to do with the "emotional appeal of the uncharted forest, the unfenced range, the trackless mountains and the open sky" (*O Strange* 352). The sense of vacancy and limitlessness embodied in the terms "uncharted," "unfenced," "trackless," "open" served to link conquest, opportunity, and Americanism all in one available territory. The fiction, then, of available land as a basis of national feeling, defined the mission of the "classic" American author from Cooper to Thoreau to Whitman, who triumphantly spatialized the nation as identical to its territory, constructed as "new" and open. This was precisely what D. H. Lawrence rejected in his sharp critique of American mythologies, especially those around "the passionate love for America, for the soil of America": "it is perhaps easier to love America passionately, when you look at it through the wrong end of the telescope, across all the Atlantic water. . . . When you are actually *in* America, America hurts. . . . It is full of grinning, unappeased aboriginal demons, too, ghosts, and it persecutes the white men. . . . America is tense with latent violence and resistance. . . . Yet one day the demons of America must be placated, the ghosts must be appeased, the Spirit of Place atoned for. Then the true passionate love for American Soil will appear. As yet, there is too much menace in the landscape" (56).[4] Lawrence gives the lie to "the special relationship to place" to underscore the unacknowledged histories and consequences of attempted genocide.

One of the important consequences of the focus on space and Soil (with an upper-case S) in the U.S. imaginary was the displacement, as it were, of history, which also served to erase the Native American presence and past. In his classic work, *The American Adam: Innocence, Tragedy, and Tradition in the Nineteenth Century*, R. W. B. Lewis suggested that the American in the novels of Cooper and others is "the hero in space." The "Adamic hero" who has "sprung from nowhere," has no history but is propelled by "American" space, is perceived to be boundless as the seas that Cooper himself had traveled as a sailor. This "space so to speak" displaces the "onslaught of time" (92–105), so that the American hero, of no parents, heritage, or history, witnesses his own birth in the forest. In his 1965 *The Americans: The National Experience*, Daniel Boorstin wrote of the independent U.S. urge to define and distinguish itself (from Europe). He suggested that while Europeans were burdened by their (feudal) past in their task to construct nations, here "space played the role of time. If American history had been brief, American geography somehow made up the difference. In the great American emptiness, varied local governments, economies, and traditions were separated from one another by wilderness and rivers and mountains, which speedily created differences elsewhere created by centuries" (401). When history is made to vanish so that indigenous precedence could also disappear, space attains the status of the singlemost important vector of identity and literary history. Unfettered by the (Indian) past, "the Americans" could submerge themselves in the love and mastery of place, founded on the erasure of the story of conquest and empire. For writers who will become "classic American authors," capturing this "spirit of place" becomes an essential contribution to American literature, whether in the depiction of the sublime forest-space of rebirth, the colonized and conquerable "territories" in the abstract terminology of Huck Finn, or regions as "colorful" synechdoches of a nation (Amy Kaplan, "Nation") imagined spatially.

If much of "classic American literature" was a particular staging of geography that emptied time and indigenousness to valorize a putatively unmarked, open place available to all, the immigrant literature that rose and began to flourish at the end of the nineteenth century provided a refracted reading of earlier spatial narratives, beginning to undo their colonizing impetus and expose the processes of spatialization—including, most relevant here, the enclosures that were part and parcel of the nineteenth-century project of expansion. As Matthew Jacobson has explained, "immigration and expansion constituted two sides of [the] same coin"; the United States sought foreign people as workers at home and consumers elsewhere in the world (*Barbarian Virtues* 4, passim). The wars of 1898 and 1899 in the Caribbean and the Philippines and the most significant European immigration ever at the end of the nineteenth century led to "a huge non-citizen population of non-English speaking peoples who were unfamiliar with U.S. political institutions and civic values. By 'Americanizing' the recent immigrants and the subject peoples the United States hoped to impose national unity and thus mitigate the demographically disruptive consequences of empire" (Cabán 25). Expansionism and imperial conquests stretching from the purchase of Louisiana to 1848 in Mexico to the 1890s with Wounded Knee, the Cuban-Spanish-American and Philippine-American wars, the annexation of Hawaii, Guam, and Puerto Rico, supplemented by repeated incursions into and wars with Latin American and Asian countries well into the twentieth century mirrored in their discursive underpinnings the immigration waves that surged at the end of the nineteenth century. As Donald Pease explains, the "doctrine of exceptionalism" has served to deny internal colonialism, external empire (1898), and neocolonial policy after World War II (203), thus obscuring "colonial wounds" (Mignolo and Tlostanova 112) and foregrounding instead moral superiority and achievement. The hypervisible narrative of immigration as the backbone of U.S. identity occludes empire, slavery, and Native Americans as well as the wounds of an immigration experience characterized by the confrontations with race, class, and gender barriers, albeit to vastly varying extents for different communities.

Dominant imaginaries around both immigration and empire were, and to a large extent continue to be, based on civilizational discourses, separating the civilized from the uncivilized; that is, the privileged white males from the racialized and gendered populations within and without who were colonized, subjugated, or ripe for conquest. The European civilizing mission, a version of the Christian mission, was adapted in the United States to shape Manifest Destiny, from the nineteenth century to the Second World War (Mignolo, *Local Histories* 280). Difference became specifically colonial difference, "the classification of the planet in the modern/colonial imaginary, by enacting coloniality of power, an energy and machine to transform difference into values" (Mignolo, *Local Histories* 13). The "values" defining racialist, civilizational hierarchies, are expressed in Manichaean terms, such as black-white, traditional-modern, backward-advanced, and so forth. Such civilizational thinking undergirds what Latin Americanist thinkers Enrique Dussel, Anibal Quijano, Walter Mignolo, and other scholars of colonialism and postcolonialism have called the "coloniality of power": that modernity, which emerged at the time of the "invention of the Americas" (Dussel) had a racist, civilizational basis that independence movements in the Americas did not eradicate. The colonial modernity that was based on imagining Indians as the Europeans' Other, helped to define the conquerors as the civilized "Old World" (Mazlish, Mignolo). Colonial modernity was spread across the globe from the Americas, with racial hierarchization continuing today to be a prime instrument of subjugation globally, even without colonial administrations (Quijano). As José David Saldívar explains, "the coloniality of power can help us trace the continuous forms of hegemonic dominance produced by colonial cultures and structures" ("Unsettling" 339). The ideology of Manifest Destiny, for example, was replaced after the Second World War with a different kind of instrument of power, but one still "continuous" with civilizational thinking. As Nikhil Pal Singh explains with examples from U.S. leaders of the 1940s, "America in [Henry] Luce's words had become the 'sanctuary of the idea of civilization' in the wake of the European catastrophe, and was thus the legitimate 'inheritor of all the great principles of Western Civilization'" (479). The mission to "spread democracy" and the concern over the "clash of civilizations" has facilitated imperial wars. Decolonization remains a goal, given that we are still confronted by the same colonial matrix within the international division of labor; that is, "the cultural, political, sexual, spiritual, epistemic and economic oppression/exploitation of subordinate racialized/ethnic groups with or without the existence of colonial administrations," as Ramón Grosfoguel (220) argues, following Quijano and Immanuel Wallerstein. Coloniality is not a synonym for global racism, but it evokes the racialist colonial structure of center-periphery relations within and among the First and Third Worlds, based on the hierarchies created at the time of the conquest and reproduced since then.

The discourses of civilization regarding indigenous people of the Americas that marked the beginning of colonial modernity also characterize the approach to immigration and domestic diaspora populations. In such varying contexts as Indian removal, immigrant labor, and the Puerto Rican colony, civilizational thinking, organized around conceptions of material and cultural progress, has been instrumental in classifying peoples racially and justifying subjugation (for examples, see Jacobson, *Barbarian Virtues* 121, 130–131). Immigrants with and without a history of direct or indirect colonization by the United States, such as the fictional Russian Jews, Bohemians, Puerto Ricans, and Chicanas/os of the works I examine, were subjected to the racialist discourse of civilization, albeit to quite different effects and extent, given that European and Jewish immigrants were legally, if not socially, always regarded as white and eventually experienced the full privileges associated with their assigned racial status. But the hegemony of the United States in the hemisphere, underwritten by the civilizing colonial discourse of Manifest Destiny, has shaped the destiny of Latin Americans viewed as inferior races in Latin America as well as in their diasporas within the United States, where they have also been segregated, exploited, and denigrated as inferior and expendable. Attitudes toward immigrants and diasporans are important prisms through which we witness the internal reproduction of external empire.

If the process of Americanizing and ruling the racialized new immigrants and colonial subjects from Native Americans to Puerto Ricans and Filipinos was and continues to be interrelated, as scholars have shown, what have been the *spatial* aspects of such discourses of empire? In the nineteenth century, the official birth of the reservation only three years after the annexation of northern Mexico exemplified spatialized colonial thinking, one based on segregation and dispossession through enclosure of specific populations considered to be of color or not entirely white, and therefore incompletely civilized. Removal to reservations in remote areas through the mid-nineteenth century and subsequent enclosures of Native common lands through "allotments" legalized in the Dawes Act served, of course, to usurp Indian land and diminish the Native population. The confinement of the indigenous population to reservations and arid areas as well as to boarding and day schools for a colonial education was legitimized through the promise that such enclosures would facilitate the civilizing and Americanizing of "the savage" and protect white Christians from their adverse influence, threats, and demands (see Deloria and Lytle; Noriega). This radical form of segregation, the creation of "Indian territory," stemmed from the said failure of civilizing Indians—that is, coercing them to become Christian individual property owners—through "contact" with whites. Their own space (of segregation), it was argued, would give them more *time* to civilize on their own without white presence to remind them of their comparative primitive status (Sheehan 250–254).

Enclosure is central to the practices and imaginaries of frontiers, putative sites of immensity, opportunity, expansion, and national identity. The enclosure of the land and its transformation into private property was the principal vehicle of establishing "civilization." The enclosure of the wilderness was not perceived the same as the British enclosure of the commons: "rather than being popularly viewed as a fall from a previous era of agricultural innocence, [U.S.] enclosures were the fiat lux which transformed the inchoate wilderness into another Eden" (Crawford 143). The New World was at once an infinite desert and a bountiful garden; indeed, in the words of William Cullen Bryant in "The Prairie," who observes that in "the gardens of the Desert," it was both at once. In fact, the wilderness was as good as its capacity to be tamed and enclosed; the agrarian and republican ideals were imagined around farms and fences. But the counterparts of these enclosures were the segregating enclosures of those deemed uncivilized, indeed, barely human. As Melissa Ryan put it, in a rare article on enclosure in U.S. literature, "civilization is fundamentally linked to disciplinary enclosure, an attempt to tame wilderness. . . . The Indian is perhaps the most culturally potent figure for untamed landscape, and the removal of native populations was the historical act of enclosure most fundamentally linked to the spirit of the pioneer" (294–295). In his helpful work *Civilization and Its Contents*, Bruce Mazlish explains the import of a spatial concept like the frontier to "civilization as a colonial ideology." Unlike boundaries, he argues, frontiers imply that there is a relationship between the "civilized" and the "barbarians" on the "other side," which entails conquering and civilizing the barbarians on the other side; as such, civilization is a "form of dominion" (23). I suggest that civilization is also perpetuated through boundaries in which the conquered and the uncivilized are contained and prevented from contaminating and burdening the civilized with their demands and visibility. Here is the primary reason why spatial segregation affects the enclosed but does little damage to the rest of the population. Urban spaces open to those on the higher end of racial and class hierarchies, for example, function well and completely independently of the zones of segregation and enclosure (now called "inner cities"). Most urban residents and U.S. citizens in general are unaffected by the existence of the sites of segregation, which are also invisible and unknown to them.[5]

From the reservation to the "inner city," national, regional, and urban places are crisscrossed by boundary lines of segregation and enclosure. These sites of exclusion are least desirable and safe, with the African American–dominant low-lying areas of New Orleans only the most recent catastrophic example. Racialized places are also the dumping ground of toxic modernity, with its residents bearing the highest, most dangerous shares of pollution, Portillo Trambley's story being a fictional telling of racialized environmental injustice (chapter 4). Although Foucault has argued that discipline and control were once realized through enclosure but have given way to "biopolitics of the population," non-spatialized instruments of control like statistics (*Discipline* 215; *History*), I am convinced that enclosures continue to be essential to the control, abandonment, and disenfranchisement of negatively racialized populations and are therefore key to the stories they tell. The long-standing enclosures of Native American and African American populations have been and continue to be documented. In this book, I foreground related enclosures in other diasporic literary contexts.

In signaling literary and social enclosures as an overarching spatiality in diaspora literature, I am not arguing that all diasporas and indigenous populations experience and tell stories about them in similar ways; I am suggesting, rather, that enclosure is a phenomenon with overlapping characteristics and effects. It is important to note that the histories and structures of reservations or other removal locations of Native Americans, border towns, and the "urban ghettos" of African Americans, Chicano/s, Native Americans, and immigrants are not necessarily isometric. The legal status of their respective residents has changed over time and were not always parallel: for example, the discourse of benevolence and reform that justified the segregation of Native Americans is not necessarily applicable to the creation of "inner cities" of African Americans and immigrants, based on exclusion and abandonment. Still, the subjection to various spatial enclosures and containment of negatively racialized populations have been motivated by common economic and racialist ideologies based on putative civilizational differences of whites and others. Such differentiations or "values" (Mignolo) have resulted in particular places of enclosure that have colonial characteristics. In *Wretched of the Earth*, Fanon writes about the starkness of the spatial division between the colonized and colonizer:

> The zone where the natives live is not complementary to the zone inhabited by the settlers. The two zones are opposed, but not in the service of

> a higher unity.... No conciliation is possible. [The zone of the colonizer is] made of stone and steel. It is a brightly lit town ... a well-fed town, an easy-going town ... of white people, of foreigners [while] the native town, the Negro village, the medina, the reservation, is a place of ill fame.... It is a world without spaciousness; men live there on top of each other.... The native town is a crouching village, a town on its knees, a town wallowing in the mire. (38–39)

The parallels between colonial regimes and U.S. reservations and inner cities of the United States have been formulated as "internal colonialism" (Blauner, Snipps; see note 2 to the introduction). Although it is not entirely possible to view the spatialized aspect of European colonialism Fanon describes as isometric with the situation of subaltern diasporans of the United States in an internal or domestic version, the overlaps are impossible to ignore, especially given the beginnings of U.S. empire. As David Goldberg summarizes, the civilizing mission of settler colonialism toward its racial others, which justified colonization, exploitation, and murder, is reconfigured in the more contemporary period as racialized separation and segregation (187).

The logic of expansion necessitated spatial contraction (including removal and enclosure) for the subaltern "foreign" populations at home and abroad. Diaspora authors telling labor and colonial migration stories foreground spatial critique. As prominent scholars have proposed, "Migrants do not arrive to an empty or neutral space. Rather, migrants arrive to metropolitan spaces that are already 'polluted' by a colonial history, a colonial imaginary, colonial knowledges, a racial/ethnic hierarchy linked to a history of empire. That is, migrants arrive to a space of power relations that is already informed and constituted by coloniality. There is no neutral space of migrant incorporation" (Grosfoguel, Maldonado-Torres, and Saldívar 8). I shall refer to the spatial exclusions and segregations that shape immigrant and diaspora communities and their narratives as "the coloniality of place" or as " spatialized coloniality."

Although diaspora narratives are often marked by an affirmation of diasporic places of resettlement, as we shall see in the following chapters, the awareness and critique of spatial coloniality is central to storytelling, challenging the conceptualization of place as a healing site of continuity, articulated by writers, geographers, and other thinkers who view place as inherently stable, positive, and grounding. For example, the renowned geographer Yi-Fu Tuan has observed that "[p]lace is a pause in movement" that satisfies the "biological needs" of humans and animals for "felt value" (139). Assumptions that place and instability are somehow antithetical and that place provides the need for constancy and "value" in a mobile and restless world, are common. Writing about place as a pregiven entity that provides a "base" for writing and the author's point of view, Eudora Welty claimed, "Place *can* be transparent or translucent, not people....

People give pain . . . but place heals the hurt, soothes the outrage, fills the terrible vacuum that these human beings make. It heals actively" (132).

This healing view of place has to do with its perceived unchanging nature, which provides comfort, or to use a term Roberto Dainotto deploys in his study of European and U.S. regionalisms, a "geographical cure" to social and other ills.[6] In more historically inflected contemporary views as well, the idea of place appears as a stable thing of the past in the context of a dramatically different present. From the commentary of the 1970s about Americans' excessive mobility (such as Alvin Toffler's *Future Shock*) to the 1999 *Country of Exiles: The Destruction of Place in American Life* by William Leach, there have been strong critiques of spatial (and other) loss and destruction, propelled by a lament for the vanished equation between place and identity and between attachment to place and well-being. This outlook is typified by the updated observations of Leach, who points to an "unprecedented alliance against place" between capitalist corporations and liberal and left advocates of cosmopolitanism (including academics). Because of these culprits, with the liberals and the Left most to blame, "many Americans . . . feel betrayed" by the "weakening of place" (6), given that, according to Leach, "the well-being of most Americans rest on a healthy connectedness to place" (7). Leach's perspective, both anticorporate and antileft, originates from an attitude critical of consumerism and capitalism as well as of the post-1965 rise of immigrants, the vociferous assertion of ethnic and racial identities, and the demands for justice. Place, then, serves as a retreat from the balkanization of identity politics and globalization.

Many migration narratives, especially those that center on ethnoracialized subaltern, colonial, or working-class subjects (like all of those analyzed here), thematize and organize themselves around places of resettlement and rediasporization. They cannot draw on place as a site of plenitude and stability, primarily because immigrant and diaspora narratives are marked so often by the coloniality of the place of settlement. The wide span between the narrative of Jewish immigration from the end of the nineteenth century in chapter 2 and of the Puerto Rican diaspora barrio in chapter 5 are testaments to the changing nature of migrant place. At the same time, they indicate an enduring preoccupation with spatial segregation and enclosure that has to do with the racialized and economic status of the migrants. While the Jewish and European-U.S. immigrant narratives have now largely gone beyond the writing of diaspora enclosures in the United States, at the time of the writing of *Yekl* and *My Antonía*, the temporarily disadvantageous racialization and spatial enclosure of people now considered white were social and political "hard facts" (Philip Fisher) that fed such works.

The spatial containment and confinement of immigrant lives, values, and cultures endure; in the case of contemporary Puerto Rican diaspora stories, such enclosures are also inflected by ongoing formal colonialism. The status of Puerto

Rico as a colony, one of the few in the world, directly affects the ongoing spatial coloniality (exclusion from most places and enclosure in a few) of its diaspora in the United States. Other Latin American diasporans, including Mexicans, also produce narratives about borders, borderlands, and barrios as loci of confinement and struggle against continuous and mounting demonization of and discrimination against migrants. Hence, although progressive observers have also pointed to a waning of place, spatialized experiences and narratives continue to be central to the experience of migration. For example, Richard Sennett has written about the impact of globalization on places, arguing that "the identity of places has weakened, becoming more hybrid in composition because of the impact of global labour migration . . . the power of place has weakened" (13). Yet, despite globalization, undocumented migrants—and even legal immigrants and diasporans who are racialized in disadvantageous ways—tell spatialized stories of ghettoization, confinement, and imprisonment. Because spatial segregation and dispossession has not waned but intensified globally through gentrification, imperial wars, and other means, diasporans cannot escape "the power of place."

Interestingly, the subjection of poor and diasporic places to the workings of coloniality and exclusion does not prevent them from being objects of curiosity in the dominant public imagination. The "special relationship" and territorial sentiment created in works about nature and land flowed later in the nineteenth and early twentieth centuries into the writing of other environments as well, including, as Jones points out, the settlers' frontier, the mining town, the slums, and others (352). The cities were especially fascinating in their phenomenal growth and capaciousness. The spaces of the "fragmented, regularized, specialized" city were mysterious "interlocking spaces occupied by functions increasingly unintelligible to each other, in short as space mystified" (Trachtenberg "Experiments" 140). The longstanding fascination of the mainstream public with the ethnic sites of the "closed and enclosing" city centered, as they still do, on the slum, "par excellence an elsewhere shrouded in awe and fear" (Trachtenberg "Experiments" 140). Lurid curiosity about the trappings of poverty, especially violence and loose sexuality, was coupled with a prying interest in a racialized foreignness of custom, culture, and language evidenced by "muckracking" texts like *How the Other Half Lives* by Jacob Riis. "Ethnic ghettos" were and continue to be viewed as not only strange and radically different but also as impenetrable by virtue of their perceived self-enclosure and exclusivity as well as their potential danger to outsiders. Thus, much cultural production that promises an "insider's view" on the ethnic place serves to affirm for the larger public (intentionally or not) mainstream values regarding ethnoracialized places and the superiority of living outside them.

Both sociological work and popular films and books have done much to perpetuate mythologies of diasporic places that accentuates their "foreignness"; that is, divergence from the more common U.S. American organization of space, culture, and language. The neat equation of ethnicity and place, propagated in various forms since the Chicago School of Sociology's "urban villages" and "mosaic" cities, remains a popular notion: an internally undifferentiated ethnoracial population inhabits a clearly demarcated site because of its unwillingness and/or inability to exist outside this place. Whatever the actual complexity of films and books on immigrant and ethnic neighborhoods, much of this cultural production is framed by marketers by the promise of a prying look at the roots of the ethnic "ghetto" dwellers' inability to partake of the project of Americanism and assimilation.[7] Publishers and studios outdo themselves in presenting, for example, "the ghetto nightmare" to "America" at substantial profit.

Indeed, as I show in my chapter on Abraham Cahan, literature and films about ghettos have been popular since the turn of the twentieth century, when the public devoured depictions of immigrant degradation in confined places. The marketing of the later narratives of immigrant neighborhoods were modeled after the publicity around African American ghetto narratives that emerged in the 1940s and 1950s, such as those by Richard Wright, Ann Petry, Claude Brown, and many others. The marketing strategies were based on presenting the "savage" and foreign nature of the ghetto environment, whose degrading circumstances naturally led to gripping narratives of crime, sex, and death. As just one example, the paratext (Genette) of Piri Thomas's 1967 *Down These Mean* Streets—a multifaceted, pioneering text about race and place I treat in chapter 5—presents the contents of the book as one-dimensionally lurid, violent, and even "savage." On the cover, just above the title, appears the enticing declaration, "The savage power of *Manchild in the Promised Land*," positioning Claude Brown's coming-of-age text as a literary precursor and drawing on civilizational discourse of savagery. Printed on the cover photo of tenement rows with laundry hanging between them, is the promise "A man from Spanish Harlem makes you live with him in hell." The word "hell" is repeated also in the back-cover blurb ("a man in hell") and in an excerpt from a *Nation* review, which appears on the first page following the front cover.

This conception of the ethnic ghetto, which belies the book's own, sophisticated presentation of the Puerto Rican neighborhood as shaped by U.S. society's racism and classism, is an enduring marketing strategy to draw a public clearly starving for the representation of radical difference—"savage" difference from the sanitary, civilized spaces of the American Dream. As the place in the book is hell, the readers will be comforted by the fact that their own is paradise by comparison. The audience is primed, by the marketing apparatus that reproduces hegemonic notions of race, place, and civilization, to perceive the enclosed ethnoracial locus as irredeemably miserable and un-American, yet interesting and comfortably distant for exactly those reasons. Such places are "unincorporated territories" of sorts, to draw on the colonial vocabulary that refers to Puerto Rico's stateless status, seemingly part of a dominant body but not fully included.

A spatialized sense of authenticity then, is central to the institutionalization and consumption of diaspora literature, marking the diaspora subjects as different, inhabiting the national territorial place and civilization but not belonging to it. While the publishing apparatus may fix the diaspora story in social and spatial stereotypes of "the foreign" (or "sites" as I am calling them), the narratives I have chosen themselves complicate such processes.

PLACE IN DIASPORA: HOMELANDS AND "REMOVAL AND REGROUNDING"

What are the places that inform the diaspora imagination, and how do authors actually represent them? Because diaspora evokes expulsion, exile, or displacement from particular places, the spatial nature of diasporas seem to be problematized infrequently, even though the rise of critical spatial studies coincided with the rise of diaspora studies. In much recent scholarship, place is assumed to be an overdetermined entity or idea in the process of diasporization. When place is not ignored, it often appears as a politically regressive entity in analyses of diaspora formations and practices. Partly, this approach stems from so much of the critical thinking on diasporas focusing on the homeland construct as the key spatial referent. Kim D. Butler put it, "It is the homeland that anchors diasporan identity" (204). Yet, there is not a singular way of perceiving and experiencing homelands in the widely varying practices of diaspora identity. The homeland informs diaspora consciousness without necessarily "anchoring" it. It is important to acknowledge the role of place-based identity in which the homeland is an important spatial referent that is not stable or fixed; indeed, it is far from being an uncontested, anchoring space and source of identification. Writing critically about diaspora thought in an article on Sikh diasporas, the anthropologist Brian Keith Axel argued, "an analytic model of *place*—central to many studies [of diasporas]—will ultimately preempt any serious accomplishments. Place has primarily been developed to identify a diasporic people's 'place of origin.' This very common analytic posits that a homeland is originary and constitutive of a diaspora, and very often it supports an essentialization of origins and a fetishization of what is supposed to be found at the origin (e.g., tradition, religion, language, race)" (411).

Axel's argument that diasporas are defined by a limiting and "definitive relation to place" (412), reduces place-based diaspora identities to a "fetishized," and presumably single, place of origin. Although he is right that the place of origin serves in some diaspora formulations as the exclusive and essential site of identification, it is important to acknowledge ways of imagining diasporas that do not posit the homeland as the fixed, primary, or only locus of identity and belonging. Jewish, European, Chicana/o, and Puerto Rican experiences in the United States, for example, illustrate myriad ways in which diasporas imagine their places of origin and resettlement. The condition of multiple rediasporization that characterizes the trajectories of many communities may make the assumption of a single place of origin impossible or moot. As we shall see in chapter 2, writing at the turn of the twentieth century, Abraham Cahan debunks the myth of a singular place of origin for "the Jewish immigrants" on the Lower East Side—all presumed to be emerging from a generic Eastern European shtetl, despite the vast variety of languages and places that they in fact claimed. Fictional texts have shown that the homeland as constructed is not necessarily fixed at the moment of displacement. Diaspora consciousness cannot be determined once and for all.

To understand how people perceive and represent places from a perspective of displacement, one must acknowledge that the diasporic spatial imagination is informed not only by contingent knowledge of and relationships with homelands, but also, and often primarily, by the places of settlement. I join James Clifford, Avtar Brah, and Jonathan Boyarin and Daniel Boyarin, who underscore the *localizing* impulses and practices of diasporas. Clifford's well-known essay "Diasporas" lays out the many historical circumstances as well as possibilities of this term. Most important, Clifford attends to the necessity of understanding various forms of dwelling, despite the prevalent association of diaspora with travel and mobility. Although I part with him on his earlier, normative stance on mobility ("Traveling"; see Cheah 291 and passim), I find the following statement very helpful in understanding diasporas as both local and translocal processes: "the term *diaspora* is a signifier, not simply of transnationality and movement, but of political struggles to *define the local* as distinctive community, in historical contexts of displacement" ("Diasporas" 308; emphasis added). In Clifford's relational model of place, "the connection (elsewhere) . . . makes a difference (here)." In the fictions of U.S. diasporas I examine, localization is affected by the experience or collective memory of places left behind; "here" is permeated with a consciousness of "there": Abraham Cahan's ghetto is a space where the Lower East Side clashes with the geography of Eastern Europe; Willa Cather's "pioneers" transplant Europe into the prairie; Mexican migrants of Chicana/o literature translate one side of the border into the other; and East Harlem may be written through the idiom of Puerto Rico. As Jonathan Boyarin and Daniel Boyarin assert, "diaspora partak[es] always of the local but [is] by definition never confined to it" (5). For Boyarin and Boyarin, as for the fiction writers of the past century, diaspora is a "process of repeated removal and regrounding" (11). Diaspora identities and narratives, then, are not necessarily based solely on a national and/or ethnoracial fixed locus that predates displacement but are formed vis-à-vis the particular conditions and places of resettlement.

The excess of attention paid to removal and mobility in diaspora-related theory has led to the neglect or simplification of the expression and practices of "regrounding," which in the U.S. context has been often treated as synonymous with the need or desire for assimilation. The association of diasporas with movement, while justified, cannot be used to de-emphasize dwelling and localization. This idealization of mobility in diaspora thought echoes some of the recent work in philosophy and critical theory that proposes systems of knowing and being centered on "the nomad," deterritorialization, "lines of flight," "travel," "migrancy."[8] But, in the spirit of many diaspora fiction writers, Paul Gilroy reminds us that in the particular condition of displacement we call diaspora we cannot dispense with the fact of expulsion; therefore, "diaspora [is] more than a vogueish synonym for peregrination or nomadism" ("Diaspora" 207). Rather than depending on an essentialized notion of place (Axel), diasporas contend with the dialectical relationship between "removal and regrounding." I am expressing this relationship through the term "migrant sites."

THE IDEA OF MIGRANT SITES

Diaspora consciousness is not necessarily bound by localities and nations, but necessarily unfolds with reference to them. Diaspora literatures grapple with local and national spatial ideologies as well as with spatialized literary genres and practices to critique, subvert, and at times to accommodate them. At the same time, they transform the coordinates of the represented places by inserting the knowledge, practices, and consciousness of other places. To encapsulate the way in which place in diaspora literature does not transcend enclosed locality but refers outside it, is at once local and translocal, national and transnational, I shall be using the term "migrant site." The oxymoronic quality of the term is intentional; I address the fixity implied by "site" as offset by a consciousness of migrancy. Diaspora literatures engage the fixed sites in spatial mythologies and practices at the same time as they destabilize them.

In deploying the term "site," I am drawing on Edward Casey's definition. In *The Fate of Place*, Casey traces the centuries-long demise of interest in place in philosophical thought as well as the more recent resurgence of place and suggests that during the period in which it was subordinated to space (and time), place in fact acquired the characteristics of a site. He suggests that a site is "the leveled-down, emptied out, planiform residuum of place and space eviscerated of their actual and virtual powers and forced to fit the requirements of institutions that demand certain very particular forms of building" (183). Following Foucault in *The Birth of the Clinic* and *Discipline and Punish*, Casey observes that the site's features of homogeneity, planiformity, monolinearity, and seriality conspire "to act as tranquilizing forces in the generation of [in Foucault's words] a 'flat surface of perpetual simultaneity,'" all of which is evident in prisons, hospitals, asylums and so on. The dynamic quality of place is suppressed in favor of fixed sites, to which individuals are assigned. Site, then, is "an antidote to place, its very antithesis—its *pharmakon*—the remedy that is its destruction. . . . Site is anti-place hovering precariously over the abyss of no-place" (186). The kinds of sites, such as the Panopticon, that Foucault analyzes are "replicable" and reduced to what Foucault calls a "generalized function" because they can be instituted anywhere. The process works "to eviscerate place itself of any adherent power, any intrinsic qualities of its own. It is to convert the concrete specificity of a particular place into the 'generalized function' of being a site" (Casey 186).

The concept of "site" as I am using it in "migrant site" refers specifically to the conception of places as spatial units that are prefigured and maintained to legitimate a particular order, whether of empire, nationalism or social hierarchies. To some extent, this concept resembles the disciplined, planned, administered, controlled spaces elaborated in Foucault's sites as well as in the work of Gilles Deleuze and Félix Guattari, Henri Lefebvre, and Michel de Certeau. In *A Thousand Plateaus*, Deleuze and Guattari oppose "smooth space," the open space of "nomadism" to the "striated space" of planning and rationality. Henri Lefebvre's "representations of space" are codifications of space created by planners and professionals to perpetuate a dominant understanding of space and order. Yet "representational spaces" are "qualitative, fluid and dynamic" (42). In "Walking in the City," de Certeau refers to the planned city as a "proper space" whose "rational organization must thus repress all the physical, mental and political pollutions that would compromise it" (94) and that "provides a way of conceiving and constructing space on the basis of a finite number of stable, isolatable, and interconnected properties" (94). As I am using the word here, "sites" with which authors of diasporic narratives contend, resemble "striated spaces" and codified, disciplined city spaces of de Certeau because they are spaces predefined by dominant discourses and practices. They are also similar to Lefebvre's "representations of space" those "conceived spaces" of planning professionals (38), in that sites are created through the reproduction of social hierarchies and the suppression of oppositional configurations of place. As such, they illustrate the coloniality of place.

The word "site" in "migrant sites" also aims to evoke the transformation of a dynamic place into a site of fixed content in the dominant imagination. In my formulation, the "generalized function" of a site is endlessly repeated, much like a stereotype, each repetition ossifying the relationship between place and content. A "site" often suggests not only a location with permanent coordinates, but also an empty container, in which things are or happen. Yet a site is more than a location or container; in fact, sites and what belongs in them are inseparable from one another. A site and its "contents" are mutually defining: with each area designated as a site, we associate a particular "content." The problem is that this content is frequently assumed to be fixed, as in the example of the "tourist site." I suggest that the places that inform hegemonic national identity as well as their purported inverts (such as "ghettos") often function as sites, in which a place is closely associated with specific "content" of events and people, represented in fixed ways. The idea of the pioneering U.S. "West" is an example of a place that has become a site of "national fantasy": it is overwhelmingly associated with heroic Euro-American pioneers, bad or vanquished/vanished Indians, open and available land, and freedom. My analysis of Willa Cather is devoted to exploring the part diasporic elements plays in her re-presentation of this site, and whether the culture and language of European diasporas she valorizes transforms the prevailing definition of the site of "the West" and thereby of Americanness during the time of her writing. I also explore the site of the "ethnic ghetto," and how Jewish and Puerto Rican diaspora authors have contended with the social facts of ghettoization, the dominant representations of neighborhoods as stereotypified "sites" rather than places, and the literary tradition of writing about "ethnic places." In feminist Chicana literature, the sites of Aztlán (when presented as a masculinist nationalist concept) and the small border town as a knowable construct are problematized through a gendered lens. These and other sites of hegemonic national(ist) fantasy are all too often ossified in their fixed "contents" and associated imagery that purport to define the spaces of "America" and "Americanness."

The spatial stereotypes, or sites, in question in this project are created in U.S. domestic discourses of the nation, race, gender, and class. I use the term *domestic* specifically because it is constructed against "the foreign" spaces, as the "national fantasy" is constructed against international or transnational ones. Hence, "the local," "the region," "the border," and the "ethnic ghetto" are all configured in the official and popular imagination in rigid and "striated" ways either to evict or condemn "the foreign" in them in order to define what is properly American. For example, "the frontier" is endlessly reproduced as a site with fixed contents that only offer one variety of Americanness. "The ghetto" of fictions, films, and social discourses, on the other hand, is a site of *un*-American life. Such site-making emphasizes the nonbelonging of diasporic, migrant, and foreign social and spatial practices and ideas and serves to reinforce the preponderance of sites that are purported to be legitimate and representative of the nation. The unequal status of most diasporic places as outside the healthy national imaginary speaks to the coloniality of place that remains in effect in the United States today. The transformation of places into sites is accomplished in great part through enclosures. Diaspora sites in the dominant political and cultural imagination are frequently "anti-places" (Casey) that enclose undesirable populations in bordered and policed geographies as well as in unchanging and damaging ideas about these social and territorial places. Enclosure, the imagined and material creation of a bordered world apart from exploitable, undesirably racialized "foreigners" is central to site-making. I am using enclosure not as a substitute for spatial segregation, a term inexplicably abandoned in recent times, but as a concept that includes social segregation, other forms of contentment (from walls to domestic confinement to class-based immobilizations), *and* the literary operation of narrating a specific and seemingly bounded place (like the ghettos, barrios, small towns, and rural enclosures that are the subject of this book).

ENCLOSING NATION, ETHNICITY, AND LITERATURE

Fictions about the experiences and legacies of immigration pivot around enclosure in several ways: they thematize the spatial segregation of rural, subaltern, or working-class communities deemed "foreign"; they designate places of enclosure, from "ghettos" to prairie gardens to small towns as primary to the experience and consciousness of the diasporic protagonists; they draw on and re-create literary genres and conventions that foreground spatial enclosure and boundaries, such as localism, regionalism, and urban writing. Of course, the kind and extent of enclosure in the works changes according to historical, social, and literary conjunctures they stem from, but they are consistently generative of diaspora narratives. How exactly does enclosure manifest itself in diasporic creative expression? In his expansive work, *An Accented Cinema: Exile and Diasporic Filmmaking*, Hamid Naficy investigates transnational cinema, observing that films conceived by exiles and immigrants feature "open forms," which involve open spaces and outside settings lit brightly that invite reflection and nostalgia as well as "closed forms" characterized by dark indoor and restricted interiors that give rise to a sense of entrapment and claustrophobia (153). Naficy observes of transnational films that much of the time open forms and the sensation of openness, limitlessness, and timelessness are found in representations of lost and remembered homelands, while phobic spaces of entrapment characterize diasporic and exilic life (150–212).

While I find Naficy's typologies helpful, my own findings about the diaspora sense of place in U.S. literature lead to different conclusions. The authors of migration narratives examined in this book represent diaspora places through irreconcilable tensions between containment and translocality. Neither openness nor closure is unique to the representation of diaspora or homeland. Each place is featured simultaneously in terms of enclosure and/or translocality, albeit through varying authorial strategies on narrating the specific diasporic experience. Although I identify many spatial representations of migration stories as gesturing simultaneously to both enclosure and translocal references, I do not mean, as Naficy does, that such simultaneity produces a "thirdspace chronotopicality" characterizing "accented cinema" (213). Naficy's term is the cinematic equivalent of "thirdspace," a concept Edward Soja elaborated on in his 1996 book of the same title, where "everything comes together" (qtd. in Naficy 212) in a zone of hybridity. In the spatialized genres, themes, languages, styles, and in the represented places examined in this book, enclosure and openness do not "come together" but clash and collide. The difficulty of migration narratives is in textual strategies often working at cross-purposes, where narratives gesture to spatial mobility and spatial enclosure in simultaneous and irreconcilable ways.

Enclosed emplacement in the writing of diasporas is often ambivalently expressed as both generative and destructive; it is countered, as I show, by translocal routes of language and culture, which is often ignored in the popular conception and reception of such works. The promotion of "ethnic literature" greatly depends on the work's ability to evoke a sense of place—imagined as affording access to a "different culture" that retains spatial and cultural separateness. Authors then "open up" the confined, invisible places of diaspora experience to the reading public largely unfamiliar with them paradoxically through literary strategies of containment such as "ghetto writing" and "local color." Naficy critiques the confinement strategy as pathological (especially in his primary case, Iranian exile cinema). But in many U.S. narratives of migration and diaspora, enclosure as a structural, generic, and thematic axis serves to emphasize social and spatial exclusion and injustice as well as providing an entry point to the literary marketplace that values representations of enclosed ethnic places.

For authors, writing the region, the local, the urban, and the small town as enclosures signifies entering and engaging the established spatialization of U.S. literature, which is largely formed around these particular places. While they change historically and according to different narrative strategies and cultural contexts, they provide a means of not only establishing a setting but also of containing and bordering their subjects. The immigrant and diasporic experience of enclosure dovetails with the bordering of the spatialized modes prevalent in U.S. fiction, whose characteristics at particular historical points I elaborate on in the following chapters. The texts with which I engage in this book both satisfy and distort the expectations of the reading public peeking through a hole, created by literature, in the curtain drawn around the exoticized, reviled, and fascinating ethnic place. Whether they take place in urban neighborhoods, small towns, or the "wide open" midwestern prairie, they speak to diasporic emplacement by drawing spatial boundaries around their subjects and depicting them in terms of enclosures, confinement, and containment. At the same time, however, the texts present these enclosures contrapuntally to the translocal spatial memories, languages, and stories that spill out from the borders that mark ethnoracial separations; that is, what I am calling migrant sites.

TRANSLOCALITIES

Implicit and explicit critiques of racialized diaspora places include the affirmation of translocalities even in enclosed places. Enclosures are not absolute in diaspora narratives, despite the evidence of coloniality that produces segregation and the literary choice of storytelling through the representation of bounded places. Such narratives are marked significantly by translocal cultures, memories, and movements, which serve as a counterpoint and critique of enclosure, without mitigating it. Leading geographers such as Doreen Massey, Ash Amin, Nigel Thrift and others have been advancing our understanding of places as interconnected, not discrete entities. Massey has observed: "The identity of a place does not derive from some internalized history," but "in large part, precisely from the specificity of its interactions with 'the outside'" ("A Place" 13). One of the revisionary, destabilizing modes of perceiving locality and place is to eliminate the perception of "places as areas with boundaries around" and to think about them "as articulated movements in networks of social relations and understandings" (Massey "A Global" 154). The translocal aspect of diaspora spatiality, for which I argue in this book, dovetails with the relational understanding of place recently advocated by geographers, philosophers, and others.[9] My use of the word "migrant" in "migrant sites" points to the ways in which places are informed by the "migrant" dimension; that is, displacement and translocal experiences and practices that are sustained despite the site-making apparatuses of enclosure or the circulation of ethnoracial and spatial stereotyping that leads some diaspora populations to be and feel "stuck." The way in which "migrant" serves as counterpoint to "site" in this book is meant to explain the heritage and memory of the displacement experience as well as the relational, translocal nature of spatialization in diaspora. The places of regrounding are represented from the perspective, languages, and geographies of the places that have been left behind, which I refer to as "translocal" geographical consciousness—the "migrant" counterpoint to enclosure. Homelands and other forsaken geographies of the past are represented from the perspective of the regrounding experience.

The writing of migrant sites shows to what extent "boundaries are transportable limits" (de Certeau 129) and stretch the borders of literature and of place-consciousness. In a critique of Doreen Massey's call for thinking about place beyond boundaries, Arif Dirlik argues that "any intellectually and politically critical notion of place must recognize some notion of boundary; porosity of boundaries is not the same as the abolition of boundaries" ("Place-Based" 22). Indeed, this recognition does not counteract but adds to Massey's argument and my own view of spatial critique. The import of the narratives I examine in the following chapters lies precisely in navigating the terrain between the acknowledgment and examination of boundaries as well as their violation. Migration stories grapple with the boundedness of enclosed places subjected to disciplinary control; at the same time, they show how places, despite their boundaries, are imagined with reference to other places. Hence, it is neither necessary nor appropriate to make a choice between fixed or boundaryless places, as Dirlik proposes (40). Migration narratives make manifest several overlapping phenomena: (1) the existing boundaries of place enforced by dominant outside forces in the ongoing process of spatial coloniality, such as the urban "ghettos" and barrios; (2) the boundaries of place as created by the communities whose collective stories are being told, with the Chicana/o imagined community of Aztlán or border towns as examples; (3) the ways in which communally defined boundaries resist, absorb, or are transformed by external pressures and internal divisions, with the gendered critique of inside and outside of diaspora communities as an example (see especially chapter 4); and (4) the ways in which places are informed by what lies outside their boundaries, with the languages, spatial memories, and histories of other places. Migrant sites in the texts I analyze indicate the persistence and import of boundaries in site-making as well as the permeability of those boundaries.

Spatial readings of immigrant and diaspora stories are instructive in showing the various effects of geographical boundaries on the subject's psyche, consciousness of collective identity, and sense of belonging. In the narratives I examine in the following chapters, these effects articulate with experiences of race, class, and gender to offer a more complete picture of "immigrant literature" and immigrant and diasporic consciousness. The fictional subjects' grappling with physical boundaries and containment help us reflect further on other narratives of mobility, openness, and the American dream.

PART II

DIASPORIZING LOCAL COLOR AND REGIONALISM

CHAPTER 2

CROSSING DELANCEY

JEWISH DIASPORA LOCALITY AND U.S. LITERATURE

"Boundaries, once conceptualized," wrote the authors of *Nations Unbound*, a volume on the transnational aspects of immigration, "are given meaning and sentiment by those who reside within them. They acquire a life of their own" (Basch et al., 33). All designated sites within boundaries, such as what is referred to as "the local," "the regional," and so forth, can be habitats of settlement, movement, as well as confinement. The circumscribed "ghetto" and the vast expanse of the prairies have equally a life and literature "of their own," constituted by seemingly opposed but in fact imbricated ideologies and practices of enclosure and translocality.

In this chapter, I examine the representation of place and displacement through the local color genre in a foundational fictional narrative about the Eastern European Jewish American community. Before I undertake the analysis of Abraham Cahan's 1896 novella, *Yekl: A Tale of the New York Ghetto*, I examine the U.S. and Jewish literary and social and political contexts that gave rise to Cahan's melding of localism, urban writing, and immigrant fiction. In the analysis of the text itself, issues of spatial representation—specifically, the construction of enclosed populations and languages in the local color genre—come to the fore and signal the importance of boundaries and boundary-crossings in the making of localized diaspora narratives and identities.

Localism and regionalism were central to U.S. literature in the nineteenth and early twentieth centuries and were not commonly associated with immigrants and immigrant stories. Empathically spatialized narratives of "local color" and "region," invested in rural or other off-center places, came to constitute literary modes in their own right through fictions about "natives" of long-established settlements. Abraham Cahan's *Yekl: A Tale of the New York Ghetto* is a significant intervention (by a newcomer to English-language U.S. literature) into not one but two narrative modes that are seemingly antithetical: immigrant fiction and local color/regionalist writing. At the end of the nineteenth and the turn of the twentieth centuries, ideologies of "the local" often bespoke of a sense of permanence, repetition, and continuity—either enduring or lamentably lost. In what manner, then, did immigrant writing highlighting mobility, change, and insecurity draw on ideologies of place as constructed by local color literature?

Through the analysis of Cahan's groundbreaking work and its contexts, I show how the master narratives of "American" place, ethnicity, assimilation, and national literary genre are transfigured in this first literary example from a community held to be a "model" for its success and assimilation. Cahan dismantles neat equations between geography and identity, diaspora and homelands by challenging the melting pot image for the immigrants. The notion of a homogeneous Jewish identity dissolves in his efforts to show the heterogeneity of what is now known as the "Eastern European Jewish" community in New York's Lower East Side "ghetto," a term then new to American literature. Cahan complicates Jewishness by pointing to the various geographical and linguistic provenances of turn-of-the-century Jewish immigrants in New York, challenging the idea that a "ghetto" is a site of homogenous or knowable ethnicity. Further, the author assembles many ingredients of a modern urban literature narrating and critiquing spatial confinement of ethnic and class groups. From Cahan's 1896 work to Quiñonez's novel of the new millennium, the writing of ethnoracialized confinement in a delineated place claims a substantial body of writing in U.S. literature. Cahan is our first example of a rigorous treatment of such confinement, showing how spatial boundedness shapes the literature, languages, and consciousness of immigrants and their descendants.

An author who attained many "firsts" in literature and journalism, Cahan was a political refugee from Russia who moved to New York in 1882 and founded the most important Yiddish-language newspaper of his time, the Socialist *Daily Forward*, which he edited for fifty years and which still survives as a weekly, mostly in English. Through his innovative journalism, fiction, and political activism on behalf of Socialism and labor, Cahan had a tremendous impact on the cultural and literary life of the Lower East Side (Chametzky; Harap 485–524; Higham, *Send These* 88–101; Sanders). He published his novels and stories in English, but reserved Yiddish for journalism, essays, and his multivolume autobiography. His 1917 novel *The Rise of David Levinsky* was highly acclaimed at the time of its publication and has been featured in college curricula, especially since the rise of ethnic studies on campuses. The seeds of that novel were sown in the 1896 *Yekl*.

The English-language literary beginnings of Abraham Cahan were also the beginnings and the (re)generation of fictional genres. In his study of Cahan's fiction, Jules Chametzky writes that *Yekl, a Tale of the New York Ghetto* was "the first novel . . . *by* an immigrant wholly about the immigrant experience" (57). Hence, Cahan was at the forefront not only of Jewish American writing but also of "immigrant literature," now an accepted genre, if still somewhat perceived as marginal. At the same time, through his editorial work, Cahan was also a literary "midwife" to the burgeoning of Yiddish literature in the United States. In 1892, he was the first to publish I. L. Peretz in this country; later Sholom Aleichem, Sholem Asch, and I. B. Singer appeared in the *Forward*. Most interesting for the purposes of this chapter, Cahan's early work has been interpreted by various critics as an unprecedented kind of local color writing. In *The Downtown Jews: Portraits of an Immigrant Generation*, in great part a biography of Cahan, the exemplary downtown Jew, Ronald Sanders writes that Cahan "was the first 'local colorist' of the New York Jewish quarter" (158). According to literary historian Richard Brodhead, Cahan "won a general American audience . . . by figuring out how to adapt the dialect tale formula to the "'region' of the Lower East Side" ("Reading" 118). Chametzky also describes the omnipresent elements of local color in *Yekl*, commending the novel for holding the local color aspects in "artful equilibrium" with character and theme, thus setting up a questionable binary (57, 61). Whatever the critical approach, there seems to be an agreement among many readers of Cahan's work that he is a trailblazer not only as a narrator of immigrant life to the wider U.S. public but also among immigrant writers in his choice of the local color mode of writing. A dominant form of Cahan's time, local color was advocated by the likes of William Dean Howells and Hamlin Garland, practiced by countless numbers of novelists and magazine writers, and previously untapped by the "new Americans."

Cahan's local colorist approach afforded him entry into the U.S. literary marketplace but was at the same time relevant to the fictional and social construction of the new Jewish America. The workings of locality and territory are central not only to U.S. literature in general, as we shall see shortly, but also to fictions of the Jewish experience, given the problematic nature and history of Jewish territoriality. For most of the turn-of-the-century Jews from Eastern Europe, the configuration of the new U.S. spaces was to be permanent: as historians have pointed out, many of these Jews were not immigrants but refugees from ethnoreligious persecution in various parts of Europe. Transnational mobility, plurilocality, and return, possible for other turn-of-the-century migrants, were denied them. In the United States, more than 50 percent of the Italians in the 1880–1924 period returned home, and many "commuted," as it were, for seasonal work (Thernstorm 1036). For Jews, the urgent task of redefining culture in the new diaspora required a shift in the parameters of Jewish and American identities and geographies in great part through new definitions of place and belonging. Cahan's "pioneer" status of being the first immigrant author to write about the immigrant experience and to represent classic Jewish immigrants in their now mythified locus of the Lower East Side, at times tends to overshadow the more provocative implications of his narrative regarding the import of geography and spatial discourses to identity. Although he used dominant literary conventions (localism) and the dominant idiom of English (he wrote *Yekl* first in

Yiddish only to translate it so that it might see the light of day), he nonetheless effectively reset the perimeters of U.S. literature, by locating it in part outside the U.S. context as well as by helping to establish a "foreign" ghetto as an American topos.

Many other notable works of the early twentieth century are also "set" wholly or in part in the Lower East Side: for example, *The Rise of David Levinsky*; Anzia Yezierska's remarkable 1925 book *Bread Givers*, breathing life into Jewish female subjectivity; and Henry Roth's expansive, Joycean novel of 1934, *Call It Sleep*. While the restricted setting of "the East Side" is also important to these works, they are primarily about the vagaries of assimilation, the coming-to-consciousness within the family romance, and the urban polyphony. *Yekl*'s distinguishing central feature is that the discourses about the neighborhood inform (though do not "determine" as in a naturalist novel) many of the key issues of diaspora literature such as Americanization, linguistic difference, new immigrants' struggles, and the sense of displacement and disorientation. As the subtitle intimates, the work draws its very language and storytelling from the ghetto, defined as an enclosed ethnic place and the immigrants' relationship to that enclosure. The novel establishes the question of boundaries as central to the narrative, so that what is usually viewed simply as "the setting" necessarily defines the language, the characters, the plot, as well as the reception of the novel. The central tension in *Yekl* between this spatial containment and the experience of past and future mobility and displacement creates a new "positioning" of Jewish America, which necessarily changed character after the tremendous influx at the end of the nineteenth century. Cahan's particular construction of the community as suspended between worlds within a bordered "ghetto" allowed the merging of existing literary genres.

Although the telling of the immigrant story through the regionalist and localist modes seems to be unproblematic for critics, these were not smooth mixtures. In *World of Our Fathers*, a massive volume on Eastern European Jewish (mostly male) immigrants, Irving Howe writes of the imbrication of genres in immigrant fiction that many have read in Cahan's early work. He characterizes the literature of the "immigrant milieu" as a "regional literature" because "after all, the immigrant neighborhoods formed a kind of region. [This writing] is regional in that it focuses on a contained locale, [and] displays curious or exotic local customs for the inspection of readers whose ways until recently have been assumed to constitute a norm" (585). But can the modes of regionalism and local color be so easily collapsed with the genre of immigrant writing? How does the immigrant, as author and protagonist, connect the local with his transnational perspective? How does the outsider gain access, literary and otherwise, to the native place and its geographic fantasies? To understand how Cahan assembled genres and staged the localization of diasporas at the same time as he showed how diasporas destabilized the idea of "the local" and turned "sites" into "migrant sites," we shall examine the social and literary contexts of local color fictions at the turn of the century.

THE "SPREAD OF LOCALITIES"

Local color fiction in the United States predates the end-of-the-nineteenth-century period with which it has come to be associated. Humorous tales of the Southwest written in the vernacular, the tall story tradition of frontier humor, and realistic narratives of the 1850s, such as Harriet Beecher Stowe's *The Pearl of Orr Island* (1862) that influenced Sarah Orne Jewett, were all pre–Civil War precedents of the mature local color genre (Trachtenberg, *Incorporation* 189; Campbell 9). The masters of this kind of writing as we have come to understand it emerged after the Civil War, in an atmosphere of preindustrial nostalgia and anxiety over the homogenizing, leveling monstrosity of industrialization and national consolidation, which Alan Trachtenberg has called "the incorporation of America." At the popular level, the period after the 1870s witnessed a tremendous burgeoning of *local* pride, especially in the form of historical commemorations.[1] All sorts of "historical pretexts" were created for celebration, from anniversaries of pioneer settlement (St. Augustine, Florida) to the centennial of the first coal that burned in the nation (Wilkes-Barre, Pennsylvania). In this way, the local and the national were intimately tied, with small, sometimes previously ignored areas vying for attention and glory in the national arena. According to the *New York Times*, "the events being remembered [in Baltimore] were of *national* importance" (Kammen 142; emphasis added). In a similar vein, John Dewey reemphasized the seemingly paradoxical mutual indebtedness of the local and the national in a 1920 article entitled "Americanism and Localism." Dewey wrote: "The only things that seem to be 'nation-wide' are the high cost of living, prohibition, and devotion to localisms. . . . The country is a spread of localities, while the nation is something that exists in Washington and other seats of government" (685). According to the "philosophy of provincialism" that Josiah Royce developed in *Race Questions, Provincialism, and Other American Problems* (1908) and elsewhere, the construction of the nation depended on "provinces," or places and communities that maintained their distinct identities but were fused together. And Howells wrote, in implicit rejection of John William De Forest's earlier call for "the great American novel," that he did not "believe the novel of the United States can or will be written. Next to the Italians and Spanish, Americans are the most decentralized people in the world. . . . There can be no national American fiction, only parochial fictions evermore" (*Criticism* 349). A "process of redifferentiation," as Lewis Mumford called it later on (294), would serve to ensure recognition of difference as well as its incorporation. Localisms or their variants ("the parochial," "the provincial") did not interrupt the grand narratives[2] of nationhood; on the contrary they consolidated the nation by providing it with distinct but unifiable parts. A variety of pre–World War II localisms culminated in the conservative regionalism of the Southern Agrarians in the 1930s.[3]

As for literary localists of the turn of the century, Sarah Orne Jewett, Kate Chopin, Mary Murfree, Charles Chesnutt, Mary Wilkins Freeman, Hamlin Garland, Owen Wister, George Washington Cable, and many others created literary worlds, mostly rural, of "contained locales" (Howe 585). According to its advocates, most famously Howells and Garland, local color writing was supposed to reflect "difference" (Garland, "Local Novel" 65) and contribute to a "decentralized literature" (Howells). Theirs was an age when the giant territories of Colorado, the Dakotas, Montana, Idaho, Wyoming, Washington, and Utah were being incorporated into the "union" (as recently as between the years 1876 and 1889), and when vastness and great numbers were overtaking the American consciousness, leading to what historian Robert Wiebe has called the "quantitative ethic": "Americans . . . saw about them . . . more tracks and more factories and more people, bigger farms and bigger corporations and bigger buildings. . . . Men defined issues by how much, how many, how far. Greatness was determined by amount" (40). By contrast, local literature promised small geographies and modest proportions. According to one critic, *size* is a distinguishing feature of local color literature: it is constricted to tiny communities, while regionalist fiction encompasses vast regional areas. This difference stems partly from the post–Civil War wariness of the old sectionalism and partly from the universalist belief in the ability to portray all of human nature through one unsung individual (Spencer 230–235). Howells argued against the notion that "our objective bigness [is] the stuff of our art" (346). Small was not necessarily beautiful: local color writing, as it reflected declining conditions in the countryside, was often about loss, diminished individual and communal circumstances, and poverty. Ann Douglas Wood referred to these fictions, especially ones written by women, as the "writing of impoverishment." But an insulated world that offered itself in lieu of the vast incomprehensibility of the new nation did seem comforting in its puniness.

From this brief description, it might make sense for a writer like Abraham Cahan to choose the local color form and why he was encouraged and publicly extolled by the likes of Howells, "the dean of American letters." Cahan too was writing about a "contained locale" (the Lower East Side ghetto). Indeed, Howells urged him to change the original title "Yankel the Yankee" and suggested the subtitle "A Tale of the New York Ghetto," spatializing the story and the central protagonist at once, foregrounding place as a source of Yekl's story. Further, local color promised to be the very embodiment of a democratic literary movement, opening up the range of fictions to previously marginalized places, people, and dialects (Kaplan, "Nation" 251). Every writer who wished to, it seemed, could earn a name in the annals of America's "decentralized literature" by adhering to the formulas of regionalism. The celebration of marginalia would then include the likes of Cahan.

However, a further look at the genre, its practitioners, and its proponents, yields a different picture. First of all, both popular localism and most of local color writing championed the *rural* milieu as a healthy predecessor and a current alternative to the large urban areas that were dictating the fate of the nation. The motif of the city as the locus of all manner of blight is clearly not peculiar to the United States in this period. Decadent writers in France and Latin America also led their protagonists out of the city into liminal suburban or rural areas for healing and regeneration. An additional basis for the denigration of the urban particular to the United States (and the continental Americas as a whole) was with the encroachment of masses of foreign immigrants, perceived to swell the cities beyond manageable proportions. These were people who had not benefited from the "republican virtue" of the U.S. countryside before the industrial period: "How could newcomers who were never exposed to the democratizing influences of the farm and the village learn the American way?" (Wiebe 65). How then could immigrant writing, with authors and protagonists who had mastered the "American way" only crudely, or perhaps not at all, having landed without any transition in the urban cauldron, draw on a genre whose primary setting is the very locus of "native" tradition?

Despite the democratic vistas that a literature of the local was supposed to unveil, localism as preached by the critics went hand in hand with another contemporaneous social and political trend: nativism.[4] "The local" functioned in part to efface the foreign and the outsider. Rootedness and continuity, with all their vagaries, were key to enduring localism and its writing; therefore, the immigrant, emblem of uprootedness and rupture, did not belong in the picture. Critics have observed that for the middle- and upper-class urban reader, the appeal of the rustic was a refuge from the alien nations now populating the cities. Amy Kaplan has written that the exoticism of the folk hero was "more familiar and less threatening than the feared flood of immigrants whose foreignness lay too close for comfort in an urban context" ("Nation" 251). Richard Brodhead argues that "nineteenth-century regionalism was produced as the upper order's reading at a time of heavy immigration and the anxieties associated with such immigration." The urge to construct regions as places with "seamless coherence of character," in geographer Doreen Massey's words, had everything to do with the perceived opposition between the supremacy of the "American-born" (of North European origins) and the undesirable immigrants. The region then, was most frequently, and even in the context of the narrative of decline, a "comforting, bounded enclosure" (Massey, "Place Called Home" 8) of the familiar, away from the disturbing, conflictive heterogeneity of the urban centers awash with foreignness.

An earlier and even more explicit discourse of the local that raises issues of nativism is found in the essays of Hamlin Garland, many of which were veritable manifestos for a literature of local color. A farmer and fiction writer of the Midwest, Garland was, with Howells, the main proponent of artistic localism in the 1880s and 1890s. In attempting to promote a new genre, Garland was turning the term "local color," viewed pejoratively then as now, on its head. Associated closely with the picturesque,[5] local color in writing signals a certain kind of framing that dulcifies its subject, evicting unpleasant elements from its purview and providing a colorful "reenchantment" of sorts to the modern reader assaulted by the rational grayness of the industrial machine age.[6] Hence, it has implications of artificiality with its focus on the likable or the beautiful. Garland's main aim, however, is what he calls "veritism," an individualized realism. For him as well as for Howells, local color means the realistic, not picturesque, depiction of local places, languages, and social customs in the United States. In both "Local Color in Art" and in "The Local Novel," Garland's "veritism" is intimately linked with an organic connection of the teller with the told. His language is couched in the ideology of nativism: in both essays, "native" and "indigenous" are key terms by which to define local writing and ideology. According to Garland, U.S. literature will be saved from its shackles of dependency on Europe by taking artful stock of what is here and now. However, only a native can know and write the here-and-now: "*Local color in a novel means that it has such quality of texture and back-ground that it could not have been written in any other place or by any one else than a native.* It means a statement of life as indigenous as the plant growth" ("Local Color in Art," 53–54; emphasis in original). Only the native can avoid the "picturesque" treatment; "the tourist cannot write the local novel" (54). Accordingly, a necessary requirement of the local novel is that it be sincere: "of all literary attempts to-day . . . it is the most sincere" (59). Garland equates sincerity with truth, natural emotions, and vitality—all of which are uncorrupted and unaffected. In *Sincerity and Authenticity*, an extensive and illuminating study of these analogous and omnipresent modern concepts, Lionel Trilling reminds us that "sincere" may mean unadulterated, as in the early use of "sincere wine." The "sincere doctrine" was that which "had not been tampered with, or falsified, or corrupted" (12–13). The local novel, emblem of sincerity, is "emotional" and at the same time unadulterated and uncorrupted, presumably by what is inauthentic, unfitting, from the outside.

The native as an escape from foreignness unquestionably invokes the immigration panic of the decades surrounding Garland's writing. He was composing these essays at the time of the greatest single wave of immigration from "southern" populations ever. The hostility and anti-immigrant fanaticism, including the literary "red-blooded" Anglo-Saxonisms of Jack London, Frank Norris, and many others (see Slotkin 159–63), brewing all those years finally led to the closing of the doors in 1924 with the Johnson-Reed Act of immigration restriction

(Higham, *Strangers* 300–330). While the demographic face of the cities was changing radically and menacingly to many, Garland focused on an unshakable understanding of "the native" and "his" exclusive ability to write the local: "The superficial work of the tourist and *outsider* will not do. The real novelist of these sections is walking behind the plow or trudging to school in these splendid potential environments" ("Local Novel" 60–61; emphasis added), with the word "potential" indicating an understanding of place as (literary) opportunity. His seemingly pluralistic vision includes "the negro [who] will enter the fiction of the South, first as subject; second as artist in his own right [and] will surely utter the sombre and darkly-florid genius for emotional utterance which characterizes him" ("Local Novel" 60). Even the slum-dweller is mentioned in a short passage about the local movement in the cities. However, any understanding of the notions of movement and change is absent. The "negro" apparently may not leave the South, and "the novel of the slums must be written by one who has played there as a child" (61), not by newcomers (like Abraham Cahan, for instance) who are neither native nor naturalized. Some years after the publication of these essays, Garland will attribute the decline in literary standards chiefly to immigration (Lutz, *American Nervousness* 111).

Mobility and heterogeneity, which in great part characterize the immigrant, were threatening to Garland's system of static local spaces, however "different" from another these localities were supposed to be. Part of "site-making"—the transformation of places into homogenous, serialized, fixed loci (Casey)—involves the draining of movement and mobility associated with the foreign and other displaced. Although we may think of it as a distinguishing feature of the U.S. experience, perhaps not surprisingly, mobility has been portrayed often as a negative practice. Political theorist William Connolly, who has shown the ways in which territorialism is essential to the definition of peoplehood for Rousseau and other philosophers (165–166), has also pointed to Alexis de Tocqueville's characterization of pre-Conquest North America as a "deserted land waiting for inhabitants" despite the presence of "some nomads"; "it is by agriculture that man wins the soil," and settled territorialism (as opposed to wandering) and civilization are mutually constitutive (165–168). Michael Rogin writes in his famous essay on the Indian question that whites projected mobility onto the Indian, called "the wandering savage" by Andrew Jackson, and characterized "the roaming from place to place" as the very mark of their uncivilized state (147).[7] And, a century after Jackson, John Dewey attributes the "failure" of the contemporary novel to the constant migrations of populations between this locale and that. He comments, "There is an immense population constantly in transit. For the time being they are not localists. But neither are they nationalists. They are just what they are—passengers" (686). According to Dewey, this "intermediate state of existence" that forces certain periodicals to "eliminate the local" (687) is at the root of the vicissisitudes of the contemporary U.S. novel, which ignores that "the locality is the only universal" (687). Dewey is rather vague about the nature of the "exploring spirit" one needs to discover to write about "home" ("we have been too anxious to get away from home," he says), and he inexplicably claims that the relationship between the local and the universal is a new discovery. What is significant, however, is his emphasis on the necessity of the local base for the novel and his perpetuation of the opposition between culture and mobility, civilization and barbarism—the very junctures at which Cahan wrote his pioneering work.

More than simply pointing a finger at localism for its nativist or anti-immigrant impulses, I am placing Cahan in a tradition with which he has been very easily identified and which, by some definitions at least, excludes his work. It seems highly incongruous for local color fiction, like Abraham Cahan's, to be telling both urban and immigrant stories to the privileged consumer of fiction who needs to revel in the preindustrial locale that is in decline, but nevertheless free of contamination by outsiders.[8] Cahan seems to have been the first to marry the fundamentally incompatible genres of the immigrant tale and nativist localism. I do not mean to imply, as some critics have, that local color literature merely chronicles preindustrial charm, a world devoid of problems. As I pointed out before, a sense of endings and loss pervades this fiction, stemming not only from a fin de siècle sensibility but also from the changing economic order. In his fictional work, Garland himself avoids constructing the local as a refuge that offers up an uncontaminated past. Nevertheless, the emphasis is on tradition and homogenous community, however much in the stage of detritus, as well as *territorial pride*, a sensibility crucial to the perpetuation of localisms (as well as, of course, nationalisms). Most of these elements are impossible for the ghetto dweller to assimilate as experience. Surely, tenement rows could not stir up much emotion of the local; nor is the local space of the ghetto identifiable with any kind of continuity or long-standing tradition. How then did Abraham Cahan become a writer of the local?

CALL IT THE "LOWER EAST SIDE"

Yekl relates the infelicitous attempt at Americanization of the eponymous hero, a Russian Jewish immigrant and sweatshop worker in the dense immigrant locality of New York's Lower East Side at the end of the nineteenth century. It is very clearly a tale about assimilation and its discontents. We meet him in his third year in the United States, when he has changed his name to Jake and is brutalizing the English language with his thick accent and grammatical contortions. He is all bravado and attitude. He hides the fact that he has a wife and child back in the shtetl, and that they are waiting for him to send a ticket so they can join him. Yekl/Jake spends his time at the dancing hall, flirting with many single working women, including Mamie, who, with her lengthier American experience and better command of English, becomes for him an emblem of social advancement; that is, assimilation. When he is finally obliged to bring his wife Gitl and their young son to New York, he is ashamed of Gitl's Old World ways, dress, and inability to speak English. The three live together, along with boarders (ubiquitous figures in Jewish immigrant life and literature of the time), one of whom is a Talmudic scholar–turned–sweatshop worker, in the flat furnished by borrowed money from Mamie. But Yekl/Jake cannot prevent himself from detesting his wife, who remains bound to the traditions of the shtetl after her arrival, and from tormenting her with his shame and repulsion. After some time, he runs away with Mamie and demands a divorce for which he pays Gitl. The sum depletes Mamie's savings, and at the end, on his way to marry Mamie, Yekl/Jake is as unhappy as before—regretful for the past and unsure of his future.

In addition to being the first Jewish immigrant writer of immigrant life with this tale of diasporic identity struggle, Cahan was also the first Jewish fiction writer to represent the Lower East Side through a realist lens and eventually take his place in the pantheon of the neighborhood's immortalizers, among the other writers, journalists, theater artists, visual artists, and photographers. As recent volumes on the Lower East Side in Jewish American memory and cultural politics have shown, the area is not simply a historical locus of initial settlement in large numbers. In the Jewish American imagination, the East Side, as it was known at the turn of the twentieth century, is ground zero of Jewish American life, its "spatial icon," representing "the essence of Jewish authenticity" (Diner 126, 118). Although the East Side was home to many other immigrant and ethnoracial groups, only American Jews have "embrac[ed] it as the Plymouth Rock of American Jewish history" (Dinner, Shandler, and Wegner, "Introduction" 6). Historians such as Morris Rischlin, Beth Wenger, Hasia Diner, Susan Wasserman, and many others have traced the transformation of the Lower East Side in the American Jewish imagination, from an area of Jewish settlement to a spatialized object of nostalgia and identity. The iconic status of the East Side has much to do with developments in American Jewish as well as U.S. and world history: the upward mobility that distanced many Jews from their spatial, linguistic, class, and cultural pasts; the Holocaust, which drastically severed ties with and destroyed places of origin in Europe; and the rise of ethnic and racial consciousness in the United States, among others (Diner, Wasserman, Kugelmass, Rischin). As Wasserman and others have pointed out, the transformation of the Lower East Side into an icon, or what I call a *site*—that is, a place imagined to have fixed, dehistoricized attributes—began not in the 1970s boom of "white ethnic" uses of the past but as early as the 1920s, initiated primarily by those who had departed from the neighborhood. By the time Henry Roth published his magnificent *Call It Sleep* in the 1930s, the construction of the East Side as an unchanging, "pre-modern and timeless" (Wasserman 160) locus representing what a consultant to the Tenement Museum called the Jewish people's "primitive experience of America" (qtd. in Kugelmass 200) was well under way and continues to this day through the efforts of writers, filmmakers, tourists, and cultural institutions.

From the contemporary vantage point, the "primitive" time of the Ashkenazi diaspora in the United States is constructed as a "primitive" place, containing the "primitive" (that is, the traditional and unassimilated) Jew, at the brink of initiation into the larger U.S. society. For the community of what has become the middle- and upper-class majority of U.S. Jews, the "semi-mythic space of the Lower East Side" (Kugelmass 194), was a site of undiluted Jewish purity, where Jews lived in unimaginable proximity and poverty but constituted a bona fide community, striving toward a better life collectively and spiritually, as yet untouched by the individualism and secularism of assimilated life in the mainstream. The "rags" part of the dominant "rags-to-riches" narrative of American life is accorded a far more representative status in U.S. Jewish history than the "riches" part that followed. I think this disproportion results not only from the obvious safety of the nostalgia for "rags," from the comfort zone of comparative "riches," but also because the Lower East Side offers an actual geography of identity in ways that the assimilated life does not. As Hasia Diner observed, in the last fifty years or so, "'Lower East Side' meant Jewish and Jewish could be best represented and assimilated through the words and pictures associated with the Lower East Side" (Diner 57) in American memory-making. According to many Jewish observers, from tourists to cultural workers, ethnic identity needs a geographical grounding: Ruth Abrams, one of the founders of the Tenement Museum established in the Lower East Side, said of Jewish immigrants: "They have never had a place to stand and say to their offspring, this is who we are" (qtd. in Diner 118). In other words, *who* we are is *where* we were.

No wonder then that Cahan, as the first to capture in English-language fiction "where we were" is perceived as essential. In addition to all his other important work, Cahan gave life to a neighborhood that has assumed the proportions of a grounding space. *Yekl* is a foundational text that helped shape two forms of identity that have been inseparable in the minds of Jewish memory-makers: the spatial and the social. Yet, while Cahan chose to write in the spatialized genre of local color with all its representational arsenal and attendant problematics and to shape the image of the Lower East Side, his foundational *Yekl* also alerts the reader to a different understanding of belonging in place. Not only are Cahan's texts devoid of the nostalgia and romanticizing that marked the later writings about the East Side; *Yekl* also disrupts the equation of the "Lower East Side" with a stable idea of Jewishness that has become prevalent. The work subtly uncouples any assumed or unproblematic relation between the spatial and the social through Cahan's references to what lies outside the purview of the American shtetl and to the heterogeneity of the enclosure itself. Read carefully, Cahan's work reveals the blind spots of contemporary memory-making and ethnic identity construction as rooted in particular geographies. At the same time, while he challenges the past and present construction of Jewishness and ghetto life, he also accommodates the dominant view of ethnoracial neighborhoods in his local color mode. Overall, Cahan occupies the same ambivalent ground regarding assimilation and difference that his protagonists famously inhabit.

"FRISKING MULTITUDES"

What are the most significant features of the Lower East Side that Cahan constructed in his writing? As one of the first to give shape to the image of the Lower East Side, Cahan first of all furthered the most prominent association of the Lower East Side with its "teeming masses." The area as a boiling cauldron of foreign immigrants spilling from all its spaces, where the public and private are difficult to distinguish, has been a staple of the literary as well as visual representations of the area. Especially vivid descriptions include the sections on the East Side in *The American Scene*, where Henry James wrote, "overflow . . . is the main fact of life" and "There is no swarming like that of Israel when once Israel has got a start, and the scene here bristled, at every step, with the signs and sounds, immitigable, unmistakable, of a Jewry that had burst all bounds. . . . It was as if we had been thus, in the crowded, hustled roadway, where multiplication, multiplication of everything, was the dominant note" (100). In addition to such written documentary accounts, photographs of the East Side in the years shortly before and after the turn of the twentieth century also served as "evidence of foreignness and economic distress" as Deborah Dash Moore and David Lobenstine have shown (Rock and Moore 29). Photographers like Joseph Byron, Lewis Hine, Jacob Riis, and many others aimed to shock as well as educate the public about the East Side's density and its corollaries of misery and exoticism with their portraits of sensational (and un-American) cramming of people into restricted space. Cahan was among the first to participate in these discourses through fiction. Granted, he furthered the dominant project in his own production of journalistic voyeurism and local color detailism in demand at the time. Yet simultaneously, as I shall explain, he challenged the strategies of containment and boundary-making essential to representations of "the ghetto" and to the local color convention.

As in other localist fiction, in *Yekl* a reportorial impetus to chronicle sights, sounds, and smells spectacularizes and primitivizes the Jewish place. On "one of the most densely populated spots on the face of the earth," "dense swarms of bedraggled half-naked humanity" pours out of "the cyclopic tenement houses" onto "the stoops, sidewalks, and pavements of Suffolk Street, . . . thronged with panting, chattering, or frisking multitudes" (13–14). The narrator's characterizations point also to a self-conscious territorializing of his topic. He uses the language of landscape to describe the human currents: "a seething human sea fed by streams, streamlets, and rills of immigration flowing from all the Yiddish-speaking centers of Europe." He also refers to the "weird kind of picturesqueness" of children dancing on the sidewalk. It is precisely the "weirdness" of this American scene that calls for attention. Pride of place, a major motivation for all localism, literary and political, is absent here; the rickety buildings and shabby streets cannot inspire the literary rendering of territorial emotion. A "native's" sense of proprietorship of place, the kind that in *Main-Travelled Roads* (1891) Garland's returning heroes experience when they behold once again the beloved panorama, is not possible for newcomers—not when the piles of garbage overflowing the barrels "[line] the streets in malicious suggestion of rows of trees," and "even these people" put "fresh air" in "mental quotation marks" (13). A sense of wonder, which Frances Bartkowski describes as a key sentiment to immigrants and travelers, is also unavailable to the "frisking multitudes" fighting for elbow space on Suffolk Street. The expansion of the U.S. empire heading for global dominance (which allowed massive immigration) is complemented by spatial contraction for its "foreigners," who vie for scraps of abject space within the metropole.

Even so, there is an attraction that draws the tourist[9] and the novelist to the East Side: it is the ghetto as a Jewish space that is a world onto itself, severed from the rest of the city, its middle-class inhabitants and its Anglo-American mores. The enclosure experienced by Jewish people in the Lower East Side was not absolute, fixed, or permanent. Yet, as early as the 1890s, writers, including Cahan and Riis, emphasized the segregation from Anglo America of the immigrant poor in New York. In *Yekl*, Cahan writes of the transformation in Jake since his move from Boston, his first stop in the United States, to New York: "The Jewish quarter of the metropolis, which is a vast and compact city within a city, offers its denizens incomparably fewer chances of contact with the English-speaking portion of the population than any of the three separate Ghettos of Boston. As a consequence, since Jake's advent to New York his passion for American sport had considerably cooled off" (24). The 1974 film *Hester Street*, an adaptation of *Yekl* directed by Joan Micklin Silver (who later made the updated Lower East Side romantic comedy *Crossing Delancey*) includes an episode absent from the novel to highlight the geography of confinement and sentiment of exclusion. During a picnic scene in the film, Yekl/Jake indulges in his usual bit of braggadocio to Gitl and their boarder about having made it in a country where a Jew can look a Gentile right in the eye and have no fear. His wife Gitl, played by the saucer-eyed Carol Kane, gently points out that where they live, there are no Gentiles to be seen and guesses that they must keep to their own quarters. Jake has no answer.

As a place in the world and in the novel, "the ghetto" is the very definition of the containment that is perceived as one of the requisites of local color fiction

(Howard 366). In confining his narrative almost exclusively to the territory of "the ghetto," Cahan, an educated, cosmopolitan author who might have offered a much larger vista of the city, portrays a bordered world created as a strange (both odd and foreign) picture to his readers. Unlike Dreiser's Carrie, who roams all about in Chicago in wonder at its offerings, Cahan's protagonists always circle around the same teeming streets. In this way, Cahan followed the geography of the turn-of-the-century city. The American city, sociologist Robert Park suggested, was "a mosaic of little worlds which touch but do not interpenetrate" (in Trachtenberg, "Experiments" 141). By the 1890s this very impenetrability—or, as Trachtenberg calls it, the "mystery" of "the city as interlocking spaces occupied by functions increasingly unintelligible to each other" (140)—had become suspicious, giving rise to demands for greater visibility and intelligibility of the urban space. The reform and settlement house movements were in full force, working to discipline the people and the social conditions of the slums and alerting the American public to the misery and needs prevalent among the marginalized neighborhoods.[10] Hence the aims of journalists, politicians, fiction writers, and politicians coincided in their quest to uncover the "mysteries" of the poor, and especially the urban "foreign" populations inhabiting seemingly impenetrable enclaves.

The "reform" movement's call to arms and characterization of "the foreign" and the poor in the domestic United States overlapped with the "civilizing mission" of empire abroad, from Puerto Rico to the Philippines. Americanization meant civilization of the "foreign" savage, from New York to Manila.[11] The reformists "at home," trying to transform immigrants into civilized Americans through the myriad activities of the settlement houses, used imperial language in referring to slums as "colonies" and themselves as brave "explorers" (Bender 11).

The exoticism of the empire at home generated repulsion and pity as well as curiosity. A spectacularization of urban "low life" in journalistic writing, partly reproduced in Cahan, became widely popular in this period. An exemplary text of this genre was, of course, *How the Other Half Lives* (1890) by Jacob Riis, Danish immigrant, crime journalist, housing reform advocate, and champion of Americanization (his 1901 autobiography was entitled *The Making of an American*). Local color and the picturesque tradition often depended on a landscape of disintegration and the nostalgia this evoked, whether in the shape of a ruin or an economy of scarcity. In the urban context, however, there was an activist agenda embedded in apprising the general readership of the condition of local spaces, so close and yet so distant. A descriptive, lurid, and highly racialized account of different Lower East Side slums that Jacob Riis toured nocturnally in search of material, *How the Other Half Lives* caught the attention of the public and spurred the interest and programs of various reformists, including Theodore Roosevelt, chair of New York's police commission between 1893 and 1895 and subsequently a friend of Riis's. Areas previously out of bounds to his readership were rendered primarily with reference to their penury and the ethnicity of the populations within.

Luc Sante argues in his history of the seamy side of Lower Manhattan that Riis's celebrated photographs documenting the predicament of tenement dwellers avoid picturesque treatment (Sante 36), but we cannot say the same of Riis's prose. Indeed, Riis has several references to "picturesque filth and poverty" of different neighborhoods. In "Jewtown," the chief theme is the crowded and unsanitary living conditions, where "the endless panorama of the tenements, rows upon rows, between stony streets, stretches to the north, to the south, and to the west as far as the eye reaches" (87). This is the kind of language that Malcolm Andrews calls "the metropolitan Picturesque," citing examples from chroniclers of mid-nineteenth-century London slums: "the Picturesque masquerad[es] as journalistic exposé . . . thereby seeming to justify its inherent voyeurism" (291).Certainly, with all his contributions to housing reform in the city, Riis went beyond mere gestures or the passive pity and class shame of Baudelaire's narrator in "Les yeux des pauvres." Nonetheless, the perlocutionary function of Riis's text—to elicit sympathy and encourage the reader to activism on behalf of housing reform—rests partly on a sensationalized panorama-making of the urban landscape[12] that takes its cues from received notions about the character of the various "races" inhabiting rigidly defined domains in the Lower East Side.

The containment of Cahan's novella within a restricted setting corresponded to the ethnically parceled structure of the city (with the slum "colonies" held at bay) and responded to the uptown public's desire to "know" downtown (which explains the popularity of Riis and other journalists). The framework of the local color genre was key in the fictional boundary-creation that was necessary to tell the Jewish immigrant story. Containment, as a narrative strategy, serves to underline the uniqueness or particularity of the people and space in the story. Such boundaries are frequently seen to indicate not only the rendering of the particular, but also a comforting enclosure. In a telling article, Michael Kowalewski reviews regionalist collections and the representation of place in contemporary U.S. literature. He writes that "smaller, more specific places" suggest what one critic calls "a welcome *limitation* of possibility," which in turn offers "what feels like *sanity*" ("Writing" 182; emphasis added). The notion that borders and compression bring sanity also echoes Eudora Welty's statement that "place heals the hurt" (131). But the abbreviated boundaries of local color literature are not necessarily comforting, healing, or impermeable. The idea that "the local" and "the region" are autonomous serves a poetics and politics of enclosure that facilitate disciplinary power and knowledge. However, as June Howard suggests in an article on Sarah Orne Jewett and literary history, all too often critics have perceived local color or regionalist writing as confined and limited (Howard points out that the image of the fence is standard in Jewett criticism) and therefore as "intrinsically minor" (366). Writing of a different, but relevant period, Howard shows how in fact Jewett's regions are not absolutely autonomous but are "crisscrossed by the tracks of *translocal connection*" (379; emphasis added). More recently, Hsuan L. Hsu has also affirmed the trespassing of boundaries, through the example of Frank Norris, who draws on regionalist themes in *The Octopus* but "undermines any sense of regional enclosure" (47). While it is certainly true that local color writing is distinguished by an intense focus on areas bounded both socially and geographically, the image of the localist's setting as an impermeable and self-sufficient container does not hold.

TRANSLOCAL SPACES AND THE LANGUAGES OF ENCLOSURE

In *Yekl*, despite the geographical enclosure in the localist manner, the gesture outward is strongly present: First, much more explicitly than in Jewett's work, "translocal connections" and "external forces" are inseparable from the locality, as Jewish Lower Manhattan is not only informed but in fact formed by migratory flows and transnational movements. Transcultural passages, such as the initially unassimilable Gitl's, are the very stuff of this paradoxical locale: circumscribed ethnically and economically, yet porous, to a certain extent, given the transitional nature of the population and neighborhood. Second, *Yekl*, a melodrama about assimilation, portrays none of the desire for history and continuity or the respect and love for inhabited space that distinguish Jewett's and Freeman's protagonists. What Yekl/Jake desires is a further rupture and a dissociation of past and present, the ghetto and the space of the future. The contained ghetto is a migrant site: the immigrants are spatially assigned to a delimited area (at the same time as they are reviled for clustering and "keeping to themselves"), and yet the outside worlds are part of the very fabric of the containment. I use the plural form "worlds" because what shapes the ghetto from the outside is not only the wider American metropolis from which it is excluded for ethnoracial and class reasons but also the many places in "Eastern Europe" that informs life and spatial perception in "America." Finally, Cahan willingly submits to the exigencies of representing bounded localities as discrete containers of culture and language (as Howells, his primary American literary inspiration, advocates). Although as an immigrant Cahan is spatially assigned, in a metaphoric sense, to write primarily about the ghetto and in the local color mode in order to enter "American letters," he nonetheless points the reader to places and languages beyond the local, destabilizing the very idea of the ethnically unified local.

The borders, fluid, fictitious, or transportable, of the local color form highlight the nexus of the social and spatial. Even so, this confluence does not necessarily indicate a unitary or definable kind of ethnicity or class. "Containment," suggests one scholar, is not only a protection of or from the outside; it "also limits and restrains forces *within* the container" (qtd. in Chilton 51). Such is not entirely true of Cahan's presentation of immigrant life. The economic and social structure of the city does of course curb the free movement of certain of its residents, and the local color form is often, especially in its feminist forms,[13] is about the restriction or reduction of mobility. However, in Cahan's story, the "contained locale" is not so "restrained" as to be ethnically unified within (as in Jewett's or Garland's stories), or to lack flows of divergent forces, by virtue of its geographical containment. Cahan writes,

> Hardly a block but shelters Jews from every nook and corner of Russia, Poland, Galicia, Hungary, Roumania: Lithuanian Jews, Volhynian Jews, south Russian Jews, Bessarabian Jews; Jews crowded out of the "pale of Jewish settlement"; Russified Jews expelled from Moscow, St. Petersburg, Kieff, or Saratoff; Jewish runaways from justice . . . artisans, merchants, teachers, rabbis, artists, beggars. . . . Nor is there a tenement house but harbors in its bosom specimens of all the whimsical metamorphoses wrought upon the children of Israel of the great modern exodus by the vicissitudes of life in this their Promised Land of today . . . people with all sorts of antecedents, tastes, habits, inclinations, and speaking all sorts of antecedents, tastes, habits, inclinations, and speaking *all sorts of subdialects of the same jargon*, thrown pellmell into one social caldron—*a human hodgepodge with its component parts changed but not yet fused into one homogenous whole.* (14; emphasis added)

The social order can only be characterized as "pellmell" because the re-diasporized Jews cannot be described as an undifferentiated group, with shared linguistic, geographical, and class origins. Cahan's characterization and description of the community as "hodgepodge" underlines the internal diversity of not only class origins and futures but also linguistic and geographical provenances, as the long list of places of origin and reference to dialects attests. By contrast, most local color literature is distinguished by either ethnic homogeneity, as in the New England or Midwestern stories, or by a clear sense of racial hierarchy, as in Kate Chopin's short fictions set in Louisiana, however much the order was liable to be upset by miscegenation or class role reversals. Cahan, on the other hand, refuses to present ethnicity as a uniform bloc.[14]

Further, in *Yekl* and in many other stories, including "The Imported Bridegroom" and "Circumstances," Cahan underlines class differences within the community by pointing to the variety and instability of class status. Yekl/Jake's assimilationism is of course partly about class mobility, and so is Gitl's "inheritance" of divorce money, though she will use it to stay in the Lower East Side. Other stories too dramatize the starkness of class differences among Russian Jews. In "Circumstances," the Russified upper-class Tanya, who is obliged to take a job in a sweatshop, is made miserable by another worker whose singing alleviates the burden of the men and women's toil. She sang "the most Russian of Russian folksongs . . . with such an un-Russian flavor and pronounced the words with such a strong accent, and so illiterately, that Tanya gnashed her teeth as if touched to the quick, and closed her eyes and ears." She is reminded of commencement day in Kieff Gymnasium where she sang the same song "but in sturdy, ringing, charming Russian." Her wretched "circumstances" among "illiterate" people make her feel, "Everybody and everything about her was so strange, so hideously hostile, so exile-like!" (222). Tanya is an exile among those who are supposed to be "her own people." In "Circumstances," assimilation is not simply about adaptation to mainstream U.S. society but to the dominant class of recently arrived Jews who have been or have become laborers in America. The Jewish diaspora then is indeed pell-mell, because the old social orders have been displaced or transposed in that most leveling of ghetto institutions, the sweatshop.

The notion of the melting pot will serve as the ideal for the "American" nation composed of varying cultures. Yet Cahan invokes a "caldron" in his narrative not to endorse the eventual Americanization of Jewish people (on this his fiction conveys significant ambivalence) but to underline the distance, at the time of his writing, of the multifarious ethnic community from constituting a homogenous group that can be added into the mix as a separate and internally consistent ingredient. Although contained in visible and invisible boundaries, "the ghetto" in *Yekl* is a migrant site that spills out of its borders. To quote from Doreen Massey again, "instead of thinking of places as areas with boundaries around, they can be imagined as articulated movements in networks of social relations and understandings" ("Sense of Place" 154). Cahan's "ghetto" is a site of boundary-crossing within a monolithically viewed but in fact internally differentiated social network of diaspora Jews, where migrants hail from vastly different places and are downwardly as well as upwardly mobile. Their "hodgepodge" composition reflects realities beyond the confines of "the ghetto," pointing to the enduring effects of a *prior social order* located in an anterior place. The local is enclosed and bounded but also *translocal.*

One of the most significant ways in which Cahan inscribes translocality within the local is through language. Whatever we may name the varieties of Ashkenazi speech produced in *Yekl*, whether "dialect" or "jargon," this diasporic language with moot origins is crucial to the making of the Lower East Side as an Eastern European Jewish locale. The debates around Yiddish highlight the shifting internal borders of new Jewish locality and identities in the making. Cahan's copious display of Yiddish in the text is often interpreted as dialect use conventional to the local color genre. Dialect is a kind of speech that defines and collapses the spatial and the social, suggesting particular locality and class as well as race and ethnicity. Cahan engages the vernacular, "the most fundamental requirement" of the regional and local color genres, as Richard Brodhead has observed ("Reading" 136). But he puts a notable accent on the *differences* within rather than displaying a unitary relationship between language and place. Vernacular, the language of *verna*, the household slave, is doubly located in terms of space (confines of the house) and social class, which complicates matters for Jewish representations. "Accent" and "voice" are indicative of specific spatial locations; until Zionism, however, Jews were constructed to be a people without a place and without a language. In a chapter entitled "The Jewish Voice" in his *The Jew's Body*, Sander Gilman writes that to "sound Jewish" to the Christian world is to conjure an image of the Jew "as possessing all languages or no language of his or her own; of having a hidden language which mirrors the perverse or peculiar nature of the Jew; of being unable to truly command the national language of the world in which he/she lives, or indeed, even of possessing a language of true revelation, such as Hebrew" (12). To spatialize this representation, the Jew's language is everywhere and nowhere at the same time; it is hidden from view.

Local color writing on the other hand, posits a concordance of place, jargon, and community in isometric fashion with nationalism's linkages of nation-state territory and national language (Hobsbawm). In a telling equation of place, race, and language, Howells wrote in his discussion of Mary Wilkins Freeman, that in her "community of character," "the people are of one New England blood, and speak one racy tongue" (qtd. in Evans 778). Local color then displays the specific language developed within a specific bordered place by a specific people for the purposes of realism and/or satire. Further, the reader receives instruction in insular, local speeches and is entertained by their idiosyncratic variations from the standard. The perceived slipperiness and migrancy of Jewish languages stand in contrast to the presentation of historically enduring, firmly localized speech that speaks to the identifiable, often place-based, origins of a group, such as "New England blood." Cahan's use of Yiddish and Jewish accent in his English text, like the entire text, both defers to the local color tradition and departs from it.

The languages of enclosure and containment had dubious status at the time of Cahan's writing, and immigrant "appropriation" of English was especially problematic. Howells, for example, had a nuanced point of view, but it was one that ultimately reproduced the idea of the one national language as key to national literature and identity. His views on dialect speech exemplify this attitude. Although many critics declared in the early 1890s that the remarkable popularity of dialect in novels, magazines, and the lecture circuit in the 1880s had exhausted itself and that dialect literature was to be avoided (Nettles 65–66), Howells, in his search for "native" literary forms, was and remained a fervent advocate of dialect use. He praised the New England, Midwestern, and other local color writers for their fidelity to local speech: "I hope that our inherited English may be constantly freshened and revived from the native sources which our literary decentralization will help to keep open, and I will own that as I turn over novels coming from Philadelphia, from New Mexico, from Boston, from Tennessee, from rural New England, from New York, every local flavor of diction gives me courage and pleasure" (*Criticism* 64). Interestingly however, in a piece entitled "New York Low Life in Fiction" Howells writes on Stephen Crane's 1896 novella *George and His Mother* and draws attention to "the parlance of the class Mr. Crane draws upon for his characters" (who happen to be Irish immigrants) yet mentions neither "courage" nor "pleasure" in this "local flavor of diction." The protagonists, he writes, "are almost inarticulate; not merely the grammar, but the language itself *decays* in their speech." No longer is U.S. English "livened and revived" by dialect; instead, it disintegrates in the mouths of the immigrants.

A much more explicit critique of immigrant English is found in Henry James's "The Question of Our Speech," a lecture to the graduating class of Bryn Mawr in 1905. In this talk, James laments the lack of a "tone-standard" in the American language, which points to the fact that "our civilization remains strikingly *un*achieved" unlike that of the French, Germans, and even Turks and the Chinese (12). The *vox Americana*, "one of the stumbling blocks of our continent" (33) is "abandoned to its fate" (34). In James's narrative, the English language "came 'over' . . . originally without fear and without guile—but to find itself transplanted to spaces it had never dreamed, . . . to conditions it had never dreamed, in its comparative innocence, of meeting" (38–39). "An unfriended heroine . . . in a dire predicament," the disoriented English language, "our transported maiden" was "disjoined from all the associations, the other presences, that had attended her, that had watched for her and with her" (39). According to James, the language has been given "away" to the "forces of betrayal"—the American school, newspaper, Dutchman, and Dago—so that "our property" is now "distracted, disheveled, despoiled, divested of that beautiful and becoming drapery of native atmosphere and circumstance" (40–41). The friendless, "unrescued Andromeda," this highly gendered, beleaguered form of "genius and taste" (39) was left in the clutches of the uncaring, and above all of "our now so profusely imported, and, as is claimed, quickly assimilated foreign brothers and sisters" (42), who wreak havoc upon James's damsel in distress by "dump[ing] their mountain of promiscuous material into the foundations of the American" (43).

While we think a more candid disdain of the dumping-happy un-American cannot be articulated, James goes one step further. An almost-comical paranoia is expressed in the vision of the innocently somnolent American, whose language gets assaulted by busy alien aggressors:

> All the while we sleep the vast contingent of aliens whom we make welcome, and whose main contention, as I say, is that, from the moment of their arrival, they have just as much property in our speech as we have, and just as good a right to do what they choose with it . . . : all the while we sleep the innumerable aliens are sitting up (*they* don't sleep!) to work their will on our inheritance and prove to us that they are without any

> finer feeling or more conservative instinct of consideration for it, more fond, unutterable association with it, more hovering, caressing curiousity about it, than they may have on the subject of so many yards of freely figured oilcloth, from the shop, that they are preparing to lay down, for convenience, on kitchen floor or kitchen staircase. Oilcloth is highly convenient, and our loud collective medium of intercourse doubtless strikes these new householders as wonderfully resisting "wear" . . .—strikes them as an excellent bargain: durable, tough, cheap. (45–46; emphasis in original)

In this passage and elsewhere, the revulsion at alien speech and values is expressed in opposition to an obviously gendered discourse of native language (with a very clear origin) and native values. The language is also framed in terms of class and ownership, which the immigrants are shown to be grabbing shamelessly. There are several references to English as "property" and "inheritance" from which "the new householders" aim to "divest" the natives. From James's diatribe, one has the sense of the immigrant posing multiple threats to the patrimony, property, and language of the "native" Americans, defenseless against the activity of the aliens. The immigrants' occupation of "American" space in their "new households" involves the transfer of property and language. The household space and its contents (the oilcloth) constitute seized and "defiled" property. While Howells and James differ in their agendas, they both recoil from alien abuse of English; more interesting, both establish a relation among language, place, and property. For James, it is the household space in its oilcloth crudeness that is a corollary of the stolen English language. For Howells, vernaculars stem from specific "native sources," whether Boston or Tennessee, and serve to "freshen" the "*inherited* English," thus adding different dimensions to the shared property, while the non-native "sources" render the language unrecognizable and incapable of pointing to specific, legitimate places.

In *Yekl* the simple revelation of one speech per group, one dialect per bounded place as dictated by the monolingualism of nations, is not possible. Here is a teeming neighborhood of Jews, one "people of Israel," some of whom can hardly understand one another, and others, like Yekl/Jake, who are inventing the English language as they go along. The complexity and multiplicity of the Jewish population and their vernaculars are staged when Yekl's "greenhorn" wife, Gitl, is confronted with Mamie, the woman she rightly suspects of having dalliances with her husband. Gitl's jealous frustration as well as intimidation by Mamie's perfumes and finery is compounded by her inability to follow the woman's speech: loquacious Mamie's Polish Yiddish mixed with English words and inflected by an American accent is scarcely intelligible to Gitl, whose mother tongue is Lithuanian Yiddish (50). In addition to the heterogeneity within Yiddish, the ghetto boasts also of "disfigured" languages in process. English and Yiddish form a strange mélange in the mouths of Yekl and Mamie. "Don' bee 'fraid. Gu right aheat an' getch you partner! . . . Don' be 'shamed, Mish Cohen. Dansh mit dot gentlemarn!" yells out Jake at the dance hall (17). Yiddish syntax and intonation enter English just as English words incorporate themselves into Yiddish. In displacement, both languages acquire an elasticity attributed to Jewish languages like Yiddish, Judeo-Spanish and many others, which evolve rapidly and are "omnivorous" as Cahan writes of the Ashkenazi language. Yekl/Jake scolds Gitl for not being quick enough to insert English words into Yiddish. Speaking Yiddish, she refers to the window as *fentzter*: "'Can't you say *veenda*?' he had growled. Other *greenhornsh* learn to speak American *shtyle* very fast; and she—one might tell her the same word eighty thousand times, and it is *nu used*" (41; we are made to understand italicized words are spoken in English and the rest in Yiddish). Cahan's reproduction of Yekl's language serves the dual purposes of displaying the centrality of Yiddish as well as the absurdity that the assimilationist impetus can reach. At the same time, however, immigrant speech itself becomes strange and even repulsive in ways that confirm James's linguistic paranoia and mirrors the non-Jewish readers' suspicions about the potential for immigrants' pollution of language, and by implication, culture.

Writing in dialect and thus "showing" a place or an ethnicity was, at the turn of the twentieth century, rife with ambiguous authorial and political implications. In *Beyond Ethnicity*, Werner Sollors positions dialect use as a playful strategy that takes "the appearance of in-group conversations and pretend[s] a little that the national audience does not exist or is merely permitted to eavesdrop." Sollors also suggests that dialect occasions authorial and narrative "passing" by allowing "non-ethnic" authors to write under assumed names (Jewish, Chicano, and so forth) without detection (251–252), thereby transgressing inside/outside boundaries. However, the dialect form does not always conform to such felicitous interpretation. The charges of minstrelsy and perpetuation of stereotype was always a threat for writers who produced geographically or racially specific speech in their works. Authors considered to be "minorities," constructing particular ethnic worlds, faced contradictory impulses: the urge to assimilate and obliterate the different voice, the resolve to preserve and disseminate aspects of cultural distinctiveness, and the penchant for avoiding exposure of the "hidden tongues." In an analysis of the works of Charles Chesnutt, an author Howells championed, Eric Sundquist writes, "For black writers . . . the use of dialect was fraught with the tension between capitulation to stereotypes and the desire to find an audience for African American literature, whether one took that desire to be rank minstrelsy or a literary act of cultural consciousness akin to the publication of dialect verse by nationalist poets such as Robert Burns and John Synge" (304).

Choice of language was crucial also for Abraham Cahan, editor of a Yiddish daily, the first person in the United States to give a Socialist speech in Yiddish (to the surprise and derision of his fellow Socialists) and the author of a multivolume autobiography in Yiddish (still not translated into English in its entirety). Cahan's linguistic options were not simply Yiddish and English, but also the variations within. To the outrage of other authors, Cahan adopted for his popular journalism not a "high," Germanified Yiddish of the educated, but the plain tongue of the working classes, which included mispronounced English words (Harap 488–489). After having been criticized in the *Commercial Advertiser* for adding Yiddish to "Negro" and Irish dialects, Cahan regretted the literary production of a Lower East Side Jewish English that straddled both Yiddish and the adopted tongue, deciding, along with many critics for whom dialect had had its day, that dialect usage is "no more than a cheap bit of comedy"; he resolved to "avoid such 'dialect' in my subsequent English stories" (in Harap 496).

In *Strange Talk*, an important study on dialect use in the Gilded Age, Gavin Jones argues for the dissociation of dialect in U.S. writing of the period from elite literary and political agendas. Jones demonstrates the various ways in which dialect was not simply an expression of the dominant class's perception of subalterns; in fact, it often contributed to the questioning of "standard" English and challenged the imposition of a unified American language and body politic. In his discussion of Cahan, Jones points to the author's complex use of multiple languages as demonstrating the difficulty of the Jewish immigrants' position, caught between the inadequacies of both the tongues available to them: Yiddish, inflected by American English, and American English transformed by the immigrants' Yiddish. Neither proves to be a proper language, accentuating the in-between status of Cahan's immigrants, ambivalent about social, cultural, and linguistic assimilation. I agree with Jones that Cahan's use of language cannot be reduced to an attempt to entertain the uptown reader. The use of language in the novel reverses the temporalization of ethnic place as "primitive" and uncivilized. As I explained, Cahan stages the complexity of a Yiddish richly varied according to region and class, pointing us to the reaches of cultural differentiation beyond the ghetto. Interestingly, those who choose to remain in "the ghetto" are those who retain their own languages *and* acquire English literacy the proper way.

At the same time, however, it is clear that the narrator's disapproval of Jake's hyperbolic performances of assimilation are reflected in the linguistic contortions that Jake produces. He observes for example that "Boston Yiddish" is "more copiously spiced with *mutilated English*" than New York English (2; emphasis added). For Cahan, what Jake refers to as the relatively more extensive encounters of Jewish immigrants with the Anglo world in Boston produces not a greater success in assimilation, but a worse degradation of the English language, which in Jake's mouth recalls "the thickest Irish brogue" (2). Ultimately, the author does not portray with sympathy Jake and Mamie's irresolvable dilemma of being caught between hybridized languages and models of identity, as Jones seems to imply. Cahan censures them for their inauthentic mimicry: he harder they try to

Americanize and upwardly mobilize, the more "mutilated" their language and selves are. The narrator's discourse encloses linguistic particularity in place: Yiddish belongs to the ghetto and not to "America." Thereby, he preserves the purity of English.

Cahan's linguistic experiments are double-edged—like every literary strategy in *Yekl*—especially in their framing of what Mignolo calls "languaging" (*Local* 226), thinking and writing between languages by immigrants in enclosures. Asserting the centrality of Jewish languages to Jewish identity and tracing their fate in the Jewish contact zone of the Lower East Side required a balancing act, in view of the hegemony of the idea of the American "national language" and English as the language of U.S. empire. Exposing the prominence and creativity of Yiddish, Cahan also has to defer to English as the language of property and propriety. In this, he echoes his mentor Howells and James and reflects his and other critics' attitudes toward "foreign" languages and English. As a "native informant," Cahan is not impartial; nor does he avoid calling attention to himself through language use. It is impossible to take for granted the author's superior command of English, even though he too is an immigrant, a fact well known to any reader of the work. Hybridized language is reflected only in the immigrants' speech and not in the narrator's own "pure" use of the language. This practice is typical of accent and dialect representation of the time, but it also endures in "ethnic literature," despite the important exceptions of civil rights–era works like *Down These Mean Streets*, as we shall see in chapter 5. Clearly, as one whose English-language writing career was a lot shorter than his Yiddish production, which lasted sixty years, Cahan does not privilege English per se, but denigrates the manner in which Yekl and Mamie throw themselves into English and the way Yekl obliges his wife to replace Yiddish words with mutilated English words.

Further, against Yekl's vocal, assimilationist Jewishness of body and sound, Cahan privileges Americanization through literacy, represented by Bernstein, which defies stereotypes of the "ghetto Jew," confined and static. The first time we meet Bernstein, Jake's boarder and fellow worker, is in the sweatshop when they are all waiting for work to arrive. While Jake is filling this idle time displaying his Gentile-like masculine bravado through speech and gesture, Bernstein is reading an English newspaper, consulting a "cumbrous dictionary on his knees" (1) This is the same Bernstein whom their neighbor praises as "smart and ejecate like a lawyer" (88) and who will marry Gitl to remain in the East Side and open a grocery store with Gitl's divorce money. In her discussion of *Yekl*, Hana Wirth-Nesher also points to the way in which Cahan deploys Bernstein as Yekl's other, underlining the value of Bernstein's education while holding Yekl at a distance. Wirth-Nesher also comments on the scenes involving Jake's illiteracy, where he has a scribe read and write his letters to and from Russia; these scenes "diminish Jake's power" whereby he "is dwarfed by the Old World of Hebrew textuality" (60). I will add that Jake, who "mutilates" English, is also dwarfed by Bernstein's

English literacy and, especially, by the narrator's perfect English, against whose written and learned command of language his remains vaudevillian, racialized as Jewish ghetto-speak. In his essay "The Russian Jew in America," where Cahan tries to redeem the immigrants and dismantle stereotypes about Jewish people and "the ghetto," he boasts of the command of English of many sweatshop workers and the strength of the Jewish press—testament to Jewish literacy at a time when immigrants in "the ghettos" were denigrated for their lack of education.

Jake is not one of Cahan's "Russian Jews in America"; he is the coarse, uneducated ghetto Jew, belonging nowhere and speaking no language properly, a stereotype created by non-Jewish as well as Jewish discourses. English is guarded by Bernstein, who will neither challenge nor deform it. Bernstein is the civilized immigrant, who would pass the literacy test proposed by the Immigration Restriction League (and adopted in 1914 in the same decade as the publication of *Yekl*). Literacy was instrumentalized as racialized gatekeeping to effect exclusion of "backward" immigrants—just as it was deployed to disenfranchise African Americans. The concepts and tools dividing the civilized at home from the savages abroad were also utilized to differentiate between "educable" and uncivilizable subalterns. Combined with illiteracy Yekl's malformed language are marks of his unsuitability and reason for his ambivalent, unhappy suspension between two worlds at the end of the novella.

Cahan's distaste for Yekl's speech as a malformed mixture is ironic given that Cahan championed Yiddish, despite its many Ashkenazi detractors denigrating the hybrid "jargon" and preferring to speak either in European languages, or, in the early Zionist movement, in Hebrew without a Yiddish accent or orthography (see Harshav). Yet Yiddish is entirely a language of mixture. The critique of Yekl's speech implies that a "pure" Yiddish, like Gitl's, is preferable to Yekl's, when in fact, Yiddish, with its own fusions of Hebrew, German, and Slavic languages is patently impure. I read this irony not only as an inconsistency of Cahan's, but also as a critique of the diasporization process that Yekl is undergoing, in which the ghetto enclosure and the pressures to assimilate make him incapable either of learning English or preserving his own culture. The Bernsteins and Gitls of the Jewish ghetto are able to withstand these pressures, while others, like Yekl and Mamie, are not. Cahan shows the many ways in which "the foreign" gets localized. Although immigrants are expected to relinquish language upon arrival and acquire English miraculously, Cahan demonstrates the variety of linguistic transitions possible in the contained space: the ghetto produced various pathways to English, from Bernstein's literate reliance on the printed word to Jake's verbal mimicries and insistence on substituting English for Yiddish even within Yiddish, to Gitl's willing yet often failing attempts at second-degree imitation, copying her husband the mimic. Hence, Cahan both confirms and destabilizes the idea of "Jewish ghetto speech," pointing to variations in the deployment of literacy and authenticity. He uses Jake to signal the absurdities of verbal mimicry that dismisses literacy and positions Bernstein and the omniscient narrator as the exemplary inheritors of language, whose foreign, immigrant, and ghetto provenance do not prevent them for according it the respect that his readers will find it requires. At the same time, in their transitional state, they do not suffer from what Wirth-Nesher calls "linguistic disinheritance," the Americanized, English-only dissociation from Jewish languages that a poet like Charles Reznikoff laments (18). They are the examples of successful integration and hyphenation, with their proper linguistic choices and their property.

The master narratives of Americanization of place, race, and assimilation occupy an ambiguous status in this first literary example from a community held to be exemplary for its success and assimilation. Cahan's champion Howells failed to observe the nuances and ironies the author inserted both into the literature of place and into the cultural logics of assimilation. In his enthusiastic review of *Yekl*, Howells wrote, " I cannot help thinking that we have in him a writer of foreign birth who will do honor to American letters, as Boyesen did. He is already thoroughly naturalized to our point of view; he sees things with American eyes, and he brings in aid of his vision the far and rich perception of his Hebraic race; while he is strictly of the great and true Russian principles in literary art" ("New York Low Life" 51; emphasis added). For the patron of the parochial, decentralization depends upon translation and requires the perspective of one naturalized. To "do honor" to American literature means to adopt the native view, embellished by other literacies. For Garland, the difference of "the local" from the national is the impetus of writing, and all the differences when put together would produce a truly American national tradition. This mosaic-making view assumes that the only difference produced by "the local" is its divergence from the national or the other locales. Cahan however shows that the local itself is heterogenous and disequilibriated, just like the roads to Americanization.

PARADOXES OF WRITING DIASPORIC LOCALITY

Cahan's reversals of local color literature and Jewish identity through the representation of a translocal and internally differentiated Jewish spatiality in a new phase of diasporization do not constitute a "pure" discourse of "resistance" to the literary and political establishments he encountered here. Although he changed the local color genre through his alternative spatializations and approach to language and dialect, he also borrowed many of the conventions of the genre. In addition to the ones I have mentioned, such as the abbreviation of space, the representation of assimilationist idioms that oppose the educated narratorial voice, and descriptive realism, Cahan drew on the prevalent discourses of racialization characteristic of the mainstream and of local color writing. While he complicates Jewish ethnicity, as I suggested, by pointing to its heterogeneity and frequently incompatible variations, he refers to Jewish racialization in more fixed and common terms.

The turn-of-the-century years were a time when the Jewish people were known as a religious, ethnic, and a racial group and as a "nation" simultaneously. The racialization of Jews in the United States often pointed to their "biological" as well as cultural differences. While their "racial" proximity to African Americans was sometimes argued, as in the much-quoted *The Jew: a Negro* (Abernethy) by a southern preacher, they were most often racialized as an intermediate group. Philosemitism did coexist with anti-Jewishness, but mostly the Jewish people were perceived as a "foreign race" with its own particular physiognomy. In writing "the local," Cahan participated in these racializing discourses differentiating "the Jew" as a "type." This approach is not surprising, given that local color often builds on the representation of types: particular people inhabiting a particular place. So, the first description of Yekl involves the demonstration of his "Jakeification"; that is, his easy adoption of American popular culture. Yekl/Jake puts himself at the center of attention by showing off his knowledge of professional boxing. Although Yekl/Jake is a magnet for the young women, it is not, the narrator informs us, his "brawny arms and magnificent form" that attracts the women who are watching him: "For a display of manly force, when connected—even though in a purely imaginary way—with acts of violence, has little attraction for a 'daughter of the Ghetto.'" Instead, the appeal is in what "those arms and form command on their own merits" and his decidedly Jewish features. "Pleasing" overall, the most central of his facial characteristics are his eyes: "Strongly Semitic naturally, they became still more so each time they were brightened up by his good-natured boyish smile. Indeed Jake's very nose, which was fleshy and pear-shaped and decidedly not Jewish (although not decidedly anything else), seemed to join the Mosaic faith . . . as soon as that smile of his made its appearance" (3). Jake's attractiveness lies in his undeniably Jewish features. Of all these, the proboscis, the stereotypically defining feature, may look neutral independently, but ultimately is marked by Jewishness upon "accentuation" by the mouth, the primary organ through which Cahan renders Yekl unattractively assimilationist, as we saw in the discussion of dialect.[15] Cahan takes pains to demonstrate that Jake has a natural penchant for assimilation through popular or official national culture in *both* Russia and in the United States. In Russia he loved military parades and martial songs and knew more Russian words than all other young men (10–11); in the United States he embraces English, albeit an immigrant English, and he is drawn to the popular cultural forms of dancing and boxing.

Cahan undermines Jake's efforts by demonstrating that he may perform his way to assimilation all he wants, through boxing moves or dancing, but his racial truth is inexorably stamped on his face. In an article on theatricality and *Yekl*, Sabine Haenni points to the performative aspects of *Yekl*. She argues that Cahan disapproves of vaudeville and Yekl/Jake's vaudevillian, "low" performance of self and of acculturation in scenes such as the one where he is showing off his familiarity with boxing. Therefore, according to Haenni, Cahan positions Jake's female spectators as having ambivalent and contradictory impulses toward Jake. On the one hand, the author represents their sexual attraction to Jake; on the other, he denies their admiration of him as good "daughters of the Ghetto," in order to make them "respectable in the eyes of his middle-class readers" (Haenni 514). Further, as "daughters of the Ghetto," they are not necessarily interested in the staging of Gentileness; what attracts them is Jake's "Jewish face" and his forms "in their own merit" (3) divorced from the performance of boxing/assimilation. In severing "violent" masculinity from Jewishness, Cahan further racializes "the Jew" and marks Jewish male difference as nonviolent—and by implication nonmasculine—according to mainstream American gendered values. Cahan locates ethnic and racial loyalty in the female audience: even though they, like the men, who mock his performance as "dog's tricks" and boxing as "fighting—like drunken moujiks in Russia" (3), are uninterested in his staging of the (badly) assimilated self, Jake's undeniable racial Jewishness draws them.

Cahan's racialization of the contained, ghetto population extends to other characters as well. For example, he creates a type out of the sweatshop owner. When the boss arrives, he is described as "a dwarfish little Jew, with a vivid pair of eyes and a shaggy black beard" who "darted into the chamber" (8) and mocked his workers who throw themselves onto the piecework they had been waiting for him to bring: "Just like the locusts of Egypt!" The exploiter deriding his workers as a plague is "the little boss" (9) who sports his Jewish features—short stature, fast-moving eyes, scruffy look—a lot less pleasantly than Jake but is nevertheless just as identifiable. Similarly, Mamie is first described as bearing "a pert, ill-natured, pretty face of the most strikingly Semitic cast" in the dance hall, "her shrewd dark eyes gleam[ing] out of a warm gipsy complexion" (19). But it is not only the morally distasteful or ambiguous characters like the boss, Jake, or Mamie, who are described in terms highlighting their physical difference and repugnance. Upon seeing Gitl at Ellis Island, Jake's heart sinks at her "uncouth and un-American appearance," exacerbated by her physique. The exposure to sun on the boat had further darkened her complexion, "which combined with her prominent cheek bones, inky little eyes, and, above all, the smooth black wig, to lend her resemblance to a squaw" (34). Although here Cahan is reproducing Jake's unkindly thoughts, his choice of words shows that he acknowledges stereotypical representations of Jewish and other races.

In negatively racializing Jewish people, Cahan conforms to the representational machinery of local color and realism as well as to the more general dominant civilizational ideologies circulating about Jews, immigrants, and other races as well as their places. The pejorative references to "gypsies" and "squaws" presumably help readers visualize the parallels among the colonized Native

Americans, the reviled, nomadic Roma, and the uncivilized (unassimilated or half-assimilated) traditional Jews, also characterized by an unsavory mobility and history of displacement. Racism and colonialism are brought to bear on the ghetto, a primitive site in the civilized Western city. Cahan may have effected the racialization of the Jewish characters in the language of anti-Semitism in order to undermine the assimilationist impulse of immigrants, of which he is critical in his fictions. That is, he may be telling his Jewish and non-Jewish readers that no matter how hard they try, Jews cannot assimilate (with the implications of simulating and being similar) to the majority; they carry the essential, unassimilable mark of Jewishness. We are left with an incomplete project of diasporic representation: Cahan offers an alternative view of the "ethnic place" and of the places and processes of diasporization; at the same time, however, he colludes with the standard representational discourses around race and place. He reproduces the expected codes of literary genres and the language of the turn-of-the-century obsession with race and biology. Cahan's text is conflicted: the stereotyping and racialization of the immigrant Jews is recognizable (distastefully so) and homogenizing as well as at odds with his social and geographic differentiation and complication of ideas about the internal homogeneity "race."

"GHETTO" SITES AND AMERICA'S DIASPORAS

Cahan entered an intensely spatialized U.S. literary tradition and marketplace through the trappings of local color conventions. He used and reconfigured the dominant literary and political discourses of place and territory to narrate the cultural fate of the most momentous Jewish immigration to the continent. Launching literature of "the Ghetto," Cahan created a new cultural locus of Jewish life in the continent, which endures till today as a "spatial icon" (Diner 126) of "mythopoetic stature" (Rischlin 16). In fashioning a new Jewish diaspora place of displacement and transition, he overturned a static interpretation of the local and of place implicit in much local color fiction and criticism. Cahan created what I am calling a "migrant site" out of the "ghetto," a place where the narratives of enclosure and translocality coexist and destabilize one another. First, he entered the local color mode from the multilingual immigrant locus and dissociated "the native" from the "the local." Thus, he inserted foreignness into and questioned the boundaries of "American" literature and its defining places. In *Yekl*, "the local" is extensive and connected outside itself at every turn, reminding us that Cahan's and the immigrants' spatial vision was shaped by what lay elsewhere: that is, a translocal layering of many places outside the locus of settlement. Like the intersecting quality of Jewish languages themselves, Jewish diaspora geography was necessarily relational. Further, the bounded space itself is far from coherent, socially and linguistically, complicated as much by spatial and social Americanization as by the geographies and languages of Eastern Europe. The Jewish populations spill out of the neatly bordered worlds of localism, with their disparate places of origin outside the United States, variant and changing social classes, and myriad languages. *Yekl* complicates Jewish identity to reveal the internal differentiation of a population at a time when Jewish and other immigrant groups were deindividualized, most frequently referred to as "teeming masses" inhabiting bounded locations. Cahan does incorporate some of the markers of a mainstream intersection of localism and nativism, including that of racialization, which is an aspect of creating "sites" out of diaspora places. As we shall see in the next chapter, on Willa Cather, many authors of the period sympathetic to diaspora groups sought to legitimize themselves as authors and the denigrated populations that were their subjects by partially adhering to literary and ideological conventions of representing place, race, and ethnicity. Yet, despite the resort to the seemingly knowable category of race, Cahan's outlook ultimately involves an unstable and equivocal conception of diasporas and their places. For Cahan, place does not equal continuous settlement and identity, as it does for Howells and Garland. This instability does not mean that the Jewish subjects are proverbially "homeless" but that displacement and localization involve a crisscrossing of spatial memories, meanings, and belongings that cannot be geographically fixed. In *Yekl* "the local," with its mobile "human throngs," can never be assumed stable; nor can its residents have even pretensions to stable identities. The "tale of the New York ghetto" shows how, despite the spatial containment, the outside Anglo/Christian world penetrates the Jewish space, influencing the immigrants and pushing them toward inauthenticity and self-display. The assimilationist urges of Yekl, or Jake-in-the-making, bring him only more discontent. Immediately after his divorce from Gitl, Yekl leaves for the marriage bureau to wed Mamie. Riding in a cable car from the ghetto toward City Hall, his ambivalence about the divorce and the impending second marriage becomes acute. The story ends in this vehicle, in the space between the Jewish place of the ghetto and the civic space of the nation in the marriage bureau. Suspended like Yekl after his divorce between two places, the protagonists of diaspora fictions emblematize the discontents of assimilation,[16] civilizational discourses, and the intersection of place and race in the age of U.S. empire and immigration.

Introducing the insider word and insider image of "the ghetto" to the reading public, Cahan also paved the way for understanding spatial coloniality in the modern city. *Yekl* stages ghettoization as a "civilizing process": it is where "the foreign" goes to hide and works on self-transformation until it is no longer "foreign." Ghetto residents stay until they are able to integrate themselves as civilized people. Unlike Yekl, the repulsive hybrid who does not know his place, Gitl and Bernstein, who prefer not to deform Yiddish *or* English and reject quick relinquishment of their traditions, are rewarded with staying put and inheriting a piece of the ghetto. Spatial coloniality makes the subaltern classes of ethnoracial others disappear into enclosures of their own. Cahan constructs an idea of the civilized immigrant, embodied by Gitl and Bernstein, as those who respect their own traditions and languages and know how to handle the dominant ones with care—and from a distance. Mamie and Yekl, on the other hand, think they have evolved and view Gitl and Bernstein as behind in the linear civilizational (assimilationist) trajectory. Mamie comforts Yekl about his wife: "Don't worry; she'll soon oyshgreen herself" (49). But they are in fact presented as deformed creatures who "mutilate" hegemonic languages and have no business stepping outside the ghetto's bounds.

In Cahan's work, the conflict is not between "native" and outsider/immigrant (as in nativism or local colorist ideology), but between the civilizable immigrant and the uncivilized one. The racialized gatekeeping involved in repudiating immigrant speech is offset by a critique of improper linguistic assimilationism: without literacy, it is one that conforms to the lowest common denominator of U.S. popular culture and language. Gitl and Bernstein, on the other hand, stay in the ghetto, affirming the viability of the diasporic place against the reformists' and the text's own repudiation of its conditions. But neither they nor the narrator confront the spatialized containment of "vernaculars" and the hegemony of standard English as national language. As Walter Mignolo explains in *Local Histories/Global Designs*, "Maintaining the links between, language, literature, culture, and territory implies reproducing imperial allocations of cultural configurations" (235). If English is necessarily the language of America, the coloniality of the social and spatial order dictates that other languages be enclosed in the "privacy" of ethnic spaces and stay in the ghetto.

In creating migrant sites, Cahan contributes to the making of diaspora place as a site; he "allocates" cultures to spatial containers by not challenging the containment of immigrants and their languages. Cahan differentiates between the successful and unsuccessful immigrants by hierarchizing them based on language, literacy, and association with "low culture," thereby reproducing racializing and civilizational discourses. But he also inserts translocal geographies and languages that cannot be discarded and compels the reader to think about immigrant and diaspora identities as complex and differentiated. Like Cahan, Willa Cather also brings immigrants, considered "low" subjects, to the center stage of U.S. national fantasies: the putatively "wide open" West of the nineteenth century. In her fiction, immigrants find a place in the vast landscape through literary regionalism and the representation of immigrants contained in small spatial units. The way that turn-of-the-twentieth-century authors, even those as different as Cahan and Cather, could foreground the spatial and social dimension of diasporas in their narratives and earn legitimacy in the American literary marketplace was through the production and representation of literary and social enclosure.

CHAPTER 3

PLURALISM IN THE IMMIGRANT PRAIRIE

WILLA CATHER'S CIVILIZED PRIMITIVES

Having discovered "the world of ideas" through the classics, Willa Cather's Jim Burden contemplates a passage from *The Georgics* in the third book of *My Ántonia*: "'*Primus ego in patriam mecum . . . deducam Musas*'; for I shall be the first, if I live, to bring the Muse into my country." Burden tells us that his mentor earlier had clarified the meaning of *patria* for Virgil, as being

> not a nation or even a province, but the little rural neighborhood on the Mincio where the poet was born. This was not a boast, but a hope, at once bold and devoutly humble, that he might bring the Muse . . . not to the capital, the *palatia Romana*, but to his own little "country"; to his father's fields, "sloping down to the river and to the old beech trees with broken tops." (151)

It is not difficult to recognize the parallels between the Virgilian invocation and authorial ambitions at hand. As Blanche Gelfant has pointed out, writing about nineteenth-century European "pioneers" and the prairie, Willa Cather was a literary "pioneer" herself (132). In an essay she called "My First Novels (There Were Two)," Cather wrote, "Nebraska is distinctly déclassé as a literary background; its very name throws the delicately attuned critic into a clammy shiver of embarrassment." She then summarized the establishment feeling: "a New York critic voiced a very general opinion when he said: 'I simply don't care a damn what happens in Nebraska, no matter who writes about it'" ("My First" 94). Cather was unique in casting not only the scorned region but also the denigrated immigrant subjects in a light previously unavailable. She wrote in the same essay, "*O Pioneers!* was not only about Nebraska farmers; the farmers were Swedes! At that time, 1912, the Swede had never appeared on the printed page in this country except in broadly humorous sketches; and the humour was based on two peculiarities: his physical strength, and his inability to pronounce the letter 'j'" ("My First" 95). Susan Rosowski has observed that Cather "was the first to give immigrants heroic status" (45) by placing them center stage during one of the most important events in the history of the United States: the continental expansion of the American empire into "the West." Although both immigration and the experience of the West continue to inform the U.S. national imaginary, these two components were seldom aligned in narrative. Particularly distinctive was Cather's favorable representations of various groups of non-Anglo immigrants, who, at the xenophobic time of her writing of the early novels, were held in low esteem and were not part of dominant national identity discourses. Frederick Jackson Turner, whose assessment of the Western experience influenced generations, disliked Cather's novels because of their sympathy for unassimilating "non-English stocks" (Handley 13). Preoccupied with the question of national, ethnic, and literary origins and inheritance, Cather mobilized her own ideas about the beginnings of settlers, American *patrias*, and "non-English stocks" through, as I explain, the contradictory discourses of primitivism and civilization as well as enclosure and translocality. On the one hand, like Cahan's localism, writing the region allows Cather to provide more complex and favorable depictions of immigrants than her readers would have found elsewhere during the xenophobic time of war. On the other hand, she encloses, as does Cahan, the possibility of a larger critique of immigration, territory, and empire; her pluralist inclusion and valorization of off-white Northern and Eastern European immigrants exclude the casualties of empire, Native American communities, as well as the other, subaltern subjects who were part of the expansion project. Reading for spatial containment reveals the deployment of (successful) immigration as foundational to national identity to cover over the "wounds" (see chapters 1 and 4) inflicted on those who were summarily excluded from this narrative. Because enclosure in Cather's works is a generative rather than confining experience of place for her heroic immigrants (unlike for others), the importance of civilizational thinking to the twin processes of immigration and expansion, separating the civilized from the uncivilized through spatial and other means, is laid bare.

In this chapter, I show that Willa Cather deploys a poetics and politics of enclosure in which place—as frontier, region ("the West"), land, and landscape—and the ideal immigrant subject are represented in terms of boundaries and containment. The translocal diasporic sensibilities of exile and nostalgia for the homeland exceed the enclosure, only to be reframed by Cather through the resort to primitivism and pluralism—through which place and culture become static entities. Cather presents the immigrants in a primitivizing frame by emphasizing their corporeality and their identification with place. Paradoxically, this emplacement, which works to enclose and contain them spatially and culturally, also underlines their superiority: they are civilized because of their bodies' primitive vigor, which parallels the characteristics of the land. Moreover, as the heirs to European civilization (which Cather considers superior to the U.S. Anglo-Saxon's), the favored immigrant characters retain and perpetuate cultural and linguistic practices; that is, their civilization and culture in their enclosed sites. While Cahan's characters exhibit an equivocal relation to immigrant sites and enclosures because of their diasporic status, Cather's chief protagonists are at one with the new place *despite* their migration experience. Through enclosures in which imported European civilization is preserved, her heroines inherit "America."

The absent Native Americans and the missing narrative of colonialism are revealed in the novel's spatial discourses, specifically in the enclosed localization of the ideal immigrant. As I argue, the substitution of the immigrant for the indigenous in *the* synechdoche for the nation, "the West," takes place through civilizational and pluralistic discourses. The immigrant in this novel is an intermediate figure possessing the "barbarian virtues" (Jacobson) of the primitive subjects of empire, namely, the primitive body full of vigor and spontaneity and the attachment to land. The enclosure of the immigrant in her land, orchards, and gardens is a reminder of other enclosures of the civilizing mission that led to the dispossession of Native Americans. Cather's heroic protagonists are heirs to "America" through enclosure, as a paradoxical means of access to the pluralist openness of America, while the Native American is disappeared from Cather's book as from the narrative of "American civilization."

Cather complicates the relation between enclosure and civilization. In one of the few critical writings that examine the idea of enclosure in U.S. literature, Melissa Ryan discusses confinement and civilization in Cather's 1913 *O Pioneers!* In her insightful analysis, she explains that while Cather's work and person are associated with "wide-open space," *O Pioneers!* shows "the theoretical relationship between civilization and enclosure" (277). Ryan examines the novel's investment in the idea of America as consisting of borders and enclosures, including the penitentiary and disciplinary kind. The novel displays the immigrant pioneer's victory over the wilderness and the establishment of civilization represented by "broken" land, fences, and the institutions of the prison and the asylum. "Ultimately," Ryan observes, "the work of the pioneer (taming the wilderness) is the work of the law (civilizing the savage) is the work of conformity (Americanizing the foreigner)" (283). Hence, the "wide-open prairie" of *O Pioneers!* is not a space of openness and freedom but a site of "civilization"; that is, taming and ordering, which, in its fenced, purchased and bordered form, parallels the institutions of the insane asylum and the prison that are its ostensible antitheses. In *My Ántonia*, enclosure works differently. I show in this chapter that in depicting the spatial and cultural enclosure of the immigrants Cather does not oppose civilization with "the primitive" but aligns them. Cather's immigrants are both primitivized spectacles and civilized Europeans, the most generative of whom—Ántonia—is a civilizing force precisely because of her primitivistic body and attachment to land. The seemingly oppositional operations of diasporization on the one hand and spatial enclosure on the other are bound up together in the body of Ántonia. In her best-known novel, Cather creates a migrant site out of the prairie by enclosing and immobilizing the idealized immigrants in land at the same time as she foregrounds their territorial, linguistic, and cultural translocalities. Her work illustrates the centrality of spatial discourses to the perpetuation of the "nation of immigrants" story that erases historical and current empire and coloniality of power in the modern United States. The enclosure of Cather's immigrants is key to the land-based claims of U.S. national identity, shaped by expansion and empire.

REGIONALISM'S NATIVES AND FOREIGNERS

Cather's dual stance toward immigrants and their relation to place make the political and aesthetic positioning of her work complex, including with regard to the spatialized genre with which she is frequently identified: regionalism. As the overview in chapter 2 shows, "local color" and "regionalism" were and continue to be used interchangeably although the former came to be instituted as a literary genre before the latter and some have argued for a differentiation between the two modes.[1] In many studies of regionalism and literature, scholars tend to offer strong critiques or else redemption of regionalism. For Roberto Dainotto, regionalist literature, whether in U.S., English, or Italian contexts, is a reactionary, nativist formation that negates history in an attempt to escape modernity. Amy Kaplan makes emphatic and convincing links among "nation, region, and empire," the title of her comprehensive essay; like Richard Brodhead, she underscores regionalism as a "literary tourism" (Kaplan, "Nation" 252; Brodhead, *Reading*) produced by and for an urban readership besieged by current realities and seeking the consolations of a remote and idyllic past. Other observers have argued for a divergent understanding of regionalist writing, suggesting that writing the region can give rise to political and literary discourses resistant to convention and dominant ideology. Cecelia Tichi suggests, for example, that "under cover of regionalism" women writers could explore gender and promote new womanhood and independent characters like Alexandra of *O Pioneers!* In two important works, *Writing Out of Place* by Judith Fetterley and Marjorie Pryse and *Cosmopolitan Vistas* by Tom Lutz, regionalism is more than a "cover"; it can provide a cogent, overt critique of oppressive ideologies. For example, Fetterley and Pryse, who contest Amy Kaplan's and Richard Brodhead's perspectives on the convergence of regionalism with nationalism, argue that "regionalism . . . is a discourse represent[ing] a general social or political strategy for resisting meaning generated by others in a nation-state" (5). In a similar reading for "resistance," Stephanie Foote concludes that "one of the most important functions of regional writing was to rectify exclusion" (13). According to these and other scholars, instead of conformity, coherence, and cultural provincialism that they might be associated with, regionalist writers actually offer a feminist and cosmopolitan outlook that derails masculinist, nationalist, and hierarchical discourses and ideologies.

Regionalism easily lends itself to such contradictory interpretations: just as its own definition and boundaries shift, its ideological stance is also often blurry or conflictingly multistranded. Rather than rescuing or condemning regionalism, I focus on the nexus of the immigrant, the West, and the land, just as I explored immigrants in the context of local color writing in Cahan's work. Like Cahan, Cather inserted immigrants into a genre largely associated with "native-born" Americans. As some have argued, regionalist and local color writing construct place by and large for the benefit of nonimmigrant readers as a comforting imaginary, one devoid of immigrants and foreignness (Brodhead *Reading*; Dainotto; Amy Kaplan, "Nation"). Roberto Dainotto has observed that as "Marxism divided society vertically into exploiters and the exploited, regionalism divided society into natives and foreigners" (26). Foote disagrees, arguing that the exoticized "natives" in regional fictions "are uncannily similar to the foreigners and immigrants in the city, and the solidity of the simple 'primitive' folk of the region is not antidote to, but instead the alibi for, alienation and self-estrangement" (15).

Cather's "prairie novels" are differently positioned from Dainotto's and Foote's examples: Cather casts the West *as* an immigrant region in which most "natives" (in this case, Anglo-Saxon Americans) are background figures. In the process, however, she "regionalizes" immigrants by ascribing to them a folk primitivism characteristic of much (though not all) local color and regional literature's "natives." She also makes regional or "native" subjects out of immigrants through their attachment to place and culture: Her heroines prefer to bypass mobility in favor of their enclosed spatial and cultural continuities enacted in the region. They are endowed with primitive vigor and identification with land; at the same time, they retain their culture as superior and uninterrupted even in diaspora. She represents them as bearers of civilization in opposition to the racializing discourses of her time that demean and denigrate immigrants.

Cather's contestation of dominant cultural ideologies around ethnicity and gender, however, rests on problematic representational means. First, although these immigrant women are depicted as creators of "new world gardens" out of the wilderness, their problematic position as "pioneers" erasing Native American presence is obscured. And, while her work attempts to "free" the non-Anglo European immigrants from the damaging prejudice and stereotypes they faced (especially at the time of her writing, around the First World War), it also encloses the perception of immigrants in a limited spatial and cultural frame, which mirrors that of pluralism, a popular if not dominant ideology of her time.

Later in this chapter, I explain how Cather's spatial ideology and the pluralism of her period dovetail and how pluralism obscures empire. Now, I shall begin to explore how immigrants came to inherit American place and represent the West in Cather's work.

"NOTHING BUT LAND"

In Cather's West, diasporic European cultures as well as U.S. identities are configured through a particular relationship to land. As the novelist of immigrant life in the prairie, Cather construes a sympathetic identification between the ideal immigrant and her landscape. Belonging in American territory defines the immigrant just as much as deterritorialization and migrancy, with which immigration is more frequently associated. Land is key to the development of the "citizen" and of "the country": Cather's model American is neither the misnamed "native" (that is, the Anglo Saxon settler), nor the Native American, but, paradoxically, the foreigner, who develops a continuous, emotional, identifying relationship with place, in which she stays.

In *My Ántonia* (1918), as in Cather's other "prairie novels," *O Pioneers!* (1913) and to a lesser extent *The Song of the Lark* (1915), the immigrant tale, associated largely with urban locations, finds its locus in "the West" of the Homestead Act. Historians and literary critics have pointed to the common perception of regions as sites of "cultural homogeneity" (see Luebke 26). According to Dainotto, "a 'region,' in fact, is a commonplace of an ethnic purity" (20). But Willa Cather's West, or what her narrator Jim Burden calls "the country," is an amalgam of clashing cultures, languages, and religions, a transposition of the multinational, multicultural urban story to the "untamed" prairie, one devoid of its indigenous inhabitants. The western region is a site of contending cultural differences that find their expression in territory. Land and landscape are the raw materials of both author and protagonist and their primary means of creating an "American" story, albeit one in which Native Americans have been disappeared and replaced by immigrants. Because Cather is trying to establish belonging for European immigrants in America, she counters the convention of deploying the discourse of the region to separate "natives" and foreigners; instead, she turns the immigrants into "natives."

How does Cather construct the settler-colonialist narrative that erases indigenous precedence and presence at the same time as she contests the anti-immigrant, xenophobic attitudes of her time? The "nativization" of the immigrants takes place through the thematization of beginnings and blankness, for "the country" (that is, the western region) and the immigrants. The immigrant novel, frequently a bildungsroman and/or a conversion story in its early twentieth-century form, appears in a different guise in Cather's work. *My Ánto-*

nia, a bildungsroman not only of individuals but also of an entire generation of settlers in the West, and therefore a story of change, development, and progress, is obsessed with origins and continuity. Like the pastorals it springs from, the novel's gaze is turned backward to its own point of origin, in the "raw beginnings" of country and people. Elegiacally recounted, the past is not another country, but the very one in which the narrator, the adult Jim Burden, continues to live. Jim looks back to the crucial "moment" of his own and Ántonia's beginnings in the West, declaring it time and again as the formative, and indeed, best possible time of his life. An orphan who was in need of new parentage and ancestry, Jim locates his past not in Virginia, the place of his and his family's provenance, but in the plains, where he moves at the age of ten and meets Ántonia, his senior by a few years. For Jim, the prairie, as wilderness or as cultivated land identified with Ántonia is an all-explanatory frame through which to observe, explain, and enjoy the world.

The narrative revolves around the originality and representativeness of Ántonia. The famous opening that frames the story, in which a friend of Jim Burden relates the origin of the novel, makes this focus evident from the outset. Both Jim, a legal representative of the railroads, and his friend live in New York and pass the long hours of their train journey through the Midwest by reminiscing about the small Nebraska town they come from, while crossing similar prairie towns in the dusty, hot landscape of Iowa. Their recollections center on the figure of Ántonia, "a Bohemian girl" who, "more than any other person we remembered, . . . seemed to mean to us the country, the conditions, the whole adventure of our childhood" (xii). The novel at hand is the one written by Jim during his travels and presented to his friend who is re-presenting it to us. Ántonia is at the core of this progression of presentations although for a time the author allows a separate space for the unfolding of Jim's own story of development.

It is important to note that the story of the representative immigrant begins in a train, as the two men reminisce in the "observation car, where the woodwork was hot to the touch and red dust lay deep over everything" and decide that "no one who had not grown up in a little prairie town could know anything about it. It was a kind of freemasonry, we said" (ix–x). For the readers, these two men are insiders who do know and have mastered the landscape and identified its representative; one of them, Jim, will be our "native informant" of this enclosed, cult-like site of the prairie town. In the chapter "Railway Navigation and Incarceration" in his *The Practice of Everyday Life*, Michel de Certeau explains that railroad travel is a regulated and "closed system" immobilizing the traveler and the traversed lands. He observes: "There is something at once incarcerational and navigational about railroad travel. . . . Contraries coincide for the duration of a journey" (113). Both insiders and outsiders, Jim Burden and his friend, frame narrators, are temporarily entrapped, beholding the framed spectacle of the prairie. This enclosure of the self and the well-known landscape is also a vehicle for the unleashing of memory. As a chronotope (Bakhtin), the train affords "the ('melancholy') pleasure of seeing what one is separated from" (de Certeau 114).

The virtual immobilization of place as a frozen spectacle in a moving object, corresponding to Raymond Williams's description of the "fly-in-amber" effect of regionalism is not simply an opening conceit. Indeed the novel throughout displays the West and immigrants as a framed picture. Cather represents the immigrants as a fascinating spectacle to Jim, who valorizes their difference in both primitivizing and civilizational terms: the immigrants' spatialization in enclosed places and their immobility is a sign both of their primitivism and their superior civilization. Hence, the "contraries coincide" in de Certeau's words, throughout *My Ántonia*; and Ántonia, the figure who represents "the country," embodies best these contradictions. I shall first describe the primitivization of "the country" itself in the works of Cather and in other prevailing discourses and turn to a discussion of civilization and primitives in the immigrant context and the attendant issues of enclosure and diasporization.

Cather's preoccupation with foundations and primitives all through her body of work begins with her now-canonized representation of place in terms of land, landscape, nature, and *patria*. The land's very foundational status, its "virginity," evokes menace and the haunted quality of the "American" soil. A vast, unpeopled, threatening, and sublime space, Cather's prairie is "nothing but land: not a country at all, but the material out of which countries are made" (8), according to Jim Burden, who surveys it on his first night in the West as a Virginian orphan about to join his grandparents in their life as Nebraska homesteaders. In keeping with early cultural and political productions of the topos of the wilderness, Cather evokes the sense of frightening desolation, thereby continuing the discourses about the "new" continent that had existed for centuries before her writing. A discourse of savagery is attributed not to prior inhabitants, whose presence is all but erased, but to the landscape. Cather writes in *O Pioneers!* "the great fact was the land itself, which seemed to overwhelm the little beginnings of human society that struggled in its sombre wastes. . . . [M]en were too weak to make any mark here, . . . the land wanted to be let alone, to preserve its own *fierce* strength, its peculiar, *savage* kind of beauty, its uninterrupted mournfulness" (15; emphasis added).

In both novels, the perception of land, which eventually "yields" to the pioneers, is at first one that inspires fear, anxiety, and insecurity. Not everyone can surmount the loneliness and other difficulties of the land: Mr. Shimerda commits suicide.[2] Cather engages in site-making here, whereby she repeats and stays in the boundaries of centuries of prior representations of an America of fearsome and sublime emptiness. In this site (that is, spatial stereotype), repeated in both *My Ántonia* and *O Pioneers!* the region as pure land is distinguished by its sheer blankness and inability to testify to human presence (that is, the signs of civilization). The narrator of *O Pioneers!* explains:

> "Of all the bewildering things about a new country, the *absence of human landmarks* is one of the most depressing and disheartening. . . . The roads were but *faint tracks* in the grass, and the fields were scarcely noticeable. The *record of the plow was insignificant*, like *the feeble scratches* on stone left by prehistoric races, so indeterminate that they may, after all, be only the *markings* of glaciers, and not a *record of human strivings*. In eleven long years John Bergson had made *but little impression* upon the wild land he had come to tame. It was still a wild thing that had its ugly moods; and no one knew when they were likely to come, or why. Mischance hung over it. Its Genius was unfriendly to man. . . . There it lay outside his door, the same land, the same lead-colored miles." (19; emphasis added)

In this description, the West before immigrants is produced as a site of primitive, uncultivated origins. Cather makes few references to Indian life, and then only in the form of traces (Mike Fischer 32), in order to cement the idealized placement of the immigrant who shall fill the "blank" foundations and origins and inherit the earth. Cather's almost total evasion of Native Americans and the takeover of their land is astounding, given that the history and identity of Nebraska, the region she championed against metropolitan snobbery (see above), and the neighboring areas is unthinkable without the history of the Lakota, the Arapaho, the Cheyenne, the Pawnees, and many other nations that the U.S. Army warred against and used in its conquests in the 1860s (the decade of the Homestead Act), and continued to fight and dispossess through treaties and war for decades after. The containment of Native American presence through the topos of the empty, unmarked, undetailed land aligns Cather with the dominant U.S. nationalist narrative of Manifest Destiny, which justifies at the same time as it denies the imperial origins of the nation (see William Appleman Williams; Kaplan "Left Alone"; Pease). Furthermore, empire-denial as a way of life also allows her a claim of originality as author. Writing about Nebraska and Swedish immigrants in ways few others would, the author's "pioneering" status mimes her material. Acknowledging Indian presence would interfere with her project of contrasting complete blankness with the European immigrants' practice of cultural continuity. It is the task of the immigrants and the writer to "fill in" details, characterize the land, and form a new narrative of the West, a site created and enlivened by diaspora cultures but eviscerated of its Native inhabitants.

Cather's deployment of erasures, in the characterization of land "as bare as a piece of sheet iron" (*Kingdom* 448) and in the narrative advocation of infidelity to detail and "atmosphere," which "should be felt and not heard" (*Willa Cather In Person* 156), speak to her obsession with origins and her desire to implant the European immigrant at the origin of the West. This "country" was, in her mind as well as that of the majority of Americans, an unpeopled, uncivilized stretch of land, even at a time when such legitimacy was actually continuously challenged by indigenous people. The arrival of the European immigrants and their transformation of the land were "the best days." Jim, whose nostalgia for the immigrants drives the novel, sits as a young man in his student apartment in Lincoln, and looks back at his boyhood time with Ántonia and the other immigrant girls in the prairie as the best of his days: in Virgil's words, "'*optima dies . . . prima fugit*,'" or, 'the best days are the first to flee' (306). That his construction of the idyllic past is channeled through his immersion in the classics is another way in which origins figure in *My Ántonia*. Several scholars have drawn attention to Cather's focus on transmission of property, culture, and language (Reynolds, chapter 3; Swift). John Swift, who suggested, "All of Willa Cather's writing involves inheritance" (107),[3] sees Jim's fascination with classical literature as "an allegory of Willa Cather's own struggles with personal identity and the dominant anxiety of her historical moment [and] a perplexing, pressing cultural question—who shall inherit America?" (108).[4] The textual discovery of the classics marks a maturation of the hero, serves to sanitize memory (through sexual repression),[5] and effects authorial legitimation. All this is achieved through Jim's demonstration of mastery over (masculine) literary tradition and his transformation into a modernist rather than a provincialist (Swift 109–110, 116). As Barbara Bair has pointed out (106), "*optima dies . . . prima fugit*" also underlines the antimodern proclivity of Cather's work, which emphasizes origins.

PRIMITIVISM IN THE PRAIRIE

The idealization of the immigrant girls as "original" and primal by Cather's narrator is a version of primitivism, a modernist antimodern construction of the world. Critics have observed this strain in *The Song of the Lark* and especially the later novels, most prominently *The Professor's House*, *Death Comes for the Archbishop*, and *A Lost Lady*. Hermione Lee writes of Cather's attraction to the exoticizing work of Gautier and Daudet and enthusiasm about Kipling in a discussion of her antidecadent "romantic primitivism," which was "reactionary and nostalgic" (54–55). *The Song of the Lark* has received scholarly attention for Thea Kornborg's self-discovery as an artist among ancient Indian dwellings and identification with the ancient women during her sojourn in Panther Canyon, Arizona (see Nealon 14–16; Reynolds 31). In *The Professor's House*, a fertile ground for a reading of primitivism, Tom Outland's identification with the "vanished" Indians bestows identity and affords the remaking of genealogy based on a "cultural," constructed family as Walter Benn Michaels reads the novel (35–38, 45–50). While these and other investigations explore Cather's primitivism in relation to Indians in other works, here I foreground the primitivizing representation of immigrants in *My Ántonia* with relation to the construction of ethnicity, race, gender, and national fantasies. I do so in order to highlight the contradictory status of the idealized immigrant, who is primitive *and* civilized in her attachment to and identification with both land (nature) and culture.[6]

Turn-of-the-century primitivism in the United States, like all primitivisms, was structured around a distaste for what was considered the ravages of modernity and progress, which inseminated moral and aesthetic decadence and degeneration. Responses ranged from what to Jackson Lears was an antimodernist evasion that retreated into martial ideals and medievalism, to, as Tom Lutz vividly recounts in *American Nervousness, 1903*, neurasthenia. Exoticism, in its germinal stage in novels like Melville's 1846 *Typee*, blossomed into a widely popular genre: from writing to song to furniture, there was an overflow of Pacific idylls, japonaiseries, Turkish taborets and narghiles, and Persian gardens in high and low cultural products, whether by Lafcadio Hearn, Gilbert and Sullivan, or John Le Farge (Jones 283–298). As in all exoticism and primitivism, the purity and difference of "the savage" was the object of fascination.

For the present purposes, what is most strikingly specific to the U.S. yearning for a purer past is that the discourse of loss in the present has a uniquely American spatial refraction. The place in question was not only the European Decadent suburban antidote to urbanism or the attainment of "the primitive springs of thought, impulse, and action" at the "weekend wilderness cottage," popular at the turn of the century (Lears 92), but also, and crucially, the *frontier* whose end-of-the-century myths equipped Americans with a vocabulary of national identity. Before Frederick Jackson Turner's 1893 declaration of the frontier's closure, a desire for nature swelled in the hearts of Americans, from Henry David Thoreau to John Muir and John James Audubon. Preservation of the wilderness, this space once seen as the bad adversary to the good frontiersman, became an obsession and "prompted a reevaluation of the primitive conditions" (Nash 145). But it was the frontier ideology, constructed ex post facto, that lent an imagined place to primitivizing impulses and the drive to identify a specific site of national belonging and national identity. The frontier formed the American, argued Turner, because it provided "primitive conditions" and the individualism (see note 3) that generated the new order—democracy. As Roderick Nash puts it, "Turner believed . . . that democracy was a forest product." This space, which served as "a fair, blank page on which to write a new chapter in the story of man's struggle for a higher type of society" (Turner in Nash 146), was lost by the 1890s, but the written chapter needed to be continually rewritten. While Turner did not see the frontier's closure as tragic but as propitious for regeneration (Bonazzi 163), a sense of loss was nonetheless inevitable. And Americans tried in myriad ways, through fiction (like Cather's), film, the writing of history, recreation, and nature conservation, to maintain the aura of the frontier long after its disappearance.

Primitivism around Cather's time, then, was based on a spatialized idea of origins, located in the frontier, *the* primal site of U.S. history and literature, whose "way of life" Americans sought to reenact. The "frontiersman's" virtues of virility, vigor, and stalwartness served as a model way of life for divergent purposes, from statesmanship to recreation. The muscular leadership of Theodore Roosevelt, propelled by the manly imagery of militancy, empire-building, exploration, and physical challenge, coincided with the martial ideal expounded earlier by the likes of Henry Adams, Brooks Adams, and Henry Cabot Lodge—all of whom detested the "overcivilized" intellectuals and culture and beheld "an attitude that was committed to life as a martial adventure" (Ziff 224). Corresponding to the Rooseveltian idea of masculinity was the popular "outdoor movement" that was to "give you good red blood; [to] turn you from a weakling into a man" in the words of one enthusiast; it was at the root of "the surge of interest among Americans in primitive environments for purposes of recreation" (Nash 153). The "thirst for the primitive" spawned outdoor clubs (the Sierra Club, the Campfire Club of America and so forth), which "provided a chance to play the savage, accept punishment, struggle, and hopefully, triumph over the forces of raw nature"; urban public parks that would relieve, as Frederick Law Olmsted put it, "vital exhaustion," "nervous irritation," and "constitutional depression." It also spawned a wide readership of natural history and literary expression of "savagery," most memorably London's 1903 *The Call of the Wild* and Edgar Rice Burroughs's 1912 *Tarzan of the Apes* (Nash 154–156). The ambition was not the perpetuation of Jefferson's yeoman ideal or a pacific New World garden (turned from desert), that Henry Nash Smith has argued was the chief self-representation of the United States by the time of the Civil War. The goal was to pursue a "strenuous life," primitive vigor, and male heroism in the remaining wilderness,[7] the simple vacationer paralleling the true-blue imperialist.

Recreational frontierism and its corollary "thirst for the primitive" also informs Jim Burden's experience of the colonized West as a ludic space as well as his narrative of the "other" Europeans. The novel opens onto the invocation of "the *adventure* of our childhood," first in the introduction by the unnamed friend of Jim Burden and immediately in chapter 1, which also begins with a train journey, the original one that takes the young Jim from Virginia to Nebraska, where he passes the time with the fantastic *Life of Jesse James*, "which I remember as one of the most satisfactory books I have ever read" (4). As an orphan boy launched into a new life in a "blank slate" of a country, he anchors himself in an idea of the frontier as the space of legend, and especially of play. Like so many literary travelers, he interprets his experiences in light of his reading (see Butor) from the very start. When Otto Fuchs, his grandfather's hired hand, comes to meet him at the town of Black Hawk, Jim finds that Otto "might have stepped out of the pages of 'Jesse James.' He wore a sombrero hat . . . and the ends of his moustache were twisted up stiffly, like little horns. . . . A long scar ran across one cheek. . . . The top of his left ear was gone, and his skin was brown as an Indian's. Surely, this was the face of a desperado" (6–7). Blanche Gelfant suggests that literature "prepares Jim for life": "Paradoxically, it precedes and takes precedence over 'real experiences' and it enhances them" (130). According to Jim, *The Swiss Family Robinson* had nothing over their homestead in terms of adventure (74). The dullness of the prairie landscape or the harshness of Ántonia's family's living conditions do not deter Jim, who, from the vantage point of his situation in his grandparents' comfortable household, perceives the frontier as an endless opportunity for play.

The frontier, a place of at least initial defeat, struggle, and poverty (for the uninvoked Indians as well as the likes of Mr. Shimerda and other immigrants), is, despite his involvement with and empathy for the Shimerdas, also Jim's ludic space. On the morning of Mr. Shimerda's suicide, Jim wakes up to sounds of unusual excitement and is thrilled. "*I looked forward to any new crisis with delight*," he remembers, adding, "What could it be, I wondered, as I hurried into my clothes. Perhaps the barn had burned; perhaps the cattle had frozen to death; perhaps a neighbour was lost in the storm" (108; emphasis added). After he finds out the news and experiences the commotion around the death, he tries to read *Robinson Crusoe* but "his life on the island seemed dull compared to ours" (115). Although Cather does not acknowledge Nebraska as Indian land, it serves Jim the way "Indian Territory" serves Huck Finn. As Alan Trachtenberg points out, "an escape from Aunt Sally's desire to 'sivilize' him lay ahead, in the Indian Territory: a place imagined as one of endless adventure, play, and freedom" (37).

But, *My Ántonia* creates a giant playpen out of the prairie by framing it as innocent of originary violence against Indians and later, as the site of Jim's "*optima dies*," as if violence and deaths had not been a part of that time. This personal enclosure of the landscape as primarily a play-space is signaled from the outset, when he and his friend gaze at "the country" from the "observation car" of the train. Despite his profound attachment to the Shimerdas and "the hired girls" in the town, Jim is more of a spectator than a participant in a frontier life that he "plays at," while others work and die in it.

The enclosure of the prairie as playpen and adventure park replaces white-settler colonialism and conquest in the Americas (Limerick). Jim constantly craves adventure and admires the Spanish explorer Coronado whose story he later tells Ántonia, Lena, and other "hired girls" when they are all living in the town of Black Hawk. Jim is beguiled by the "romance" of "discovery" and conquest. From his initial moments in the prairie, Jim perpetuates for himself the age of exploration and adventure, sought in organized form at the time of Cather's writing by the Boy Scout movement, established in 1907; within thirty years sales of the *Scouts Handbook* would be second only to those of the Bible (Nash 148). The "boundless" frontier as enclosed locus or playpen is, as with the Boy Scouts, gendered as male, despite the novel's glorification of women and Jim's attraction toward them. Although later he has ambient desires toward Ántonia as a woman, in the countryside, as Hermione Lee and others have pointed out, "'Tony' and he are like boys together" (Lee 156) adventuring in the wild. Sex is frequently evicted from the pastoral genre, which is to a large extent about childhood and early life or a longing to regain beginnings. There have been many interpretations of Jim's sexuality, the main discussions revolving around his androgyny, homosexuality, and repression of desire (see, for example, Judith Butler; Sedgwick).[8] Whether we might read Jim as lesbian tomboy and masked Cather, or as closeted, melancholy gay male, it is clear that the frontier as space of play is a boyish ideal. Like a Peter Pan of the West, Jim never relinquishes the idea of the frontier countryside as an immense amusement park and the immigrant settlers as playmates. At the end of the book, as a middle-aged man with a wife, career, and apparently prosperous but unsettled life, Jim visits Ántonia's large family, and hits it off with her sons and husband. Indeed, this last chapter is entitled "Cuzak's Boys," after Ántonia's husband's last name, and not "Ántonia's Boys" or, given that she has many daughters as well, "Ántonia's Children." After he leaves them and visits his old town, Black Hawk, he walks "into the pastures where the land was so rough that it had never been ploughed up" to stave off "the curious depression that hangs over little towns" (417). A species of the turn-of-the-century neurasthenic (see Lutz, *American*), Jim is romantically, sexually, and professionally unfulfilled, we find out at the outset. His relations with his wife are strained, and his work does not fill his life. Now however, he feels "at home" and happier, and his mind turns to pleasant prospects: "trips I meant to take with the Cuzak boys, in the Bad Lands and up on the Stinking Water. There were enough Cuzaks to *play with* for a long while yet. Even after the boys grew up, there would always be Cuzak himself!" (417–418; emphasis added).

From the very beginning of his story until the end, then, Jim's perception of play as the defining frontier experience stands in contrast to and undermines the story of the heroic immigrant subduing the landscape at great pain. Despite his sympathy with this story and its protagonists, it separates him from them and turns them into eternal boy-playmates, who remain in their rustic setting and help fulfill Jim's recreational fantasies. Making the classic linkage between the primitive and the child,[9] Jim and Cather both enlist the immigrant to enact perpetually the uncontaminated state of childhood and the nation's early beginnings in soil (although, as we shall see, immigrants are also "burdened" with civilizing the prairie through their diasporic attachments). As Amy Kaplan suggests in regionalist literature and the writing of the West, the representation and sensibility of childhood satisfies the "nostalgia for pre–Civil War innocence" which "comes together with a scientific view of childhood as an earlier stage of evolutionary development; as G. Stanley Hall put it, 'the child revels in savagery.' In this formulation the boyhood of white settlers comes to displace the history of Indian settlers" ("Nation, Region" 255). Jim is the "white settler" whose boyhood is enhanced and even defined by the immigrants, who are, in Cather's early novels, the ones through which Indians are disappeared.

As Cahan separates his immigrants into the civilized and uncivilized, Cather divides the "natives" from the immigrants, save for the intermediate figure of Jim. What most emphatically embodies the rawness and adventure of the land paralleling the childhood state in *My Ántonia* is the primitivized immigrant presented in contrast to the Anglo-Saxon "natives." Living in the town of Black Hawk, the young Jim Burden is deprived of the wilderness, the ready-made landscape of adventure, with snakes, wild characters, and dramatic events that were his domain in the countryside. He feels stifled by small-town life. After dinner, he recounts, "I used to prowl about, hunting for diversion. There lay the familiar streets, frozen with snow or liquid with mud" (247). As he "pace[s] up and down those long, cold streets, scowling at the small, sleeping houses on either side," flimsily built, containing much unhappiness:

> The life that went on in them seemed to me made up of evasions and negations; shifts to save cooking, to save washing and cleaning, devices to propitiate the tongue of gossip. This guarded mode of existence was like living under a tyranny. People's speech, their voices, their very glances, became furtive and repressed. Every individual taste, every natural appetite, was bridled by caution. The people asleep in those houses, I thought, tried to live like the mice in their own kitchens; to make no noise, *to leave no trace*, to slip over the surface of things in the dark. The growing piles of ashes and cinders in the back yards were the only evidence that the wasteful, consuming process of life went on at all. (249–250; emphasis added)

Jim's small town is a topos in U.S. literature, as we shall see more extensively in the next chapter. While historically they have represented the ideal site of "American life" and values, in many literary and cinematic representations small towns appear as dull and stagnant—or worse, creepy, corrupt, and inhabited by a prejudiced, duplicitous, and relentlessly homogenous group. Against the panorama of Black Hawk's sterile banality stands the dynamism of the immigrant spaces and immigrants themselves, toward whom Jim throws himself. In Jim's mind, Black Hawk stands in contrast against the prairie, which is less ordered and civilized but certainly lively and unrestrained. Along with the Indians, Cather's Anglo-Protestants, who frequently appear in her work as a small-minded lot at best, will disappear "to leave no trace" having set immobility and restraint as their highest goals. Jim's portrayal of Black Hawk as a place of stasis stands in sharp contrast to one of his first impressions of the prairie: Although he notes, riding in the wagon to his grandparents' house for the first time, there is "nothing to see, no fences . . . nothing but land (7–8), the next day he observes of the red grass of the prairie, "there was so much motion in it; the whole country seemed, somehow, to be running" (16).

The unregulated vitality and metaphorical mobility of the country is embodied in the immigrant women, Jim's cure for the repressed propriety of the Anglos is the company of the "hired girls," including Ántonia, Lena, "the three Bohemian Marys," and the unnamed four "Danish laundry girls." He is not alone in finding them irresistible; he describes "a curious social situation in Black Hawk" (225), where young men were captivated by the determined, self-sacrificing young women, who had traveled from "the old country" to the Western countryside and finally to town to get into "service" and help their families. "The country girls were considered a menace to the social order," Jim writes, "but anxious mothers need have felt no alarm. They mistook the mettle of their sons. Their respect for respectability was stronger than any desire in Black Hawk youth" (229). The sexual attraction Jim himself feels toward the girls in Black Hawk is insinuated and largely unfulfilled, aside from the stolen kisses from Lena. But despite the censuring voice of the community, which "said there must be something queer about a boy who showed no interest in girls of his own age, but who could be lively enough when he was with Tony and Lena or the three Marys" (246), Jim places "the girls" at the very center of his life, which would have been otherwise dominated by the restrained company of his own people. The young immigrant women are the very picture of spontaneity and joy—sorely lacking from the life around Jim—with the irrepressible Ántonia, who is frequently depicted running, jumping, or gesticulating, as the archetypal image of vigor. Ántonia is in constant motion in her own strong body, whose first loving description includes "a glow of rich dark color" and "curly and wild-looking" dark hair. The words "wild" and "crazy" are in reference to the Shimerda children (26, 73, 83, 84): Jake, the farmhand who had "crazy" spells (76), Pavel the Russian's gesticulations, and Ántonia's "crazy" brother who had webbed fingers. The "queer bodies" of the prairie (Lindemann) are the less-than-civilized, nonconforming bodies that are rough and difficult to contain, like the land itself, despite the conditions of enclosure in the prairie's caves or in Black Hawk's domestic quarters.

In the gendering and racialization involved in the civilizing process that was part of the conquest of "the West," non–Anglo-Saxon immigrant women occupy intermediate status between the "natives" and the Natives. Ántonia's "queerness" extends to the gender ambiguity her body is capable of, which is disturbing to Jim and his grandmother. In the dark period following her father's suicide, Ántonia, who has to give up school and work the land with the men, loses her manners and "civility." Wearing her father's boots and hat, burned brown from outdoor work, she brags about her strength, competes with her older brother in plowing, eats noisily, and constantly stretches her aching arms (143). Although Jim and his grandmother regret that she "can work like mans now" regretting the loss of "her nice ways" (143), Ántonia declares proudly, "I not care that your grandmother say it makes me like a man. I like to be like a man" and asks Jim to feel her muscles (157). While the frontier-as-play scenario ends because of necessity, the primitivistic sexual indifferentiation and gender ambiguity of Ántonia moves to a new phase. In *Manliness and Civilization*, an innovative cultural study on masculinity, gender, and race in the 1880 to 1917 period, Gail Bederman reminds us that

> one could identify advanced civilizations by the degree of their sexual differentiation. Savage (that is, nonwhite) men and women were believed to be almost identical, but men and women of the civilized races had evolved pronounced sexual differences. Civilized women were womanly—delicate, spiritual, dedicated to the home . . . Savage women were aggressive, carried heavy burdens, and did all sorts of "masculine" hard labor." (25)

Shifting between the roles of "savage" or primitive earth woman and the civilized, storied European (she, not the narrator, is the novel's primary storyteller figure), Ántonia becomes domesticated again: she moves to town as a "hired girl" and learns "feminine" skills from her lady employer. Even then, however, she retains the corporeal and emotional vitality that invigorates Jim and the town itself.

Ántonia's shifting, in-between identities reveal the instability of gender and ethnicity constructions in the context of immigration as well as recalling the deployment of immigrants as in-between replacements of the conquered. In the novel, it is not only affect but also the nature of the body that serves to distinguish sharply the immigrant women from the "native" Anglo townswomen. In the narrative of his memories of "a score of these country girls," Jim notes that "Physically *they were almost a race apart*, and out-of-door work had given them a vigour which, when they got over their first shyness on coming to town, developed into a positive carriage and freedom of movement, and made them conspicuous among Black Hawk women" (226; emphasis added). The latter, and especially the daughters of prosperous families, were physically confined: "When one danced with them, their bodies never moved inside their clothes; their muscles seemed to ask but one thing—not to be disturbed" (226). In an analysis of Josephine Baker's career and its context, Wendy Martin writes of the black body as a receptacle of "unrestrained, illicit desire" that is "irrepressible and uncontainable" (318). African Americans are seen to embody "spontaneity itself" and their dance is an expression of "freedom from restraint" (320). In very similar ways, Ántonia's hunger for dancing at the tent the traveling Italians have set up, is irrepressible. When her employer asks her to choose between her job and the tent, where the town boys pursue the hired girls, "'Stop going to the tent?' she panted. I wouldn't think of it for a minute! My own father couldn't make me stop!" (235–236). After this exchange, she quits and takes a job, against all advice, at the house of Wick Cutter, whose rape attempt she later escapes. Even in the last chapter of the book, when we meet Ántonia, "a battered woman now" (398), Jim reflects that despite her missing teeth and flat chest, she "had not lost the fire of life"—unlike women he knew who were missing nothing but "whose inner glow has faded." For Jim, "Her skin, so brown and hardened, had not that look of flabbiness, as if the sap beneath it had been secretly drawn away" (379). A primitivized body, hard and dark in color, suits the life force that has not been subjected to the feminized constraints of (Anglo) civilization.

The primitivization of the immigrant body in this projection of naturally flowing emotions, love of dance, and ease of movement as testament to their strength and spontaneity is another site of the in-between positionality of the immigrant: overlapping but distinct and superior to the victims of empire, the unnamed Native Americans and the African Americans. The brief episode about Blind d'Arnault, a "Negro pianist" who plays in town for a night, abounds in racist condescension. D'Arnault had a "soft, amiable Negro voice," Jim remembers, "with the note of docile subservience in it." Jim continues: "He had the Negro head too; almost no head at all; nothing behind the ears but folds of neck under close-clipped wool. He would have been repulsive if his face had not been so kindly and happy. It was the happiest face I had seen since I left Virginia" (209). In the next few pages, Jim recounts the musician's life, and the quasi-miraculous tale of little blind Samson's initiation to the piano, in which he had simply "found his way to the Thing . . . [,] approached this highly artificial instrument through a mere instinct, and coupled himself to it" and started playing what the young mistress had been practicing (213–214). Thereafter, "He was always a negro prodigy who played barbarously and wonderfully. As piano-playing, it was perhaps abominable, but as music it was something real, vitalized by a sense of rhythm that was stronger than his other physical sense—that not only filled his dark mind, but worried his body incessantly. To hear him, to watch him is to see a Negro enjoying himself as only a Negro can" (215).

Other readers have pointed to the racist, stereotyped representation of Blind d'Arnault (for example, Handley 148–149). It is important to note also that Cather draws a parallel between him and the young immigrant women. The passion of his music inspires the immigrant girls, who are listening from another room at the hotel where he is playing, and they spontaneously burst into dance in their segregated quarters. Blind d'Arnault, feeling that there are "little feet" dancing somewhere, starts playing for them, looking "like some glistening African god of pleasure, full of strong, savage blood" (217). The abandon of the "Negro" is matched by the "handsome girls, [who] had the fresh color of their country up-bringing" (218). The primitivism of the robust, spontaneous, resilient immigrant female body, transforms womanhood and foreignness in Jim's eyes into a spectacle play and fantasy, like the idea of the frontier itself.

Racialization and primitivization, then, is key to the representation of the play-space of the frontier and of immigrants. Like Jews and many European immigrants, Slavs were not altogether racialized, socially speaking, as white at the time of Cather's writing. In a comprehensive history of whiteness and European immigrants, Matthew Jacobson suggests that at the turn of the century, Slavs were (like "Hebrews" and Italians, for example) "becoming less and less white in debates over who should be allowed to disembark on American shores, and yet were becoming whiter and whiter in debates over who should be granted the full rights of citizenship." The tensions between immigration and naturalization discourses led to debates on "color-quality" and comparative civilization (*Whiteness* 77). Considering East European immigration in 1891, Henry Cabot Lodge

> announced that "these Slovacks are not a good acquisition for us to make, since they appear to have so many items in common with the Chinese." Not only would their presence in large numbers "interfere with a civilized laborer's earning a 'white' laborer's wage," but indeed, representing "races most alien to the body of the American people," they would be "very difficult to assimilate" and hence "do not promise well for the standard of civilization of the United States." (Jacobson, *Whiteness* 77)[10]

As most of the non-Anglo European populations were in the early phase of the transition from savagery to whiteness, their representations were suitably barbarized. In his infamous *The Old World in the New*, the sociologist Edward A. Ross wrote, "Slavs are immune to certain kinds of dirt. They can withstand what would kill a white man" (qtd. in Roediger 191). An 1895 newspaper article by Cather expresses her primitivistic view regarding specific "races" in quite clear terms:

> Some day, perhaps, when our civilization has grown too utterly complex, when our introspection cuts off all action . . . , when sincerity and simplicity have utterly gone from us and we are all a bundle of nerves, then *the savage strength of the Slav* or the Bushmen will come upon us and will burn our psychologies and carry us away into captivity and make us dress the vines and plow the earth and teach us that after all nature is best. ("Kingdom" 232; emphasis added)

In this fantasized captivity narrative, the fin de siècle desire for an escape from civilization and degeneration can only be guided by the primitive life force alive in certain "races." During a 1921 interview with a Lincoln, Nebraska, newspaper, Cather voices again her modernist penchant for the instinctual and savage as opposed to "the prevalence of a superficial culture": "The nigger boy who plays by ear on his fiddle airs from *Traviata* without knowing what he is playing, or why he likes it, has more real understanding of Italian art than [the women who run about from one culture club to another] with a head and a larynx, and no organs that they get any use of, who reel you off the life of Leonardo da Vinci" (*Willa Cather in Person* 46–47). While "naturalness" is a primitivizing value Cather bestows on both immigrants and blacks, it is the European immigrant whose naturalness is expressed best in nature; that is, in the land that defines national identity.

ENCLOSING PRIMITIVES IN LAND

Cather asserts both rootedness and diasporization in the process of Ántonia's inheritance of "the West." The heroine's beginnings in the harsh countryside are inauspicious: her father, like many of the immigrants around them, does not know much about farming; the land is unyielding; their living conditions are "primitive," to say the least. Indeed, theirs is a *cave*like dwelling, "no better than a badger hole" in Jim's grandmother's esteem (23) with Ántonia and her sister sharing a smaller cave on its side, "a round hole, not much bigger than an oil barrel, scooped out in the black earth" (85). In this enclosed space of poverty, she and her family become un-civilized and revert to a primitive mode of living. Despite the harsh conditions of "the country" that afflict her and all the other "immigrant girls" Jim comes to love, at the end of the novel, we find Ántonia close to the earth. In *My Ántonia*, a self-consciously cyclical novel,[11] return to earth from sojourns elsewhere is presented as nature taking its course. When Jim returns to the *patria* twenty years later, having heard before that Ántonia was poor and had a large family, he finds an overworked Ántonia, with missing teeth, a flat chest, and close to a dozen children. Yet, "I belong on a farm," she says, and beams with enthusiasm and pride about her family and way of life. Jim contemplates this Ántonia, no longer a delightful girl but a "battered woman" who still "had only to stand in the orchard, to put her hand on a little crab tree and look up at the apples, to make you feel the goodness of planting and tending and harvesting at last. All the strong things of her heart came out in her body, that had been so tireless in serving generous emotions" (353).

Ántonia's robust spirit and body are at their best in the state of nature. She tells Jim, "I'm never lonesome here like I used to be in town. You remember what sad spells I used to have, when I didn't know what was the matter with me? I've never had them out here. And I don't mind work a bit, if I don't have to put up with sadness" (387). The vitality of the countryside parallels Ántonia's: they are at one in spirit and body. She had told Jim the last time they saw each other as young people, "I'd always be miserable in a city. . . . I like to be where I know every stack and tree, and where all the ground is friendly" (362–363). Twenty years later, exuberant in her love of the earth, she shares with him that she "love[s] the trees as if they were people." The trees were "like my children," Ántonia says; indeed, she is the one who transformed the treeless ground she found and created out of it orchards—enclosed places of enchantment.

Fertile like the land itself, Ántonia is an original and originator. From the beginning we know there is something special about her; she is entrenched in the memory of everyone who has known her. Jim tells her children, "I was very much in love with your mother once, and I know *there's nobody like her*" (390; emphasis added). Not only is she an original (part primitive, part civilized), but she also establishes origins, through her earthy vigor and fecundity: "She was a rich mine of life, like the founders of early races" (398), Jim thinks to himself on the first night of their reencounter. She is both a founder of the "race" of hybrid, Bohemian-speaking Americans and a "pioneer" of the plains, who could, with a small gesture, "make you feel the goodness of planting and tending and harvesting" (398). Unlike Tiny, the Swedish contemporary of Ántonia and Jim, who has abundant financial success, and Lena, who becomes an established dressmaker (both of them childless), Ántonia has chosen to labor in the hardest, most physically demanding conditions. But Cather's triumphant immigrant is Ántonia, whose body has proven to be as hardy and bountiful as the soil she works. Like Alexandra of *O Pioneers!* she is a cultivator, but the productivity of her body corresponds to the bountifulness of the earth: the land had responded twenty years before; when Jim surveyed it, he noted that "all the human effort that had gone into it was coming back in long, sweeping lines of fertility" in ways that were "beautiful and harmonious" to him (346). Now, in perfect harmony with the land sculpted in her image, Ántonia neither wants nor needs a place larger than her orchard. Her brown, labor-worn yet strong, primitivelike body, are encased in this idyllic site of what Cather considers to be the foundational moment of the West.

The experience of the prairie with Ántonia is one of enclosure—the pastoralizing eviction of all evil and the encasement of Ántonia and her fruit (her children and her plants) in it. It is no wonder that Jim finds "the deepest peace in that apple orchard": "It was surrounded by a *triple enclosure*; the wire fence, then the hedge of thorny locusts, then the mulberry hedge which kept out the hot winds of summer and held fast to the protecting snows of winter" (385; emphasis added). Unlike Alexandra's (see Ryan), Ántonia's enclosure gestures not only to a taming of the savage land but also to the transferral of the non-Anglo immigrant's primitive vigor and spirit and creativity to the landscape itself. In Ántonia's hands, the orchard and the prairie are the antithesis of the urban setting that looms in the adult Jim's and the novel's background, characterized by the hollow, socially ambitious, barren wife of Jim's. As Andrew Ettin observes in *Literature and the Pastoral*, the pastoral space is a "privileged spot marked and enclosed from the world at large" with "the natural world" as "the proper field of reference" for humans (131). Ettin explains, "Pastoral art records our longing for a life bounded by friendliness and goodness, at once contained, enclosed and at the same time infinite" (71). Ántonia's feelings, which she imparts to Jim, are those of "peace, contentment, belonging, and long association as well as of easy possession" (129).

Cather thus feminizes the pastoral, a classically male-centric genre (Ettin 146), and inserts foreignness into it, indeed, making the immigrant the privileged center. Further, in Cather's novels, the women overturn the masculinist appropriations of territorial discourse through the recourse to feminizing the landscape. As scholars like Annette Kolodny have shown, the representation of the New World territory as a gendered, womanly site normalized conquest. Cather draws an identity between "virgin land" and women (as raw but full of potential), eschewing the language of domination. The relationship between the land and the women is one of identification based on love and labor, rather than male conquest. But in fact, Ántonia *is* part of the conquest, one in which she is deployed to obscure the fact that "settlement" for Anglos and other Europeans spelled genocide and removal for Native Americans. Ántonia's invasion seems benevolent because she is "a race apart," in Jim's words, closer to the primitive, and sharply distinguished from the true conquerors, the un-dynamic Anglo-Saxons, who are affectively, corporeally, and culturally different and inconsequential in this novel to the story of the building of the West. Unlike them, Ántonia is the rightful inheritor of the land because she becomes one with the land *and* preserves her "original" culture.

In Cather's novel, the feminized, beloved "new world garden" is presented as a migrant site, a product of the western soil *and* importation of "old world" civilization. As David Weisberg notes in an article on Cather and Margaret Mead's narratives of adolescence and modernity, Cather accords "the status of the aboriginal woman" to Ántonia (165). Unlike anthropology's aboriginals, however, Ántonia is identified with soil and nation not only because she owns and belongs to it but because she has cultivated it specifically through the knowledge of and attachment to a prior and superior place in Europe. Her orchards are a product of this relational sense of place. The representation of the eponymous protagonist serves to negate Native American precedence; it also works to counter the erasure of non-Anglo immigrants from the mythologies of the nation and insert the culture and labor of continental Europe into the region. Cather creates a migrant site out of the prairie, drawing on fixed discourses of "virgin land" (Nash) to turn the region into a site by "emptying" and "eviscerating" it to use Casey's words (13). Yet Cather also inserts a "foreign" dynamism and relational culture and sense of place to the Western landscape. Enclosure affords the preservation of (superior, European, not Anglo-Saxon) civilization.

Because they retain their identities, assimilating themselves only to land and not to dominant Anglo culture, it is the immigrants who inherit the earth in *My Ántonia* (as in *O Pioneers!*). The Bohemian immigrant's representative status as the emblem of the prairie is invoked in the frame narrative, as I indicated earlier: "Ántonia . . . seemed to us the whole country." While dominant discourses would position the Anglos as the rightful inheritors of the West and the nation as a whole, in Cather's works, the region (which stands for the origins of the nation as we know it) and the non-Anglo European immigrant belong to each other. In the second book, Jim remembers that the snobbish Anglos of Black Hawk had disregarded the fact that Lena Lengard's grandfather was a respected clergyman in Norway; to them, "All foreigners were ignorant people who couldn't speak English" (200–201). Now, he notes with satisfaction, these nonimmigrant town residents cater to the very people they scorned. Jim writes, "I always knew I should live long enough to see my country girls come into their own, and I have. Today the best that a harassed Black Hawk merchant can hope for is to sell provisions and farm machinery and automobiles to the rich farms where that first crop of stalwart Bohemian and Scandinavian girls are now the mistresses" (201).

The immigrants master the garden, and the state of nature is in their hands; the Anglos are reduced to service them. This vision has little to do with the real events in the West. The 1862 Homestead Act lured many immigrants to large-scale speculation; however, "rather than fostering a region of family farmers [the act proved] instrumental in furthering the incorporation of Western lands into the Eastern industrial system," including railroad interests (Trachtenberg 22), which also employ the adult Jim. But in Cather's vision, the heroic immigrant who stays close to earth inherits and truly represents the country as region and nation. Cather fosters the recognition of immigrants—their labor, languages, and cultures—and reconstructs the western settlement story in response to the discursive Anglo-Saxonizing of past and present by those in power. For this insertion of certain immigrants into the national imaginary, the idea of the immigrant in harmony with nature is necessary. In Cather's early novels, it is only (by staying) in place that the immigrant can fulfill herself and be what she already is. The containment mechanism, where the protagonists are culturally and spatially enclosed and reproductive in settings ranging from caves to orchards, defines the immigrant and justifies her right to the land.

For a novel framed by railway journeys and revolving around the consequences of migration, *My Ántonia* is tremendously invested in immobility and return in a seemingly paradoxical way. Some critics have read a strong sense of "rooted identity," in western literature, though the examples given, such as "John Muir in the Sierras," "Mary Austin in the Mojave desert" and "Mari Sandoz in Nebraska" (Kowalewski, "Introduction" 14) indicate an inclination to divorce the literature of migration, such as Cather's, from formulations of "rooted identity." Rootedness, despite the migratory history, is precisely what distinguishes Cather's primitivized protagonists (in contrast to the other countryfolk) as heroic. What Richard Brodhead observes to be the tendency of regionalist writing to evict the industrial, the urban, and the transforming elements of American life (*Reading*) is true for *My Ántonia*. Even though the novel is framed by industrialism (represented by the adult Jim's work), change (from desert into garden), and movement (of immigrants), at its center, diasporic existence is immobilized and frozen in "groundedness" and enclosure. While movement is integral to Cather's western stories, the European immigrants who define and inherit the western experience are ultimately those who stay put.

The story of "the tramp," one in Ántonia's stock of tales, is illustrative of the perils of mobility in contrast to the settlement of the immigrant. While Ántonia is a "hired girl" at the Harling house, she recounts the story of the tramp, who comes up to the Norwegian farm where she worked one summer, complaining about the ponds' being so low in water now that a man couldn't drown himself. He then asks the Norwegian for a job on the threshing machine. After a short while of working on it, the tramp throws himself in the machine after the wheat, ending up in pieces before the men can stop the horses. Tony ends the story with the comment, "and the machine ain't never worked right ever since" (203). The gruesomeness of the suicide is passed over rather lightly; and the dispossession of the tramp, who exclaims "My God! . . . So it's Norwegians now, is it? I thought this was Americy" (202–203), is taken for granted.

While the "native" tramps around destined for self-annihilation, the immigrants tend their cattle and thresh the wheat, assuring survival and success. Similarly, successful immigrants seem better off than Jim, who travels for a living, yearning for vitality, wholeness, place, and belonging: they are comfortable in their success and not prone to Jim's melancholic backward glance. In *The Age of Energy*, historian Howard Mumford Jones writes, "Mobility, which had been a mark of a westering society from the beginning, became an absolute virtue in an industrial democracy wherein mechanism put a special premium on speed and movement and a special disadvantage on standing still" (145). Jones adds, "For the majority of Americans mobility was progress" (146). However, there were those who were part of "the Great Restlessness," whose only mobility was not upward, but horizontal, including squatters, migrant workers, the quack doctor, the prostitute, the traveling salesman, the comic hobo, and the sinister tramp interrupting middle-class lives. Many of them, and the people portrayed in works such as Josiah Flynt's *Tramping with Tramps* (1899), Walter Wyckoff's sociological studies, and Jack London's *The People of the Abyss* (1903), were, observes Jones, "parodies of the great central theme of mobility" (147). Cather, on the other hand, chooses to portray mobility through its melancholy (Jim Burden, the railroad man) and dreadful (the suicidal tramp) representatives to emphasize the virtues of settlement, rootedness, and enclosure—enacted not by region(alism)'s Anglo "natives" but by immigrants.

Enclosure and movement are "dual rubrics" that characterize place-making, as Cunningham and Heyman have argued with reference to the contemporary period (295). Through Cather's work, we see that they also coexist paradoxically in the writing of the West, but they are hierarchized: despite the broad movements within Cather's vast social panorama, it is the *contained* immigrant, in place and the happier for it, who emblematizes the ideal citizen. While we learn in *My Ántonia* that the Swedish immigrants Tiny and Lena become successful businesswomen, making their way in Lincoln, Alaska, and finally San Francisco, the novel's most important character is the one who stays put, save a brief and unsuccessful venture. Similarly, Alexandra in *O Pioneers!* is the unchanging character who stays in the wilderness she tames, while characters like Carl (another melancholic man) roves a long while only to return to Alexandra and her land. Alexandra likes neither traveling nor hotels (287). Both female characters stay in place by choice, against the preference of their men, who are ultimately proven wrong in their impatience with the land and desire to leave.

Inversely to Abraham Cahan's strategy, in which the local was made mobile and the enclosed ghetto revealed its translocality, Cather inserts rootedness, enclosure, and immobility into the immigrant story. If at the origins of "America" lies nature, literal and metaphorical, for Cather, the people who are to naturalize themselves become American originals through land and emplacement. It is the European "landed immigrant" and neither the Native American nor the crassly commercial contemporary Anglo-American who stands to inherit the heartland, the sentimental locus of belonging.

The representation of the ideal immigrant in primordial settings, which takes its cues from a primitivist glorification of the natural widely circulating at the turn of the century, relates in multiple ways to the nativist context in which Cather wrote. The primitivized immigrant body and setting are informed by the politics of nativism, a phenomenon I touched on in the chapter on Cahan. As a form of social consciousness, nativism had drawn inspiration from jingoism and nationalism and solidified in the period of economic depression in the 1890s.[12] The imperialism that sought regeneration through external conquest and met the Spanish-American War with enthusiasm had as its complement (or, as Walter Benn Michaels argues, its flip side)[13] the internal hostility to "foreignness," whether in the form of Catholics or immigrants. Early in the twentieth century, the sociologist Edward A. Ross disseminated the term *race suicide*, which encapsulated the fear that the civilized Anglo-Teutons would become extinct, once overtaken by immigrants of savage customs and habits. Nativism was actually quelled for only a few years between the end of the century and the prewar revival years. Its most egregious form appeared, of course, during the First World War. By the time Cather took up the pen to write *O Pioneers!* and *My Ántonia*, the age of immigration restrictions and militant nativism was in full force. The charge of divided loyalty was the gravest; Germans, citizens or not, received most of the venom. The rubric for designating treachery was "hyphenated American," with Theodore Roosevelt leading the "unhyphenated Americanism" movement and Woodrow Wilson following in his heels. Once the United States entered the war, "100 percent Americanism," offered a positive twist on the "unhyphenated" movement and became a powerful slogan. All this repugnance for foreignness, enveloped in the discourse of national security during the war, led to more curbs on immigration.

Cather's publication of a book like *My Ántonia*, in 1918 no less, counters nativist and nationalist public opinion with a pluralist outlook that, I shall argue is the lens through which her spatial enclosure of immigrants should be viewed. In her time, two opposing trends, assimilationism and pluralism, were vying for legitimacy, the former's adherents being more vociferous and influential than the latter's. The "incorporation of America" as described by Trachtenberg and "the search for order" portrayed by Wiebe entailed not only economic but also social and, significantly, ethnic integration. Americanization programs and ideologies implemented throughout the first decades of the century pushed for a new civic American consciousness, one that left limited space for the expression of ethnicity in the public sphere,[14] despite some claims that immigrants found freedom to practice and further their culture in the United States.[15] Cather's sympathetic depiction of non-Anglo immigrants, disliked by Frederic Jackson Turner, went against the occlusion of immigrant labor, culture, and politics from the core national narratives. The novel is also a testament to Cather's Europhilia and her dissatisfaction with the political and social pressure for "amalgamation" and the philistine dismissal of European cultures and languages. It was part and parcel of what has been viewed as the "cosmopolitan" outlook of regionalism (Lutz, *Cosmopolitan*), a literary spatialization and a mode of reading (Dainotto) more closely associated with the converse of cosmopolitanism; that is, with a denigrated provincialism and quaint or exotic localism. But regionalism as a genre and an ideology is based on forms of spatial, cultural, and political boundedness and enclosure—which is not the opposite of pluralism but its complement and partner in suppressing other, indigenous spatial narratives of "the West."

CIVILIZED PRIMITIVE PLACES

Cather's work sought to change the national imaginary about the West by emphasizing the frontier not as a place of assimilation, amalgamation, or Americanization, as Jackson Turner suggested, but as a locus of retention, specifically of European civilization. Cather's prairie novels reflected some of the diversity of the West, which makes it very difficult to argue for the internal social homogeneity of regions or even of "European Americans." Cultural pluralism "was a fact before it became a theory" (Gordon 135) in the Midwest and the West. In an influential article on Western history, Friedrich Luebke wrote that "patterns of migration hold the key to regional culture" (26) and suggested it is necessary to study the cultures in the migrants' places of provenance as well as their reinvention of tradition and identity in the United States for a richer and more accurate picture of the West. Cather's own attentiveness to the "patterns of migration" was informed by her advocacy of European culture and its preservation. Critics have noted that Cather had "a nostalgia for a Europe-in-America" (Nealon 5), and she extolled in her novels and elsewhere the virtues of retaining and emulating Europeanness. Christopher Nealon and Hermione Lee both discuss Cather's attachment to Yehudi Menuhin and his family, who represented refinement and cultivation of a higher order than to be found in a United States besieged by modernity, mass production of culture, and xenophobia. While Cather's initially dispossessed, laboring Europeans seem a far cry from the Menuhins, her representations of their particular culture as well as their cultivation of the soil are admiring and vindicating.

As a result, despite the primitivistic imprint on their suntanned bodies at hard labor and instinctive, spontaneous natures, the immigrants are shown to possess a worthy culture and civilization. One of the primary means by which Cather asserts the validity, and indeed, superiority, of European civilization, is their enclosure in cultural "orchards" of self-perpetuation. The most emblematic immigrants of all, Ántonia and Alexandra, are the ones who do *not* Americanize, do not hyphenate themselves, and do not change. They are loyal to place and do not venture very far from the land with which they are identified; they "preserve" their customs; they can be counted on to stay and "become" (see below) themselves. Ántonia in particular is a vehicle of nature (the primitively corporeal, foundational life force) as well as of culture that is perpetuated spatially, in the landscape that she creates and possesses. Cather's elevation of the immigrant to center stage of the U.S. regional and national narrative works through spatial and cultural enclosure and containment—and their counterpoint, translocality.

The Shimerdas' confinement in cavelike dwellings during the period of their misery and Ántonia's later, contented enclosure in "the country" parallel the circumscription of their familial and collective memories of Bohemia and their cultural practices. The primary representative of a superior culture is the father, whose suicide symbolizes the death of Europe (that is, civilization) in America. Unlike Ántonia, Mr. Shimerda is not close to the earth in any metaphorical or literal way. An artist at heart, he fails at working the land. He retains dignity, however, through his elegant, clean clothes, the memory of a better past, and mild manner. Mr. Shimerda is not a "civilized primitive" like his daughter and other immigrants; he is a pure representative of European civilization—its music, clothes, and "beautiful talk, like what I never hear in this country" in Ántonia's words (269). Years later, Jim asserts that despite their contempt for the immigrants, "There was not a man in Black Hawk who had the intelligence or cultivation, much less the personal distinction, of Ántonia's father" (228). His continuous backward glance at his homeland, unwillingness to forget, and inability to make America his own by working and merging with the land makes it impossible for him to go on. Mr. Shimerda cannot accommodate his country to "the country" as Jim calls it, and turn over his body to the new land. He cannot produce the dual and relational sense of place that his daughter will. His very grave is situated at a location that Jim's grandfather had predicted would be a "crossroads" once "the country was put under fence" (113). Jim reports proleptically in the chapter entitled "The Shimerdas" that "when the open-grazing days were over . . . when all the fields were under fence, and the roads no longer ran about like wild things, but followed the surveyed section-lines," the grave, "with a sagging wire fence around it," remained because of a surveying error and was "like a little island" (135, 136). A cordoned testament to the death of European culture and its inability to be part of the American land, the grave remains as the "unploughed patch" at the crossing of the roads. The grave is an emblem of Mr. Shimerda's unredeemed exilic condition: unlike Ántonia, who becomes part of the landscape *through* her translocal attachments, Mr. Shimerda is unable to localize. He rests at the crossroads that migration produced—his life and death have been enclosed onto "a little island" and severed—a part of and apart from the land in which he found himself.

The life force remains instead with Ántonia, the character who can maintain in diaspora both civilization and primitive vigor, at one with the land, in which she localizes with the cultural and emotional apparatus of the prior homeland. Ántonia's escape from the despair that killed her father and her redemption as an adult do not arise from her avoidance of enclosures. To the contrary, Cather depicts her freedom to be herself *through* enclosures. Immersed in the land and in her own culture, Ántonia is able to perpetuate what Mr. Shimerda could not—cultural continuity—because she is spatially entrenched and has created an enchanted, though hard-laboring world of orchards, fields, and children. When her husband wants to cease enduring the hardships and abandon working the land, she persists (386). At the same time, she is able to maintain the language, culture, and stories of Bohemia, which she is passing down to the U.S.-born generation. In their cocoon of cultural survival, Ántonia has forgotten English and is perpetuating Bohemianness. As she did with herself and her children, she also contained her husband: despite the husband's urban tastes and attraction to crowds, Jim relates, she had "managed to hold him here on a farm, in one of the loneliest countries in the world" (412).

Ántonia's loyalty to the land corresponds to her loyalty to her culture and father's memory. Ántonia and Alexandra of *O Pioneers!* are at one with the soil; they are also model cultural preservationists who resist the tide of Americanization and commercial culture. While Alexandra's sullen, ambitious, and self-righteous brothers adopt "modern" ways unequivocally by refraining from speaking Swedish, indulging in crass materialism, and bearing no tolerance for difference, Alexandra preserves the "old world" through Swedish, furniture, and daily habits. An old relative who makes yearly visits to Alexandra's house to indulge her language and customs, exclaims "now we be yust-a like old times!" as she crosses Alexandra's threshold (189). Although the father figures more prominently for Alexandra, she also inherits from Mrs. Bergson, who is always conserving fruit, the ability to store and use: "Alexandra often said that if her mother were cast upon a desert island, she would thank God for her deliverance, make a garden, and find something to preserve. Preserving was almost a mania with Mrs. Bergson" (29). That is exactly what happens to Alexandra, of course: she is cast on a desert (as the West was commonly referred to) and she makes a garden of it, partly through her business acumen but also in great part by her uncanny preservation of self exactly as she was, despite cataclysmic changes that she makes happen and that happen to her.

Although the novels draw on distinct discourses of civilization with Ántonia as a "civilized primitive" (while Alexandra is an agent of civilization in a less complex way), Cather's penchant for the conservation of culture is an essential feature of both works. These emblematic characters are enclosed in the gardens and orchards they have created and perpetuate themselves in islands of civilization and cultural continuity in the vast deserts, open or fenced, of the American landscape. As Ryan argues, enclosures in *O Pioneers!* evoke the enclosure of reservations and "allotments" of the Dawes Act and the opposition between civilization and the wilderness. In *My Ántonia*, while the emphasis is also on gardening and cultivation, the opposition is not so strict, given that the eponymous heroine emblematizes both the primitive and the civilized tendencies. Between natives and Natives, her enclosure and primitivistic attachment to land evokes the asymmetry of how immigrant and Native spatiality are imagined in the expansion of the empire. Ántonia's is the inverse of the reservation model: while Indians were removed and segregated to be dispossessed in the name of "self-development," the heroic immigrants enclose themselves to stay the same through translocalizing cultural practices that make prior places and cultures bear on the present one. Native Americans were expected to shed themselves of their cultures and economies in enclosure in order to become civilized (Sheehan), whereas Cather's immigrant in her enclosure is rewarded with land and representational, heroic status because she *retains* her culture in primordial American place. Although the logics of the reservation and of the allotments were different, the era ushered in by the allotments following the 1887 Dawes Act, based on individual ownership of land is also embodied and modeled by the immigrant's ownership and cultivation of a piece of America. Needless to say, the allotments of the Dawes Act intended to civilize and assimilate only caused the further dispossession of Native Americans, whereas, in Cather's narrative, the "allotments" of the Homestead Act led to the already civilized white immigrant's inheritance of America's land and national narrative. The profitable and positive containment of the immigrant in the novel also serves as a beacon of the pluralist ideal, based on preservation and self-separation. Attending to Cather's wilderness and civilizing enclosures shows the importance of spatialization to pluralist ideology and its occlusions, at least until the 1920s, of the subjects of empire who were deemed to have no culture worth preserving.

PLURALISM AND PLACE

Cather's model of culture and place echoes the pluralist position, an alternative to the dominant nativism and assimilationism that characterized her times. As an ideology, cultural pluralism competed for prominence with integrationist patriotism. Among its many influential supporters were William James, Randolph Bourne, Jane Addams, and Horace Kallen, all of whom advocated forms of multiculturalism and the preservation of tradition. In such publications as "Democracy *versus* the Melting Pot" (1917), *Culture and Democracy in the United States* (1924) and many more throughout his life, Kallen, the secularized German-Jewish immigrant and self-proclaimed inventor of the term "cultural pluralism," argued against assimilating Americanization, what William James called "the sniveling cant" of Anglo-Saxon conformism (in Mann 147), and for the many over the one. His ideal was an "orchestra" of cultures perpetuating themselves ad infinitum and coexisting in harmony and freedom. More complexly than Kallen, Randolph Bourne, who used the terms "trans-national" and "post-modern" before the 1920s, was also committed to a cosmopolitan ideal. He vacillated between the fixity of the elements of the mosaic and an understanding of hybridity and fluidity of cultures. Many of the pluralists, especially those writing in the period of toxic xenophobia during the war years, were avid to overturn the nativist mistrust and fear of "foreignness." Bourne's cosmopolitanism in his well-known essay "Trans-National America" (1918) is in great part a corrective to nativist trepidation and dogma: "Against the thinly disguised panic which calls itself 'patriotism' and the thinly disguised militarism which calls itself 'preparedness' the cosmopolitan ideal is set" (260). Bourne reminds us, "We are all foreign-born or the descendants of foreign-born, and if distinctions are to be made between us they should rightly be on some other ground than indigenousness" (249)—forgetting altogether of course about the indigenous themselves. As for the suspicion the immigrant's devotion to the homeland arouses in "the native American," Bourne states cannily, "The truth is that no more tenacious cultural allegiance to the mother country has been shown by any alien nation than by the ruling class of Anglo-Saxon descendants in these American States" (251), an observation about history and immigration that bears repeating today, given the manufactured fear of multiple loyalties and diasporans, which led to the recent designation of the United States as "the homeland" (Amy Kaplan, "Homeland"). The antihyphenist Anglo-Saxon, Bourne argues, who accuses other people of loyalty to other countries and desire to take over "betray[s] the unconscious purpose which lay at the bottom of his heart" (253), which is "the imposition of its own culture upon the minority peoples" (252). In a similar way, Kallen was also perspicacious in exposing the said "neutrality" of the Anglo-Saxon. Priscilla Wald underlines his observation that "a hyphen attaches, in things of the spirit, also to the 'pure' English-American" (in Wald 245).

The pluralist valorization of difference and "nuclei of nationalistic culture" that petrified Anglo-Saxonists who denied their own hybridities and historical mixed allegiances, has something to do with mass culture: difference is positioned as a remedy for the blandness, destructiveness, and tastelessness of the rabble. Distinction, Bourne says, would "be washed out into a tasteless, colorless fluid of uniformity," and the immigrants who do not maintain their "color" are "hordes . . . without taste" (254) and get submerged into "our civilization with its leering cheapness and falseness of taste and spiritual outlook, the absence of mind and sincere feeling which we see in our slovenly town, our vapid moving pictures, our popular novels, and in the vacuous faces of the crowds on the city street. This is the cultural wreckage of our time, and it is from the fringes of the Anglo-Saxon as well as the other stocks that it falls" (255). As a contrast to the "falseness of taste" and the "masses of people who are cultural half-breeds [who] have lost the foreign savor," we have the authenticity of the "national colony" that "retains" a "central cultural nucleus" (254).

Willa Cather similarly recoiled from the masses and their culture. All over her writings is an admiration for things European, from food (Cather considered the preparation of food the most important thing in life) to art as well as a denigration of three facets of American culture: its small-mindedness in relation to art and the related belief that it can be bought, its xenophobia, and its mass banality. She decried "cultured ladies" as she did inferior, ready-made American cooking and popular novels and cinema (see *Willa Cather in Person*). She raged against forced Americanization and spoke out against the state of Nebraska, which in 1919 prohibited foreign-language instruction before the eighth grade and brought one educator before the Supreme Court for teaching German (Reynolds 79–80). Like Bourne, Cather also wanted Americans to refrain from inauthenticity and imitation and to appreciate what they already had.[16] In many ways, both Bourne and Cather relied on a dichotomy between the folk and the mass, a binary that continues to be a point of reference and departure for cultural studies today.[17] Bourne was concerned that "in our loose, free country, no constraining national purpose, no tenacious *folk-tradition and folk-style* hold the people to a line" (255; emphasis added), suggesting yet again the conservative view of "tradition" and "the folk," which, by "holding them to a line" and "constraining" them, ropes people in and makes them consistent. Such is precisely what the immigrant offers: a tightly secured culture, as an alternative to the bland (or "tasteless"), "vacuous," and "loose" U.S. mass formation.

Current critics have argued against the tenability of the cultural pluralist position and the problem that ethnicity for the most part appears in this body of thought as a fixed, unchanging entity that needs preservation, (like the fruits in *O Pioneers!* that Alexandra's mother ceaselessly captured in jars). In their arguments against the unchangeability of ethnic identity in Kallen's brand of pluralism, Werner Sollors and Walter Benn Michaels both highlight Kallen's dictum, in *The Structure of Lasting Peace* (1918), that "an Irishman is always an Irishman, a Jew always a Jew. Irishman or Jew is born, citizen, lawyer, or church-member is made. Irishman and Jew are facts in nature; citizen and church-member are artefacts in civilization" (in Sollors 183). As a more complex thinker, Bourne did not advocate unadulterated repetition of the past; indeed, he asserted that "we are not dealing with static factors, but with *fluid and dynamic generations*" (Bourne, 250; emphasis added). But, contradicting himself, he did repudiate, in crude terms, "the Jew who has lost the Jewish fire and become a mere elementary, grasping animal" and "the Bohemian who has made money and has got into ward politics" (254). For Bourne, the Americanized Bohemian is more dangerous than the one who conserves Bohemian culture, because then "he" is truly among "us," and when "we" are at our worst. While I am not convinced that Bourne makes only an "argument for homogeneity and ethnic purity in the service of cosmopolitan diversity" (Sollors 185); there *is* a certain immobility assigned to foreign cultures, despite the argument for fluidity, evident especially in his disapproval of cultural "half-breeds" (254). While Cather represents many immigrants who contest what Kallen thinks is the naturalness of their identity through strategies of assimilation and deculturation (think especially of Alexandra's brothers), she valorizes those who choose not to change and reject both assimilation and hybridity. Her heroic immigrants are as purely Bohemian or Swedish as they can be, all the while they are enmeshed with the soil that they inherit and Europeanize.

The pluralist notion propagated by Bourne, Kallen, and others, that the immigrant carries a civilizing mission and influence, is found in emphatic forms in Cather's writings and constitutes the flip side of her penchant for primitivizing the immigrant. Such does not belie her exoticism, nor is it a paradox or contradiction at the heart of her work. In part, the immigrant is civilized precisely *because* she is primitive. In *My Ántonia*'s concluding chapter, Jim, who works for the company that makes mass transportation possible and travels far and wide, is set against Ántonia, who retreats into a life far removed from the influence of any type of mass culture; she hardly sees anyone outside her family. Yet, clearly, she is the happier for it, living in a modified state of nature, engendering new "races" at the frontier, and by implication serving as a model "American." The maintenance of tradition marks and separates the immigrant and provides her with a dynamism that Jim's "own people," the Anglo-Saxons, lack. As Wallace Stegner has suggested, the frontier, with its extreme hardship and deprivation, can be a site for "deculturation" (147), in which an artistic person like Mr.

Shimerda can find no outlet. Yet Ántonia, in her primitive state, living in caves and subsequently deep in nature, can transmit her past and culture through language, the storytelling that enthralls generations (including Jim, the children whose parents employ her, and especially her own progeny), and her love of land. The more immigrants remain "like themselves," and avoid the Americanization that leads to "the downward undertow of our civilization" (Bourne 255) the more cultured and civilized they can hope to be, beyond the threat of the masses.

Kallen's and Bourne's advocacy of a "federation of cultures" mirrors, as Sollors implies, the ideology of regionalism, in which equal parts form an organic whole (184). And it is at this intersection of ethnicity and regionalism, that, in my view, Cather joins the orchestra of pluralists. Cather's particular contribution is the positioning of *place* as a crucial category in the formation and, more significant, *preservation* of a pluralistic universe of cultures. For Cather, emplacement experienced through enclosure is just as important as the perpetuation of language and other cultural practices in which Kallen and Bourne put so much stock. The West transforms itself greatly in the course of Cather's narratives, in which immigrants become self-sufficient and sometimes even rich, towns grow by leaps and bounds, and the railroad crisscrosses the former wilderness. But through all this the ideal immigrant inhabits a perpetual time-space. Other immigrants, of course, are successful; however, they are not glorified as representative of the West and central to the narrative. Only characters like Ántonia and Alexandra, who stay in place, are one with the place that informs national fantasies.

It is especially at the end of the novel that Cather's pluralism converges with Walter Benn Michaels's description of it as *identitarianism*, the obligation to be yourself: Cather's heroines are "themselves" in land and spatial enclosures they create. According to Michaels, many modernist authors echo Calvin Coolidge's claim that "we have a great desire to be supremely American" (3). Michaels observes that "becoming what you already are" is a tenet of modernism. In the special section of the journal *Modernism/Modernity* devoted to Michaels's *Our America*, Robert von Hallberg disagrees with Michaels's argument about the modernist pursuit of self-sameness with regard to specific authors (especially William Carlos Williams) and with modernism at large. Hallberg observes that Michaels overstates the case and disregards countertrends within the "movement." But Michaels's insight does apply to Cather, even though he does not mention her in this regard.[18] In Cather's work, "becoming what you already are" necessarily happens *in place*, which provides both identity and the medium for identity, exemplified by the narrator's description of Alexandra: "it is in soil that she best expresses herself" (84). Cather's pluralism, which glorifies the non-Anglo European, posits rootedness and enclosure in place as quintessential to the maintenance of true distinction.

In both *My Ántonia* and *O Pioneers!* as well as in other works, it is clear that the author venerates the idea and practice of difference: The very first line of *My Ántonia* directs us to a footnote that tells us, "The Bohemian name *Ántonia* is strongly accented on the first syllable, like the English name *Anthony*, and the *i* is, of course, given the sounds of long *e*. The name is pronounced An'-ton-ee-ah" (3). Diacritics are at the center of Cather's stories of the West, made up of "various grain," as the epigraph from Adam Mickiewiz indicates in *O Pioneers!:* "Those fields, colored by various grain!" In that novel, the "queer" Ivar launches into a bitter discourse about the intolerance for difference in the "new" world, where "if a man is different in his feet or in his head, they put him in the asylum" (93). After Alexandra's youngest and favorite brother returns from Mexico, he tells his sister that he sang Swedish songs to the Mexicans, who "like anything that's different" (238), unlike the judgmental, small-minded Protestants represented in *O Pioneers!* by many of the Swedes and in *My Ántonia* by the townsfolk in Black Hawk. Against the critics, from Lionel Trilling and Granville Hicks to Harold Bloom, who have characterized the author's work as backward-looking, irrelevant, and nostalgic,[19] in *Willa Cather in Context: Progress, Race, Empire*, Guy Reynolds presents her as a multiculturalist *avant-la-lettre*, an author "unusually receptive to *difference*, weaving into her novels a broad-minded acceptance of the foreign or the strange" (16). Recently, Tom Lutz has also argued for the "openness to difference" of *O Pioneers!* (*Cosmopolitan* 114).

And yet, while pluralism provides a prospect for the possibility of maintaining and respecting cultural difference, it fails to address power differentials with respect to place among groups. Further, the opportunity for positioning of the United States as a place of "overlapping diasporas" (Lewis) is foreclosed in favor of a mosaic, whose components do not cross-pollinate. Cather's work is an example of both of these shortcomings. It is true that Cather's pluralistic approach celebrates difference, but the author clearly eschews the power differentials among immigrant groups; she also occludes representations of those who do not comply with the immigrant model, most relevant here, Native Americans. Most pluralists, like Cather, had a very Eurocentric lens through which they looked at immigrant and foreign populations. As Sollors notes, Kallen's orchestra of nations and Bourne's transnationalism have no place for the black American (186) and certainly not for the Native American. In an article subtitled is "Willa Cather and the Burden of Imperialism," Mike Fischer observes that Cather's account of origins in the West in *My Ántonia* is a whitewash of history, from which Native Americans are almost completely excluded, even though "as late as the 1870s . . . much of western Nebraska had still been under Sioux control" (33). Indian presence or removal does not concern Cather very much, nor will she address at all, for example, the stories of the large East Asian migration in the period that interests her. Moreover, Fischer suggests that while in the jingoistic context of her writing Cather's portrayal of immigrants was "courageous," at the time of her writing Czechs were a privileged group, who "were used throughout World War I by American propagandists to underscore the United States government's commitment to the right of self-determination." Given this context and "the Wilson Administration's sudden concern for the Czechs' plight" (while true self-determination went by the wayside for other nations), Czechs were "the most Western and consequently least threatening of the Eastern European peoples" (Fischer 41). Cather played it quite safe, then, in contrast to the portrait Guy Reynolds draws: he claims that, despite "lapses," such as anti-Semitism in her writings, Cather was ultimately progressivist and genuinely sympathetic (24). Yet Cather's use of the tenets of pluralism to rewrite the story of the nation's origins against the Anglo-Saxonist grain, all the while evading the Indian, is predictable and befits the racist circumscriptions of pluralism. Perhaps the Slavs provided only the *juste milieu* of distance from the American Anglo: not close, but not too far, as well as more "productive" in enclosures than the Indian, who was stereotyped as culturally nomadic, idle, and rebellious.

Cather's selective and Eurocentric consideration of difference is part and parcel of her pluralistic outlook that is expressed through enclosures. The spatial and cultural containment of the selected immigrant group that keeps to itself and perpetuates itself is the one that is separated from Native, Black, Asian, and other groups that are at the foundation of the Western region's history. The enclosure of the immigrant in on herself prevents her from claiming difficult but multiple identifications by which the diasporic experience is defined. The immersion in the telluric, a distinguishing feature of both reading and writing early twentieth-century regionalism, enforces an immobilization of identity and culture that belies the migrant's unstable, bifocal, displaced experience of life and place and turns place into a site, while transforming the immigrant into a still representative of a fixed, unchanging culture. Cather does delegitimize Americanization and the forgetting that assimilation requires. But in representing the perpetuation of collective memory and the self in isolation and spatial containment, she also freezes diasporic existence. Localization in *My Ántonia* and *O Pioneers!* focuses on an important aspect of the diaspora experience: the shaping of the region and the nation in the image of the non-Anglo immigrant and newcomer, instead of the other way around. But the heroines' determination to stay in place and their feminized status as the perpetuators of culture, in their different ways, mirrors the immobilization of their culture and their lack of connectivity. What Cahan refers to as the "pell-mell" nature of transplanted cultures and collectivities that find themselves enclosed in the same place is absent from Cather's prairie, where Ántonia and Alexandra draw on homeland customs and language unproblematically and without the mixed signals and crossed wires that usually characterize diaspora lives (such as those of Gitl and Yekl). Ántonia is safeguarded from assimilation but also by contact with others.

The intersecting quality of diaspora existence—where both productive and damaging relations with dominant, subaltern, and other groups defining the experience of the West as well as of the United States as a "diaspora space" (Brah)—thus becomes immobilized. Despite the transmission of Bohemianness, the homeland is a static entity represented by the framed picture on Ántonia's wall, which she acquired through the mediation of Jim, who sent it to her following his visit to her hometown, where she will never go. While technology and transportation did not facilitate so vast and intensive transnational networks and lives as they do today, transnationality was also part of the turn-of-the-twentieth-century migration process, as Nancy Foner has argued. Many immigrants returned to their countries more than once and retained contact through much of their lives. In *O Pioneers!* Marie briefly mentions the Bohemian anarchists in their midst, who were part of a European and international political movement, but they are dismissed quickly in that novel and never mentioned in *My Ántonia*. There is little to indicate that Ántonia and her family are part of any diasporic or other networks. They remain isolated "pioneers," enclosed onto themselves in time and place. Cather divests the immigrants of the complexity of diasporic attachments, which are conflicted, productive, and generative of new forms of culture and identity. Instead, she invests Jim with one aspect of diasporic in-betweenness and frequently encountered sense of nonbelonging. It is Jim, the "native" who does not belong and is constantly in search for identity. Cather projects onto him the immigrant desire and necessity for assimilation into the dominant culture. Jim is constantly attempting to attach himself to immigrants and feel whole through their ability to belong. In the process, her idealized immigrants appear healthy and wholesome, at the expense of the emotional and existential struggles that mark diasporic experiences.

While literary regions in general have been interpreted as representing the nation as a prelapsarian America before urbanization and large-scale immigration, Cather's regionalism redefines this conception of the nation by centering the narrative on the immigrant's emplacement in America. By rewriting history from the perspective of the immigrant love of land, Cather redefines prevailing ideas around immigration, region, and nation for the period she writes about as well as for her own. Like Cahan, Cather transforms the idea of the local, including its nativism, by inserting the immigrants at the center of the geographical and literary creation of the nation. However, Cather's places are migrant sites quite different from those of Cahan: his protagonists are depicted in the site of the immigrant ghetto, but their languages, cultures, and desires exceed the invisible walls of the neighborhood confines and indicate an internal noncoherence and mélange. Cather's heroines are in the proverbial wide, open spaces of the West, but the location of their culture and selfhood vacates the dynamic, complex, frequently disjointed aspects of individual and cultural transformation that come to the fore in the works of Cahan and other authors we examine here. Cather may have been eager to redeem and valorize maligned immigrants and their cultures and therefore counteract nativist and assimilationist ideologies and practices.

Topophilia (Tuan) and attachment to place on the part of the immigrants serve to legitimate the immigrant and bring the Muse to the country. Cather strives not to pit "a place-based identity against a transnational or diasporic one," to use the words of Arif Dirlik from another context ("Bringing" 93). But in that process, she encloses her protagonists spatially and culturally and obliterates the prior and continuing presence of Native Americans to present a static image that conforms to the pluralist perspective's image of self-contained, self-perpetuating culture untouched by others, spatialized in the enclosures of the Shimerda and Cuzak families.

Both Willa Cather and Abraham Cahan spatialize stories about intermediately white subjects not yet accepted into the top echelons of the racial hierarchy. Their civilized immigrants are those who are properly enclosed spatially and culturally (they do not Americanize through low, popular language and entertainment) and retain their identities in that place of enclosure, which they come to "inherit" and own. While Cahan's picture of the diasporization process is more equivocal and complex, neither author's narratives of migration challenges the civilizational terms that the assimilables and the unassimilables are subjected to or the colonialities that disappear Native Americans from contested spaces and contain immigrant workers within bordered areas. As Foote writes of Gertrude Atherton's *The Californians* and George Washington Cable's *The Grandissimes*, the "imperial foundations" as well as "local historical conflicts" (100) of the local and the region are suppressed. At the same time as it foregrounds foreignness and difference, then, the region can also be a site of exclusion and reproduce metropolitan grand narratives.

Pluralism, the static retention of original culture and Americanization through inheritance and property, cannot redeem empire. The pluralist discourse of the salad and the mosaic, which current multiculturalism draws on, does not address the injuries inflicted in the quest for global hegemony through immigration and expansion, spatialized in terms of segregations and enclosures. Further, discussions of pluralism and multiculturalism are incomplete without discussing how space is allocated and organized in terms of class and race of the various cultures in question. The spatial lens (or, put simply, who is placed where) is an effective one to understand asymmetries produced in the "empire of liberty," which multiculturalists and pluralists tend to avoid. The specific spatialization that was the focus of chapters 2 and here, enclosure, for example, is the corollary of the expansionism and continental hegemony that propelled large-scale immigration and "settlement" in the West. Cahan and Cather try to shift literary and social parameters of inclusion by redeeming as valid subjects of fiction certain immigrants whose diasporic translocalism is legitimate and civilizing. But they stay true to the enclosures of local color and regional genres' boundaries and reproduce ideologies of enclosure as a civilizing place and process (as in reservations) without incorporating a wider critique of manifest destiny and Americanization, reaffirming the colonialities of power involved in social and spatial assignments of individuals and communities.

The privileged female relationship to land and enclosure in Cather's work is different from the connection to land and territory we shall see in the Chicana context. The communion between Chicanas and territory, whether conquered or inherited, also bespeaks a felicitous female space. But that link between woman and place, whether in an imaginary homeland or the present-day border town, is politically inflected against the discursive formulations of Anglo and male conquest and economic and cultural hegemony. Although Cather "sidesteps the vocabulary that merges 'the feminine' with the inert and insentient landscape awaiting the male intervention that will shape it into meaningful form" (Carden 283), her heroines do not question the power structures that facilitated their own relationship to the land and their own triumphant status as originators who are unaware of what and who preceded them. The operations of enclosure in the homelands and borderlands of Mexican America, emblematic in the alternative cultural imagination of contact and mobility, is the subject of the next chapter. The authors we meet make manifest what Cather's narrative hides. While the term "frontier" obscures the facts of conquest (Limerick), empire, and coloniality, the Chicana *frontera* places them center stage.

PART III

WRITING ENCLOSURE AND TRANSLOCALITY IN THE CIVIL RIGHTS ERA AND AFTER

CHAPTER 4

"CUANDO LLEGUEMOS/ WHEN WE ARRIVE"

THE SMALL TOWN AND THE POETICS OF CHICANA/O PLACE

The title of this chapter, taken from one of the fragments that constitute Tomás Rivera's . . . *y no se lo tragó la tierra* (1971), is emblematic of much of the fiction I discuss in this book. Most of the works that I analyze invoke the condition of a migrancy terminable and interminable ("*when* we arrive"), are vested in some way in the life of a collective body ("when *we* arrive"), and are concerned with temporal and spatial points of transition ("when we *arrive*").[1] We have seen how Cahan's and Cather's fictions of communities in transition are told through spatialized genres and the production of spatial ideologies, including critiques of ethnoracialized enclosures and the immigrant's foundation of land, region, and nation. But more pointedly and consistently than most of the other diaspora literatures in the Americas, it is the Chicana/o literary output that speaks to the arrivals and departures of populations, languages, cultures, and nations by pivoting its narratives around spatial representations and ideologies. The abiding trauma of 1848, immigration upheavals past and present, borderland hybridities, and regional and ethnic identities are some of the most important contexts of spatial removal and disjuncture that continue to inform Chicana/o culture and literary production in fundamental ways.

Chicana/o literature has been constituted by space and spatial discourse from within and without. Externally, the literary traditions were domesticated and denigrated through their construction as a "merely" regional body of writing encompassing stories set in and about the Southwest and the West. That it was only recently relieved of this reputation is attested to in a blurb on the jacket of Ramón Saldívar's important 1990 book *Chicano Narrative*. The potential reader is assured that the writing discussed is "no longer a regional literature," but "part of American literature." Despite this presumably complementary despatialization of a "minor literature" in order to emphasize its arrival, Chicana/o politics and literature have been and continue to be shaped significantly by spatial issues. Spatially determined expression reached a radical point during the civil rights–era flourishing of contemporary Chicana/o literary arts and resistance politics, when images, symbols, and narratives of the physical and mythical lands of Chicana/o and Mexican peoples served as the very grounding of cultural identity. Chicana/o activists, students, novelists, and poets created a region, Aztlán, in and through which Chicana/os and Mexicana/os could write and rule their fate in the past, present, and future. In this border-defying, territorialist discourse, the space of Aztlán, the legendary homeland somewhere in what is now the "southwestern" United States from which Chicana/os' ancestors are said to have moved southward and established the Aztec empire, became central to political struggle, collective identity, and literary expression. The call to understanding and unifying Chicana/o cultures has been more recently formulated along the lines of borderland hybridities and multiple territories, which also informed new conceptualizations of Aztlán and homelands.

Contemporary Chicana/o literature is informed by multiple frames of reference to origins and current struggles. Scholars have debated whether Chicanas/os are a colonized people; their roots date to the 1848 annexation of Mexican lands and their current situation as a racialized, minoritized group is an indication of ongoing coloniality. Authors and activists like Rudolfo Acuña and Mario Barrera have focused on the past and present colonial situation of Mexican people, who were not "immigrants" in 1848 and who have legitimate historical and territorial claims that are unrecognized. For these and other scholars, Chicanas/os constitute an ongoing "internal colony" within the United States. Because the assimilation-integration model is not applicable to the racialized Chicanas/os, whose origins may not be outside of the current territorial boundaries of the United States, it is difficult to consider them an immigrant group like the archetypal, European immigrants whose fictional stories we discussed in the preceding chapters.

Indeed, in literature, the status of Chicanas/os appears often as a conquered people. The groundbreaking Chicano writer Américo Paredes, Renato Rosaldo observes, grew up near the Texan border and "was forced to live, as his ancestors were not, under a dominant aggressive group that spoke a language not his own." Rosaldo warns that Paredes was not an immigrant: "Not unlike the experiences of blacks and Native Americans, Chicano history cannot readily be assimilated to a tale of immigration and displacement" ("Politics" 69). This is certainly true, especially of those Chicanas/os whose forebears were among those who ended up on the "wrong" (that is, the U.S.) side of the border in 1848. At the same time, as Gilbert González and Raul Fernández have pointed out, the origins of much of the present Mexican population in the Untied States dates to late nineteenth-century migrations. The U.S. pursuit of economic hegemony over Mexico at that time led to the displacement of Mexicans onto the other side of the border as immigrants. Controversially, González and Fernández dismiss the idea that the Chicana/o community was constructed in 1848 and has continuously existed since then in what became U.S. territory.

Although González and Fernández pit racial and cultural issues against what they see as the imperial underpinnings of Mexican migration, many critics and fiction writers draw on both the empire and immigration frames to tell the Chicana/o story. Most cogently, Emma Pérez proposes a "decolonial imaginary" in discussing the migrations spurred by the Mexican Revolution, when "a kind of colonial diaspora emerged, created by colonial relations historically inherited in the Southwest" (76). In the "decolonial imaginary" the Chicana/o is viewed as a diasporic subject who "reminds us that Aztlán, the mythic homeland, shifts and moves beneath and around us." In lieu of the linear trajectory of the immigrant, "time is traversed, and a mythic past entwines with a future where a decolonized imaginary has possibilities" (78). With a symbolic homeland that fosters the sense of belonging and hope of return, Chicanas/os are a diasporic people (78). Instead of assimilation, enforced by racism, argues Pérez, we have diasporic and oppositional subjectivities that blend the old with the new (81). To describe Chicana/o cultural productions as diasporic is possible because of the elasticity of the term, which allows us to explain these histories and the varied displacements, whether through conquest, immigration, U.S. economic domination of Mexico, or the "transnational migration circuit" (Rouse), as interrelated phenomena. Unlike "immigrant," the term "diaspora" does not erase the coloniality of the Chicana/o past and present; it evokes the centrality of place and of translocality ot Chicana/o cultural production.

The "tactics of habitat" (Foucault, "The Eye of Power" 149) that the Chicana/o movement and writings have produced during and since the civil rights era speak to long histories of conquest *and* migration in American terrain. As scholars like José David Saldívar, Mary Pat Brady, and Raúl Hómero Villa have shown, Chicana/o literature has had what Brady has called "a longstanding engagement with space" and a "sense of spatial urgency" (Brady 11, 7). Villa has explained that the experience of displacement and deterritorialization has figured as a central theme in Chicano expressive culture (1). What I show in this chapter is how Chicana literature's spatial orientation converges with the thematics of displacement and "lost lands"; that is, how place and displacement come together, specifically in the context of enclosures produced by colonialities external and internal to Chicana/o culture as well as of translocality. Through two important works of Chicana literature, "The Rain of Scorpions" by Estela Portillo Trambley and "Woman Hollering Creek" by Sandra Cisneros, I argue that translocality and territoriality go hand in hand in the Chicana/o imagination. Even the originary myth of Aztlán, the primordial domain, is inseparable from the story of migration southward of its inhabitants. The writing of territory, community, and identity by such groundbreaking writers as Portillo Trambley and Cisneros offer a particular perspective on im/mobility and belonging. While in Cather the immobility and enclosure of the immigrant serves to claim ownership of land and territory, in "The Rain of Scorpions" and "Woman Hollering Creek," enclosure is a consequence of injustice. Cather's work has immigrant women triumphantly embracing place and nation from their enclosures, while Portillo Trambley's and Cisneros's characters struggle with the legacy of 1848 and ongoing coloniality; that is, a racialized and gendered subjugation that displaces and encloses. The authors' decolonizing engagement of the historical and mythical narratives of place imagines prevailing over the injustices of enclosures, class, and gender without recourse, à la Cather, to the discourses of property and primordial territoriality.

THE SMALL TOWN

In their focus on the relationship between place and displacement, and enclosure and translocality, the "migrant sites" of Chicana/o diaspora stories overlap with other narratives I examine in this book. But they are nonetheless unique: Chicana/o literature's engagement with territory draws on the particularities of conquests and U.S.-Mexico relations and literary and cultural tropes that speak directly and give new meanings to these histories. Aztlán, the borderlands, and the barrio, variously, are Chicana/o topoi that have been the subjects of considerable study. One context through which Chicana literature has *not* been examined frequently is that of the "small town," even though an overwhelming portion of Chicana/o writing draws on this locus, usually as "border town." The lens of "the small town," a historically pivotal site of U.S. literature and culture, on Chicana/o literature helps relocate the idea of U.S. "American literature" geographically and ethnoracially, as the representations of "classic" small towns rarely place the stories of immigrants, diasporans, and people of color at the center.

While the frontier is foundational, the imaginary of the small town has been central to the subsequent development of U.S. identity and literature. The concept of the "American Dream" is frequently localized in the site of the small town, fixed in the literary and social imagination as a place where individual freedom and collective harmony can be achieved in a pleasant environment. The small scale of this idyllic setting does not inhibit prosperity and keeps at bay the anonymity and the evil tendencies of larger places as well as the poverty of rural life. Hence, the association of innocence and virtue with the small town, expressed nostalgically in the work of popular authors like Zona Gale and recreated in contemporary architecture like Celebration, Florida. Of course, the transformation of "the small town" into such a fixed site has not gone unchallenged: Literary works as various as *The Spoon River Anthology*, *Main Street*, and *To Kill a Mockingbird* have demythologized the small town by exposing its underbelly of prejudice, paranoia, conformity, and conservatism, belied by a veneer of peaceful communal existence. Cinema has reinforced both of these dichotomous tendencies, portraying idyllic small towns as in *Mr. Deeds Goes to Town* and the darkness just below the surface, as in *Blue Velvet*. Further, the postwar decline of the small town (see, for example, Davies) has been registered in films like *The Last Picture Show* and in novels like Richard Russo's *Empire Falls*. Although "small-town America" is now considered, by and large, an anachronism, its hold on the U.S. imagination continues, as evidenced by the setting of films like Peter Weir's *The Truman Show* (1998), which locates the illusion of "America" in a small town of the imagination, or Dutch director Lars Von Trier's *Dogville* (2003), which situates collective violence in a "village" and shows also the enduring importance of the small town as representative of "America" to the world.

While local color, regionalist, and small-town literature overlap both in terms of literary strategies and their reception, there are some important differences. As we have seen in previous chapters, literary localism and regionalism, like the writing of the small town, can be both written and interpreted synechdochically as a representative unit of the larger national identity, history, and politics. They build from the strategy of writing through a bounded area in order to magnify what lies within the confines and to draw attention to the border lines themselves. Often, localism and regionalism are informed by an ethnographic impulse, presenting, from an outsider's perspective, the cultural and linguistic practices of a social group presumably unknown to its reading audience. The literature of the small town is also concerned with the mores of the community, but marking the difference of the population (as "ethnics" or as "rural folk") is not primary. The subjects of small-town literature are most often "all-American," and do not need to be designated as unique or apart. Rather than cultural and historical peculiarities, what becomes central in this writing are the prevalent moral and ethical values and practices, which serve as barometers of Americanness—done right or gone wrong, depending on the author's perspective.

Small towns in Chicana literature are rather different from those of the popular and canonical texts that depict largely homogenous white populations and an "all-American" insulation from linguistic, cultural, and political "foreignness." While some works like Sarah Orne Jewett's *A Country of Pointed Firs* (Howard) and Carson McCullers's *A Member of the Wedding* do remind the reader of the connection of "the local" to the world, in many well-known novels and short stories, the small town is represented as sealed off from what lies beyond its own limits. Such containment is often the basis of the town's innocence and enchantment (as in the novels of Zona Gale), which may be subsequently violated by outside forces ranging from big-city interests to body snatchers (on film, see Tibbetts). Conversely, many authors from Sinclair Lewis to Shirley Jackson have pointed to the town's self-enclosure as the very reason for its bigotry, ignorance, and violence. Chicana/o writing of the town is informed less by such dichotomies than by issues of the cultural and political crossings of the Mexico-U.S. border; most frequently, therefore, it describes small towns as places where the oppositional categories of "foreign" and "domestic" do not hold. Chicana/o literature's small towns are bilingual spaces where Americanness and Mexicanness mingle, often uneasily. The works draw on several historical contexts, including the U.S., the Native American, and Mexican, which clash in the body of these spatialized narratives. For example, in Aristeo Brito's 1976 *El diablo en Téjas* (The devil in Texas), the town is violently split in two by the border and tormented by "the devil," which thrives on the malevolent partition of a once-integral community. This work, written in Spanish by an author on the U.S. side of the border, violates the secure-enclosure scenario of the fictional mainstream small town by pointing to the cruel artificiality of containment in the context of borders and conquests. In works by other Chicana/o authors, such as Ana Castillo, Denise Chávez, Sandra Cisneros, or Estela Portillo Trambley, small towns are economically and socially limited and restrictive, especially, but not only, for their female protagonists.

Cisneros and Portillo Trambley's texts register Chicana/o literature's conversations with and radical difference from the "classic" small-town fictions. I show in this chapter how the two authors create the small town as an ethnoracialized enclosure of Chicana/o-Mexican communities and of women through social and economic oppression internal and external to Chicana/o communities. Enforced enclosures are also accompanied by enforced displacements so that the tension between rootedness and migrations are much more acknowledged, explicit, and central to the conception of "the small town" than in classic U.S. fictions, drama, and cinema. Most significant, the stories underline the enduring legacy of conquest in small places invisible on the national agenda as well as the ongoing spatial coloniality that produces racialized and gendered inequalities and immobilizations.

Although they draw on the trope of the claustrophobic small town, these writers also produce an alternative spatial consciousness in which the towns' complex history of cultural crossings, ethnoracial mixtures, and conquests are central to the narratives. It is not homogeneity and the sense of stagnation afflicting the inhabitants of the classic small-town fictions that causes the protagonists of Chicana/o literature frustration and dissatisfaction. Their lives are informed by Mexican popular culture, the relationship between new immigrants and original inhabitants, Mexican and syncretic religious practices, pre-Columbian narratives, and multiple border-crossings. The dissatisfaction and suffering that the protagonists experience are caused by injustice: sexism, poverty, economic exploitation, and anti-Mexican and other racisms, all of which have a specific relation to the towns' particular histories and geographies.

Trambley's "The Rain of Scorpions" and Cisneros's "Woman Hollering Creek," examined in this chapter, are two such works, in which individuals and communities are constrained by their spatialized circumstances of subjugation but rely on narratives of translocalizing strategies. By this I mean that the stories build on reference points outside of the everyday limitations of small towns and the circumscribed nature of the Chicana/o inhabitants' lives even as they emphasize enclosure. Cisneros's and Portillo Trambley's stories include historical, folk, and mythical tales of Mexico and the U.S.-Mexico border, which historicize the present-day enclosures and spatialized exploitation and disenfranchisement. In Chicana literature, the literary strategy of "containment" common to the writing of "the local," the region, the neighborhood, and the small town, does not involve bracketing the outside world but registering the resistance to enclosure through the evocation of historical and mythical memories and practices, which reveal the small town to be not an isolated, unchanging unit but a locus of competing narratives and cultural and political crossings. In "The Rain of Scorpions" and "Woman Hollering Creek," the residents appear as victims of the dominant spatial and socioeconomic order of the town; at the same time, however, as they invest themselves in their spaces by exploring the ways in which narratives of the past, including of empire, conquest, and indigeneity, can change the spatial order in the present.

Although Portillo Trambley and Cisneros belong to two different generations of Chicana/o authors, the narratives I analyze in this chapter overlap significantly: both depict the physical environment of the towns as generative and indicative of cultural and individual destinies. Portillo Trambley, a novelist and playwright, as well as an early feminist Chicana writer, was the first woman to win the prestigious Quinto Sol prize, which sought to create a canon of Chicana/o literature. Cisneros, a poet and fiction writer, also well known for her feminist perspective, is a foremost author of the first generation of Chicanas to be published by the big houses, to receive acclaim in the press, and to arouse much interest among a wide range of scholars. Both "A Rain of Scorpions" and "Woman Hollering Creek" are quest stories, pivoted around the protagonists' seach for idealized place informed by past and present Chicana/o spatial stories about conquest, enclosure, exploitation, and the border. Drawing on the actual towns of Smeltertown and Seguín, both in Texas, Portillo Trambley and Cisneros reinvent them in their works and expand the Chicana/o spatial imagination. They offer new imaginary spatial narratives to change the way we see the historical and mythical spatializations of Chicana/o lives and cultures in small towns, bodies of water, borders, and utopian spaces. In each story, the injustices and the suffering of the present are reconfigured through the spatial histories and myths of the past, such as those of Smeltertown and Seguín as well as of La Llorona and gods of nature. Hence, both authors create migrant sites, acknowledging the site-making apparatus that enclose working-class Chicanas/os (Portillo Trambley) and Chicanas specifically (Cisneros) within places of exploitation and injustice but also suggesting different kinds of displacement and translocality that lead to the critique and reconfiguration of that confinement. Further, both authors gesture to the reigning places of their contemporaneous cultural discourses—Aztlán for Portillo Trambley and "the border" for Cisneros—each of them pivoting their story around the places that animate contemporary Chicana/o literature and culture. Before beginning my discussion of their texts, I trace below the various ways in which Chicana/o literary and cultural productions have been spatialized.

THE PLACES OF CHICANA/O LITERATURE

In Chicana/o cultural productions, the politics and aesthetics of place are inextricably locked together, as is befitting a literature that flowered at the very same time as a class- and ethnicity-based political movement. Writing in 1980, prominent literary historian Bruce-Novoa noted that the "recent phenomenon" of Chicano literature was "a by-product of the Chicano Movement" (*Chicano Authors* 4), and anthropologist José Limón emphasizes that it is "impossible to conceive of the Chicano movement from 1965 to 1972 without its artistic literature, particularly, its poetry" (84). While Chicana/o politics has changed significantly, the poetics of place and displacement remain interwoven and persist in constituting a core problematic of Chicana/o writing and politics.

The historical dispossession of the annexed Mexicans, the continued border-crossing of peoples under quasi-colonial conditions of economic dependence, and the exploitation of ethnoracialized subjects as disposable, cheap labor in the United States and Mexico—as well as resistance, rebellion, and folk, experimental, literary, and popular cultural traditions as founts of resistance and rebellion spanning borders—are the backbones of Chicana/o history and literature. The authors' treatment of spatialized coloniality is informed by this Chicana/o history and culture, which are deployed as challenges. Specifically, while Portillo Trambley and Cisneros depict very restricted settings of small towns, they draw on the love of land, Aztlán, and the borderlands topoi of Chicana/o literature to take their stories out of their own boundaries, as it were. The enclosures of gender, race, and class are mediated by other spatialities that feed the "decolonial imaginary" (Pérez).

At the center of this imaginary is the awareness of the role of U.S.-Mexico relations in shaping Chicana/o lives and literatures; specifically, the impact of the U.S. pursuit of empire in Mexico and the domestic production of conquest and expansion through the exploitation, marginalization, and demonization of immigrants. U.S. expansion did not end with the wars, treaties, and purchases of the 1840s but has continued to inform the Mexican economy and politics, from the Mexican Revolution to NAFTA (North American Free Trade Agreement). The removal of President Lerdo to install Porfirio Díaz, which resulted in the phenomenal spread of U.S. investments in Mexico, was the first instance of a U.S.-supported overthrow of an elected government; as historians have explained, the Revolution was the "first major political challenge to American hegemony in

Latin America during the modern era" (Hart 68, 303). Since 1848, the continuing hegemonic practices of the United States over Mexico have shaped the fate of the Mexican diaspora in the U.S. territory, with Mexican-origin populations experiencing segregation and proletarianization (especially in California and Texas), as well as, more recently, "illegality," incarceration and deportation, even though their labor is necessary and their most recent migrations in great part a consequence of NAFTA (see, for example, Horsman, David Gutiérrez). Both the legacy of the dispossessed annexed Mexicans of 1848 and the migrations that have been largely the fallout of this imperial relationship characterize the spatial discourses of Chicana/o literature. The spatializations of land, Aztlán, and the borderlands contribute, in different ways, to the decolonial imaginary challenging the forced displacements and regulated exclusions and enclosures to affirm claims to national, transnational, and border-crossing space and time.[2]

CHICANA/O LANDMARKS

Land and territory have always been of prime importance for Mexican peoples, whose ancestors, native and conqueror, peasant and landholder, derived livelihood, riches, and tradition from working and owning the land. But in terms of the Mexicano presence in the United States, land and place have been particularly forceful nodes of conflict and identity since 1848, when the United States conquered and absorbed a third of Mexican territory following war and the Treaty of Guadalupe Hidalgo. Without crossing any frontiers, about 100,000 Mexicans found that the frontier crossed them and made them strangers in their own land. A primal wound (a notion elaborated later in this chapter), 1848 as event and symbol was central in early, oppositional Chicano politics and remains a crucial reference. The lands that have had continuous Mexican presence before and after the war with the Untied States have come to epitomize cultural resilience; they provide a salient node of identification for Chicanas/os even though many, including some of the most prominent writers, like the Chicagoans Sandra Cisneros and Ana Castillo, hail from other parts.

An articulated love of and union with land as recurrent theme has often served as a grounding feature of Chicana/o culture and literature. In Miguel Méndez's Chicano "classic" *Peregrinos de Aztlán* (1974), the narrator voices a passionate love of desert and land, which "burns" in him (52). In Arturo Islas's 1984 *The Rain God: A Desert Tale*, a New Mexican family saga, the novel lives up to its subtitle in its creation of embodied places and placed bodies. The desert, locus of family, is part of, a backdrop to, and at the heart of the stories of family members. Sentimentally described, the desert is made one with the body so that it frequently enters the mouth, the eyes, the hearts of the protagonists. References to sandstorms and the need to keep the desert out of the house abound, metaphorizing the discontents of desert-belonging and assimilation. And for the

Mexican Trini in Portillo Trambley's 1986 eponymous novel, a primary motivation is to acquire a piece of land for herself and her family, as their salvation.

But the unquestioned reverence for land is perhaps at its most emphatic in Rudolfo Anaya's oeuvre, in which the desert is a "green valley." One of the most esteemed Chicano authors, Anaya has built his writing and reputation on representing the terrain and culture of his native New Mexico. From the first pages of his most widely read 1972 novel *Bless Me Última*, references to singing rivers, and the "throbbing," "living earth" populate the novel, in which natural elements, used in the mythical, symbolic, and archetypal registers, are in communion with those sensitive to their transcendent "presence." Anaya's 1976 *Heart of Aztlán* reads like a paean to the territorial pride espoused in "El Plan Espiritual de Aztlán" (see below, this chapter). In this novel, "the power of the earth surged through" the main protagonist, who "felt the rhythm of the heart of Aztlán beat to the measure of his own heart . . . and he cried out I AM Aztlán! . . . I am the earth and I am the blue sky! I am the water and I am the wind" (3) .

In his essay "The Writer's Landscape: Epiphany in Landscape," Anaya explains that the epiphanic sentiment results for him from a communion with "the raw, majestic, awe-inspiring landscape of the southwest" (99). For Anaya, a sense of place is elementary to writing and belonging, and in describing its importance, he enlists primordial and transcendent qualities: "So the landscape of the southwest has been very important to me as a writer. Here time, or a sense of timelessness, permeate the earth-features" (101). Anaya underlines his belief in the "actual healing power which the epiphany of place provides" (101) and describes characters in *Heart of Aztlán* as those "who have become separated from their land and sense of place" and are consequently "frustrated, alienated human beings" (101) suggesting that "this separation also bode[s] ill for the writer" (101). Further, Anaya believes, "it is our task as writers to convey our landscape to our readers and to work through the harmony of this essential metaphor" (102). As I shall discuss in the section on "Woman Hollering Creek," many Chicana feminist authors have also developed such discourses of land and landscape but changed their terms by placing women at the center of territorial sentiment.

THE SPACE OF AZTLÁN

Although place-based aesthetics such as Anaya's seem apolitically timeless, it echoes, through a rather different discourse, other Chicana/o challenges to dominant territoriality, specficially those that demand legitimation of precedence in the land and reversal of the continuous disenfranchisement of Mexican peoples, whether self-identified as diasporic, indigenous, mestizo, or immigrant. In the civil rights era, Chicana/o spatialities articulated in politics and poetry drew on the love of land discourse but one transformed into the specific formulation of Aztlán as an originary site, a historical and mythical reference point and a repository of pride and power: "In the spirit of a new people that is conscious not only of its proud historical heritage but also of the brutal 'gringo' invasion of our territories, we, the Chicano inhabitants and civilizers of the northern land of Aztlán from whence came our forefathers, reclaiming the land of their birth and consecrating the determination of our people of the sun, declare that the call of our blood is our power, our responsibility, and our inevitable destiny" ("El Plan" 1).

At the first national Chicano conference in 1969 in Denver, this nation-based claim for land and spirituality set the tone for much activist and literary discourse, and Aztlán became "the symbol most used by Chicano authors who write about the history, the culture, or the destiny of their people" (Leal 11). The authors of the groundbreaking "El Plan Espiritual de Aztlán," named by Alfred Arteaga "the birth certificate of the Chicano" (146), called for a kind of nationalism as "the common denominator that all members of La Raza can agree upon" ("El Plan" 2), one based on blood and soil. A shared territorial past was a prime agent of cultural cohesion, and identity equaled geography: "we are a nation, we are a union of free pueblos, we are Aztlán," the poets (most notably, Alurista) declared in the Denver manifesto ("El Plan" 1). Thus, the locus of yesterday was translated into the nation of today, and a spatial designation became the definition of collectivity: Aztlán now referred to not only to a place but also to a nation. An emotion and rhetoric of dispossession based on the loss of terrain and sovereignty, which led to a reconsideration of U.S.-Mexican history as well as the origins of Chicana/o people, is partly what informs the interpellation of Aztlán as organizing myth and unifying symbol. The authors of "El Plan Espiritual de Aztlán" rejected separations between Mexicano people and land, asserting, "We do not recognize capricious borders on our bronze continent" (1). Chicano magazines established in the 1970s were called, for example, *Aztlán* and *Sin Fronteras*.

Despite the "obsession" with history, the Chicano reclamation of identity and territory in the 1960s and 1970s, as with other cultural and political nationalisms predicated upon territoriality, produced a narrative of naturalized homeland and negated the importance of historical constructs, such as "capricious borders" in the quest to reclaim land and indigenous identity. Instead of locating homeland in Mexico, Chicano activists and poets chose a transcendent site of origins positioned as a predecessor of current states and politics. The poets Alurista and Rodolfo "Corky" Gonzáles, the authors Rudolfo Anaya and Miguel Méndez were only some of the most prominent writers motivated by the usable past of this interpretation of Chicano identity, which, armed with the mythical and historical symbolic apparatus, aimed to translate itself into current political action. Reies López Tijerina's land-grant movement in the 1960s, which unsuccessfully sought to restore southwestern territory to New Mexicans cheated out of their rights by the Treaty of Guadalupe Hidalgo, was a concretization of the recuperative spatial claims of the Aztlán ideology.

The utopian ethnonationalism based on the symbol of Aztlán has been extensively critiqued by literary critics, historians, and others, including feminist scholars (Chabram and Fregoso; Cooper Alarcón; Pérez-Torres, *Movements*; Saragoza). Chicano thinkers have pointed to the construction of Aztlán as an ahistorical, androcentric site that denies internal differences of the Chicano "nation" (Cooper Alarcón 39; Chabram and Fregoso 206; Andouard-Labarthe)[3] As for the geographical specificity of Aztlán, it is a moot issue: most scholars maintain it was in the Southwest, but others place it near Mexico City (John Chávez 9). Cooper Alarcón further points out that it may not be realistic to try to "fix Aztlán firmly in the Southwest, while claiming its universality for Chicanos everywhere" (61) as there are significant Chicana/o populations in the Midwest, New York, and elsewhere.[4] This is the kind of diasporization relying on the primacy of a homeland whose geographical and racial coordinates are fixed, or, as I indicated in chapter 2, essentialized and fetishized according to some critics (Axel). As with many other ethnonationalisms, the boundaries drawn around a definitive homeland and its people can be restrictive even while aiming at cultural and political liberation.

However, because its reclamatory, resistant impetus overlaps with other Chicana/o decolonizing practices and theories, Aztlán remains a powerful spatial symbol for many thinkers and writers. Even those like Cherríe Moraga and Gloria Anzaldúa, who are critical—from various gendered and class perspectives—of the Chicano movement from which Aztlán sprang, draw on the mythic homeland to assert belonging in the borderlands and decolonization. In her 1993 book of essays and poetry *The Last Generation*, Moraga considers Aztlán "tierra sagrada" and writes, "Aztlán gave language to a nameless anhelo inside me" (150). The indeterminacy of the location of Aztlán and the Chicana/o homeland (is it in Mexico or in the mythical Southwest?) causes Moraga to deterritorialize Aztlán and to vacate its spatial aspect. Nonetheless, she insists on referring to "the invasion of Aztlán" (153) and "our Indian blood . . . that made us rightful inheritors of Aztlán" (154) taking an ambivalent stance, between locating and deterritorializing Aztlán. But unlike the Aztlán of indigenists, who insisted on recuperating the pre-Columbian (in territory, spirit, and blood), Moraga's Aztlán, onto which she maps her unnameable desire, "had nothing to do with the Aztecs and everything to do with Mexican birds, Mexican beaches, and Mexican babies right here in Califas" (150–151). Attributing the waning of the movement partly to its homophobia and sexism (156), she proposes "Queer Aztlán" (147–148) in an attempt to rectify the colonization of women's, lesbians', and gay men's bodies within the colonized Chicano "nation." Land is equated with the body so that "Throughout las Américas, all these 'lands' remain under occupation by an Anglo-centric, patriarchal, imperialist United States" (173). Aztlán has become a useful "empty signifier" (Pérez-Torres, "Refiguring" 36) that refers both to the enclosure of lands as of 1848 and metaphorically to Mexican bodies since then in conditions of minoritization, deportation, and other colonialities. But it is the border that became the primary locus, articulating both the spatial and the migrant consciousness of Chicana/o literature and culture.

BORDERLANDS: "TABULA DE LA RAZA"

The border, which eclipsed Aztlán as a spatialized marker of Chicana/o identity and cultural politics in the 1980s and 1990s, in great part due to the inspired intervention of Gloria Anzaldúa in her book *Borderlands/La Frontera*, evokes both the history of annexation and the continuous struggles around Mexican migration and diasporization without recourse to a nation-based, masculinist imaginary that the Aztlán-centered Chicano Movement embraced. Border thought does not abandon Aztlán to its own place-based resistance against current colonialities, but its transnational, mestizo, queer, and multiclass scope has appealed to those within and outside of Chicana/o studies as the more radical spatiality, both geographically and metaphorically. As such, the border became the master trope of Chicana/o identity, or as Carl Gutiérrez-Jones playfully calls it, the "tabula de la raza" ("Desiring" 99). Further, in many other areas of cultural studies, the "border" became a key concept that expressed in-betweenness, hybridity, and fluidity as a form of resistance to monological cultural and political formations. In the U.S. context, the Chicana/o experience is often positioned as its paradigmatic case. Chicana/o writers and scholars repositioned the U.S.-Mexico border, as a place on a map and a potent symbol as a complex place of division and regeneration, oppression and resistance. Unlike earlier stories of the border that only saw the imaginary line as a locus of desperation and misery,[5] Anzaldúa's borderlands emerged as a more nuanced place in and through which to decolonize both dominant and Chicana/o colonialities around race and gender/sexuality. The border is a 2,000-mile "open wound," but it "hemorrhages continuously to produce a third country" (Anzaldúa 2–3). As a place of simultaneously painful and productive *mestizaje*, liminality, in-betweenness, and multiple crossings, it is quite different from the fixed, if mythical, place of Aztlán, whose certainties occlude difference. Scholars like José David Saldívar, Ramón Saldívar, Sonia Saldívar-Hull, and others have explained that authors of the borderlands provide "a counter-discourse to the homemade nativist discourses of U.S. imperialism" (José David Saldívar, *Border* 49) and constitute a resistance literature. Moreover, feminist writers like Portillo Trambley and Sandra Cisneros engage gendered and ideological differences not only between "occupier and occupied," but also within the Chicana/o communities of the borderlands. For them, as for Anzaldúa, the border signifies a locus of displacement and difference from dominant ideologies as well as one of reimagining internal, gendered and other colonialities reproduced within the Chicana/o body:

The love of land, Aztlán, and the borderlands are three of the most important spatializations that shape Chicana/o literature and Portillo Trambley and Cisneros reimagine. Each author who draws on these tropes rewrites them and contributes to the ongoing critique of spatial forms that serve to oppress and exclude Chicanas/os and Mexicans and to the continuing redefinition of Chicana/o belonging and home. In the small towns of Portillo Trambley and Cisneros's texts, the tropes combine and change character in order to redefine place and community within constricted contexts. The simultaneous deployment and critique of "master tropes" of home and the shifting nature of homeland, from Mexico, U.S., the transfrontera region, Aztlán, "queer Aztlán" and other feminist homelands of the imagination, are testaments to the malleability of the idea of place and homeland in Chicana/o culture. Constructing the homeland as unstable and multiple is a decolonizing strategy: Chicana authors' approach to territorialities of geography and the imagination challenge the cultural instruments that shrink places and convert them into immutable and delimited sites for diasporic subjects.

"RAIN OF SCORPIONS"

In "Rain of Scorpions" Estela Portillo Trambley writes a new narrative of Chicana/o belonging and struggle against injustice without anchoring the diasporic enclosures, emplacements, and displacements in a fixed homeland of belonging and unity. Originally written in 1975, at the height of resurgent Chicano politics and literature, the work engages the possibility of Aztlán, or a utopian space of the past that can be transformed into the present, but ultimately offers an alternative narrative on the idea of a Chicana/o place. The title story of a collection, "Rain of Scorpions," appeared in 1993 in a revised version for the "Clásicos Chicanos/Chicano Classics" series of Bilingual Press/Editorial Bilingüe with some plot changes. The story brings together mythical as well as political expressions of Chicanas/os and their histories. The small town that is subjected to a "rain of scorpions" is a real site of exploitation and enclosure that is marked by past and imminent migrations. But the suffering around involuntary displacement is offset by the idea of home and belonging as trans-spatial, an Aztlán of the mind of sorts, shaped by a narrative of the resilient Chicana/o people belonging to the borderlands and to many migrations.

Portillo Trambley's novella takes place in Smeltertown near El Paso. The toponym is a brutally direct reflection of this settlement built around factories spewing toxins into the air and poisoning its workers and the town as a whole. The fate of this border settlement, which industrialists plan on evacuating in lieu of changing their practices, is the chief concern of the central protagonists. While the narrative does shed light on the private endeavors of the young boy Miguel, the crippled Vietnam veteran Fito, the talented Lupe who adores Fito, and the "pagan" Papa Át, "Rain of Scorpions" is primarily a story of a small-town community on the brink of dissolution. Unlike many of the other early Chicano works now considered "classics" (Tomás Rivera's . . . *y no se lo tragó la tierra*, Rudolfo Anaya's *Bless Me, Última*, Ernesto Galarza's *Barrio Boy*, and so forth), "Rain of Scorpions" is not a bildungsroman centering on the young Chicano male coming to terms with ethnoracial and class struggles and artistic identity as a writer in the United States; the story concerns principally Smeltertown's destiny. Bridging the four protagonists, as well as some of the minor characters, is the determined caring for community. The young Miguel and the older Fito decide to take direct action against the company's decision to uproot the residents of Smeltertown and relocate them wherever housing was to be found in order to stave off lawsuit threats resulting from the new environmental consciousness. Fito attempts and fails to organize the residents against the company. Miguel's quest for the paradisiacal "green valley" of the Indian past, as related to him by Papa Át, concludes differently from what he had expected but provides Smeltertown with alternative conceptions of a utopian homeland.

In imagining the communal troubles of Smeltertown and the journey of Miguel to "the green valley," Portillo Trambley was speaking to the contemporaneous social and political issues in Chicana/o lives. The exploitation of the laboring class of Mexican origin, like the population of Smeltertown, was, of course, the cause of mobilization among Chicana/o workers and the foundation of the movement that gave life to the Chicana/o literary renaissance. Notwithstanding the fable-like qualities of the story, "Rain of Scorpions" is based on the history of the real Smeltertown, a company town twenty-five miles outside of El Paso, Texas. Established by ASARCO (American Smelting and Refining Company) in 1887, Smeltertown employed mostly Chicana/o workers, who made homes around the smelter, despite the sulphurous clouds and arsenic-and-lead–streaked soil created by the company's operations. After decades of allegations, ASARCO finally settled a lawsuit with El Paso in 1972: it would take care of Smeltertown's problems by evacuating the town. As Mary Romero has explained in her aptly titled "The Death of Smeltertown," instead of changing its practices by decontaminating and reducing the pollution, the company chose to condemn the town and set its long-term residents, many of them second- and third-generation workers, loose in inferior housing situations, most frequently, projects. Romero emphasizes that the longtime residents were strongly against removal and dispersal but lacked the resources to battle against the giant corporation. As a community based on propinquity (Romero), the Smeltertown community did not outlive the scattering; its story is part of a historical body of Chicana/o displacement and disenfranchisement narratives.[6]

"Rain of Scorpions" takes place at a time when dispersal is imminent, and the community, like so many in Chicana/o and other diaspora literatures, is enclosed and "stuck" at the same time as it is informed by past and future displacements. Portillo Trambley's Smeltertown is a migrant site: the product of many migrations from Mexico and from within the United States and a bounded site of corporate exploitation. The author innovatively merges the quest narrative and fable elements with the writing of environmental injustice, an issue vital to minoritized, racialized, and contained populations. The author was the first of the Chicana feminist fiction writers in contemporary times to address the dissolution of Smeltertown and to address environmental issues in Chicana/o places. Important longer works followed, like Helena María Viramontes's *Under the Feet of Jesus* and Ana Castillo's *So Far From God*, which told stories of toxic workplaces and their workers. Chicana/o environmentalists, like other activists and writers of color, have focused less on the more visible environmental issue of conservation and more on linking environmental and social and economic justice explicitly (see, for example, Peña and Pulido). Chicana fiction writers, in their turn, have exposed conditions in the fields, factories, and living spaces that have poisoned Chicanas/os, as they created characters and Chicana/o places of the imagination.

Portillo Trambley's Smeltertown, a seemingly enclosed unit like many small towns in U.S. literature, is also set apart from it. Many of the archetypal towns in U.S. fiction either are idyllic or *seem* idyllic in their communal, architectural, and political unity and simplicity. Even when this premise of idyllic serenity is disassembled in the course of the narrative so that its dark underpinnings or contamination by outside forces are revealed, the idea that small towns represent the ideal American locus is the most frequent premise or point of departure. In "Rain of Scorpions," the representation of the small town is informed less by the idea of it as an inherently corrupt or assaulted entity. Polluted and toxic since its beginnings, Smeltertown is neither innocent nor a bland facade. Indeed, Smeltertown looks very little like the idealized towns: A poor place, it was also subjected to "sandstorms black with ash from the smelter, poisoned air, and the threat of flash floods. Not three miles away on a high plateau was the city of the affluent with its twenty-two-story concrete buildings, scattered shopping centers, and well laid-out suburbs, with parks and easy access to the freeways, a land totally alien to the people of Smeltertown, except for the few who had made it to the university. . . . To the city fathers Smeltertown was an eyesore, an arroyo sometimes flooded by heavy rain where in some mud hut an anciano lay dead from pneumonia or black lung" (133). The place is also sometimes referred to as a barrio, but the logic of Portillo Trambley's representation is neither "socially deforming (barrioizing) [nor] culturally affirming (barriological)," as in the urban barrio narratives that Raúl Homero Villa studies (8). While the inhabitants are Chicana/o, their beliefs, practices, and politics differ widely: there is no consensus, say, on how to resist ASARCO or on cultural identity issues of indigeneity that Papa Át raises.

What ties the inhabitants together is neither American small-town unity, nor barrioizing pathologies, and not even direct cultural affirmation, but a sense of place and of belonging. ASARCO's decision to evacuate the town, with no thought given to "the breaking up of a human nucleus of life, the warm web of human daily existence that identified a community," was a "deathblow" to Smeltertowners: "The breakup of the town was the breakup of their spirit, their identity, their very soul. . . . They were awakened to the reality of their helplessness" (114). As the young Miguel thinks to himself, "Smeltertown was like a giant mud hole." And yet, "to him it was also as beautiful as the green valley where nature gods lived. He thought of the poison, of being poor. These things were not as important as the good things" (118). Perhaps unimaginably to outsiders, Smeltertown emerges also as a place whose central characters love it. Unlike the naïve protagonists of small-town fiction and film, who are unaware of the rotten core or who suddenly become vulnerable to overwhelming outside forces, most Smeltertown residents hold no illusions. Returning from Vietnam, Fito looks out from the bus onto the landscape and explains to the man sitting next to him about carbon disulfide and how "our souls are covered with ash" (121). And yet, he, like the many other real and fictional Smeltertown residents, resists being uprooted from the town. A community born of toxic fumes, Smeltertown emerges in the story as a wholly different "small town" that is nevertheless part of the story of capitalism, environmental injustice, and diasporic populations consistently subjected to spatialized colonialities.

The two characters most actively opposed to complying with the company's decision to vacate Smeltertown are in search of a promised land, a home for community, an Aztlán. Fito is embittered by his war experience that has left him without a leg, but is roused to feeling by the injustice of this decision that will scatter Smeltertown inhabitants away from one another. He decides, on the spur of the moment, to call a town meeting and resist this move. However, he lacks a clear strategy and without much thought, suggests simply that they all "decide to leave together, like the Israelites left Egypt." But when someone in the audience laughs and asks where their promised land is, "Fito spoke haltingly, 'The gesture of leaving together.' An angry voice protested, 'A gesture? What in the hell will that do? The whole town leaving together with no place to go? Only fools would do that.'" Although Fito comes up with a plan to make a media event out of this "gesture," the residents are not convinced, as they believe the company could afford bad publicity: "Fito had thought his plan majestic, grand, but now, seeing the reaction of his neighbors, it seemed impractical, all in disarray. One more meeting had come to an end" (128). An Aztlán does not exist for people who are unimpressed by the idea of "gestures" and metaphors.

It is only the boy Miguel who derives real inspiration from this meeting, despite its failure. He convinces his two friends—all of whom grew up hearing stories from the beloved community figure, the "pagan" Papa Át, about El Indio Tolo, the playful god of water Gotallama, and the Edenic "green valley"—to follow the Indian's journey to the valley in order to find a place for the town. They undertake the journey the next day, and, following the cues from Papa Át's stories, travel through a cave in which the map to the valley is to be found. The story of the boys' adventure through myth is intercut with the description of the disaster that befalls Smeltertown in their absence; the barrio partially sinks under a mudslide and a downpour of dead scorpions. By the time the community recovers and presumes dead the three boys who are missing, Miguel and his friends have come upon a stone with an unintelligible inscription that is supposed to be the map. Armed with the slab, they return to Smeltertown, to find that they are being mourned at a church service. The "pagan" Papa Át, who acts as a spiritual guide to Miguel as well as a seer, translates the mysterious word on the stone. Instead of providing a map, or a clue to the location of the green valley, the word simply means "you." Papa Át explains that El Indio Tolo "had journeyed, looking for a place to belong, a place of peace. He found it inside himself. He was the green valley" (169). Miguel appreciates this explanation, as he understands that "every breathing being was a miracle, a green valley" (169).

This vision of the individual carrying a paradise or a promised land within herself flies in the face of the collectivist dream of a primordial Aztlán that seemed to be the consensus at the time of Portillo Trambley's writing. The centrality of community in the story is at odds with its individualistic conclusion; hence, the author's dispute with the primacy of a geographical and metaphorical consensus regarding the topos of Aztlán. While the story takes place near the border of Mexico and the United States, and the three children cross the state line between Texas and New Mexico during their underground journey through the cave, there is little in the story that represents a borderless, unified community coming together in the "tierra sagrada" (Moraga) of Aztlán. In the last pages of the story, the children and adults in the communal space of Pepe's Bar discuss the boys' adventure and the rain of scorpions. One man wants to turn Smeltertown into a tourist attraction, as a site of dead scorpions, while another is suspicious about whether a rain of scorpions has ever taken place; the boys are disappointed that few take true interest in their journey and experiences. Far from being united under the banner of Aztlán, the townspeople are simply "unbelievers" (186), who mostly scold the boys for their irresponsible behavior. While a caring spirit is present, community is far from a model unanimity, homogeneity, and concurrence of purpose.

Smeltertown residents, about to be uprooted and relocated by outside forces, or "scattered to the winds" (128), cannot realize Fito's dream of collective departure without the "promise" of a concrete space. Miguel's discovery of the internal "green valley" does not change their reality. After the landslide, they scrub the dirt off for weeks, some investing in new paint even though they know they will have to leave everything behind shortly. Although the message on the stone relocating the "green valley" from the exterior to the interior heartens Miguel and adds an encouraging note to the story's conclusion, Smeltertown is still to be subjected to the will of exploitative outsiders, and community will soon be evicted. Aztlán, as metaphor for unified nation or as geographical reality is unattainable: the community is in limbo; there is no land for collective belonging. Portillo Trambley, as previously mentioned an early feminist author, registers her dissent from the male-authored plans of Aztlán, territorial primordialism, and absolute collective unity, in which women were rendered invisible and the ideal of cohesive community became, in Bruce-Novoa's words a "monological practice," rhetoric that sought to "catalyze unity based on strict adherence to communal customs" ("Dialogical" 229).

While there is no Aztlán, Portillo Trambley suggests that it is possible to overcome the enclosures and evictions common to the borderland experience of poor or working-class Chicanas/os through recourse to pagan, Indian, pre-Conquest narratives. The sentimentalized paganness and "Indianness" of Papa Át and the playful nature gods provide a utopian exit from the reality of spatial and communal extinction. Indian myths and Indian blood are unproblematically accessible to these present-day border dwellers: "Most people did not believe in the nonsense of a green valley. Yet, somewhere deep, deep in ancient instincts, something was felt, a tremor of their own earth, their own organic being" (166–167). In the cave, Miguel achieves communion with the god Gotallama "who flowed into him" (147). Papa Át, the paganized former Catholic, to whom "one day the Great Security was no longer the church, but the mountains, wind, and rain" (162), derives comfort from nature because "that's the Indian way" (113). Moreover, references to a "lost heritage" of Indian beliefs abound, doubling as a criticism of the Christian faith.

In dissenting from the "spatial cures" dictated by the male-dominated forms of the movement that sought to carry the Chicano voice during the time of her writing, Portillo Trambley provides a different solution (the personalized "green valley" that exists in the collective) to the vagaries of Chicana/o labor and locality. Given the real and discursive problems of environmental injustice and corporate exploitation Chicanas/os face as a collective, the utopian impulse of the story is a gesture to transcend the contemporary borderland narratives of injustice and enclosure by deploying the Chicana/o migration story and Indian roots as a personalized source of purpose and courage. The utopian original homeland discourse, distanced from the needs of the community, is put aside in favor of diasporic survival and continuity in the current place of a community, without anchors in an original, primordial place.

As in so many border stories, "Rain of Scorpions" is a narrative of spatial crisis: at the edge of two countries, communities and individuals are seldom securely placed. Notwithstanding the problematic nature of the indigenist impulse, the story registers the dialectic of enclosure and translocality we have observed in other U.S. narratives of migration and displacement. In Chicana/o literature, as in Portillo Trambley's story, the prevalence of the border space as setting, motif, and character provides both a unique and exemplary case of this dialectic. Chicana/o narratives, like many Chicana/o lives, revolve around enclosures in urban barrios and small towns; they also register cultural memories as well as the realities of daily border-crossings informed by what lies outside the zones of confinement, the myths and realities of Mexico, Aztlán, and utopian green valleys. Portillo Trambley's quest narrative is about remembering the alternative locations, beliefs, and stories that are translocal and lie beyond the enclosure. Although there is no utopian green valley and no national or ethnoracial geography to reconquer, alternative spaces do exist in the imagination, which is what the inhabitants will take out of Smeltertown with them.

"WOMAN HOLLERING CREEK"

Like "Rain of Scorpions," Cisneros's moving "Woman Hollering Creek," in her eponymous collection draws on translocal indigenous and historical narratives as an exit strategy to escape confinement and injustice in a small town in the Mexico-U.S. borderlands. Cisneros's story reflects the contemporary prevalence of the border in critical, fictional, and political discourses just as "Rain of Scorpions" draws on the theme of the lost homeland central to Portillo Trambley's cultural moment. Unlike many cultural and critical discourses that tend to overinvest in these topoi, in these writers' works, homelands and borderlands are not redemptive; at the end of each text, the protagonists' material situation remains the same. But the stories provide new spatial narratives of Chicana/o culture and identity that reimagine the existing conditions of enclosure and belonging and offer a more hopeful, though not utopian, way of seeing. In the case of "Woman Hollering Creek," the rewriting of Chicana/o places and spatial stories reveals the gendered ways in which borderland small towns and Chicana/o icons are constructed. Cisneros exposes the physical confinement of women and their metaphorical confinement to unchanging plots of femininity. At the same time, she constructs these gendered sites as translocal. Cisneros reimagines the eventless border town designed against women and the poor as a transnational place that connects seemingly buried and disconnected translocal histories and mythologies. Such connections do not so much destroy the boundaries of enclosure as provide new narratives of exits.

An ordinary girl from an ordinary Mexican town, Cleófilas watches *telenovelas* (soap operas) and awaits passionate love. Immersed in the program *Tú o nadie*, she muses, "You or no one. Because to suffer for love is good. The pain all sweet somehow. In the end" (45). Her reveries do come to an end with the marriage that takes her across the border, near San Antonio. Before the wedding, she dreams of the life ahead her: "Seguín. She had liked the sound of it. Far away and lovely. Not like Monclova. Coahuila. Ugly. Seguín, Téjas. A nice sterling ring to it. The tinkle of money. She would get to wear outfits like the women on the tele, like Lucía Méndez. And have a lovely house, and wouldn't Chela be jealous" (45). What she finds out is that "far away" is far from lovely. Her husband quickly reveals himself to care little for romance or beauty, mostly preferring the company of men and sometimes other women as well. Worst of all, he abuses her physically. Cleófilas is almost completely isolated, not allowed even to be in touch with her family back home, and her movements are restricted. She ponders her new environment but cannot find an interlocutor with whom to share her curiosity. Cisneros registers Cleófilas's growing doubts, disappointments, and desperation through a lyrical, understated narrative style that mimes the sensitive, quiet watchfulness of her protagonist.

Cisneros's representation of small towns from her protagonist's perspective underscores a uniform sense of limitation and enclosure on both sides of the border. Cleófilas realizes soon enough that the town she has left and the town she has chosen are grimly alike. As she considers returning to her home of no mother, a father, and "six no-good brothers," she knows she will be met there with censure, as a pregnant woman with a small child and no husband:

> The town of gossips. The town of dust and despair. Which she has traded for this town of gossips. This town of dust, despair. Houses farther apart perhaps, though no more privacy because of it. No leafy zócalo in the center of the town, though the murmur of talk is clear enough all the same. No huddled whispering on the church steps each Sunday. Because here the whispering begins at sunset at the ice house instead. (50)

While the term "border-crossing" is frequently used as a metaphor for the encounter with difference, her own crossing "al otro lado" (to the other side) has not produced much "difference" for Cleófilas. The same oppressive elements have been translated into the new locale with slight spatial differences.[7] But those small differences make her life more difficult, rather than less; in Texas, she is more confined in space than in Mexico. Back home, "there isn't very much to do" for women besides playing cards at each other's houses, watching soap operas, going to the cinema, or taking a walk to the center of town for a milkshake (44), but there is at least sociability and the public space of the "leafy zócalo." But in her new environment, there is "nothing, nothing, nothing of interest. Nothing one could walk to at any rate. Because the towns here are built so that you have to depend on husbands. Or you stay home. Or you drive. If you're rich enough to own, allowed to drive, your own car. There is no *place* to go" (51; emphasis added). Here is what we rarely encounter in U.S. literature: the "small town" from an immigrant's perspective; specifically, an immigrant woman's perspective, to whom the famous mobility of U.S. American life is as unattainable as its mythical riches. Displacement and migration, paradoxically, may inhibit mobility and lead to stasis and enclosure in place.

Michel de Certeau has suggested that a range of practices on the part of "the pedestrian" resists the disciplinary power that spaces produce. For him, "walking in the city" is a "process of appropriation of the topographical system on the part of the pedestrian; it is a spatial acting-out of the place" (98). For many, however, such a "use" of space can be impossible. Janet Wolff has shown that there could not be a freely roaming *flâneuse* (lounger, saunterer) no matter what her class, because she could not circulate so freely in social space. While it is true that women are not always simply "fixed in locale" (Probyn, "Travels," 182), they can be severely limited by it. For Cleófilas, public space is always already appropriated by car culture or patriarchy and is therefore unavailable. Or, because it lacks "interest," it leaves nothing to be "acted out" in de Certeau's words. As Mary Pat Brady has also pointed out, her confinement at home is only reproduced outside of it by town planning (133).

Female confinement is a theme that runs through feminist and socially informed U.S. literature, from Charlotte Perkins Gilman's canonized *The Yellow Wallpaper* (1892), an account of a genteel woman driven out of her mind by the isolation and restraint imposed by a "rest cure," to less well-known contemporary Chicana/o tales of agoraphobia and spatial enclosure. In Tomás Rivera's . . . *y no se lo tragó la tierra*, an agoraphobic woman who never ventures beyond the few streets surrounding her neighborhood, loses consciousness in the city center (54–60); in Helena María Viramontes's short story "Neighbors," Aura's life is limited to her house and garden and a bit of vicarious living through voyeurism; and, there is "unrelenting claustrophobia" (Debra Castillo, *Talking Back* 266–268) in Denise Chávez's stories, one of them evocatively named "Space Is a Solid." Cleófilas, one in a long line of enclosed female protagonists, does have some access to the public realm, but she is severely limited by the geographical organization of space in the auto-centric U.S., which, for her, endorses both patriarchy and the prerequisite of material prosperity that curtail women's mobility. The routes to desire, as for most fictional small-town protagonists, are clogged in Cleófilas's world. But, as a migrant subjected to abuse, her sense of alienation, entrapment, and enclosure is heightened.

The narrative and Cleófilas are both framed by her prospective displacements, which we understand to limit her mobility, from one side of the border to the other. Mobility does not generate release; on the contrary, for Cleófilas, it perpetuates and exacerbates enclosures based on gender and class. The repetitive plot of Cleófilas's life, like the repetitive plots of her beloved romances, is announced at the outset. In the opening paragraph of the story, the father "divines" that it will not be long before her daughter wants to return "to the chores that never ended, six good-for-nothing brothers, and one old man's complaints" (43). As predicted, at the story's end, Cleófilas and her son are in the pickup truck of a woman who is helping her escape her husband and get back home. The feminist philosopher Iris Marion Young has written that for women "location is about vulnerability" (qtd. in Rose 146), producing what Gillian Rose describes as "a sense of space something tricky, something to be negotiated, a hazardous arena" (146). Cleófilas's border-crossing through the hazardous geography of power she encounters disempowers her. But despite the bookend journeys to unpromising situations of enclosure and entrapment, Cisneros's narrative is also about openings.

Although the patriarchal organization of life and place is similar for Cleófilas across the transnational borderlands, "Woman Hollering Creek" is ultimately about the emergence of new spatial narratives. In the absence of other stories that had shaped her hopes, from the passions and luxuries of *telenovelas* to the prosperity that "the other side" of the border would provide, Cleófilas is drawn to the only available locus, a creek near her house, which has a semblance to what Gaston Bachelard calls "felicitous space" (xxxi), a refuge from her home and an alternative to the confining, drab spaces of the town. The only thing that still holds mystery for her is this creek called "Woman Hollering," which her husband translates as "La Gritona." She tries to investigate the origins of this name, but no one in the town cares to think about it; her questions are shrugged off. Her proximity to the arroyo, the riddle that it poses, and its position as one of the few places accessible to her, pull Cleófilas toward the body of water. She sits by its banks with her son at sundown and wonders whether the woman cries "from pain or rage" (47).

Woman hollering—this is precisely what she cannot do. The first time her husband hits her, still as newlyweds, she is immobilized by shock, though she, who had never been hurt by her own parents, had always sworn to herself that she would fight back if a man were to try. Her silence continues until the day she bursts into tears at the doctor's office, her body black and blue, and asks for help from the attendant, Graciela, who is moved to help her escape. But more than a from-silence-to-voice trajectory common in feminist narratives, "Woman Hollering Creek" situates the protagonist's awakening through her engagement with place and spatial narratives as counterpoint to her enclosure. In so doing, the story not only locates itself in Chicana/o literary and cultural tradition of strategically spatializing narratives through articulations of the love of land or of constructing border identities; it also positions enclosure and migrancy in a historical as well as translocal context.

Cisneros's protagonist finds a place for herself and for a complex collective history in the one place that is a refuge for her. Cleófilas admires the stream in its springtime radiance; it is "a good-size alive thing, a thing with a voice all its own, all day and all night calling in its high silver voice" (51). She wonders if "La Gritona" is really La Llorona of the childhood stories she remembers, the woman in the cautionary folk tale of greater Mexico and the Americas. Cleófilas thus transforms this body of water into "an intimate space," a refuge, a site of daydreaming, as Bachelard describes a house. For Bachelard, as for Heidegger, "dwelling"—that is, enclosure and shelter—which a house provides, produces well-being, intimacy, and memory: "The chief benefit of the house," is that it "shelters daydreaming . . . , protects the daydreamer" and "allows one to dream in peace" (6). For Cleófilas, however, the house frustrates daydreaming; it contains the inversion of her telenovelesque fantasies of passion and riches. Her enclosure in the home only generates repetition: of limits, of abuse, of disappointment. Thus, she relocates her capacity for daydreaming and fantasy to the free-flowing water that gives an audible, feminine voice to her own despair.

Yet even the reverie, unlike Bachelard's house, does not allow "dream[ing] in peace." The voice that Cleófilas, the silent woman, is attracted to recalls La Llorona, the iconic Latin American figure embodying the maternal and the monstrous at the same time: she is said to have drowned her own children in anger at her husband's betrayal. Her neighbors, Dolores and Soledad, warn her against going to the creek after dark, recalling the way the legend of La Llorona, the weeping, howling woman who is said to haunt riverbanks, is used to frighten children to keep them from wandering after hours. Hearing "La Llorona calling to her" and watching her young son play by the creek, Cleófilas, in her unhappiness, wonders what if "something so quiet as this" leads women to do dark things. Cleófilas identifies with La Llorona as another betrayed weeping woman, who lends the creek its identity and its "voice."

The correspondence between Cisneros's protagonist and this body of water does not emerge from the masculinist tradition of conflating representations of woman and landscape, the female and the natural, as I noted in the previous chapter. In such imagery, whether in painting, literature, or advertising, women and nature might be mapped onto each other from the patriarchal perspectives of ownership and domination, division between nature and culture, and Oedipal erotics. In Chicana prose and poetry, the relationship between women and place registers a different and very powerful note. We have seen how in Cather's work the feminization of land and landscape is not for the male gaze or appropriation but for asserting the literal and metaphoric fecundity and primacy of European immigrants. In the Chicana context as well, land is wrested away from the masculine discourses and feminized to posit a relation of identification with woman—ecifically Chicana womanhood. In her book, *The Desert Is No Lady: Southwestern Landscape in Women's Writing and Art*, Tey Diana Rebolledo surveys past and present Chicana writing about the Southwest and suggests in an analysis of contemporary work, that there is "return to a sense of integration with the land, with nature, with the cosmos seen in their landscape" (115).

Chicana authors reclaim land and deploy it for self-definition to create it in their own image. They also make the formerly masculine border their own (Rebolledo; McKenna). As Teresa McKenna writes, "Within the gaze of these writers, the border is reformed and renamed as a woman, . . . as a person who glories in the sensuality of the life she draws from the arid sand" (124). For the woman in Pat Mora's poetry, observes Rebolledo, "Nature and land are a kind of talisman that enables her to make her way through the alienations of male society" ("Tradition" 123), thus underlining the "relationship between sexuality and the land" in Chicana poetics.

The female body commemorates and celebrates historical, collective landscape, registering those stories that are specifically women's. On Gloria Anzaldúa's body the border is a wound, inscribing the pain of cultural doubleness as well as women's and lesbians' separation from the male-dominated homespace. In Pat Mora's poetry (*Borders*) in which the desert is a leitmotif, women are likened to cactus ("Desert Women" 80), the narrative voice speaks of "my desert eyes" ("Portland" 81), and an erotic poem is named "Mi Tierra" (79). Portillo Trambley's work is rife with identifications of women and landscape. In her well-known play *The Day of the Swallows*, Josefa, a strange, tragic figure who commits suicide upon her intolerant town's discovery of her lesbian love, is identified with the lake in which she drowns herself. In the same author's *Trini*, an indigenist novel replete with imagery of the Indian as "noble savage," the eponymous heroine is repeatedly described as having the earth in her (115, 125, 170, 244). Moraga writes:

> I am a river cracking open. It's as if the parts of me were just thin tributaries. Lines of water like veins running barely beneath the soil or skimming the bone surface of the earth—sometimes desert creek, sometimes city-wash, sometimes like sweat sliding down a woman's breastbone. Now I can see the point of juncture. Comunión. And I gather my forces to make the river run. (Moraga qtd. in McKenna 118)

The metaphorization of land as woman and woman as land may take at times a conventional indigenist turn, as in Portillo Trambley's *Trini*, or may poetically wrest land from the male gaze and masculinist nationalism to imbue it with a feminine/feminist consciousness, as in Pat Mora's poems and Moraga's politically motivated work. Whatever its tendency, the relationship between landscape and femininity in Chicana letters often takes the form of an identification and "comunión," as Moraga writes, as well as of struggle and suffering, as in Anzaldúa's wound, thus forming a body of writing that stems from but reinterprets, from a gendered perspective, the love-of-land tradition in Chicana/o literature and culture to which I referred earlier.

While the Edenic Aztlán and the destructive borderlands ceased being a binary in the Chicana/o imagination, suffering still characterizes much of the experience and representation of locational in-betweenness. A prevailing image used to represent the border/lands is that of the wound. In fact, it is virtually impossible to read anything recent about American border cultures without encountering Gloria Anzaldúa's description of the U.S.-Mexico border as a 2000-

mile "open wound" that hemorrhages continuously to produce a third country (2–3). Anzaldúa is hardly unique in her choice of metaphor. Arguing that "the border as metaphor has become hollow," Guillermo Gómez-Peña writes, "the border remains an infected wound on the body of the continent" (qtd. in Mendoza, 120). The wound is not only a metaphor of a Mexicano space; it is also used to characterize the very identity of Chicanas/os. In his article "Cut Throat Sun," composed, curiously enough, in the second person, Jean-Luc Nancy suggests that the Chicanas/o's very identity is a wound, emerging from a series of "cuts": the very term "Chicano" ("cut" from Mexicano; mestizaje as "cutting"), the name of El Pueblo de Nuestra Señora de Los Angeles de Porciúncula, the Chicanas/os' capital city, cut to "L.A.," and so on.

Elsewhere in *Borderlands*, Anzaldúa refers to the "wounding of the India-mestiza" in documenting the injuries inflicted upon the Indian woman and her representation in history (22–23). Cherríe Moraga recounts the Aztec myth in which the goddess of war Huitzilopotchli cuts her sister Coyolxauhqui's head, informing us that in her own work, she writes the wound symbolizing this "machista myth . . . enacted every day of our lives," thus reading a wound into her experience and renderings of Mexicano patriarchy. Like other "in-between" postcolonial cultures, observes José David Saldívar, Chicana/o culture and identification are "hybridized and ruptured." Quoting Homi Bhabha, Saldívar says, they are "splitting wounds," that "are wounds of my body [but] also a form of revolt" ("Américo" 308). In his work on the image of the wound in Derek Walcott's *Omeros*, Jahan Ramazani refers to the "postcolonial poetics of affliction," in which the wound is an unremarkably appropriate metaphor. In Ramazani's reading, Walcott's use of the wound image surpasses the "experiential uniqueness" of Caribbean suffering to make intertextual and crosshistorical linkages with the pains of other peoples.

Whether or not Chicana/o culture is postcolonial per se, its writing has often partaken of a poetics of pain. I would argue, however, that its articulations do refer to a unique kind of suffering, because the Chicana/o allegory of the wound stems from the oscillation between a continuous history of painful migrations and conquered rootedness. Most relevant, unlike any other visible group in the United States, Chicanas/os have a literal dimension to their "poetics of affliction," split identity, and cultural bifurcation, in the form of the Mexico-U.S. border. Place being a primary category in formulation of Chicana/o belonging, it is not surprising that spatial and identitarian discourses draw on the same image of cutting, separating, hurting, and suffering. Using the corporeal metaphor of cultural self-division, Anzaldúa writes, "1,950 mile-long open wound / dividing a pueblo, a culture, / running down the length of my body, / staking fence rods in my flesh, / splits me—splits me / me raja—me raja" (2). The poetics of affliction derives its metaphors from an actual space, which is, not unlike the spatial concept of Aztlán, part of the rent consciousness of Chicanas/os.

In "Woman Hollering Creek," the ideas of the wounded subject *and* place as the marker and the generator of the wound are not abandoned, but they are revisited. The representation of the female relationship with the environment is different from other feminist approaches in rewriting the patriarchally inscribed places of belonging. "Woman Hollering Creek" does not build on a feminist identification with land or on an expression of perpetual suffering. Instead, a nonidentitarian relationship with the creek and the town emerges, one based on shifting perceptions of the places in question and on what Carl Gutiérrez-Jones calls "critical humor." Humor and play, argues Gutiérrez-Jones, are neglected in ethnic and racial studies, even though they are crucial to "working through the injuries so often represented in Chicano Culture" ("Humor" 121). Much has been written about Cisneros's transformation of the icon of the weeping woman into the laughing, hooting, hollering woman (see Brady, Doyle, Saldívar-Hull). Within this story, which consistently gestures to storytelling itself, there are many tales of the silent, suffering, wounded woman that echo one another: the television melodramas dear to the heart of the women; newspaper articles about battered women; gossip around Cleófilas's husband's good friend who is reputed to have killed his wife; and the story of La Llorona. As Jacqueline Doyle points out, they all converge to the same plot about double-crossed or abused women (56). In Cleófilas's mind, they begin unwinding shortly after she arrives in Texas as a newlywed.

By the end, however, these plots have been rejected. Cleófilas leaves behind Dolores and Soledad, her neighbors, the only people she has contact with and who spend their time mourning their abandoning and dead men. She embraces Graciela and Felice, another, contrasting, pair of allegorically named female allies, who help her escape. Several scholars (Brady; Doyle; Saldívar-Hull) have explained that Felice, an unmarried woman who drives her own pickup truck with much pride and swagger, embodies "a different plot of Mexican womanhood and a different type of subjectivity" (Saldívar-Hull 258), which "amazed Cleófilas" (Cisneros 54). Moreover, Felice provides an alternative interpretation of place and gender, challenging the constrictions of both place-stories (about riverbanks haunted by women suffering for love) and of femininity by transforming pain and rage into defiant laughter. As they cross the arroyo, Felice begins hollering, which startles Cleófilas and her son. Felice explains that since it is named "Woman Hollering," she yells every time she crosses. She adds, "Did you ever notice . . . how nothing around here is named after a woman? Really. Unless she's the Virgin. I guess you're only famous if you're a virgin" (55). Given that the county in which Seguín is located as well as its river are actually named after Guadalupe, the virgin patron saint of Mexico, Felice is far from wrong. The way Felice affirms the creek's name, Cleófilas remarks to herself, is not with a scream of pain or rage, which she herself had attributed to La Llorona and the arroyo, but it is a "hoot." Woman Hollering creek "makes you want to holler like Tarzan,

Felice had said" ("Humor, Literacy" 56), recounts Cleófilas later. When Felice starts laughing again, "it wasn't Felice laughing," writes Cisneros in the concluding lines of the story, "It was gurgling out of her own throat, a long ribbon of laughter, like water" (56). In his article on "critical humor," Gutiérrez-Jones ends his brief discussion of "Woman Hollering Creek" with the important observation: "Chicana feminist humor . . . help[s] promote healing and enfranchisement, first by using laughter to foster a critical distance from one's experiences, especially those experiences that would reduce a person to a racialized body in pain, and second, by facilitating community in a context otherwise defined by women's isolation from one another" (122). As the two women convert a desperate situation to an audaciously joyous one and Cleófilas becomes a "hooting" woman, spatial meanings also change, so that the creek can be associated with a defiant and hilarious femininity and assume a humorous, rather than dark and sad, identity. This is humor about place and femininity that arises from the context of crossing and borders, which are frequently imagined as tragic and painful.

Along with humor, the entrapping plots and images of suffering are displaced though the instability of spatial meanings. While the female plots, from La Llorona to soap operas, always tell the same story, the meaning of place shifts and is sedimented by changing histories. Woman and nature are not collapsed into one in this story, because neither the name nor the voice of the stream is to be moored in meaning. "Woman Hollering" is but one name for the creek in a series: "The neighbor ladies, Soledad, Dolores, they might've known once the name of the arroyo before it turned English but they did not know now" (46). For Cleófilas, who does not speak English, it is "La Gritona," but it could also be "La Llorona" of the legend. As for the mysterious sound that emanates from the river, it may be one of pain and rage as Cleófilas imagines, but Felice turns this interpretation upside down, by speaking back to the arroyo with free-flowing hilarity. Cleófilas is not identified with water as Pat Mora's "desert woman" is likened to cactus with its "deep roots" and ability "to hide / pain and loss by silence" (80). The identity of the creek is all too shifting, now perhaps bespeaking rage, and then roaring with merriment, to fix in this particular kind of feminist metaphorization. Instead, a *site*, associated with iconic femininity, changes into a migrant, mobile entity that can be re-created in the defiant imagination that struggles against enclosure. At the end, then, Cleófilas's site of daydreaming truly turns into a "*felic*itous space." Cisneros thus moves away from articulations of pain and wounding as well as of fixed territorial identities at the end of her story. Laughter takes over near the border, in the form of a continuum (but not a "comunión" or identification with landscape) from the river, to Felicity, to Cleófilas. Just as Cahan's "ghetto" story and, as we shall see in the next chapter, barrio narratives like Quiñonez's *Bodega Dreams* are about enclosing their protagonists in the established genres of local color and noir, so Cleófilas is entrapped in the plot of abused women. Quiñonez and Cahan provide exits from the spatialized plots through indeterminate endings, melancholy, and ungovernable cultural translocalities and heterogeneities in the contained place. Cisneros rewrites the genre of female confinement through laughter and free-spirited, feminist interpretations of place.

The emphasis on spatial meanings also transforms another conventional plot: the rescuing of Third World women by First World women, or more specifically the Chicana's liberation of the Mexicana or other Latin American refugees from political and patriarchal violence (see Ana Patricia Rodríguez). The border between Felice and Cleófilas, Chicanas and Mexicanas, is made quite obvious at their first encounter. Exhorting Felice on the phone to give a secret ride to her patient so she may escape her abusive husband, Graciela explains that she is "another one of those brides from across the border" (54). Her name, she mistakenly assumes, refers to "one of those Mexican saints, I guess. A martyr or something" and has to spell out letter by letter to Felice, who had apparently never heard of it (54). Later, riding in Felice's truck, Cleófilas is "amazed" by the Chicana, her "Spanish pocked with English" and unwomanly "talk" such as her reference to Pontiacs as "pussy cars" (55). The diasporic use of hybrid language and unconventionally gendered behavior seem to reduce the immigrant woman to a position of the silent, grateful, awed refugee. But the reading of Felice as her savior, guide to unorthodox behavior, and subversive interpreter of patriarchal spatial meanings and toponyms should be nuanced in view of Cleófilas's own impulse to understand and reinterpret the spatial markers around her. Although Graciela and Felice imagine Cleófilas to be just "another bride" from "over there" whose story evokes, in Graciela's words, "a regular soap opera" (55), Cleófilas's own investigations into the spatial history of the creek have the potential of unearthing histories and memories that other Chicanas she has met "over here" are unaware of.

Many on the U.S. side of the border seem to care little for the spatial significances underlying Anglo toponyms. When Cleófilas asks about the name of the creek "before it turned English," she is brushed off with "what do you want to know for?" and "pues, allá de los indios, quien sabe?" (well, it's an Indian thing, who knows?) as "it was of no concern to their lives how this trickle of water received its curious name" (46). Yet, of course, it has everything to do with their lives, as post-Conquest citizens of the United States and inhabitants of greater Mexico. But they suffer from the collective amnesia imposed by conquest and ignore the names and other particularities of Mexican presence predating 1848, and the Indian names further predating the Spanish ones, in this town named after Juan N. Seguín, a *tejano* who fought for an independent Texas on both the U.S. and Mexican sides. Cleófilas does not simply adopt Felice's reinterpretation of spatial meaning in feminist terms. She *shares* with Felice an investment in the historically sedimented meanings of the places around her.

Moreover, it is through reference to the gendered space of the creek that the diasporic Chicana and the Mexican immigrant can share experience. While Cleófilas's curiosity is quieter than Felice's bolder defiance, the two women, representing some of the many forms of Mexican womanhood, join together, at the moment of bridge-crossing, in laughter. Although some have understood the transfer of laughter from Felice to the "gurgling out of her own throat" as Cleófilas's finding of her own voice, given the nonverbal nature of the exchange, I prefer to interpret this union as a *fusion* of Chicana and Mexicana women and a contingent, gendered exit from the patriarchal organization of place and enduring spatial narratives. I say "contingent" because the border between Mexican women on either side is not eliminated at the story's end: when Cleófilas returns home, she becomes the storyteller of "the other side" to her brothers upon her return and talks about Felice as an amazing, hooting woman, punctuating her narrative with "who would've thought," which marks Felice's difference. But the stereotypical bordering of femininity on either side, with Cleófilas as "another bride" and Felice as a *loca* becomes irrelevant as the two women unite over the reinterpretation of female belonging in everyday and storied places. When the immigrant Cleófilas meets the diasporic Chicana, the recourse to knowable, fixed homelands as a point of identification, such as Aztlán or even Mexico, is less relevant than the reimagined places they create together through reinterpreted histories and myths at the borders of their different and overlapping consciousness of place and belonging.

"Woman Hollering Creek" alerts us to the critical question of how to think about the borderlands and their inhabitants: separate or continuous? To take the border, and more recently, the fences, literally by overemphasizing cultural, economic, political, linguistic differences between the U.S. and Mexican contexts is to capitulate to the monological conception of nation-states as discrete formations and ignore legacies of conquests and crossings. Further, as Angie Chabram-Dernersesian argues in reference to "U.S." as a qualification of "Latino," "What is also visible here is an affirmation of the borders and the boundaries of the nation (as a category of social identification) that is contrary to the sensibilities of oppositional forms of transnational Latina/o social identification that posit a decolonizing, antiracist, anti-sexist, antiglobalization (anti-capitalist) movement from below"("Latina/o" 109–110). Chabram-Dernersesian's observation is aligned with Chicana/o thought's refusal to take existing politico-spatial markers and separations for granted—from the Chicano nationalist denunciation of "capricious borders" on "our bronze continent" to Anzaldúa's invocation of "unnatural boundaries." At the same time, the production of disparities under the regime of "unnatural" borders has to be addressed, as does Cisneros through the representation of significant and subtle differences between Cleófilas's hometown and Seguín and between Cleófilas and Felice. Under different hegemonies, the mutual production of place and culture and subjects changes. However, these differences are not reducible to the official identities and ideologies of the places or regimes. Stories like "Woman Hollering Creek" complicate the versions of transnationalism that rely on the ignoring of differences on either side of borders at the same time they challenge absolute separations.

Through the contingent union of Felice and Cleófilas, Cisneros does not attempt to transcend the borders between places and between women but forms a transnational feminist understanding of place, in which the gendered sites of enclosure, restriction, and taboo have their counterpoints that women on both sides of the border can draw on as resources. These topoi are the places that the new imagined community of hooting diasporic women can claim and define for themselves without recourse to mythical or actual homelands of patriarchal discourses. While other differences remain, the reconfiguration of place in the image of a bold and humorous female subject position provides a point of critical connection. Rosa Linda Fregoso provides a helpful formulation of the Chicana and Mexicana "intersection": her term "meXicana draws attention to the historical, material, and discursive effects of contact zones and exchanges among various communities along the Mexico-U.S. border . . . meXicana refers to the processes of transculturation, hybridity, and cultural exchange—the social and economic interdependency and power relations structuring the lives of the inhabitants of the borderlands (xiv). In Cisneros's story, these "meXicana" intersections and what Fregoso calls "cross-border feminist solidarities" occur around the meaning of places.

In addition to the creek and its toponym, whose significance to the story is apparent, there is another place-name that is important but underexplored. It is no accident that Cisneros chose to set the story in a town named after Seguín, this borderland figure, who is condemned or co-opted by one side or another in the context of monological conceptions of nationhood and identity. The name of the town appears but briefly in what we know of Cleófilas's consciousness, and yet is foundational to her imaginings of what "the other side" is like as a place. In her media-informed idealization of love and life on the U.S. side, Cleófilas thinks that, unlike the place-names closer to her, Seguín sounds "far away and lovely," carrying the "sterling ring" of the American Dream. The pre-migration Cleófilas is drawn to dominant readings of place, just as she subscribes to dominant constructions of women and gender. Cleófilas's pre-migration conception of the town as "far away and lovely" with a "sterling ring" points to the erasure of histories: for Cleófilas, the name Seguín is completely divorced from the originary naming and figures as just another, undistinguished localization of the "American Dream," which colludes with the victors' point of view. Her subsequent experiences with migration and marriage make her ideas about place and gender relations untenable, and Cleófilas becomes our guide to spatial meanings that are buried and unacknowledged.

Seguín, like the town that owes its name to him, had little to do with the

"American Dream." An iconic figure of intermediation and the vagaries of class privilege and nationalism, Juan Seguín was an elite *tejano* who fought on the U.S. side against Mexicans for the independence of Texas in 1836 and survived the Alamo. In 1841, he became the first *tejano* mayor of San Antonio (and the last, until Henry Cisneros's election in 1981). Disillusioned by Anglo racism against *tejanos*, he moved to Mexico, where he was considered a traitor. He fought with the Mexican army against Texas shortly after, becoming a "traitor" to both sides. Despite his status as a landowning elite, whose *tejanocentrism* (Olguín) had much to do with maintaining his own economic position, Seguín's suspect position in both national contexts mirrors the enduring and frequent positioning of diaspora and conquered populations as possible internal enemies or perpetual aliens.

The name of the town is emblematic of the particular transnational histories that underlie the making of Texas (as well as of Mexico and the United States) and the dichotomous way in which two national narratives are conceived so that those who are shaped by their intersection are perceived to be anomalous. The erasure of the contradictions of Seguín, the man and the town it is named after, continues today: the town's current Web site, where there is a link to an image of his statue entitled "Lone Star Legend," reveals little of the complex history of the town and the man himself, who is described as having participated in the "great victory at San Jacinto." His fighting against Texas is not mentioned. Both the "history" and "demographics" sections of the Web site exclude the Mexican history and heritage of the area. Even the link to the Seguin [*sic*] Family Historical Society, which explains that Seguín had fought for both sides because "circumstances forced him," is an uncritical recuperation of his reputation ("City of Seguín"). The name of the town, then, evokes the strict divisions informing the formation of borderlands and the nations that claim them. Seguín's seemingly irreconcilable allegiances continue to be erased or to offend. B. V. Olguín criticizes Genaro Padilla for "pathologizing" Seguín's life as "schizophrenic" and suggests that, though "myopic," Seguín's *tejanocentrism* contested the nationalism not only through war-making but also through (failed) efforts to "build cross-cultural alliances" and a bilingual government bureaucracy (87).

The exploration of toponyms and spatial meanings in "Woman Hollering Creek" suggests that as much as it is a story of overlapping plots of female entrapment (from the melodrama of La Llorona to the *telenovela* to Cleófilas's own life), it is also a story of borders between countries, genders, and the inhabitants of the lands on both sides of the imaginary Mexico-U.S. line. Borders among Mexicans and Chicanas/os and between women and men function to enclose each entity upon itself and restrict intersections at the same as they create a world of real and metaphorical migrants struggling with the visible and invisible fences and hostile patriarchal and nationalist domains. Although we know there is no "happy ending" to the story of Cleófilas, who only returns to chores and tiresome if supportive relatives, the union between the two women provides the hope that women's solidarity can be a tool of survival and eliminate, at least in a contingent fashion, the narratives of patriarchal and Anglo domination that divide them. One of the most frequently quoted parts of Seguín's memoirs is his statement that he "became a foreigner in my own land" (Seguín 103). Felice's observation that nothing in the town is named after women unless they are virgins, points to the fact that women are always potentially "foreigners in their own land," whichever side of the border they inhabit.

The border between Felice and Cleófilas does not disappear; each goes back to her original place of belonging after the ride. But they share a refusal to be abused or confined in actual places and spatial meanings as well as a vibrant interest in creating new spatial narratives: Cleófilas takes flight while Felice disobeys. They laugh away the narratives of weeping women, virgins, and patriarchal occupation of space, with their solidarity over re-engendering spatial meaning. Without collapsing differences and borders, Cisneros rewrites the legacy of Seguín, which is in great part about the discontents of a single dominant narrative of place and belonging to the exclusion of others. Felice and Cleófilas's subversion of borders and enclosures allows for the critique and the thawing of such spatial meanings congealed with the victory of expansion. Without recourse to originary homeland geographies or the representation of seamless, borderless diasporized communities, Cisneros points to shared histories and present struggles at the nexus of gender, place, and empire.

Female solidarity and the reinterpretation of sedimented mythologies of place through topographical renaming revises the prevailing critical paradigms of both borderlands and territorial identification. First of all, while place and spatial meanings are central, "Woman Hollering Creek" does not gesture to the transcendent love-of-land tradition. Not having "the earth in her" à la Portillo Trambley's Trini, the primordial significations of land are irrelevant to Cisneros's protagonist. Instead, what she is keenly aware of is the gendered, confining, and conquered histories and practices of place across the border in the United States. Second, while the story seems to privilege border-crossing and spatial in-betweenness as the site of personal transformation (they hoot as they are *crossing* the bridge), it is attentive not simply to the act of crossing but also to its aftermath. We know of the protagonist's dim fate after the first crossing. But the second crossing is also only a return to an unchanged familial situation. Thus, the heady, exhilarating quality critics sometimes assign to in-betweenness and border-crossing, such as the "cultural vertigo of living in a multilingual / multiracial society" Gómez-Peña mentions (*New World* 21), is absent here. Migration in and of itself does not lead to an improved or even adventurous relation to her physical and social environment. Her cross-border spatial and social experience is not one of fluidity, mestizaje, and metaphysical migrancy but one largely defined by repetition and transformation in the feminized spaces of confinement and felicity. The Mexican and pan-American iconography of La Llorona and the

Chicana feminist literary tradition of writing landscape inform Cisneros's writing of borderlands as places that are conquered and gendered at the same time. And at the moment of her departure, Cléofilas redefines the character of the creek, the gendered site in a town redolent with historical defeat and forgetting.

At the end of Cisneros's and Portillo Trambley's texts, there are no unexpected events, but there is a major shift in the characters that leads to the emergence of new kinds of narratives: an alteration of spatial consciousness unmoored from the patriarchal histories and collective myths, from the conqueror's spatial history to Aztlán and gendered legends of place. Viewed by its outsiders, a child and an immigrant woman, both small towns and their reigning spatial narratives take on new meanings: we not only understand the "real" Smeltertown and Seguín differently from the sites that they have been transformed into by official discourses, but we are also led to rethink the topoi of Aztlán and the borderlands. Diaspora narratives, like diaspora lives, need not anchor themselves in the certainty of fixed homelands or meanings, whether of "the green valley" or the "el otro lado de la frontera." Enclosed in spatialized colonialities, sites of exploitation and restriction, the protagonists reconfigure their spatial worlds to uncover and reimagine translocalities and invent alternative meanings that reconfigure both place and identity. Instead of the absolute unity sought by the discourse of utopian homelands, Miguel locates "green valleys" within the individual Chicana/o; instead of cross-border difference or seamlessness, Cleófilas finds solidarity through the reinterpretation of place. While Cather's heroines maintain themselves and civilize their environments through homeland places and identities preserved intact and transposed onto the place of settlement, Cisneros's protagonist remains unmoored but unearths buried spatial histories and incorporates alternative spatial meanings. Without anchoring homes or homelands, the subjects and collectivities remain diasporic, and their small towns become what I have been calling migrant sites, gesturing not only to a heritage of displacement and localization but as well to the instability of the topoi (place and theme) in dominant and masculinist writing. The works of these groundbreaking authors, in which the migrant sites of diasporas and homelands serve to form feminist Chicana identity, are singular contributions to the spatialized consciousness of Chicana/o literature.

As Chicana/o writing contends with a geographic dimension to the wounds of racism and conquest at the Mexico-U.S. border, Puerto Rican island and diaspora conditions and cultural productions are shaped by another unique political situation in the Americas: Puerto Rico as a "special" place, a colonial possession unnamed as such. Puerto Rican diaspora literature is produced through the spatial politics of the urban enclosure in "the mainland," refracted through the island.

CHAPTER 5

THE POETICS OF *AQUÍ*

BARRIOCENTRISM IN PUERTO RICAN DIASPORA LITERATURE FROM *MEAN STREETS* TO NEO-NOIR

Both Chicana/o and Puerto Rican diaspora literatures, marked by enclosures, conquests, and labor exploitation articulate the struggle for place in the United States through their engagement with dominant spatial representations of belonging as well as the spatial articulations specific to the Puerto Rican and Chicana/o experience and cultural imagination. We have seen Chicana authors critique systemic enclosure and coloniality as well as rewrite the Chicana/o topoi of homelands and borderlands. Unlike Chicana/o writing, which spans spatially from rural areas to small towns to urban neighborhoods, Puerto Rican diaspora literature written in the United States since the civil rights era is a body of primarily urban writings that overlaps with and differs from other urban immigrant narratives as well as from African American city literature in its representation of place. It parallels other writing of immigration in its poetics of displacement, including bilingualism and other linguistic stylistics and politics, depiction of marginality with respect to the dominant socioeconomic and spatial arrangements of the city, and frequent thematization of the homeland as an entity that gives meaning to immigrant consciousness. Diaspora Puerto Rican literature of the twentieth century also intersects with African American writing, which is not surprising, given that in the urban settings of a good part of the twentieth century the two social groups often inhabited the same places and shared cultures as well as politics. Further, Puerto Rican and African American authors often have similar localizing impulses and choose as their narrative engines the politics of class and chromatics as they unfold in restricted spaces within large urban areas. In so doing, they point to marginalization within cities *and* make a claim on urban life and literature. As urban studies scholar Luis Aponte-Parés has observed,

> for the new majority of New Yorkers—people of color and immigrants—the built environment of New York City has no apparent relationship to their history, i.e. they are guests in someone else's city. Except for a recent

> attempt by New York City's Landmarks Commission to begin to recognize important places in the South Bronx, Queens, and in Harlem, the City's preservation efforts have concentrated on the History of European descendants. ("What's Yellow" 278)

Many Puerto Rican, African American, and other authors have redressed these erasures in their writing by claiming place and re-creating literary and ethnic history.

Boricua literature differs from these and other traditions, however, in significant ways: in its frequent depiction of "in-betweenness" in a binary black-and-white world and the consequences of Puerto Ricans' particular ethnoracialization in spatial, literary, and linguistic terms. Further, the distinctly ambiguous status and consciousness of Puerto Ricans on the island and in the diaspora as a colonial population shape the spatial stories that Puerto Ricans have told about themselves to the world. In her contribution to an anthology of Latina/o feminist *testimonios*, Liza Fiol-Matta refers to her "uneasy" citizenship as a Puerto Rican (149). Given the quasi-oxymoronic quality of Puerto Rican citizenship, Fiol-Matta's characterization of national belonging is not surprising. A Puerto Rican is a citizen who is not one: the "homeland" is a nation that is neither a nation-state nor a U.S. state. Her consciousness and the way she is perceived by others is structured by the dependent colonial status of the island, which was determined by the U.S. Supreme Court in the early twentieth century to be "foreign in a domestic sense."[1] If she relocates to New York, she is then an immigrant who is not one in a space that is considered not hers, despite the trappings of (unequal) citizenship and passports. It is no wonder that the Puerto Rican diaspora writer, viewed as "foreign," inhabiting "foreign" ethnoracial spaces on the mainland, makes *place* central to her concerns:

> Like many Puerto Ricans, I struggle to inhabit a place that can hold the contradictions of nationalism, *patria*, migration, exile, and diaspora. But there is no place for me on my island, nor am I totally comfortable in the United States. The geography of my world is as much conceptual as territorial. It is as much Northeastern United States as it is Caribbean, as much Army bases as island, as much the subway as ocean and horizon. Chicana poet Lorna Dee Cervantes's words resonate for me when she writes: "Every day I am deluged with reminders / that this is not / my land / and this is my land." But sometimes I mean both my island and this land. (149–150)

In this passage, the Puerto Rican poet-scholar living in New York expresses the vagaries of Puerto Rican belonging in spatial terms; the predicament of being a citizen who is not one and an immigrant technically not crossing nation-state boundaries, is precisely about how to belong in what space. The available spaces are organized so as to dislodge any belonging that is not mediated and infiltrated by the colossal presence of the United States. Puerto Rican diaspora literature and politics carry the tasks of imagining and asserting independent, viable, multilingual places in which Puerto Ricans can have a future.

As Chicana/o literature distinguishes itself through such spatial paradigms as the Mexican homeland, the homeland of Aztlán, and the border that separates homeland from diaspora (see chapter 4), U.S. Puerto Rican writing establishes itself through two principal locations: the island homeland and the urban diaspora. These two places, lived and imagined, overlap with and differ from the kind of places that form the axis of Chicana/o writing. Despite the common legacy of conquest and colonialism and relations of domination with the United States, the island of Puerto Rico, as a current colonial possession, signifies differently from both places of symbolic and historical portent for Chicanas/os; that is, the nation-state of Mexico and the "Southwest" and other locations of Mexican America. That Puerto Rico is a "commonwealth" nation has much to do with the status of the Puerto Rican diaspora in the United States and the representation of Puerto Rican places. Further, at least until the civil rights era, the island informed Puerto Rican diaspora literature to a greater extent than Mexico did Chicana/o literature. As we have seen in the previous chapter, the assertion of indigeneity and historical belonging-in-place has meant that the primary spatial references in recent Chicana/o writing are the borderlands and Aztlán rather than Mexico. Relatedly, in Chicana/o literature the homeland and the space of displacement may coincide for historical reasons, whereas in the Boricua imagination, the U.S. urban space is often represented as severed from the place of origin. Hence, although the Chicana/o and Puerto Rican literary and cultural practices draw on a place-based consciousness and narratives of spatial conquest, they differ in their approach to places that signify the homeland and diaspora.

In this chapter, I locate Puerto Rican narratives in the urban barrio, which I see as a central topos of the Puerto Rican diasporic imagination, one that has generated multivalent forms of writing and signification. This variety is not surprising, given that the socioeconomic reality that much of, though not all, Puerto Rican life in the continental United States has been produced in barrios and that New York City's Puerto Rican population rivals San Juan's. And yet what I shall be referring to as *barriocentricity* in cultural expression is not a simple reflection of this reality, but a choice to position Puerto Rican diaspora literature and consciousness in a particular urban geography. Certainly, the Puerto Rican experience outside of the island, varying in location from Hawaii to Hartford, has been wide-ranging. Even so, many (though not all) of the most recognized authors of the Puerto Rican diaspora have created what I think of as a barriocentric literature, oriented toward the practices, languages, and conditions of barrios, New York City barrios in particular.

Because such a significant portion of Puerto Rican diaspora literature is barriocentric, I cannot address the entire range of works. I shall focus on the narrative representation of the East Harlem barrio in the "third stage" of diaspora writing (Cruz-Malavé, "Teaching") after 1965. This period is important because it is when fictional works not only represent the contemporary conditions of the Harlem barrio but also approximate "subaltern strategies of localization," a term I borrow from Arturo Escobar's 2001 article on place and globalization. In that essay, Escobar underlines the importance of place-based resistance movements in a regime of globalizing capitalism that builds on placelessness as practice and ideology. Although my focus here is not on globalization, I also argue that the authors I have chosen, Piri Thomas and Ernesto Quiñonez, as well as Nuyorican poets, assert a place-based imagination in which the barrio is a site of Puerto Rican and Latina/o community and vitality against the forces that revile and devastate the neighborhood. These authors locate themselves and the future of the Puerto Rican diaspora *in* the barrio and not in the escape from it. While some narratives of upward mobility may emphasize the overcoming of barrios stemming from the exceptionality of the individuals (e.g. Linda Chávez's work), and others choose not to represent collective diasporic loci but focus on Puerto Rican experiences (for example, the fiction of Judith Ortiz Cofer), there is also a powerful tendency in diaspora writing to localize in the barrio as a literary and political strategy seeking to overturn the coloniality that shapes it, that is, racism and economic exploitation that give rise to its worst conditions.

Notwithstanding its boundaries and enclosures, the writing of the barrio is a crossroads of many literary traditions, including the African American, Chicana/o, and different immigrant fictions, including the Jewish. In reading Thomas's *Down These Mean Streets*, I make connections to African American literature, and the consciousness of the colonized island that Quiñonez invokes echoes the awareness of conquest and history of U.S hegemony I underlined in Cisneros. Socially and politically the African American, Puerto Rican, and Chicana/o communities have overlapped in terms of developing a common culture out of propinquity (African Americans and Puerto Ricans in New York City, for example) and by way of sharing a history as conquered subjects of the Americas with Chicanas/os. Puerto Rican literature has reflected these commonalities, as we shall see in the discussion of Thomas and Quiñonez below. The links to Jewish American literature seem less tangible, given the different racialization processes of the two groups as well as the greater prominence of Jewish American literature in the literary marketplace. Yet, when asked about the future of Latina/o literature, Quiñonez compared the "heavyweights" like Sandra Cisneros and Junot Diaz to Jewish American writers he named, such as Henry Roth, Bernard Malamud, I. B. Singer, and Philip Roth, thereby linking the fates of diasporic writing in the United States. Jonathan Freedman has argued in *Klezmer America* that Jewish American literature and culture have been paradigmatic for many other diasporic cultural productions of the United States. Jewish immigrant literature stands in as a "model" of ethnic alienation and integration struggles. Although they are separated by a century, the writing of the Lower East Side ghetto and El Barrio overlap in their exposure of enduring spatial coloniality: the segregation and enclosure of racialized migrants to exploitative ends.

But the most important difference between the writings is not simply the more vociferous expression by Quiñonez to the creation of these conditions, but that Cahan's critique is self-contained. Quiñonez is explicit, as we shall see, about the segregation and abandonment of the barrio residents by those in power; Cahan, in contrast, does not attribute the ghetto's conditions to hegemonic forces, choosing instead to critique those within the Jewish world who conform to that power. Hence, the coarse Jewish sweatshop boss and Yekl the mimic are the figures who assimilate into the power structure through crude means and mimesis, but systemic spatial segregation and economic exploitation are not addressed. Moreover, the affirmation of the diaspora place that is present in both *Down These Mean Streets* and *Bodega Dreams* is largely absent from Cahan's text.

Thus, while Cahan's ghetto is enclosed to reveal only internal power dynamics, Quiñonez's barrio is more complexly a product of outside forces *and* a locus of home-making for Puerto Rican and Latina/o communities. The transitional ethnoracial status of Yekl, Gitl, and other characters in Cahan's novella speaks to the transitional status of Jewish Americans who were affected by spatial and other racial colonialities relatively briefly. In contrast, Thomas and Quiñonez mark enduring enclosures as well as lasting place-based social and political struggles and aesthetics gesturing to the island as well as to the diaspora: hence the continuing barriocentricity of Puerto Rican diaspora literature. The comparison of Cahan's localism with Thomas and Quiñonez's barriocentricity indicate the overlapping imaginaries of writing the urban diaspora place across time and origins; at the same time, however, the distinctions are instructive in understanding the asymmetrical processes of spatialization, social exclusion, and entry into U.S. literature as a diaspora space. Such comparisons undo Jefferson's "empire of liberty."

Just as thinking through the similarities and differences between Cahan's tenement rows and Quiñonez's projects tells us about the transformation of U.S. literature, the differences between Thomas's 1967 text *Down These Mean Streets* and Quiñonez's 2000 *Bodega Dreams* also point to some of the shifts in the narrative representation of the barrio. Although the barrio is central to both works, their differing spatial aesthetics and politics indicate not only generational differences between the authors but also changing spatial politics and aesthetics in Puerto Rican diaspora writing. In Thomas's text, a narrative of multiple returns to East Harlem, or El Barrio, emphasizing a place-based identity despite the ravages of racism that threatens it, the future of both the protagonist and the neighborhood remains uncertain. While Quiñonez also critiques the neighborhood's marginalization, he offers a self-help program to combat gentrification and promote ownership in what comes closer to a happy ending. The texts' differential approach is also apparent in their ethnoracial connectivity and diasporic aesthetics: Thomas's text is in generic and thematic dialogue with African America; Quiñonez's novel emerges from a pan-Latina/o context emergent in both politics and the publishing world.

In addition to delineating the changing spatial imaginary of Puerto Rican diaspora literature, I intend in this chapter to demonstrate that place-based aesthetics and politics are part of, and not contrary to, diaspora consciousness, as has been argued. In his critique of the diaspora concept, Arif Dirlik has suggested that place-based identities and politics differ from diaspora identities and politics. For Dirlik, diasporic identification reifies interethnic distinction and obliterates intraethnic differences. Additionally, he proposes, "One of the dangerous consequences of undue attention to diasporas is to distance the so-called diasporic populations from their immediate environments, to render them into foreigners in the context of everyday life" ("Bringing" 118).

Yet, the representation of ethnic places in diaspora and immigrant literature, including, as we shall see, of El Barrio, shows us that it is not necessary to pit place-based identities against diaspora identities. In writing El Barrio, U.S. Puerto Rican authors struggle to define the local, to use Clifford's words ("Diasporas" 308), for themselves, against the site-making apparatus of dominant society that "eviscerate" (Casey 187) ethnic places, constructing spaces of foreignness in fixed and endlessly repeated terms like "ghettos" and "inner cities." In their works, Piri Thomas and Ernesto Quiñonez transform El Barrio from a site of pathology and criminality and re-create it in order to offer new politics and aesthetics that are both place-based and diasporic. Reading these works in a diaspora frame does not cause an estrangement of these practices from the U.S. context from which they emerge (as suggested by Dirlik); rather, it explains the origins of spatial containment and the place-based eruption of new artistic and social forms and languages. At the same time, the diasporic reading allows for the conception of barrios as relational entities that, despite their status as contained and enclosed places, with their residents subjected to contemporary colonialities of economic subjugation, are created with reference to what lies outside them, in this case, the island of Puerto Rico. Further, as I show in this chapter, Dirlik's concern that the emphasis on ethnic and diasporic particularity inhibits bridge-making (118) does not necessarily hold: place-based Puerto Rican diasporic narratives also allow the articulation of connectivities among diaspora populations and cultural expressions, between African American and Latinas/os and among Latinas/os of varying backgrounds (as well as with other urban diaspora literatures, like Cahan's).

In the works of Thomas and Quiñonez, El Barrio is a place of both confinement and translocality; that is, a "migrant site," as I have been using this term. As in other narratives of diaspora we have seen, irreconcilable tension results from representing place as both an ossified site (Casey) of containment and "migrant" in terms of the possibilities of movement and spatial relationality of even enclosed places. In the specific context of Puerto Rican diaspora writing, the neighborhood is a migrant site in which the local is translocalized through the island. Literary East Harlem is a spatialization of the status of the Puerto Rican diaspora as a colonial population on the island and a negatively racialized, marginalized one in the United States, the "racial/colonial subjects of empire" to use terminology that distinguishes among different "newcomers" to the United States (Grosfoguel and Georas). The barriocentric narratives of Puerto Rican United States bespeak the practices of enclosure as well as of translocality and displacement.

The East Harlem barrio, known as Spanish Harlem as of the 1940s, is at the heart of Puerto Rican literary and cultural geographies. The other New York neighborhoods of the Lower East Side, Brooklyn, and the Bronx (not to mention Puerto Rican strongholds in Chicago, Hartford, and so forth) are pivotal to Puerto Rican life, but in terms of concentrated population and geographic extent, East Harlem is central. A classic "ethnic succession" neighborhood, East Harlem was home to the largest Italian population in the United States until the arrival of Puerto Ricans, who had been in the neighborhood since the early twentieth century and whose numbers soared as of the 1940s and 1950s with the unprecedented emigration from Puerto Rico, becoming its largest group. Despite the arrival of subsequent Latin American populations, most recently Mexicans, Puerto Ricans are still the most numerous population in East Harlem. With institutions like *la marqueta*, El Museo del Barrio, and many long-standing restaurants, East Harlem is not only a living neighborhood of Puerto Rican life but also a heritage place for the larger Puerto Rican diaspora. Those with roots in El Barrio can return there for a bit of nostalgia and food. Unlike the Jewish Lower East Side, however, which we examined in chapter 2, El Barrio is a place of ongoing Puerto Rican life and not primarily a site of heritage tourism primarily institutionalized in museums and history. Despite the recent problems of gentrification in El Barrio and the increasingly dispersed geography of the Puerto Rican diaspora, it remains a core Puerto Rican space[2].

PUERTO RICAN PLACE

A literary barriocentrism, drawing on East Harlem as well as other barrios, has spoken to political movements of Puerto Ricans as to other communities of color since the 1960s. The civil rights era was a time of demands for equal treatment that had an emphatic spatial dimension. Not only did communities assert the rights of people of color to all public space; they also launched unprecedented programs for and raised consciousness about the positive aspects of ethnoracial spaces—the ghettos and barrios of African Americans and Latinas/os in particular. Political action, such as that of the Young Lords and social programs were barrio-based (see Aponte-Parés, "Lessons"), which went hand in hand with the affirmation of barrio culture, art, and people. Piri Thomas's emergence as an East Harlem writer and activist takes place in the context of this purposeful localization that sought to counteract the spatial containment imposed from above. The legacy of civil rights–era barriocentricity continues, although in a rather different form, as we shall see, in contemporary fictions such as Quiñonez's *Bodega Dreams*. The novel addresses specifically the urban neglect and the literal and metaphorical gutting of infrastructural investment and social programs in East Harlem. Quiñonez also writes from within the context of the changing "pan-Latina/o" demographics of the neighborhood and its aggressive gentrification seeking to displace low-income Puerto Ricans and others.

Barriocentric texts are often double-edged: they attempt to address and represent the causes and consequences of racial and economic exploitation, yet at the same time, they risk reconfirming prejudices about Puerto Ricans and Puerto Rican places circulated through the news and other media, including popular works like *West Side Story* (on the film see Negrón-Muntaner; Sandoval-Sánchez). The mainstream social and cultural representations of "Spanish" barrios as sites of crime, pathology, and foreignness have often been reinforced by scholarly ones, beginning, most infamously, with Oscar Lewis's *La Vida*. In a review essay on ethnographies of U.S. Puerto Ricans, the anthropologist Arlene Torres argues that studies of East Harlem and Puerto Ricans that emphasize the extreme problems of crime and addiction receive more attention than those that focus on the vast majority of Puerto Rican lives and struggles, which are unrelated to crime and drugs. Hence, writing the barrio is often a delicate enterprise negotiating spatial stereotyping, literary institutions' containment strategies through the assignment of labels, genres, and themes to writers of color, and the writers' own aesthetics and politics regarding place.

Localization in the barrio for the literature of this period does not eliminate the other spatial axis of Puerto Rican diaspora discourses—the homeland. Barriocentric literature also represents homelands, in a complex and ambivalent manner. The translocal identification or even disidentification with the island also shapes the literary geographies of the Puerto Rican diaspora so that the barrio is a migrant site in which localizing aesthetics and politics are often undergirded by *trans*local consciousness of the island and of migration.

BARRIOCENTRIC LITERATURE

While Puerto Rican life and cultural practices outside the island continue to be informed by the island heritage and/or "the flying bus" syndrome of continuous movement between north and south, the tendency toward localization in fact and imagination and a barriocentric outlook and aesthetics have been central to U.S. Puerto Rican politics and literature. Because the diaspora subject can often claim belonging in neither the homeland nor in the places of resettlement, placelessness is often thematized in diaspora fiction. But Boricua writing has insisted on localizing despite the awareness of a seemingly perpetual in-betweenness of the race and place of the Puerto Rican. In writing "the local," diaspora authors have emphasized both its forced enclosure and marginalization and its translocal, multiple, bilingual dimensions. Although there have been "out of the barrio" narratives of upward mobility (for example, those of Linda Chávez), much of the discourse of belonging has insisted on its barrio-based forms. I shall devote the remainder of my analysis of place in Puerto Rican diaspora literature to the different literary forms that barriocentrism has taken. The writing of "the local" has not been a one-dimensional enterprise. Subaltern literary strategies of localization have been framed by both protest *and* upward mobility, both artistic experimentation and the documentary urge, both progressive politics and measures of accommodation.

The writing of the barrio has been a constant feature of diasporic expression, but after 1965 it becomes particularly complex and willfully localizing. The main impetus of the pre-1965 writing about East Harlem, the Lower East Side, and other Puerto Rican neighborhoods in New York was to draw attention to, usually through a realistic style, the misery and depravity of life in diaspora through narratives of Anglo racism and exploitation and degraded physical conditions of the housing and built environment. As Rafael Falcón has shown in his *La enmigración a Nueva York en la novela puertorriqueña*, Puerto Rican authors who lived on the island but had some experience in New York wrote about the experience of migration and ghettoization as blight as early as the 1920s. In novels such as *El negocio* (1922) and *Redentores* (1925), Manuel Zeno Gandía represented New York as a locus of failed dreams, with his disillusioned protagonists returning to the island by the end of the narratives (see R. Falcón 12–14).

But it was after the greatest wave of Puerto Rican migration to the United States that Puerto Rican authors engaged in many works the tremendous social fact of mass departure from the island and focused on their lives in marginalized neighborhoods on the continent. As Juan Flores has indicated ("Puerto Rican Literature"), fictions about Puerto Ricans in New York were at first written in Spanish by island authors from an outsider's perspective by such authors as Jose Luís González, René Marqués, Enrique Laguerre, and Pedro Juan Soto. Thomas's *Down These Mean Streets*, the first English-language Puerto Rican novel, won wide recognition upon publication in 1967 and became the first in a long line of English-language novels about barrio experiences by diaspora Puerto Ricans born and/or raised in Puerto Rican/Latina/o neighborhoods across New York, including those by Nicholasa Mohr, Edward Rivera, Ed Vega (Edgardo Vega

Yunqué), Esmeralda Santiago, Abraham Rodríguez, and others. While the barrio experience is central to these authors' protagonists' consciousness, narratives by Piri Thomas and Ernesto Quiñonez are examples of Puerto Rican diaspora literature in which the barrio is not only a significant part of storytelling but also a source of narrative identities, aesthetics, and politics.

POETICS OF *AQUÍ*

In the post-1965 fictional worlds of U.S. Puerto Rican literature, the barrio is a space of blight that is nevertheless the space of the diaspora's future. A space of claustrophic enclosure created by institutional and everyday racism, it is also a place of belonging. A deictic tendency of diasporic Puerto Rican literature is revealed in the number of important works that locate themselves "here," creating what I am calling the poetics of *aquí*. The *aquí* of Puerto Rican prose and poetry shifts in meaning, but frequently it asserts *localization* in utopian as well as material places for a diasporic people struggling with spatial disenfranchisement and incomplete citizenship. The neat balance that obtains in the dominant narrative of migration, in which the loss of the old place is offset by the gain of a new, does not apply, in many instances, to the migrants from the colonized island. As scholars of the Puerto Rican migration have argued, in the post-1945 period, the colonial government, collaborating with the mainland, exported its most marginal (rural and/or impoverished) populations in order to transform the island more easily into a "showcase" of Third World development under capitalism. Thus disposed of, they arrived in the North only to find themselves transformed into urban proletariat, indeed, "the reserve of the reserve" (Juan Flores, *Divided*), quickly entrenched in spaces undesired and disregarded by others. Yet, despite all, diasporic writing has asserted and claimed to be *aquí* in imagined and real spaces of belonging. From Piri Thomas to Pedro Pietri, from Sandra María Estévez to Ernesto Quiñonez, *aquí* has taken on the multiple resonances of political critique (esp. Pietri and Thomas), cultural validation through space and time (Estévez), and real estate as the Puerto Rican's ideal estate (Quiñonez). Whatever the differences among visions of *aquí*, they are nevertheless all impassioned expressions of how deeply spatialized Puerto Rican diasporic consciousness is and the extent to which the struggles for justice and belonging are place-based.

In "Puerto Rican Obituary" Pedro Pietri's characters, from Juan to Milagros to Olga, who toil in North American factories and are seduced by the American dream, die broke and unfulfilled, estranged and alienated from one another and from themselves, "never knowing / the geography of their complexion." Once dead, however, Pietri allows them a zone of belonging in a mythical, utopian, unlocated locus of belonging he refers to as *aquí*:

> Aquí se habla español all the time
> Aquí you salute your flag first

Aquí there are no dial soap commercials
Aquí everybody smells good
Aquí tv dinners do not have a future
Aquí the men and women admire desire and never get tired of each
 other
Aquí Que Pasa Power is what's happening
Aquí to be called a negrito
 means to be called LOVE. (11)

Aquí is nowhere-utopian, though it is clearly a national site where "you salute your flag first," Spanish is the first language, and racial dynamics are Puerto Rican. Relatedly, it is also a place uncontaminated by consumer capitalism, which, with its soap commercials and TV dinners, characterizes what Pietri names "this dept store / named America" earlier in the poem.

While different in tone and focus, Estévez's poem entitled "Here" is also about a place that does not necessarily exist in a world divided into the dichotomies that the first lines of the poem enumerates. "Here" registers the impossibility of recovering the island heritage but the possibility of reconciling island and diaspora identities. Despite the "theft" of island heritage, "that reality" (362) is going to reunite the separated selves. Pietri's "here" is bounded by oneness of language and community and fullness of belonging. Estévez's "here," on the other hand, is not delineated by a sharp anaphoric construction like Pietri's. Her "here" is not a place but a locus of betweenness and reconciliation at the same time: the mythified and codified palm-tree *isla* and the "ghetto stairways" are seemingly irreconcilable places and sources of identity that nevertheless "bring me back to me" (363).

The location of *aquí* may vary, but asserting belonging in terms of "here" affords a spatial way of being, "real" or utopian, for a diaspora consciousness shaped by displacement and conquest. In their different ways then, these examples from two of the most influential of the Nuyorican poets demonstrate the centrality of a "poetics of here" for the diaspora imagination. The emphasis on "here" does not necessarily eliminate "there" (that is, Puerto Rico), but serves to ground the imagination in local identities and struggles of the diaspora. This "subaltern strategy of localization" (Escobar) as a diaspora population associated with a prior locus does not, as Dirlik argues, "make them foreigners in their everyday life" but responds to the preexisting condition of treatment as undesirable foreigners.

In many Puerto Rican narratives "here" refers specifically and primarily to the lived and imagined locus of barrios, especially, though not exclusively, in New York's Lower East Side, East Harlem, and the Bronx. The elaboration of a Puerto Rican aesthetic unfolds in many writers' works with reference to the language and everyday life of the barrio. While island writers such as Pedro Juan

Soto and José Luis González, who penned impressive stories about the Puerto Rican experience in New York in the postwar period, and René Marqués whose play about the immiseration of Puerto Ricans in diaspora, *La Carreta* (1963), made Puerto Rican literary history, among others, wrote about the urban mainland experience as primarily one of misery and exploitation, Piri Thomas is one of the first authors who, while critiquing ghettoization, also embraced El Barrio in his narrative.

THESE *MEAN STREETS*

The very title of Thomas's book, which influenced many subsequent U.S. Puerto Rican works, points to El Barrio as the locus of Puerto Rican belonging. In fact, at the same time as the work reinforces the title's sensationalized premise of violence and promise of a narrative of descent *down* those streets, it also reverses them in the course of the narrative by asserting the neighborhood as *the* place of the present and future. The novel ultimately belies its marketing apparatus, including its title, to offer a progressive critique of social and spatial relations in the United States and to inaugurate a new writing of the barrio that privileges its idioms.

As I suggested in chapter 1, the promotion of the novel's first editions depended on conjuring in the mind of the readers its "savage" power and "hellish" setting. The paratext (Genette) promises to satisfy the reading public's ethnographic curiosity for representations of "different" cultures and the need to reinforce the perception of violence as primarily localized in ghettos. It is important to note that *Down These Mean Streets* appeared at a time around urban rebellions (for example, Watts [Los Angeles], 1965) and the crisis of urban violence were perpetuated discursively to emphasize "the ghetto's" "increasingly violent and absolute separation from the metropolis" (Rotella 239). Both the fear of and the fascination with ghettos were heightened by the "violent crime and the fear of it [that] rose to the status of a defining urban problem, flowing as such into the racial logic of the urban crisis" (Rotella 230). Narratives of "the ghetto" promised insight into this "racial logic" that depended on the "territorial logic" (Rotella 228) of containment. Jane Jacobs observed in her *The Death and Life of Great American Cities*, that the "barbaric concept of Turf" is first and foremost practiced by the powerful urban "developers," who parcel the city into zones of exclusivity walled off from the lower classes and protected fiercely (qtd. in Rotella 227–228). Many ghetto and barrio narratives attempt to underscore the enclosure of the neighborhoods and the violence around turf not as an expression of the "savagery" of marginalized populations, but as a mirroring of the spatial order, based on race and class, of the city as a whole. And yet, even a text like Thomas's can be promoted as confirming the dominant perception of turf and violence in the ghetto as endemic to its "savagery."

Thus any novel of "the ghetto" is easily subjected to what I have been calling the site-making apparatus of the dominant literary and political institutions: one that transforms a diaspora place into a site with a fixed identity determined primarily by those outside of it looking in. One way of site-making is to generalize the condition of the place so that spatial specifics can be vacated and one place becomes an echo of the other. For example, the reader is informed in a blurb that Thomas's work is reminiscent of "the savage power of *Manchild in the Promised Land*," another tale of the ghetto. El Barrio and African American Harlem are collapsed into each other. This collapsing not only allows the publisher to ride on the success of another writer but also gives the impression that the writing of ethnic places can be interchangeable in their "savagery." The binary discourse of civilization versus barbarism serves to fix spatial identity. "The ghetto" is a monolithic site, always already referring to ethnoracial and class marginality and of course "savage" violence.

How does the text overturn its original paratext? What kind of spatial imagery, language, and story does Thomas develop, and how does he transform El Barrio from a discursive site subjected to mechanisms of economic and social control into a migrant site? How does he narrate El Barrio as a place in which these mechanisms cannot be completely overcome but can be destabilized? How does he position "Spanish Harlem" as home? Unlike some protest novels of the 1940s, Thomas's denunciation of East Harlem's conditions and racist and classist marginalization does not end in inevitable disaster and escape (as does, for example Ann Petry's *The Street*). Nor is the work an indictment of East Harlem and the larger society as its reason for existing. The novel is ultimately a narrative of return, positioned between the critique of place and its affirmation; its suffocating enclosure and its liberating feeling of belonging, its containment and connectivity.

The novel spurs the interrogation of not only the borders of East Harlem but also of ethnoracial identities and their localization. As a narrative of the experience of a dark-skinned Puerto Rican in Harlem, *Down These Mean Streets* is claimed by more than one tradition, including African American literature, Puerto Rican literature, and diaspora literature.[3] In her *Boricua Literary History* Lisa Sánchez González, positions Thomas as a premier Boricua or Puerto Rican writer, and Robert Reid-Pharr refers to Thomas as among "the most prominent chroniclers of Black urban male experience" (378). Reid-Pharr suggests that "Thomas and [James] Baldwin attempt to push against the confines of American Blackness altogether" (374), and Marta Sánchez and Lisa Sánchez González underline the ways in which Thomas tries to create a Puerto Rican identity beyond racial dichotomization. The "confines" Reid-Pharr mentions, I argue, are about racial as well as spatial identities. Further, at the same time as it is a pioneering work of the Puerto Rican diaspora, for example, Thomas's book is also at the intersection of African American and Puerto Rican literature and identity.

Race and place are the central axes of *Down These Mean Streets*, in which the protagonist Piri struggles with the dichotomous black-white matrix of U.S. society in the iconic loci of Harlem and the South. Inevitably, his narrative tips a hat to African American tellings of localization in the urban setting, which vary from what Toni Morrison calls the "love of neighborhood" tradition to narratives of enclosure by authors as varied as Richard Wright, Ann Petry, and Claude Brown. The imaginative creation of Puerto Rican place in the city and in literature entails the positioning of El Barrio at a particular literary and social juncture, in dialogue with other spatialized diaspora imaginings of ethnicity, race, and belonging.

Down These Mean Streets is organized around the representation of places that shape the story. Thirty-five chapters come under eight headings in the following order: Harlem, Suburbia, Harlem, Suburbia, Down South, Harlem, Prison, New York Town. Although the story is told retrospectively and chronologically, the headings and many of the chapter titles give weight to the defining spaces, some of which are repeated to demonstrate the cyclical nature of the "journey" and to lend weight to the phenomenon of return. The book's title signals only descent and points to a spectacle of violence. Interestingly, the back-cover blurb on the thirtieth-anniversary edition of 1997 is expurgated of references to the "savage" and the "raw" foregrounded in earlier editions. Yet it also presents, against the book's own grain, a narrative of vertical ascent: "As he recounts the journey that took him from adolescence in El Barrio to a lock-up in Sing-Sing to the freedom that comes of self-acceptance, faith, and inner confidence, Piri Thomas gives us a book that is as exultant as it is harrowing." Nowhere from this description, the likes of which Marta Sánchez calls "the white mainstream narrative of rehabilitation" (44), can the potential reader discern the novel's structure and politics, its investment in the narrative not of ascent and relinquishment but of return, however uncertain.

The novel begins and ends on a rooftop, an important topos of barriocentric literature, from Thomas to Quiñonez. The "Prologue," both a spirited paean and a challenge to the neighborhood, begins with the storyteller's own positioning in it:

> YEE-AH!! Wanna know how many times I've stood on a rooftop and yelled out to anybody:
> "Hey World—here I am. Hallo, World—this is Piri. That's me.
> "I wanna tell ya I'm here—you bunch of mother-jumpers—I'm here, and I want recognition, whatever that mudder-fuckin word means."
> Man! How many times have I stood on the rooftop of my broken-down building at night and watched the bulb-lit world below.
> Like somehow it's different at night, this my Harlem.

There ain't no bright sunlight to reveal the stark naked truth of
    garbage-lepered streets.
Gone is the drabness and hurt, covered by a friendly night.
It makes clean the dirty-faced kids.
This is a bright *mundo*, my streets, my *barrio de noche*,
With its thousands of lights, hundreds of millions of colors
Mingling with noises, swinging street sounds of cars and curses,
Sounds of joys and sobs that make music.
If anyone listens real close, he can hear its heart beat.

(ix)

The voice, exuberant, high, and angry, releases itself from a rooftop to jolt the reader. Alone up above, a young Piri whose story we are about to know, writes of himself and of "this my Harlem:" narrator and neighborhood shaped by one another. He, a self-described "skinny, dark-face, curly-haired, intense Porty-Reecan. Unsatisfied, hoping, and always reaching," his head "growing bigger than my body as it gets crammed full of hate" and El Barrio's streets "like a great big dirty Christmas tree with lights but no fuckin presents" (x). The view from above is not only appropriate for a speaker "high on anything" (x) but also exemplifies the space of the Barrio storyteller-protagonist, who stands apart and above to tell his story. Nineteenth-century literature is full of such topoi of the (male) individual placed on a height, looking down on the city, his space of self-invention and future success, including *Père Goriot* by Honoré de Balzac, a writer admired by at least two contemporary Puerto Rican authors of urban life, Abraham Rodríguez and Ernesto Quiñonez. In *Down These Mean Streets*, however, the protagonist's surveying of the city is localized in a Harlem that promises nothing: "*Get angry, get hating angry, and you won't be scared. What have you got now? Nothing. What will you ever have? Nothing. . . . Unless you cop for yourself!*" (x). In the narrative that follows, the young Piri takes his rooftop consciousness of an indeterminate mesh of love, hate, fear, and bravado from the rooftop to the streets below and to the U.S. South.

Appropriately for a narrative of enclosure, the first chapter of the book is not so much about mean streets but the desire to run away from confinement and its attendant injustices, which only ends in a return. The chapter is entitled "Cutting Out" and is concerned with the twelve-year-old Piri's failed attempt at running away from home as a result of the racial dynamics of his family, in which he, as the darkest-skinned child, is subjected to unfair treatment and neglect by his father. Here too, he ascends to a tenement rooftop, this time in the hopes of sleeping there; in an experience that foreshadows his future addiction, he witnesses two junkies shooting up under the stairs and running away when they hear Piri's footsteps, which they mistake for a policeman's. The negative feeling following this brief episode leads him to reconsider his escape in terms of the impact it will have on his mother (she will be beaten by his father who will return from work to an absent Piri). The boy goes back home only to discover to his dismay that no one had realized he had been missing: "all that running away for nothing" (6–7). Although this chapter presents the narrative of escape as one of failure, read in the context of the work as a whole it becomes clearer that the chapter does not signal, as would a nineteenth-century naturalist or twentieth-century noir novel, the inescapability of the social conditions of "the ghetto" but of the limitations of running away and "moving out and up" on one's own. Further, in retrospect, it becomes clear that many of the conditions of the neighborhood, especially with regard to racism, are only duplicated and not overcome outside its limits.

Localization in *Down These Mean Streets* is shaped by translocalization as much as by the "hard facts" of tough neighborhood life. During the time the Thomas family lives under the strained condition of poverty and immobility, the crucial spatial reference is of the island and displacement from the island, which shapes Piri's self-conception and the very writing of the book. It is significant that the second chapter, following "Cutting Out," is entitled "Puerto Rican Paradise." Both chapters are about escaping spatial confinement and transgressing the invisible yet palpable boundaries of the neighborhood. Although Thomas neither runs away from the neighborhood nor chooses the island over diaspora, his narrative journey is informed by the places that lie outside El Barrio, which complicates his understanding of the neighborhood and his position within it. In *Down These Mean Streets*, the island appears as if magically in the narrative of the East Harlem family's struggles under severe conditions of inadequate housing, hard labor, war, Depression, and discrimination in New York. On a freezing cold day in 1941, the father is out digging ditches in the snow for the WPA, and the mother and children are warming up from the exercise of beating the radiator with a hammer to force some heat out of it. Over hot cocoa, "Moms copped the wet-eyed look and began to dream-talk about her *isla verde*, the verdant landscape of Moses's land of milk and honey"(18). The father's return home from his labors, with parts of his body frozen, interrupts the warmth these stories provide and brings the northern chill indoors once again. The literature of migration is rife with such images, Juan Flores argues, of colors and warmth on one side and grayness and ice on the other (*Divided* 187). The warm *isla verde* narrative of Moms, Piri's mother, is told in a context diametrically opposed to the cold, unfeeling conditions of the storytelling situation so that the present and the past are juxtaposed:

> "When I was a little girl," she said, "I remember getting up in the morning and getting the water from the river and getting the wood for the fire and the quiet of the greenlands and the golden color of the morning sky, the grass wet from the *lluvia* . . . *Ai, Dios*, the *coquis* and the *pajaritos* making all the musica." "Mommie, were you poor?" asked Miriam. "*Si, muy pobre*, but very happy. . . . In Puerto Rico those around you share *la*

> *pobreza* with you and they love you. . . . I like *los Estados Unidos*, but it's sometimes a cold place to live—not because of the winter and the landlord not giving heat but because of the snow in the hearts of the people." "Moms, didn't our people have any money or land?" I leaned forward, hoping to hear that my ancestors were noble princes born in Spain. (9–10)

The young Piri's intervention into the mother's memory of community and solidarity bespeaks his own preoccupation as to his status within the family and the current diaspora community. Because the darkness of his skin sets him apart not only from dominant U.S. society but his own family and the *gran familia puertorriqueña*, he is eager to find out about a heritage of whiteness that he can appropriate. While his siblings' questions are about economic disadvantage, Piri's inquiry into origins and original place is simultaneously about race, place, and class, as the darkest-skinned child in the family.

Although the stories of his mother's "Puerto Rican Paradise" does not improve his position in the racial and economic hierarchy in diaspora, the nostalgic narrative serves to unite the family, fractured by difficult conditions and the differential racial identifications. It veers from the usual deployment of nostalgia in the depiction of the homeland, in which past places are invoked only to critique or devalue the present. Although neither the present nor the past allows for a narrative of total belonging or security, the juxtaposition of the mother's reveries about the homeland and the father's reality (of unemployment and exploitation the father brings home upon arrival) in fact affords a moment of unity. When the conversation turns bitter, Piri takes stock of his family members looking at one another, full of questions and no answers: "And Miriam, James, Jose, Paulie and me just looking and thinking about snowballs and Puerto Rico and summertime in the street and whether we were gonna live like this forever and not know enough to be sorry for ourselves. The kitchen all of a sudden felt warmer to me, like being all together made it like we wanted it to be. . . . I looked at the clock and it was time for 'Jack Armstrong, the All-American Boy'" (11–12). The reference to this juvenile adventure hero, who travels the world rooting out evil as boys listened avidly in the 1930s and 1940s (and later read in comic strips), provides further contrast to the spatial confinement of the family. Even more important, at this moment the family recognizes the contrast between the pastoral image of the island and the urban reality and the unresolvable nature of this contrast. The unresolvability is what destabilizes the way we are to think of each locus: if the diaspora reality blasts in from the cold so readily, what is the meaning of the *isla verde* memories? If the island is so idyllic, then why suffer in diaspora? The very difficulty of answering these questions and the incertitude as to how to make meaning of each of the places that informs their lives unites the family momentarily.

"ON THE RIM OF BELONGING"

As a young man, Piri continues to dream of a maternal "Puerto Rican paradise." The conjuncture of gender, ethnicity, and place in Piri's long-lasting love for the young woman he calls "Marine Tiger," thinking about whom sustains him even in prison, speaks back to the earlier chapter in which diaspora and homeland stand in such stark contrast.[4] Significantly, the chapter in which we are introduced to her, entitled "My Marine Tiger," begins with Piri's walk through Harlem, to which he returns from Babylon, Long Island, where his family had moved. The suburbs were particularly unwelcoming to Piri, who is excluded and maligned in its social spaces. As a result, he decides to leave his beloved mother and move back to El Barrio. "This Long Island was a foreign country. It looked so pretty and clean but it spoke a language you couldn't dig," he explains, ". . . and you always felt like on the rim of belonging" (88). Belonging was back home in Harlem: "I was swinging in Harlem," he writes, "my Harlem, next to which Babylon was like cotton candy—white and sticky, and tasteless in the mouth. In the daytime Harlem looks kinda dirty and the people a little drab and down. But at night, man, it's a swinging place, especially Spanish Harlem. The lights transform everything into life and movement and blend the different colors into a magic cover-all that makes the drabness and garbage, wailing kids, and tired people invisible." Revealing the most significant aspect of his attitude toward Harlem, he observes, "The daytime pain fades alongside the *feeling of belonging* and just being in swing with all the humming kicks going on around you" (105).

The streets in Harlem and his "boys" are thus the only refuge of Piri, who has been marginalized within the family realm, ill-treated by his school principal, and finally discriminated against in Babylon. It is here he becomes smitten with the young woman passing by,"the prettiest, softest, widest-eyed Puerto Rican girl in the whole world." He names her Marine Tiger, "after the ship that brought so many Puerto Ricans to New York" (109), during the Operation Bootstrap period of U.S.-led industrialization on the island in the 1950s—which also "pushed" out Puerto Ricans, who migrated in huge numbers, largely to New York. That Piri falls in love with this "nice girl from the old country" at the time of his separation from his adored mother, is not coincidental. Marine Tiger is a transitional object that mediates the separation; she is to him a mirror image of Moms, represented as a loving and long-suffering woman. Marine Tiger embodies the feminine ideal as well as serving as a synecdoche of the island, whose stories Piri has heard from his mother. Mother and motherland merge in a woman named after a ship that brings Puerto Rico to New York. Through gendered means, Harlem's status as home is amplified by its connection to Puerto Rico.

For Piri, East Harlem streets are migrant sites, then, that afford both local belonging and translocal affiliation with an island-homeland perceived through its feminine and maternal embodiments. At the point of his departure from Long

Island and his family home, Piri explains to his mother, "this Long Island ain't nuttin' like Harlem, and with all your green trees it ain't nuttin' like Puerto Rico" (91). The bucolic setting is not enough to afford the belonging and plenitude that Piri, like so many others who developed postmemories, envisions about the island. Postmemory is inherited memory or the memory of stories about the previous generation's traumas and experiences that are central to identity formation. Such memories are based on the recollections' of others and on "projection, investment, and creation" (Hirsch 9). The most common postmemories in Puerto Rican diaspora narratives are of familial memories of the island. For example, Rosario Morales's expression of the impact of immigrant nostalgia on the generation born or bred in the United States is based on just such a postmemory. In an account of her Bronx childhood, she writes, "I grew up with nostalgia for a place I did not grow up in, nostalgia for the family I'd missed. . . . I grew up with nostalgia for green landscapes and tropical fruit, . . . for the smell of coffee roasting, the sound of cocks crowing and hens scratching behind the house, I grew up wanting blue skies and rain falling in hard punishing drops. I grew up yearning for trees, yearning for trees" (87–88). The adult Morales, then, is writing the memory of nostalgia for an object that never had an experiential referent for her, the child of the displaced. As Hirsch observes, the parental experience creates a "postmemory" for a child who grows up with stories "so powerful, so monumental as to constitute memories in their own right"(8).

But the influence of postmemory wanes for barriocentric Piri. Despite its diametrically opposed built environment, Harlem is closer to the maternal Puerto Rico than tree-lined Babylon, Long Island. Harlem for Piri is not the "site," an ossified locus of pathology, that it is for mainstream observers. Thomas depicts a beleagured but enveloping barrio, at once confining and translocal. That is, although Harlem is a locus of containment to which people of color are assigned and instructed not to transgress its boundaries by spilling out into forbidden racial zones, Thomas reminds us that its residents perceive it not only as a limited world onto itself but in relation to other places.

Far from being diametrically opposed to the maternalized green island, Harlem is in fact analogous to it for the sense of belonging it affords. Although at the beginning of *Down These Mean Streets* Thomas stages the classic opposition between the warm, maternal homeland and the drastically cold, urban reality (found in many Puerto Rican diaspora texts, as discussed above), in the course of the novel, this opposition unravels to suggest that Harlem is also home, in what Piri feels its welcoming embrace. It is not surprising that an early version of the book, destroyed in prison, was called "Home, Sweet Harlem" (Hernández 177). Further, the presence of Marine Tiger and the likes of her arriving by the thousands to El Barrio confirms that "the ghetto" is not a site of enclosure severed from the surrounding city and the world; in fact, like Cahan's Lower East Side, it is a global "contact zone" (Pratt, *Imperial Eyes*) of people and cultures, the

U.S.-born, and the immigrant, which it continues to be today, despite gentrification. It is a locus of containment and translocality, simultaneously.

In her article "City Limits, Village Values: Concepts of the Neighborhood in Black Fiction," Morrison argues that unlike the anti-urbanism that prevails in U.S. texts by Melville, Hemingway, Cheever, and Updike, African American writing exhibits a love for "village values," which are transposed onto the urban setting. These are primarily social values that prioritize community life above the individualism dear to mainstream white authors. For authors like Thomas and Miguel Piñero, who instructed in his famous "A Lower East Side Poem" that his ashes be scattered not on the island homeland but on the Lower East Side, Puerto Rican barrios represent home, not its antithesis. Despite the drastic change in title from the original version written in prison, Thomas's poetics of *aquí* remains true to place, without idealizing or sentimentalizing it, but rescuing it from the site-making operation that presents the barrio as a "savage" place to escape from and not return to. Harlem becomes another "island," in diaspora; it is "home."

IN THE "TWO-TONE SOUTH"

In most texts the primary spatial reference that links diaspora place with what lies outside of them is the homeland. But in Thomas's text, El Barrio exists not only in close relation to the island but also to the American South, a crucial topos in African American literature, through the use of which Thomas connects the fates of black people, whether African American or Puerto Rican, as well as Puerto Rican diaspora narrative with African American writing. The novel lays bare the complexity of racialization and racial identifications that are held to be mutually exclusive. In exploring psychosexual aspects of an identity that is, as he puts it in a chapter title, "hung up between two sticks," Thomas creates a narrative that is both "black" and Puerto Rican, categorized in literary criticism as either one or the other, as I explained above. Yet Thomas's work is crucial in demonstrating how these categories overlap. *Down These Mean Streets* depicts complex social identities that defy categorization as well as integrating African American and diaspora Puerto Rican textual and linguistic modes and topoi.

All of Piri's forays into the world end with his return to Harlem. One of the most significant of his sojourns is in the U.S. South, where Piri travels in order to explore his blackness. Although he defines himself as a Puerto Rican and not as black, in a world where these are separate and hierarchized categories, he is perceived as "a Negro." The discrimination he feels subjected to within his own family as the only dark-skinned child and the general agreement, including especially by his African American friend Brew, born and raised in the South, that the South is the ultimate locus of racism leads Piri to undertake this journey of discovery. The South, he hopes, might cure of him of his confusion as to his racial identity and help him "come in on a right stick" (127). Instead, his experiences with racism, including the African American experience of eviction from a lunch counter, in the South and all over the world confirms Brew's argument that skin color overrides any other attribute. At the end of his chapter on traveling with the Merchant Marine, which he joins for passage to the South, he reports that he told himself prophetically, "Dear God, dear God. . . . I am going to kill, I am going to kill somebody" (191). Hence, the rage that fuels the inevitable decline into serious crime, a sine qua non of the protest novel that shaped a good part of African American writing, is triggered in the South, presented as the quintessential locus of black oppression.

Thomas's representation of the South converged with those in the urban-centric African American writing of the 1960s, which was largely denunciatory of that region as a place blacks needed to forget and transcend. This attitude did not anticipate the resurgence of literary depictions of the South in the 1970s—especially by feminist authors—as a historical place of black autonomy and creativity (Dubey). Even his experiences in the Merchant Marine encapsulate another foundational African American experience: as a coal fireman, Piri writes, "Damm-sam, I never knew what a slave was until I began to shovel that black crap" (189). The ship serves as yet another locus that bridges his own history to African American experience, through which he acknowledges his own African ancestry.

Thomas's use of the topoi of the South or the ship is not, however, a simplistic superimposition of the African American literary and historical experience onto the Puerto Rican. In fact, Thomas complicates what he calls "the two-tone South" (186) and his place in it in more than one way. Even though as Brew warns him, Piri finds out that "any language you talk, if you're black, you're black" (191), Piri's "Spanish" roots, linguistic and other, serve to challenge the "two-tone" make-up of U.S. identity. As El Barrio is lived in Spanish, Thomas's South becomes a place in which Spanish is currency, albeit of a very different kind. Thomas's groundbreaking written language blends Spanish words, phrases, and syntax with 1960s "smooth talk." Lisa Sánchez González observes that in many works that deploy grassroots languages, dialogue or certain characters' idiom is rendered in "dialect," while the omniscient narrator's English is "standard." This is true, as we have seen, of *Yekl*. Thomas, on the other hand, writes in barrio language throughout the text and not only in dialogue or interior monologue (Sánchez González 107). He renders the South in the same way, entitling his Southern chapter "Las Aguas del sur." Piri's "languaging" strategies (Mignolo) not only legitimizes barrio expression, devalorized in the world at large (see, for example, Urcioli; Zentella, *Growing Up*); he also takes it outside of its geographical enclosure and maps it onto the presumably separate, unconnected space of the U.S. South. Given that Puerto Rican English is laced with African American Vernacular English (Zentella, *Growing Up* 45), the very barrio language of *Down These Mean Streets* is itself a negation of the geographical and racial separation of African America from the Puerto Rican world and of the walls among Spanglish, Standard English, and AAVE.

Piri's experience in Texas points to the differing valences of race and language in distinct places, specifically of Spanish and of Puerto Ricanness outside of New York. In an unforgettable episode, Thomas "passes" for a Puerto Rican in Texas in order to gain access to a brothel from which blacks are barred. By pretending to be a man from Puerto Rico who speaks only Spanish he manages to convince the clerk that he is not black. The clerk then tells Piri's Mexican companion, "Well, you know, we got all kinds of people coming in, all kinds of foreigners, and Spanish people who come from Argentina and Colombia and Peru and Cuba, and that's all right, but we got to keep these damn niggers down" (188). The terrible irony is that because of the virulence of antiblack racism, Piri accomplishes what he could not anywhere else: to be identified as a Puerto Rican. Piri avenges his injuries through the body of the white prostitute, who does not know that she has slept with a black man until his triumphant postcoital announcement that she has done so. While doing so allows Piri to trick and outwit racial hierarchies, as Marta Sánchez has observed, his revenge also twins "femaleness and passivity" (51). This event reinforces gender hierarchies as it points to the phantasmatic construction of race. Perceived solely as a black man in most other contexts, in the South, Piri transforms himself into a non-"Negro" through the use of Spanish and Puerto Rican identity. Thomas shows how the imaginary fixity of race and racial attributes vanishes, if blackness is attributed contextually. The South is another locus then, like El Barrio, where Piri again blasts open the racial dichotomization at the root of antiblack racism and Puerto Rican marginalization. He also provides a link between colonialism and slavery and reminds us that the plantation and the barrio are more proximate than their spatial and temporal differences indicate. Piri's experience shows that the plantation and the reservation are refracted through time and space in the production of new spatial confinements and inequalities affecting the colonized, racialized people of color today.

The final link that Thomas's work creates between the topologies of African American and Puerto Rican diaspora writing is in the prison setting, the most extreme spatial assignment and confinement.[5] There are significant overlaps with African American male narratives of crime, punishment, and rehabilitation published in the 1960s and 1970s, including a brush with Islam. But Thomas emerges from prison not a nationalist but with only El Barrio in his thoughts. Although he knows he cannot bear returning to prison, he is no less "hung up between two sticks" and no more certain of his destiny. What structures his post-prison narrative is the nature of his return to Harlem. That the neighborhood is a substitute parental figure that welcomes and envelops is apparent once more in the title of the chapter that treats Piri's release: "Hey Barrio—I'm Home." Piri does not romanticize the barrio:

> I breathed in the air; it was the same air that I had breathed as a kid. The garbage-filled backyards were the same. Man, everything was the same, only I had changed. I wasn't the grubby-faced Puerto Rican kid any more; I was a grubby-faced Puerto Rican man. I am an *hombre* that wants to be better. Man! I don't want to be nuttin'. I want to be somebody. I want to laugh clean. (32)

Indeed, as he looks out at the Harlem scene from his aunt's apartment, he is grabbing the bars of the iron gate, which mentally transports him back to prison. As Arnaldo Cruz-Malavé ("What a Tangled Web" 139–140) and Lisa Sánchez González have pointed out, Thomas's is an equivocal text, in which certainty and resolution are elusive. El Barrio can be the mean streets in the way that outsiders conceive it. And it may not even offer the womblike feeling of security-in-confinement that Naficy points out as a feature of the enclosed spaces of exile and diaspora film (see chapter 1). Yet El Barrio is the space of the future, however uncertain. Thomas's subsequent novel *Savior Savior, Hold My Hand* is about staying on and working with Harlem youth.

Thomas's representations of El Barrio, the South, and the prison are all migrant sites, as I have been defining the term. In his use of each of these topoi, Thomas is able to dislodge received ideologies about certain places, those sites, maligned, misrepresented, and marginalized in a majority of spatial discourses. Thomas also creates migrant sites by connecting the different topoi to one another and establishing links between African American and Puerto Rican diaspora racial and class discourses, laying bare the continuum of spatial and other colonialities that affect "racial/colonial subjects of empire" (Grosfoguel and Georas) like Puerto Ricans and other "domestic others." At the same time, Thomas creates a new locus of belonging that questions the representational mechanism of enclosure and marginalization. He develops an aesthetics and politics of connectivity, which he has continued in his life's work. In spatial terms this means that the barrio may be defined by containment as much by translocal connection and closure as by openness, through its connections with the island of Puerto Rico and African America. In *Down These Mean Streets*, the site of the barrio became a migrant site, one that laid the groundwork for subsequent narrative explorations of Puerto Rican diaspora place and identity.

BODEGA'S AMERICAN DREAMS

Bodega Dreams comes in a line of what is now decades-long writing of the Puerto Rican barrio in English by diaspora authors. Published in 2000, the novel continues the legacy of barrio writing and pays homage to Piri Thomas and the Nuyorican poets, all the while charting a separate course in the representation of El

Barrio. As Thomas's work was of its civil rights moment, born of both anger and affirmation, Quiñonez's novel speaks to the current juncture of more abundant self-representation by Puerto Ricans and other Latinas/os, social critique, and literary marketing. An heir to the work of Piri Thomas and the poets of the 1970s and 1980s, Quiñonez establishes a different conjuncture of writing, spatial politics, and cultural representation.

Quiñonez is writing at a time when his barrio narrative not only satisfies the readership's abiding interest in "mean streets," "the ghetto" (or, to use the most recent description that is now treated as a genre, the "urban"); it also coincides with an unprecedented "boom" in literature about Latina/o life, the likes of which was unimaginable when Thomas emerged as an author. Out of all the so-called ethnic literatures in the United States, Latina/o writing was the ethnic literature of the moment at the time of the novel's publication. Following the "Latin explosion" in pop music in the late 1990s and the reverberations of the 2000 census construing Latinas/os of the United States as a population that mattered, trade and mainstream publications trumpeted the "arrival" of Latina/o literature, the Latina/o reading public, and the Spanish-language market. As a 2002 *New York Times* article on Latina/o publishing put it, "Maybe the most important thing that ever happened in this country for Hispanics wanting to read relevant books was the 2000 census. It said, hey, publishers, there are 35.3 million Latinos out there. So book publishers started to awaken from the somnolence that often embraces them when it comes to the new and started to take notice" (Arnold). Of course, Latinas/os are emphatically not a "new" demographic force in the United States; there has been Latina/o literature in the United States since the nineteenth century. But in the presentist mentality of the publishing and marketing sectors, the novelty of the Latina/o aesthetic as well as the Latina/o market is their most prominent marketing feature. It is true that mainstream interest in Latina/o literature has been growing for some time and especially since Hijuelos's 1992 *Mambo Kings Play Songs of Love*, but the post-2000 census interpellation of Latinas/os as a "new" force to contend with has helped publishers expand their attempts to transform the Latina/o and Spanish-language publishing sector from a serious niche into a phenomenon. In addition to many other developments in the last few years in big-business publishing, 2003 was declared by the Association of American Publishers to be "the Year of Publishing Latina/o Voices for America."

Now, within this terrifically hyped and streamlined literary marketplace for Latina/o writing, how do we read Latina/o texts that have mainstream appeal? And how do these texts position diaspora places and spatialize their writing within this literary market? I shall explore these question through an analysis of Quiñonez's *Bodega Dreams*, published by Vintage and extremely well received in the mainstream press. The novel—whose sources range from F. Scott Fitzgerald, Miguel Piñero, and Piri Thomas to noir writing and film and the *Godfather* movies—takes place in Puerto Rican and Latina/o East Harlem and concerns the involvement of a young man nicknamed Chino with Willie Bodega, a former Young Lord turned drug lord, who envisions a "great society" of social programs in East Harlem funded by his illicit business. Most of the novel, including the eventual murder of Bodega, the charismatic and tragically marked character modeled after Gatsby, by his associate and best friend takes place in and around East Harlem. Despite its evocation of *The Great Gatsby*, it is a novel of the barrio, and that, of course, is part of its appeal.

Like much of so-called ethnic literature, Latina/o literature is promoted for its ethnographic value, for its said ability to convey aspects of a culture otherwise inaccessible or invisible to wide audiences. *Publishers Weekly* hailed the book as "the novel East Harlem has been waiting for since the days of the Young Lords" and Quiñonez as having a "brujo's gift for describing [the neighborhood's] alma" (Steinberg). Quiñonez was also praised for portraying El Barrio with "zest and authenticity" (Friedman), having the reader "almost taste the piraguas, pastels, and empanadas" (*The Source*), for "know[ing] this 'hood" so well that "readers may have to remind themselves that this is a work of fiction and not a memoir" (Philadelphia). As *Entertainment Weekly* sums it up, "Urban Latino Culture springs to life in this debut novel, rich with the sights, smells, sounds, and Spanglish dialect of the heavily Puerto Rican neighborhood" (Johnson). No matter how damning African American and Latina/o novels (and films) have been of the imbricated conditions of race and place in the United States, the mainstream's fascination with texts that are marketed as peeping holes to the cultures of poor, enclosed, and exploited communities, has not abated.

In the face of demands for representational machinery that churns out the same ghetto in different guises, the cultural politics of writing El Barrio is complex. Quiñonez's telling of the barrio narrative through the noir genre has particular implications in this regard. As we shall see, at the same time as the noir features help solidify the critique that Quiñonez undertakes, they also affirm the codified ways in which El Barrio can be represented as a site. Despite the promotion of Latina/o literature as "hot" and "new," what is privileged within this category are not, for example, the oppositional aesthetics of Nuyorican poetry of the 1970s and 1980s, but old stories of violent barrios, upward mobility, the assimilation of a chosen few, and Latina/o "twists" on conventional genres. It is no wonder that a text like *Bodega Dreams*, both marketable and progressive, is promoted as an edgy yet palatable work with recognizable aesthetics and an easily digested vision of purchased upward mobility. The author attempts to extricate the barrio narrative from the sensibility of entrapment endemic to both barrio and noir narratives by reconciling the critique of barrio conditions with a more familiar narrative of uplift, which mitigates the relevance of his critique. Ultimately, however, Quiñonez follows Thomas in leading his characters not "up from the ghetto" but into a place-based future *aquí*, in El Barrio.

LOCATING BARRIO NOIR

The touristic language in the reviewers' promise of "the sights, smells, and sounds" of Spanish Harlem, coupled with the violence promised in the paratextual material, make Quiñonez's novel ripe for mainstream consumption as a "ghetto novel." The book is described as a noir thriller in the blurbs and reviews and indeed is marked significantly, although not exclusively, by noir features. The novel of the barrio dovetails nicely with noir and crime fiction; one always already implies the other.[6] Noir fictions and films are intensely spatialized: in urban noir, protagonists are forever running through shadowy streets and wrong neighborhoods and hiding out in decrepit tenement apartments. Both the noir and the "slum novel" build on a sense of entrapment, in which the doomed protagonists and their condemned spaces mirror one another. One of the attractions of "slum" noir fiction is that it provides a sense of authenticity to those mean, unlit streets. In "classic" noir, the white male heros "cross borders to visit Latin America, Chinatown, or the 'wrong' parts of the city" (Naremore 13), but the protagonists of novels like *Bodega Dreams*, not to mention its author, are *from* the wrong parts of the city, which intensifies for the readership the sense of entrapment and constant potential for violence inherent in noir. Unlike classic noir's outsiders, the principal protagonists of works like *Bodega Dreams* live a noir life in noir neighborhoods.

Quiñonez draws on the implied noirness of the barrio narrative in a work like Thomas's, which only gestures to that crime genre in its title, and makes it central to his own work.[7] The violence begins on the first page of the novel, with a close-up on the aggressive behavior of Sapo, the narrator's friend, zooming out to the brutality in school and on the block, and on the second page, to the general conditions of poverty and violence in East Harlem produced by social and political marginalization:

> It was always easy to get into fights if you hated yourself. . . . Your life meant shit from the start. . . . You lived in projects with pissed-up elevators, junkies on the stairs, posters of the rapist of the month, whores. . . . You lived in a place where vacant lots grew like wild grass does in Kansas. Kansas? What does a kid from Spanish Harlem know about Kansas? All you knew was that one day a block would have people, the next day it would be erased by a fire. The burned-down buildings would then house junkies who made them into shooting galleries or become playgrounds for kids. . . . Fires, junkies dying, shootouts, holdups, babies falling out of windows were things you took as part of life. (5)

With this, the author establishes for the reader the setting as a locus of degradation as well as the novel's own path into the landscape of violence and noirish entrapment, already familiar to the reading and moviegoing public.

The noirness of the novel emerges not simply from its barrio setting as a potential site of crime, but also through its narrator, who tells the story as in a cinematic voice-over. The narrator is an ambivalent character with divided loyalties and in search of identity. Like many noir protagonists, he gets embroiled in a dangerous situation involving drugs and murder without much agency of his own; nonetheless he has a crucial role as the one who tells the story in its aftermath, following Bodega's death. The language of the characters itself is reminiscent of wise-cracking classic noir films, albeit with a Spanglish accent and vocabulary—what the reviewers praise as the "edgy" language of "the street." The most explicit noir element of the novel is in the obligatory femme fatale character, Vera, who causes the downfall of the vulnerable, Gatsby-like eponymous hero. Willie Bodega takes the blame for his beloved and unattainable Vera's crime, as Gatsby does Daisy's. But unlike Daisy's, Vera's crime is no accident; in a classic noir move, her motive is to set up and kill Bodega, which she engineers with his best friend Nazario, her secret lover. Duplicitous in every way, the femme fatale is a sine qua non and indispensable to the novel's construction and reception as noir, one that dovetails with the "infinitely more evil and dangerous than her classic noir counterpart" frequently found in the "neo-noir" of the 1980s (Martin 54). Ingeniously combined with his obvious borrowings from Fitzgerald's novel, the noir clichés that Quiñonez draws on affords his novel an easier entry into what Ishmael Reed once called "the American literary scene": "a white settler's fortress."

As James Naremore has written, the "term [noir] . . . has now become a major signifier of sleekly commodified artistic ambition" (10). Part of the "sleekness" of this particular novel as of the neo-noir genre of the last few decades is the self-consciousness of the narrative *as* noir through irony and allusions to other noir works. For example, in *Bodega Dreams,* Doña Ramonita, who is a seer at the local botánica, tells Chino the narrator that the woman Bodega is in love with will soon arrive with "a lot of trouble." Deliberately pointing to the stock nature of the femme fatale "full of trouble," Chino then informs us that "Doña Ramonita [as a visionary black woman, another stock figure found in many familiar genres] was right. Vera would arrive, fading in and fading out of the neighborhood as if in a film. A character so out of focus that it was hard to know when you had her just right" (53). The cinematic language and self-conscious references to iconic images and characters create out of the novel a pastiche of different media and genres.

In addition to noir, *Bodega Dreams* draws heavily also on gangster and Mafia films as a novel that revolves around a drug lord who rules over a good portion of East Harlem. The novel parades hitmen, a don, a grisly murder, Mafia-style turf wars stretching from the Lower East Side all the way uptown, references to more than one Al Pacino film, and Bodega as a tough-yet-vulnerable gangster character who is betrayed by those he loves. This is the kind of intertextuality that increases the chances of marketability: it domesticates a marginalized community through the familiar, and very much gendered, codes of violence, sex, betrayal, and resolution that are the stock in trade of noir and gangster films. As a result, not only are mediatic stereotypes of violence in the barrio reinforced; the barrio also becomes a familiar site interchangeable with other mean streets known to audiences from crime films and fictions. The references to such films make the book strongly visual; indeed, my students like it because "it reads like a movie."

NUYORICAN DREAMS

The promotion and reception of the book, which focuses on the novel's noir and gangster elements reinforce the novel's own incorporation of generic conventions that invite large-scale appeal, commercial movie potential, and the outsider's touristic gaze. But the literary strategies in *Bodega Dreams* are more complex than its conventional frame. Although the criminal barrio is present as a recognizable figure from the very beginning of the novel, the explicit rejection of stereotypes is also part of the novel's project: Referring to his Puerto Rican teachers, the narrator explains:

> Most of them were young, the sons and daughters of the first wave of Puerto Ricans who immigrated to El Barrio in the late forties and fifties. . . . At times they spoke to us harshly, as if they were our parents. This somehow made us fear and listen to them. They were not Puerto Ricans who danced in empty streets, snapping their fingers and twirling their bodies. Nor were they violent, with switchblade tempers. None of them were named Maria, Bernardo, or Anita. (7)

Although East Harlem is not on the "West Side," the narrator is well aware that *West Side Story* has infected and continues to affect the perception of Puerto Ricans anywhere, and he unequivocally debunks the film's, and the larger culture's, simplistic and damaging characterizations of Puerto Rican ethnicity, race, and place.

In addition to such explicit and at times didactic demythifications, the literary lineages established in the novel also distinguish it from conventional urban fiction. Simultaneously as it jockeys to capture the reading market with its noir barrio, *Bodega Dreams* is also a progressive novel, critiquing racism and the barrio's economic conditions and positioning itself within the genealogy of radical Puerto Rican diaspora aesthetics. Although *The Great Gatsby*, noir thrillers, and gangster films inform the work, the novel is also, as the author himself has asserted in interviews, an homage to the radical politics and aesthetics of Nuyorican literature of the 1970s and 1980s. The title of the novel is a reference to Miguel Piñero's poem "La Bodega Sold Dreams." Moreover, a character named

Willie Bodega appears in Piñero's play *The Sun Always Shines for the Cool* and is given the name Bodega, the convenience store, because like Quiñonez's hero, he provides for his friends. The novel's epigraph is from *Puerto Rican Obituary*, a signature work of Nuyorican poetry, Pedro Pietri's ode to Puerto Ricans stuck in the mire of U.S. capitalism and the consumerism of the American dream, which defines for Pietri "this dept store / called America." In a respectful nod to the crucial 1960s–1970s period in U.S. Puerto Rican politics and culture, the Young Lords are presented as heroes in a brief history offered by way of Willie Bodega's biography. And Quiñonez has a whole coterie of what he calls the "East Harlem aristocracy" show up at Bodega's funeral at the end of the novel, including former Young Lords, Taller Boricua artists, Nuyorican poets from Miguel Algarín to Martín Espada to Miguel Piñero who "cried their eyes out next to Piri Thomas, Edward Rivera, and Jack Agüeros" (208)—well-known New York Puerto Rican authors, artists, and cultural workers all.

Like many of these authors he salutes, Quiñonez approaches the diaspora story spatially, where, as in many urban and "ghetto" novels, place is at the center of storytelling. El Barrio is not only a location in which the noir/crime plot can unfold; it is also a diaspora project. The neigborhood fuels the eponymous hero's imagination and ambition and in turn the narrative itself; it is about the downfall of a heroic figure whose mission is to transform the diasporan neighborhood. The barrio as a whole and the places that constitute it are at the center of the novel, beginning with its title. A bodega is not only a convenience store but often a social space where people gather; similarly, the character Bodega aims for East Harlem to be a place, like the store itself, in which the community's dreams can unfold despite the hard reality of its streets.

"WE NEEDED MORE SPACE"

An early chapter in which the narrator justifies his involvement with Bodega is entitled "We Needed More Space," and it stages the daily coloniality of place for Puerto Ricans and Latinas/os in New York. Bodega, the drug and real estate king, offers Chino a larger apartment in return for his collaboration in Bodega's "program" and for helping locate Vera, who is Chino's wife's aunt and Bodega's own Daisy, straight out of Fitzgerald. What the chapter reveals about the title is that it refers to more than the couple's concrete need for more apartment space for themselves and the baby they are expecting. The chapter begins with Chino taking a walk in the streets geographically close to East Harlem but worlds away in every other sense. On Museum Mile, part of ultra-wealthy Fifth Avenue, Chino recalls being viewed with suspicion at the Museum of the City of New York, of exploring Fifth Avenue with his friend Sapo, and accompanying his mother to her cleaning job at a fabulous apartment, which leads him to see for the first time what separated the haves and have-nots. This is the part of town, the narrator explains, whose residents never cross the boundary to the adjacent barrio and who, in his early days, petitioned to rename the wealthy part "East Central Park" to distinguish it from East Harlem (44–45). Crossing the invisible borders meant danger to East Harlemites who were viewed as trespassers, although their own living spaces were only a short distance away. Chino's walk down the rich neighborhood serves to recall his early experiences as well as to further delineate for the reader the boundaries of the neighborhood and the racialized origin of place that recalls colonial arrangements of "reciprocal exclusivity" between the zones of the privileged and their others (Fanon 38–39). It is after this stock-taking of the neighborhood's literal situation, "a world without spaciousness" (Fanon 39) that Julio decides to accept Bodega's offer for more space. Clearly though, it is not only Chino who "needed more space." What the book subsequently makes clear is that *all* East Harlemites need more space, confined as they were to substandard housing and a reviled neighborhood. Stepping out of the barrio was perceived as trespassing and entailed perhaps even more danger than being in it. The project that informs the novel and its title is alluded to in the title of this early chapter: the necessity for "more space" where a Puerto Rican can belong.

LOCATION, LOCATION, LOCATION

In the spirit of those who created a unique aesthetics of the Puerto Rican diaspora informed by trenchant critiques of capitalism and racism, *Bodega Dreams* explicitly attributes the noir conditions of the neighborhood to racism and economic exploitation of Puerto Ricans and other Latina/o immigrants. In one scene, the narrator beholds Manhattan from an approach to the 59th Street bridge, observing that

> Manhattan at night seen from its surrounding bridges is Oz, it's Camelot or Eldorado, full of color and magic. What those skyscrapers and lights don't let on is that hidden away lies Spanish Harlem, a slum that has been handed down from immigrant to immigrant, like used clothing worn and reworn, stitched and restitched by different ethnic groups who continue to pass it on. . . . East Harlem had no business being in this rich city but there it was, filled with broken promises of a better life, dating decades back to the day when many Puerto Ricans and Latinos gathered their bags and carried their dreams on their backs and arrived in America, God's country. But they would never see God's face. Like all slumlords, God lived in the suburbs." (161)

In this and other such passages, Quiñonez registers the exploitation of immigrants, the marginalization of the neighborhood, and the utter neglect of the city whose presence is emblematized more than anything else by the wrecking ball that eventually destroys abandoned buildings (167, 171) on vacant lots. The dereliction and abandonment that has characterized the "policy" toward New York City's poor neighborhoods in Harlem and the Bronx in the postwar period are among the more egregious examples of spatial coloniality and the continuous reproduction and consequences of segregation. For Puerto Ricans, at once citizens and immigrants upon arrival, the coloniality on "the mainland" is an extension of colonialism at home. The author depicts a neighborhood under the baleful control of religion (especially the evangelical) and the economic establishment as well as in permanent daily battle with roaches, rats, children playing with garbage cans, fires, and many other ills. But he also details the spaces that give meaning to its residents' lives, many of which speak to languages and histories that predate the barrio. The paradoxical sense of being migrants with a language and a homeland beyond the barrio and being stuck *in* it is captured throughout the novel.

In *Bodega Dreams*, the noir plot's predictable twists and turns unfold in the social spaces of El Barrio that serve as institutions of ethnic pride and particularity that legitimate both diaspora and homeland identities. When Chino gets summoned to a meeting with Bodega, he is surprised to find out that Bodega is waiting for him at the Museo del Barrio, open before regular hours just for their encounter. Without explaining the reason for their meeting, Bodega, a benefactor who is welcome at the museum at any time, takes Chino on a private tour of the galleries. All he tells Chino is that he will ask the younger man for a favor upon Vera's arrival, and for this reason he would like Chino to know him better. The choice of the museum as a meeting place for an unsaid anticipated request allows Quiñonez to stage Bodega as a wealthy, generous donor to a barrio institution who consolidates his power with such dispensations and to magnify his image for the narrator and reader, who mirror one another in their incomplete knowledge about Bodega at this early point in the novel. Even more important, the museum as a settting serves Quiñonez to help present the barrio as a place with authentic institutions that presents and legitimates Puerto Rican and other Latina/o cultures in the past and in the diasporic present. He describes paintings by Taller Boricua artists, including one that was "entitled *Despierta Boricua* and depicted a Taino Indian tied to a New York City fire hydrant." Bodega responds to this painting by saying "So much was promised to us when we left our little island. . . . They gave us citizenship and sent us to the garment district. I am going to make sure they make good on their promises" (78). Bodega's self-image as a political leader and an activist Gatsby is bolstered in this public space, established by politically involved artists in the Young Lords era of his past. Looking at the paintings with Bodega, Chino notes that the museum imparts a sense of well-being and belonging to him as well: "The tiles were beautiful, new. El Museo had just gotten a face-lift. The floors were shining, the walls a cool, soothing white, and the titles of the painting were written in Spanish, with the English translation only as a secondary thing. El Museo del Barrio was the only museum where I could look at the paintings without having a guard follow me from wing to wing. At the Met I got suspicious looks. . . . When they saw my worn sneakers, they treated me like I might pull a knife from my back pocket and go slashing Goyas" (79).

While Latinas/os in the "white public space" are viewed as intrusions who violate established spatial coloniality through their color, bodies, and language,[8] the barrio provides an alternative place of belonging and cultural immersion. The museum emerges from the novel as a cultural and a social space that legitimizes the barrio, its people, and its cultures. As a place where Spanish comes first and the diaspora's politics and creativity are on exhibit, the museum makes it possible to reflect on "our little island," Bodega's experiences with the Young Lords, and the future. The museum is a place that counters dominant images of El Barrio as a place ruled solely by "the culture of poverty" that has long been associated with Puerto Ricans. Here, those belonging to a "lower-case" culture—in the words of the author Abraham Rodriguez (qtd. in Juan Flores, *From Bomba*, 180, 184)—can see their own history as "upper-case" in a renovated museum without feeling alienated, as they would in the dominant upper-case Culture and its institutions, like the Metropolitan Museum. The museum serves as a monument in a nation that has not erected monuments to Boricua diaspora history. Like the Jews, Chicanos, and Eastern Europeans we have examined, Puerto Ricans have made their stories and their art and music their most enduring monuments to the heritage of displacement. In *Bodega Dreams*, El Museo emerges as an institution to be venerated, a solid paean to the island and diaspora. Hence, Quiñonez corrects the barrio's image: despite the socioeconomic conditions imposed on the Latina/o space, its artists and other visionaries are able to destabilize the idea and the experience of the barrio, the barrio as a *site* of blight and violence. The site of the barrio, then, is transformed into a place of trans/locality that creates a nexus where Latina/o, Latin American, Puerto Rican, and East Harlem cultures and histories intersect.

A second museum scene also serves to connect the diaspora to the island to envision a future beyond enclosure. At the Museum of Salsa with Nazario (later revealed to be Bodega's enemy), Chino is impressed to find out that "there's two museums in Spanish Harlem" (105). This little one with the salsa memorabilia, reflects Chino, "had a deep association with my parents' time, when the neighborhood was still young and full of people and not projects" (104–105) Here, Puerto Rican, Carribbean, and diaspora histories connect once again, this time through the music of Willie Colón, Hector Lavoe, Celia Cruz, and many others. The music was, Chino explains, "a symbol of past glory, of early migration to the United States and the dreams that people brought over along with the music" (105). After they leave the small museum, Nazario reveals more of Bodega's uplift program for the neighborhood through the purchase of territory, on which I shall reflect further below. At the end of his persuasive talk about upward mobility following their time at the salsa museum, Nazario makes an explicit linkage between the plan to "build a strong professional class and accumulate property" in diaspora and the view to the island: After destroying the projects, Nazario muses, "we'll free our island, without bloodshed." The museum is a conduit for this discussion as well as the locus for the histories and the fates of the diaspora and the island to conjoin, more precisely, for the articulation of the role of the diaspora in bringing an end to colonialism. The salsa museum is a synecdoche of this Puerto Rican continuum, in which the diaspora place and the island always refer to each other, each a migrant site that incorporates both settlement and uprootedness, as their music and the history were formed in the back-and-forth movement between the two places. Nazario and Bodega's project, however misguided, imply also that the liberation of Puerto Rico will be linked to the diaspora.

THE "PROGRAM"

There are contradictory impulses, then, in *Bodega Dreams*. On the one hand, El Barrio appears as a *site* of degradation and is contained through the idiom of noir and marketing as a place of "thrilling" murder, love, and betrayal. On the other, the author creates a migrant site, forcing open the enclosure of El Barrio by foregrounding its relationality to the island and affirming its connective alternative social spaces within. Quiñonez's novel, like *Down These Mean Streets*'s Piri is "hung up between two sticks." Unlike Thomas, however, Quiñonez attempts to provide a resolution, one with a political vision that departs from the novel's own explicit gestures to progressive politics. The young author is highly skillful in his smooth interweaving of genres and literary traditions, from Fitzgerald to noir to Nuyorican creativity, but the politics do not flow easily from this blend. Willie Bodega does not seek to reinvent or revolutionize the American Dream but to appropriate it from a Latina/o space. Referring to the lack of respect Puerto Ricans receive, Bodega argues,

> Now, you don't want to consider me an American, I got no beef with that. You want to keep me a bastard child, I got no beef with that, either. But when the spoils of the father are being divided, I better get some or I'll have to take the booty by force. East Harlem, East L.A. South Bronx, South Central, South Chicago, Overtown down in Miami, they're all the same bastard ghetto. (26)

In other words, incomplete citizenship or not (in the reference to Puerto Rican's "bastard" colonial status), what matters is the "spoils," the division of the pie. Further, if the American Dream was built by Anglo thieves, Bodega proposes (quoting Balzac's "behind every great man there is a crime"), it can just as well be built by a Puerto Rican drug lord who plays by the crooked American rules and dispenses housing and other services to his people. At the center of Bodega's dream is the vision of a barrio populated and uplifted by middle-class professionals. As Nazario explains, Bodega "plans on building a professional class, slated to become his movers and shakers of the future. . . . But it goes deeper than that, Julio. It's about upward mobility. It's about education and making yourself better. It's about sacrifice." This is when Chino/Julio becomes convinced that Bodega and Nazario have a legitimate dream; they "had seen what guns could do. They knew you could not attack the Anglo like that. You had to play by his rules, and like him, steal by signing the right papers" (106). Ultimately, Bodega's "program," which Chino the narrator inherits, is trickle-down economics and upward mobility for some, without a vision of political and economic empowerment of the vast majority of Puerto Ricans and Latinas/os or changes in the social and political structures that shape the barrio. What Augustín Láo-Montes describes as "Latino grassroots populism" in an article on Latina/o social movements and ideologies helps illuminate the novel's political project. Láo-Montes explains that

> in Latino liberal urban populism, there is no systematic analysis of the sources and mechanisms of social power. This implies an understanding of the status quo of social and political inequality in terms of elite control, corruption, and bad leadership. It also involves an instrumentalist view of the state and *a fuzzy notion of domination in which subalternity is seen as a temporary moment of subjection to be surely solved by ethnic self-organization and a proper representation in the political system*. . . . [T]he key principle of political identification is still a notion of ethnic solidarity that tends to marginalize the political significance of internal differences (such as gender and sexuality). (135; emphasis added)

As a political plan, this view is quite different from the legacy of the Young Lords and Nuyorican poets that Quiñonez invokes repeatedly. Indeed, it neutralizes the author's own social and economic critiques of the marginalization, racialization, and exploitation of Latinas/os in New York and diminishes the challenge to the very order that continues to devastate the barrio. Quiñonez allows his reading public to envision a barrio salvaged by the appropriation of the American Dream and the creation of a *new* "East Harlem aristocracy," the professional class of movers and shakers.

Although Bodega and Nazario do not survive to fulfill this "new hope," the legitimacy and potential of their dream is borne out in the last gesture of Chino, the successor figure of the tragically slain Bodega, when he takes in two newly arrived Puerto Ricans from the island, who are disoriented and shelterless. The hospitality of the diaspora elite toward the immigrant and the working classes displays the model of the middle-class Latina/o diasporan as inheritor of the American Dream, who shares generously with his fellow ethnics. The anthropologist Arlene Dávila wrote, "*Bodega Dreams* represents the ultimate neoliberal novel. The context it speaks to is one where the purchase of place is presented as the only alternative for lasting power, even when the feasibility of such a dream is quickly fading" ("Dreams of Place" 114). Although Dávila does not analyze the novel, she begins her article on the recent gentrification of the barrio with a paragraph on Quiñonez's work as a paradigmatic illustration of the elite-led ideas and programs of privatization. These, according to Dávila and other critics, have been inadequate measures that not only failed to address but actually exacerbated the problems: the devastating cuts in social programs and housing funds, the decrease in affordable housing construction, increased rents, and other ills of neoliberal urbanism since the late 1970s.

While Dávila is harsh in her description of the novel, the convergence of Quiñonez's vision with the accommodationism of neoliberal policies is hard to ignore. Nazario explains to Chino, "This neighborhood will be lost unless we make it ours. Look at Loisaida, that's gone. . . . All those white yuppies want to live in Manhattan, and they think Spanish Harlem is next for the taking. When they start moving in, we won't be able to compete when it comes to rents, and we'll be left out in the cold. But if we build a strong professional class and accumulate property, we can counter that effect" (107). It is not simply that Bodega and Nazario's vision of buying up East Harlem is unrealistic (as is well known, and as Dávila meticulously documents and analyzes in her book *Barrio Dreams*, little is left to "buy up"), but the vision of an elite-led (and bought) reconstruction only mimes the workings of the very system that devastated the barrio. Bodega does not want to challenge it; he wants to buy (or "steal with the right papers") a piece of the system, in which the disenfranchised are handed favors by those who own space.

Bodega's dream then, *is* the American Dream, not its reversion or subversion, as its Latina/o dimension is supposed to imply. Early in the novel, Chino reveals that the novel is about Bodega, who "for a small while . . . would create a green light of hope. And when that short-lived light went supernova, it would leave a blueprint of achievement and desire for anyone in the neighborhood searching for new possibilities" (14). But the "blueprint" does not offer "new" possibilities. A professional class, a Latina/o talented tenth, accumulating property and apportioning resources to the rest is an old, worn-out vision long endorsed by the mainstream and already carried out by elites, as Láo-Montes, Dávila, and many others have argued, to little effect for Latinas/os or others.

"A NEW LANGUAGE BEING BORN"

The novel ends on a hopeful note that reinforces the idea of resolving the contradictions in representing El Barrio. Although the narrator begins his story reflecting back on a time when he was seeking self-reinvention and a world larger than the neighborhood (14), at the close of the novel, he asserts the viability of the barrio as a place of his and others' future, a pan-Latina/o space that can work if someone carries out Bodega's vision. In the dream sequence of the last few pages of the novel, the now defunct Bodega appears in Chino the narrator's own dream, and from the fire escape the two look out onto East Harlem: "See it's alive, he said and right that minute, at a window next door to us, a woman yelled to her son down on the street. 'Mira, Junito, go buy un mapo, un conten de leche, and tell el bodeguero yo le pago next Friday. And I don't want to see you in el rufo!'" (212). Laughing, Bodega says to Chino,

> You know what is happening here, don't you ? Don't you? What we just heard was a poem, Chino. It's a beautiful new language. Don't you see what's happening? A new language means a new race. Spanglish is the future. It's a new language being born out of the ashes of two cultures clashing with each other. You will use a new language. Words they might not teach you in that college. Words that aren't English or Spanish but at the same time are both. Now that's where it's at. Our people are evolving into something completely new. (212)

After Bodega's departure, Chino looks down at the neighborhood and articulates the meaning of this final section's title, "A New Language Being Born": "Tomorrow Spanish Harlem would run faster, fly higher, stretch out its arms farther, and one day those dreams would carry its people to new beginnings. . . . The neighborhood might have been down, but it was far from out. Its people far from defeat. They had been bounced all over the place but they were still jamming. It seemed like a good place to start" (213). *Aquí* then, is "where it's at": the barrio is not a place to abandon; here, one can begin anew. The novel's conclusion is in explicit contrast to its outset, in which the young man reflects on self-reinvention: "Shedding your past. Creating yourself from nothing" (113). Quiñonez proposes a barrio-based future for the Latin American diaspora of East Harlem, a destiny undergirded by the very hybridity and mixture of language and culture for which it is usually denigrated. The author joins generations of poets, activists, and scholars who have tried to understand and validate language mixing. Ana Zentella, whose study *Growing Up Bilingual* proved the grammatical competency of her Spanglish-speaking subjects, observes in a later article that her "approach is aimed at de-stigmatizing [code-]switching in the minds of teachers and other gatekeepers, but I fear that the emphasis on proving that '*aquí no pasa nada*' (nothing's wrong here) obscures the power and beauty of mixing various dialects of Spanish and English, and the positive statement about embracing several languages and cultures" (57). Quiñonez celebrates precisely this creativity and skill involved in bilingual practices, which Zentella likens to expertise in sports or dance (57). Spanglish, like the Yiddish of Cahan's characters, points to the ways in which "Spanish Harlem," viewed as a *site* of foreign monolinguals who refuse to learn English, exceeds its own geographical, social, and political borders. As Azade Seyhan comments on Gloria Anzaldúa's deliberate and proud heteroglossia, "living multilingually is the best revenge" (117)! Quiñonez places Spanglish at center stage to flaunt and assert its "natural" fit for a pan-Latina/o neighborhood that may be enclosed but where worlds and languages cross and blend nevertheless. Indeed, his faith in Spanglish as the expression and fulfillment of a diaspora people endorses the words of the Nuyorican poet and cultural figurehead Miguel Algarín: "A new day needs a new language or else the day becomes a repetition of yesterday" (Algarín and Piñero 18).

Quiñonez emphatically *locates* the new day, *aquí* in El Barrio, rejecting the narrative of "moving up," and displacement as progress. Thus, in one way, he creates what I view as a migrant site: the re-creation of a site; that is, an unchanging representation of place with fixed attributes and dimensions, into a place defined by the sensibilities, languages, and ethnoracial identifications of a people with a heritage and literature of dislocation. In his representation of a range of barrio loci, from the roofs (where Sapo and Chino sabotage other people's kites and confer about their lives), to the streets, the botánicas, the evangelical churches, and the museums, Quiñonez attempts to wrest the barrio from the dominant discourses that marginalize and criminalize it. Through the languages of migration (Spanish, Spanglish, English), Quiñonez, a half-Ecuadoran, half–Puerto Rican East Harlemite—like his narrator—creates a present and future space that is not only Puerto Rican but also pan-Latina/o, reflecting the lived reality of East Harlem, whose Latina/o population is still primarily Puerto Rican but also now Mexican and Central American. While Puerto Rican culture and history are at the center of their consciousness, Nazario's, Bodega's, and the author's vision includes the discourse of pan-Latina/o solidarity in a place-based context, *aquí* in El Barrio.

At the same time, there is a disjunction that results from the combination of conventional noir, uplift politics, and the homage to Nuyorican creativity. As Norman Klein wrote, "a critique that uses a noir aesthetics can transform the agonies of the inner city into an exotic descent"(236). Quiñonez's writing, despite its use of noir, is more complexly a double-edged sword—like his politics. On the one hand, he is ingenious at creating migrant sites by overturning perceptions of "the ghetto," offering the barrio's spatial and cultural meanings and power beyond stereotypes. He also valorizes Spanglish by not positioning it as the "bastardized" language of those hopelessly in-between languages and places but as a new, beautiful whole. Like the barrio itself, Spanglish belongs to the future; it is not an interim phenomenon destined to be forsaken at the first chance of "Americanization." Unlike Cahan, who deplores Yekl's efforts at crossing English with Yiddish to create an imperfect and impure language of assimilation (and contrasts it with his own educated narrator's idiom), Quiñonez's character destigmatizes Spanglish to signal its creativity. But at the same time as Quiñonez is rewriting diaspora space as a space of the future born of migrant languages, desires, and cultures, and destabilizing the stereotype of the barrio as a blighted space of the past, he also draws on existing models that reinforce barrio regeneration through uplift by the few. The critique of exploitation and racism in Latina/o spaces along with the debunking of concomitant dominant literary and cultural representations of barrios and Puerto Ricans is at odds with the desire for "the spoils of the father" obtained through the ownership of territorial (and by implication) literary space.

"GHETTOS" AND "ETHNICS" IN U.S. LITERATURE

Despite their stylistic, ideological, and generic differences, our texts show that Puerto Rican barriocentricity both overlaps with and differs from the larger body of neighborhood, ghetto, and migration narratives in the United States, an early example of which is Abraham Cahan's work. Cahan and the Puerto Rican diaspora authors create an aesthetics of place-based stories and languages that narrate the twin processes of international migration and ghettoization. Yet, despite certain continuities and the critique of spatial assignment that they share, Thomas's and Quiñonez's spatial representations differ from turn-of-the-twentieth-century works like Cahan's: they assert a place-based politics and vision of belonging for migrants and their descendants. In *Yekl,* ethnic identity may be "preserved" in the ghetto by the likes of Gitl, but such is not a real alternative to the dominant society's simultaneous, irreconcilable demands for ghettoization and assimilation. Nor is Gitl's choice about a self-conscious assertion of autonomy and resistance. For Thomas and Quiñonez, on the other hand, El Barrio is not simply the space of a past contained and perpetuated by an as-yet unassimilated (or unassimilable) group; it is the space of the Puerto Rican and Latina/o future, a marginalized and yet vital community in which narrators are witnesses to "a new language being born."

In great part, the difference between the Jewish immigrant writing of the turn of the twentieth century and the Puerto Rican diaspora writing of the more recent period stems from their different historical circumstances of production. The works of "the third stage" were published during and after the civil rights era, when ethnoracial self-affirmation and critiques of racism became prominent. Further, questions of assimilation and passing that troubled Jewish immigrants did not have the same centrality for Puerto Ricans, for whom assimilation has been largely a more distant possibility and desire, despite the successes of visible politicians, entertainers, and authors, and the existence of a Puerto Rican middle and upper-middle class.

Immigrant-neighborhood texts have been genres of choice in U.S. literature from the end of the nineteenth century to our day, from Cahan to Quiñonez. My analysis of examples that are about a century apart, however, makes it clear that there is no transcendent "immigrant story" or "immigrant-neighborhood novel." The circumstances of immigrants, their descendants, and literary production change significantly over time. Further, the origins of the immigrants in terms of their home country and diaspora relations to the United States and in terms of linguistic and literary traditions shape how the narrative of place will intersect with the narrative of migration. In the case of Puerto Rican diaspora literature, barrio-based aesthetics and politics have remained crucial throughout the years since the mass migrations from the island. Thomas's is only the first literary articulation of this aesthetics in the English language, while Quiñonez's is one of the most recent.

Despite the greater opportunities to voice dissent in the writing of diaspora, race, and place, "the ethnic writer" continues to be in a bind: narrating "ethnic place" is politically important and socially relevant, but also potentially marketable. The containment imposed on ethnoracialized migrants is mirrored in the literary strategies of containment, such as the use of the noir genre and the discourse of urban uplift, both of which have wide appeal. This literary and political enclosure coexists in tension with the novels' attempt to unbind representations of barrios through new languages, affirm the places of pride (for example, museums), and pay homage to an alternative, diasporic literary tradition. In the work of Quiñonez as with the work of other authors writing about diaspora and immigration, the containment strategies effected by literary establishments as well as by the authors themselves are in irresolvable contrast to the open and dynamic nature of the represented places.

TOWARD CONCLUSION: PUERTO RICANS IN NEW YORK

Quiñonez published a novel that sought to reinvigorate Puerto Rican space and community in the same year as an article entitled "Puerto Rican Presence Wanes in New York" by Mireya Navarro appeared on the front page of the *New York Times*. The piece, which provoked the displeasure of the Puerto Rican community, reported a substantial decrease, for the first time in many decades, in the population of Puerto Ricans in the city. The article explored such "puzzling" issues as the decline of Puerto Rican income levels during the strong economy of the early 1990s, continuing poverty at 40 percent of the population, a 10 percent level of college education, high incidence of return migration, and the persistence of low-level socioeconomic indicators despite the advantage of citizenship. The answers were found in "bad timing": the arrival of mass numbers of Puerto Ricans at a time of industrial decline in New York, the export of poverty from the island, and competition from other groups in a New York that is increasingly "Latinized" by non–Puerto Ricans, especially Dominicans, Mexicans, and Central Americans. A senior executive of the Puerto Rican Legal Defense and Education Fund contested the numbers and pointed out that even worst-case scenario statistics means that Puerto Ricans are about 800,000 strong; at 40 percent of the Latina/o population, they remain the largest community anywhere (Angelo Falcón). The damage that the headline and insufficiently analytical article did, however, was to perpetuate the marginality of Puerto Ricans, positioned historically against African Americans and now against the more visible Dominicans and Mexicans in the city. Fortunately, Quiñonez makes Puerto Rican literary and political history more visible and asserts the centrality of the spatial struggle and the poetics of place to Puerto Rican diaspora consciousness, following the legacy of Piri Thomas and Nuyorican creativity.

Against the notion that in our current mobile, wireless, globalizing modernity, we live in a placeless world, Puerto Rican diaspora writers like Thomas and Quiñonez have asserted the ways in which Puerto Ricans and other Latinas/os are place-bound by external forces at the same time as they reformulated their relationship to place. As Luis Aponte-Parés has observed in his article on Puerto Rican *casitas* (makeshift structures reminiscent of those in the Caribbean constructed in New York City): "Paradoxically, in 'Cyber-city,' the city ostensibly with no material spatial needs, the 'virtual' electronic city of computers, modems, and electronic highways linking together any place in the globe, the need for meaningful and precious places validating cultural identities in space may have increased" ("What's Yellow" 272). Hence, in literature of the city and its diasporic spaces, the emphasis on the poetics of *aquí* endures.

Further, even though mobile subjectivities are central to diaspora Puerto Rican consciousness and expression as Sandoval Sánchez ("Puerto Rican Identity") and Cruz-Malavé ("Colonial Figures") have pointed out, the literary and political strategies of localization persist through the changing economic and literary contexts. The perennial marginalization and the recent gentrification of East Harlem and other Puerto Rican barrios in New York City, for example, have not lessened activists' and writers' commitment to represent and transform them, despite the overwhelming forces of conquest and expulsion through real estate. In an essay of the 1940s (unpublished till the 1960s) tellingly entitled "Harlem Is Nowhere," Ralph Ellison wrote of disorienting ghetto life: "One 'is' literally, but one is nowhere; one wanders dazed in a ghetto maze, a 'displaced person' of American democracy" (300). Knowing much about American democracy, colonialism, and displacement, Thomas and Quiñonez narrate Puerto Ricans' multiple dislocations by accentuating place as central to the cultures of displacement and asserting barrio-based futures despite exploitation, hatred, and, most recently, expulsion through gentrification. Far from being deformed expressions of nonbelonging, multilinguality and code-switching are in *Bodega Dreams* and *Down These Mean Streets* essential to the representation of a place that is both enclosed and a crossroads at the same time.

The diaspora condition as enclosure and containment on the one hand and spatial relationality and translocality on the other emerges in the work of Thomas and Quiñonez, as it does in the works examined in previous chapters, even though their localization and translocalization is shaped by the specific position of Puerto Ricans and Puerto Rican diaspora literature and by the particularities of literary institutions (genres, publishing practices) of their time. Less widely recognized than other diaspora literatures, Puerto Rican writing complicates social and literary categories in special ways. The experience and legacy of Puerto Rican migration to "the mainland" is not, strictly speaking, an immigration and legalization of citizenship status or a diaspora dispersing from a sovereign nation-state. Yet, it *is* widely considered a diaspora, from policy statements to the poet Mariposa's "Ode to a Diasporican," which overturns definitions and critiques of diasporas and their links to nation-based belongings (see, for example, Soysal).[9] Moreover, although localization, including barriocentrism, is central to diaspora narratives, the consciousness of the island permeates most of the works, drawing attention to the ongoing colonial activities of the United States in Puerto Rico and elsewhere in the world. Because East Harlem and Puerto Rico do not figure into the mainstream discourses sufficiently, Puerto Rican creativity serves also as a reminder of the colonial present in an environment that still, despite all the recent acknowledgments, largely denies the identity of the United States as empire, disseminating instead the image of the civilizer and democratizer. The Puerto Rican barrio story is about "regrounding" in New York neighborhoods; at the same time, it is a story of power and resistance linking the Americas. Localized in Puerto Rican diaspora politics and aesthetics and connected to other diaspora writings and U.S. literature and culture at large, El Barrio is a migrant site and a locus of Puerto Rican literature, diaspora writing of the Americas, and U.S. American literature—all at once.

CONCLUSION

The narratives of migration and diasporization that inspired this book are testaments to the myriad ways in which literature has imagined the seemingly contradictory operations of displacement and enclosure. The enclosures are effected through genre in local colorist, regionalist, and urban writing and through themes of geographical exclusions based on culture, race, class, and gender. The counterpoints of these spatial containments, restrictions, and segregations are in geographies and languages beyond the thematic and generic boundaries the texts stage. Although I have argued that the dialectic of enclosure and translocality is common to all the texts featured in the chapters, I am not generalizing about the literatures of all ethnicities and diaspora formations of the United States. Rather, the preceding chapters together suggest a new way to look at the role of place in diaspora writing. I have argued that complicating place-based identities and aesthetics in the literature of migration and diasporization through the lens of enclosures compels a rethinking of the boundaries both at the contours of and within the national literary and social formations. My readings revealed not only the transnational, boundary-crossing dimensions of U.S. literature but also the ways in which lines are drawn around the lives and literatures of immigrants and diasporans within the American national frame.

Focusing on diaspora spatiality as I have urges critical thinking about the sites that give meaning to U.S. national identity. In the popular imagination, an iconic "American place" is frequently the majestic canyonlands and the vast prairies but never a border factory town like Smeltertown in "The Day of Scorpions." A symbol of America is the skyline of Manhattan but never its barrios, though represented to powerful effect by Thomas. The nation's location is more often than not a site of awe, grandeur, beauty, and immensity, and not containment, insecurity, and poverty. Diaspora narratives alert us to other spatialities that have created national history and experience at the same time that as they signal what lies outside of them. Migration and diaspora literatures are a self-evident place from which, to use Carolyn Porter's words, we could be "remapping American literary studies" in terms of crossings and convergences with other bodies of writing. Especially from a spatial point of view, many diaspora literatures produced in the United States push against the borders of the national imaginary by bringing the world to "America" and its literature. It is true that some narratives of migration reinforce the teleological story of the United States as an "immigrant nation" that has followed the displacement-adjustment-incorporation path. As Pease explains, immigrant narratives can reinforce exceptionality: "Each story that represented the US as a safe haven from colonial oppression abroad eclipsed the history of US colonial relations. The myth of the US as a promised land erased the middle passage narratives of slaves . . . , and the stories of migrant laborers the state had newly colonized, and of immigrants who felt their conditions worsened" (215). But, in other narratives, such as the ones I have analyzed in *Migrant Sites*, the languages and knowledges of other places often interrupt discourses of exceptionality and grandeur through which U.S. national identity is produced. In Cather's novels, even the relatively marginal cultures of Europe (the Bohemian, the Swedish, and so forth) are held in greater esteem than the Anglo American. Cisneros's narrative shows that, especially from a gendered point of view, the U.S. side of the borderlands is not necessarily very different from "the other side," shattering the myth of superiority by which America sustains its identity and rules the world. Frequently, if not always, the "foreign" geographies evoked in U.S. diaspora literature also serve to underscore the spatial operations of imperial "America" *in* the world, as with my transamerican examples from Chicana and Puerto Rican diaspora writings.

Although the narratives analyzed in this book are by no means exemplary of U.S. diasporic cultural productions in toto, together they provide a way in which to think about national literature as a "diaspora space," to use Avtar Brah's term. In *Cartographies of Diaspora*, Brah argues: "In the diaspora space called 'England,' African-Caribbean, Asian, Jewish and other diasporas intersect among themselves as well as with the entity constructed as Englishness, thoroughly reinscribing it in the process" (209). The intersections and divergences regarding spatial consciousness among migration narratives and the national narrative "constructed as Americanness" is an organizing feature of the book, as well as of what we think of as U.S. literature. Diaspora writing should not be treated as a separate and unequal literary compartment, but as a literary practice that exposes diasporic confluences and conflicts in the United States.

Diasporic reading differs not only from hegemonic nationalist interpretations but also from the flattening, multiculturalist approach. In unspatialized multiculturalism all stories are presumably equivalent and have the same access to representation. But the diasporic interpretation as I have proposed it means reading for the complexity of place. Once we begin from that standpoint to consider the "placement" of the groups said to make up the American mosaic, the unequal dynamics of race, class, gender, and culture reveal themselves in relation to hegemonic structures and ethnoracial hierarchization. Who lives where, and who owns place? Without asking those questions, we do not have a complete picture of racialization, integration, or social justice. What are the discourses about the places in which we live our lives, and how do they include and exclude segments of those with whom we share our cities and towns? In the real estate–crazed world of the last fifteen years, for example, we have witnessed the languages and practices of colonization inflicted time after time on the urban poor of color, when the "ghetto" turns into middle-class "frontier" and gentrifiers become "pioneers." As a result, in the gentrifying city, it is a quick step from being enclosed to being evicted. Place becomes a site, one ripe for incursion, and its inhabitants a burden destined for removal. Such colonialities are not considered in pluralist and multiculturalist thinking, which emphasizes equivalencies.

I used the term "spatial coloniality" to explain the parceling of place in order to create, accommodate, and enforce dominant practices of race, class, and gender. The term refers to the "coloniality of power" perspective (Quijano), emphasizing a world system of domination and exploitation justified by ideologies of racialist "colonial differences" (Mignolo). "Coloniality of power" as a model is useful because it emphasizes the colonial character of our world from the time of the conquest of the Americas to today and the enduring centrality of civilizational discourses in maintaining power locally and globally, without falling into the debates as to whether particular nation-states are colonial, postcolonial, or neocolonial. Coloniality is pervasive, from imperial wars to the present national and global division of labor, and, as I suggest, to spatial organization. Spatial readings of works like those I have examined reveal the intersection of the colonial literary and social categories that constitute "America." We might think about "ethnicity, race and place" as an inquiry about the spatialization of "minorities," but our works instruct us that place *is* race, insofar as race is an invention that serves to separate the civilized from the uncivilized. Races and places are mutually constructed in the U.S. social imaginaries to enforce separation and maintain social and literary hierarchies. Nationcentric spatial representations rarely leave room for viewing the "sense of place" as sites of coloniality.

This book has argued throughout that a key form of spatial coloniality pertaining to diasporas and their literatures is spatial enclosure. Enclosure is an insufficiently studied but central form of spatialization in U.S. literature about migration. The sense of spatial containment, segregation, and restriction in migration narratives produced through thematic and generic means critiques the grand narratives of monological, monolingual American civilization and multiculturalism. From Cahan to Quiñonez, the works have shown that despite the rhetoric of openness and opportunity that undergirds the mythos of the "immigrant nation," spatial enclosures have served to contain working-class and racialized immigrant and diaspora populations. Spatial restriction and containment prevent the encroaching of diasporas on triumphant "American civilization."

Discussions of what Leach calls "the destruction of place in American life" frequently eschew the destruction that *made* American place. Attending to enclosure in literary and social contexts reminds us of the exclusions entailed in the *con*struction of place as a "site," a locus of fixed attributes ("the West," "the metropolitan center" of master narratives) that masks its colonial nature. The plantation and the reservation are at the origins of other spatial containments such as ghettoization (called "American apartheid" by influential scholars Douglas Massey and Nancy Denton). More research is needed that examines enclosures in narratives of immigration and diaspora together with Native American and African American enclosures in literature and history.

The comparative approach of *Migrant Sites* has made it clear that enclosure's effects are not symmetrical. While staying in enclosure ultimately benefits the protagonists of the works from the early immigration period, in the fictions of the second period, for the displaced Chicana/o and Puerto Rican protagonists, the vexed relation to place is not similarly resolved. In many ways these differences mirror the "real-life" situation that divides immigrants who are immediately or prospectively white and the racial/colonial immigrants of color. How do the diaspora narratives convey different experiences of enclosure? What we have seen in the novels is that ownership and property afford some of Cahan's and Cather's protagonists to "inherit" place by dispossessing others. As the more proper immigrants, Gitl and Bernstein "inherit" from Mamie and Yekl the right to own a piece of diaspora space, and Cather's heroines "inherit" land, the West, and its mythos through the unacknowledged disinheritance of the indigenous inhabitants. As such, the stability and success of the whitening immigrants is ensured through property ownership and the protagonists' transformation into successors of and substitutes for the less civilizable. The Chicana and Puerto Rican narratives are also concerned with spatial dis/inheritance, but without the same outcome: although eviction from place (Portillo Trambley), erasure of spatial history (Cisneros), and conquest and loss of homeland (Thomas and Quiñonez) are key to diasporic identities and destinies, none of the protagonists stand to inherit or own place. Diaspora texts, then, register these divisions that conform, broadly, to the historical and continuing segmentation and stratification by race and class of diasporans' access to and ownership of place. It is well known that despite initial negative racialization and spatial separation, the European immigrants' Americanization experience, deemed to be representative of all immigration, concludes with "spatial assimilation" (Massey and Denton, 10), characterized by the move outward from the preliminary, protective "immigrant enclaves." Immigrants of color, on the other hand, including many Latinas/os, experience long-term spatial apartness (though this is variable by class and skin color and often not so stark as the segregation of African Americans; see Alba et al.). Although the logics of enclosure are part of the wider application of coloniality of power on diasporas and other "foreign" and marginalized entities, we have seen through the preceding chapters that the effects are far from homogenous.

At the same time as they lay bare material processes of diasporic spatialization around race, class, and gender and register their varying effects on individual and collective psyches, diaspora texts, especially from the second period, also offer alternative spaces of the imagination to counter site-making enclosures. I have called this effect *translocality*. All the authors bring to bear on the local sites and localization processes that the protagonists grapple with the knowledges, memories, and languages of places outside of and prior to enclosures, from actual and imaginary geographies. Cather and Cahan tweak the national spatial imaginary by inserting immigrant speech and prior forms of knowledge about foreign cultural spaces, thereby complicating the histories and subjectivities of misunderstood "foreign" communities and their spatialization processes in rural enclosures and urban "ghettos." But they do so without extensively questioning the dominant spatial narratives that link immigration and empire through ideologies of property, virgin land, and Americanization. Chicana literature's translocalities consist of the convergence of borderland spaces of myth and lore with the representation of restricted places of exploitation and eviction that also shapes Chicana history and spatiality. Our Chicana and Puerto Rican authors foreground, respectively, decolonizing feminist and antiracist critiques that reassert connectivities such as the intersections between African America and the Puerto Rican diaspora and between Chicanas and Mexicanas, otherwise foiled by spatial, racial boundaries created to control and dispossess.

Translocality, then, involves a boundary-crossing and intersectional imagination that counteracts enclosure. Our texts have revealed that key to diasporic intersectionality and translocality is the issue of language. We have seen in almost all the chapters that bilingualism and multilingualism are represented not only for the sake of realistic rendering of immigrant and diasporic communication, but especially to characterize the heterogeneity and mixture that characterize place, from the various Yiddishes of the Jewish ghetto to the Bohemian of the prairie to barrio and borderland Spanglish. These languages are preserved, created, and reconstituted in diasporic places; through literature, they emerge out of their enclosures, are validated instead of disdained as "ghetto languages" (see Zentella, *Growing Up* and *José*), and re-created. Diaspora languages' clashes with English and with one another (such as the different Yiddishes) are emblematic of the insertion of foreignness into place and U.S. literature. Language is a key marker of the "foreignness" of the diasporic enclosed place and literary genre: it is not, as in varieties of regionalist and local colorist narratives of white rural residents, temporalized to evoke preserved folky origins dating from the nation's own distant past, but it reminds the reader of the continuous infusion of foreignness into the enclosure in the depiction of new immigrants—or, to borrow from Quiñonez, "new languages being born" as a result of diasporization in contained places. Our texts' uses and representation of different languages indicated not only the authors' and the communities' linguistic creativity and heterogeneity but also the mutual constitution of language and place in diasporic literature.

Confirming the centrality of place to American literature, Philip Fisher in *Hard Facts: Setting and Form in the American Novel* designates three "privileged settings" in which U.S. history and fictions have been created: the wilderness, the homestead, and the city, each with its own "hard fact" of conquest, slavery, and capitalism. In this book, I have explored less privileged narratives of place and displacement, specifically those that accentuate the "foreign," the immigrant, and the diasporic places within the national geography, all of which are shaped in part by connections to other "settings." Narratives of displacement and eviction shake up the static nature of "sites" created in fiction and literary criticism. The coupling of "migrant" with "site"—that is, of translocal consciousness with enclosed stasis in diaspora literature—has several implications. First of all, the fixed sites of "the frontier" or "the city" and so forth are defamiliarized by the insertion of diasporic or migrant referents, including "foreign" spatial identities and languages that belie the monological triumphant narrative of national space. Relatedly, scrutinizing the making of sites through the migrant imagination reveals the connections between empire and immigration. For example in the work of Cahan and Cather, the civilizing mission to assimilate immigrants, paralleled by other such missions in the external and internal empire (Cabán; Jacobson, *Barbarian Virtues*), is inflected through the immigrants' own cultural, geographic, and linguistic references and attachments prior to relocalization. In Chicana/o and Puerto Rican literature, there is an open contestation of the literary and spatial enclosures of diasporas shaped by empire (1848, 1898), immigration, and modern coloniality; that is, the ongoing containment and removal of those at the low rungs of the racial classification system. Further, "site" evokes the limitations placed on the presumed mobility, upward and spatial, of the migrant: "foreign" (im)migrants and other diasporans have to struggle with spatial organization and definitions generated in reaction to their arrival in order to exclude and limit their presence. This is true of both lived places of re-settlement as well as spatialized literary discourses of "American" literature into which authors enter. Moreover, literary and political enclosures (of regionalism, pluralism, racism, and so forth) *assign* subjects to particular sites. Spatial segregation and enclosure are among the "hard facts" that diaspora narratives address in their representation of "migrant sites," where a consciousness of displacement from previous locations and of being *stuck* in place coexist in no easy terms. Diasporic literatures unfold in that paradoxical place where "migrant" and "site" clash but are also mutually constitutive, each redefining and destabilizing the other.

Reading for diasporas in U.S. America means redefining American literature at the juncture of connective, expansive translocalization and restricted, contained localization. In the hardening of attitudes and policies toward immigrants in recent years—and especially since September 11, 2001—diasporas and immigration have been tainted by association with criminality (of "illegality" and threat to national security). As Amy Kaplan has argued, "homeland" has entered the U.S. national vocabulary via "homeland security." In her perceptive article "Homeland Insecurities," Kaplan asks, If the United States is designated as a homeland, what does this mean about those who identify with homelands outside the United States? Divided loyalties, treason, and insecurity are conjured through this particular bordering of "America." The domestic restrictions and removals that have accompanied the war have shown that enclosure is the flip side of expansion and empire. Now, it is all the more important to assert the contingent and multiple possibilities for homelands as well as other diaspora places within and without the nation and to resist enclosures of diasporic lives and narratives.

NOTES

INTRODUCTION (PAGES 3–24)

1. Arguing—as do Latin Americanist scholars Anibal Quijano and Walter Mignolo—that the present is a colonial one, run without colonial administrations but with the "New World" colonial legacy and continuous practices of racialized subjugation, Grosfoguel and Georas taxonomize newcomers to U.S. space into three categories. First, "colonial/racial subjects of empire," those who are long-term subjects of U.S. conquest, colonization, and slavery (Native Americans, African Americans, Puerto Ricans). Second, "colonial immigrants," those without a direct history of colonization but are treated as colonial subjects after arrival (for example, Haitians as African Americans, Dominicans as Puerto Ricans). Third, "immigrants," those racialized as white (for example, Europeans, European Latinas/os).
2. On South Asian American Studies, see, for example, Shankar and Srikanth, whose edited volume is tellingly entitled *A Part Yet Apart: South Asians in America*. On queer diasporas, see Gopinath. On Puerto Ricans in the "Latino" and "Hispanic" construction, see Juan Flores, who explains that while viewed as a "Hispanic" group, Puerto Ricans are also "cast as the bottom rung, the 'exception' to the Hispanic rule" (*From Bomba* 8–9). Despite a continuous historical presence and considerable size, "it is the Puerto Rican population that is most commonly pointed to as the most nagging 'problem'" and at present we have "age-old social pathologies and theories of cultural deficiency now buttressed by the loudly touted success stories of so many of their presumed 'Hispanic' cohorts" (ibid.).
3. The Chicana/o and Puerto Rican diaspora movements of the 1960s and 1970s in the United States were informed by the historical conquest and colonization of Mexico and Puerto Rico; they rethought the struggles of Mexican and Puerto Rican diasporans as anticolonial processes in continuum with the decolonizing Third World. The conceptualization of the Third World within the United States found expression in the idea of "internal colonialism," proposed by Latin American social scientists in the 1950s and 1960s to explain the disenfranchisement and spatial confinement of exploited peoples within "domestic" territories. African American, Native American, Chicana/o, and Puerto Rican activists and scholars

adopted this term to think about racialization in the United States and of oppressed minorities as "nations" in need of liberation. Although "internal colonialism" has been criticized for adhering too closely to the national model and for occluding divergences between internal and external colonialisms, it remains compelling as an analogy. As Ramón Gutiérrez has summarized, "internal colonialism offered minorities an explanation for their territorial concentration, spatial segregation, external administration, the disparity between their legal citizenship and *de facto* second class standing, their brutalization by the police, and the toxic effects of racism in their lives" (282).

1. REFORMULATING DIASPORA SPATIALITIES (PAGES 25–45)

1. As the historian Richard Hofstadter put it, "What developed in America was an agricultural society whose real attachment was not to land but land values" (41).
2. As Turner puts it at the beginning of his phenomenally influential 1893 address, "The Significance of the Frontier in American History," "The existence of an area of *free land*, its continuous recession, and the advance of American settlement westward, explain American development" (Turner 1; emphasis added). The concluding choice of words regarding the "closure" of the frontier, are a testament to the utter, effortless brutality of erasing history and peoples: "But never again will such *gifts of free land* offer themselves" (38; emphasis added).
3. It is not surprising that U.S. conceptions of national (that is, collective) identity such as Turner's frontier hypothesis is based on an emphasis of the individuality of the "frontiersman" and "yeoman farmer." Turner writes, "the frontier is productive of individualism. . . . The tendency is anti-social. . . . The frontier individualism has from the beginning promoted democracy" (30); he goes on to detail the positive and negative aspects of this individualism (32). How the strenuous individualism yields a communal identity is a question elided.
4. Lawrence the modernist primitivist defines Spirit of Place in blood-and-soil terms: "Every people is polarized in some particular locality, which is home, the homeland. Different places on the face of the earth have different vital effluence, different vibration, different chemical exhalation, different polarity with different stars: call it what you like. But the spirit of place is a great reality. The Nile valley produced not only the corn, but the terrific religions of Egypt. China produces the Chinese, and will go on doing so" (12). Americans, for Lawrence, have defiled this essential sense of place and deny that they have done so.
5. David Goldberg discusses how it is taken for granted that the "the racially marginalized" are compelled to shop in white spaces, while whites would never cross into the ghettos to do the same (196).
6. Positioning place as synonymous with continuity, enchantment (*locus amoenus*), and stasis all too often has converged with hegemonic or reactionary projects. Such ideologies of place have been enlisted, variously, by the early anthropological drive to envision "native cultures" as unchanging and place-bound (Gupta and Ferguson), the disturbing meditations of Martin Heidegger on authentic dwelling in the Black Forest (*who* really could dwell, *who* could be authentic there?), and reactionary regionalisms in Europe and elsewhere (see, for example, Dainotto).

7. The use of the word "ghetto" has changed in both academic and mainstream discourses. Abraham Cahan was the first to "import" this European term into English to apply to an immigrant population, namely, the Jewish people of the Lower East Side at the end of the nineteenth century. In the first decades of the twentieth century, the word "ghetto" was used in a similar way to indicate immigrant enclaves. The sociologist Loïc Wacquant explains that a ghetto is more than simply an enclave as the earlier sociologists like Louis Wirth had used the term: for most immigrants eventually accepted as "white," the ghetto is a temporary gathering place until upward and outward mobility takes place. Wacquant defines a ghetto differently, as "a highly peculiar form of urbanization warped by asymmetric relations of power between ethnoracial groupings: a special form of collective violence concretized in urban space"—a definition that does not apply to most "ethnic places." See Wacquant's history of the term. Here, I use the term that the novelists themselves use in their works: "ghetto" for Cahan and *el barrio* for Thomas and Quiñonez.
8. Displacement, for modernists and some poststructuralists, is a universal condition as well as a normative ideal, as both metaphor ("nomadic thought") and concrete action. Caren Kaplan has provided a useful critique of many of these theories, most cogently of Gilles Deleuze and Félix Guattari's romanticizing appropriation of "the gypsy" and "the nomad," the generalized, antiterritorial, mobile other of metropolitan ontology. Of course, mobility, along with speed and technological revolutions, has been a feature of Western modernity for the last two centuries. Particularly cheerful celebrations of "migrancy" and wondrous displacement can be found in Iain Chambers's *Migrancy, Culture, Identity* and Rosi Braidotti's *Nomadic Subjects*. For a useful overview of movement and speed and the concomitant changes in subjectivity and perception, see the last chapter ("Inhuman Geographies") of Nigel Thrift's *Spatial Formations*, in which he elucidates these developments through discussions of their major commentators from Marx to Simmel to Virilio.
9. Ash Amin has summarized the relational perspective on place succinctly: "cities and regions" are perceived as "places overlapping—but not necessarily locally connected—relational networks as perforated entities with connections that stretch far back in time and space, and resulting from all this, as spatial formations of continuously changing composition, character, and reach" (34).

2. CROSSING DELANCEY: JEWISH DIASPORA LOCALITY AND U.S. LITERATURE (PAGES 49–80)

1. In *Mystic Chords of Memory*, an extensive work on how Americans remember their history, Michael Kammen describes the parades, banquets, concerts, pageants as well as edifices and monuments in cities and towns that honored the importance of the locality to the nation. Kammen argues that although this period was one of national definition and jingoism, "local pride was much more likely to energize the observances that really engaged people; place-specific activities served as strongest impulse to memory" (141).
2. See Jean-François Lyotard, *The Postmodern Condition: A Report on Knowledge*,

trans. Geoffrey Bennington and Brian Massumi (Minneapolis: University of Minnesota Press, 1984), and Clifford Geertz, *Local Knowledge: Further Essays in Interpretive Anthropology* (New York: Basic Books, 1983) for influential statements on the necessity of "local" and contingent knowledges in order to subvert hegemonic discourses. For a critique of "local knowledge," see Alan Liu, "Local Transcendence: Cultural Criticism, Postmodernism, and the Romanticism of Detail," *Representations* 32 (1990): 75–113.

3. See Louis D. Rubin, Jr., *I'll Take My Stand: The South and the Agrarian Tradition, by twelve southerners* (Baton Rouge: Louisiana State University Press, 1977 [1930]).
4. See John Higham, *Strangers in the Land: Patterns of American Nativism, 1860–1925*, for a historical overview of this phenomenon.
5. There is a large body of literature on "the picturesque" as an aesthetic category. For "classic" statements in the English-language context, see, for example, William Gilpin, *Observations on the River Wye* (1789) and Uvedale Price's *Essay on the Picturesque* (1796–98). Recent criticism includes *The Politics of the Picturesque: Literature, Landscape and Aesthetics Since 1770*, ed. Stephen Copley and Peter Garside (New York: Cambridge University Press, 1994); "Nine Revisionist Theses on the Picturesque," by Kim Ian Michasiw, *Representations* 38 (1992): 76–100; Sidney K. Robinson, *Inquiry into the Picturesque* (Chicago: University of Chicago Press, 1991).
6. In "Dialectics of Modernity: Reenchantment and Dedifferentiation as Counterprocesses," sociologist Edward Tiryakian discusses the media of "reenchantment" within modernity previously constructed to occlude "enchantment" in favor of rationality. "The enchantment of the exotic" with its strong "local colors" is a feature of modernity that provided an outlet from the "life that was becoming increasingly sublimated and inhibited with the advance of 'the Victorian ethos,' an ethos of sobriety and somber clothing" (88).
7. I appreciate Shari Huhndorf's reminder to me that the attribution of mobility to Native Americans does not remain constant. The romanticized representation of the Indian, who, toward the end of the nineteenth century is constructed to be unthreatening and even "noble," included a projection of the native as "place-based" and a feature of the landscape. This projection further illustrates that mobility is frequently configured negatively to be used in representations of threatening social or racial/ethnic entities. See Gail Guthrie Valaskakis's 1996 article "Indian Country: Negotiating the Meaning of Land in Native America" on representations of the relationship between Native Americans and land.
8. See Sandra Zagarell for an analysis of the exclusion of otherness in Jewett's *The Country of Pointed Firs*.
9. The Lower East Side, with all its poverty and misery, was in fact a tourist attraction. It was the perfect locale for what was then called "shudder journalism" as well as a favorite site of uptowners for "slumming" for a night's entertainment. In *The Downtown Jews*, Sanders describes slumming as a popular turn-of-the-century activity:

> the Jewish quarter had become a prominent leisure-time attraction to many New Yorkers from the middle and upper classes, and "slumming" there was a favorite pastime. They would come on Saturday evenings and Sunday after-

noons and "aristocratically scrutinize the poor neighborhoods with 'artistic curiosity,'" as Cahan wrote. "In this way, two restaurants grew up in the poor East Side, in which millionaires would spend their evenings. This supposedly meant that they were scrutinizing the poor 'other half.'" But in reality they were just scrutinizing one another (178).

10. See Jane Addams, *Twenty Years at Hull House, with Autobiographical Notes* (New York: Signet, 1981 [1910]) for a first-person account by an outstanding leader of the movement. Paul McBride's *Culture Clash: Immigrants and Reformers, 1880-1920* (San Francisco, Calif.: Rand, 1975) and Mina Julia Carson's *Settlement Folk: Social Thought and the American Settlement Movement, 1885–1930* (Chicago: University of Chicago Press, 1990) provide useful histories.
11. See Bender on the specifics of the reformists' discourse on immigrants. He points out that the "civilizing mission" was practiced not only in the empire abroad but also domestically through the institutionalized reform movements directed at "savage" immigrants.
12. Alan Trachtenberg ("Experiments") argues that Riis's rhetorical tactic is "to place the reader in a moral relation of outrage, indignation, or pity" but that the reader is neither allowed an inside view of the slums nor to adopt the perspective of one within, thereby dissolving the possibility of a exchange between the two halves (144). He contrasts Riis's reporting with Stephen Crane's fictions of the "low life" and suggests that Crane "forces the reader to free his own point of view from any limiting perspective" (147). Although I do not concur that it is quite possible to "free" the reader, it is true that Riis's omniscient narrating perspective makes him the sole master and raconteur of his subject, thereby lending him the status of sole author(ity) on the misery of the ghettos.
13. In the fictions of Jewett, Chopin, and many other local colorists, mobility becomes an important issue. In *The Country of Pointed Firs*, narrated by an urban outsider, women speak of their former travels, in their youth and before Dunnet's Landing ceased to be an important port and their mobility became restricted. In *The Awakening*, Edna Pontellier's restricted movement in traditional society, as in much feminist writing, is a focal point. See chapter 4 for a treatment of immobility in the work of Sandra Cisneros.
14. His original audience read *Yekl* as if it were about an undifferentiated ethnic corpus. An editor at *McClure's*, the most popular magazine of the time, turned down *Yekl*, telling Cahan, "you describe only Jews. Someone who reads your novel is likely to think that there are no other kinds of people in America than Jews" (in Chametzky 67). Clearly, no editor would have said to Jewett or Freeman that their novels make it seem like there are only small-town New Englanders in the U.S. The editor as well as others who considered the novel a failure could not look beyond the exoticism of the singular Jewish life they read, mistakenly, in *Yekl*.
15. Henry James does not hesitate to mobilize the cliché and adds his bit to the art of Jewish physiognomy in his vivid, incredulous description of the Jews of New York: "at the bottom of some vast sallow aquarium in which innumerable fish, of overdeveloped proboscis, were to bump together, for ever, amid heaped spoils of the sea" (*American Scene* 100).

16. Even the happily integrated subject Mary Antin in *The Promised Land* (1912) is not immune to "a painful double-consciousness" (Wald 250) that immigrants can experience. See chapter 4 of Priscilla Wald's *Constituting Americans* for an in-depth analysis of the ambiguities involved in the construction of (immigrant-) American selfhood in the writing of Gertrude Stein and other turn-of-the-century writers.

3. PLURALISM IN THE IMMIGRANT PRAIRIE: WILLA CATHER'S CIVILIZED PRIMITIVES (PAGES 81–118)

1. Judith Fetterley and Marjorie Pryse have argued that local color literature draws sharper distinctions between the insider and outsider perspectives, while in regionalist writing, those belonging to the region make their voices heard. Regionalism, they suggest, is a more elastic and unpredictable mode than local color, which reproduces more readily discourses of the nation.
2. In a later novel, Oleg Rölvaag's *Giants in the Earth* (1927) the terrifying desolation, barrenness, and solitude of land leads the mother of the Norwegian immigrant family to insanity. While Cather's West is no prelapsarian paradise, Rölvaag's novel relates much crueler conditions and personal fates. Not only does another Norwegian woman become insane, at the novel's unforgettable end the main protagonist (the paterfamilias) is found in the aftermath of a snowstorm, frozen in a seated position still wearing his skis.
3. One piece of evidence for this escapes Swift's attention: coming to know his stately grandfather, Jim is awed by his intonation of the biblical word "selah," in his reading of the Psalm, "He shall *choose our inheritance for us*, the excellency of Jacob whom He loved. Selah" (13; emphasis added).
4. In his discussion of the debates on classical education in the universities, Swift reproduces a 1917 statement by Princeton University's president, which includes the declaration, "Ours is the civilization that has come directly from that original civilization of Greece and Rome" (113). Michaels's book includes a quote from Calvin Coolidge: "Modern civilization dates from Greece and Rome," and Americans are now their "inheritors" (37).
5. See also David Stouck's "*My Ántonia* as Pastoral" for an examination of the classical sources in the novel and an exploration of pastoral imagination's attempt to "exclude sex" to avoid encroachment upon childhood, which is the ideal state in pastoral. On Cather and pastoral, see also Lee, 90–96.
6. In an interesting article on Margaret Mead and Willa Cather, David Weisberg also discusses primitivism in the novel, but he focuses on the representation of incest, kinship, and the construction of sexuality as part of the authors' antimodern discourses. For Weisberg, "Cather's apparent intention was to make the image of primitive womanhood impinge upon and ameliorate the modern, [and] detach sexuality from the ideology of heterosexual romantic love" (165).
7. Alan Trachtenberg's *The Incorporation of America*, Robert Wiebe's *The Search for Order*, and Frederick C. Jaher's *The Age of Industrialism in America* provide histories of the corporate and industrial "landscape" that actually replaced the wilder-

ness in a short time and led to all the nostalgic discourse and organization around Nature. See Leo Marx's classic *The Machine in the Garden* for an account of the imbrication of the technological and pastoral ideals in the U.S. experience.

8. Much commentary has also been made on Alexandra's celibacy and passionless, yet close relationship with Carl in *O Pioneers!* See Lee 111–112; Murphy 121–122.
9. See Jackson Lears's *No Place of Grace*, 142–149, on late nineteenth-century U.S. notions of childhood and the search for a primitive infancy in the Middle Ages.
10. See also Thomas F. Gossett's *Race: The History of an Idea in America* (1997 ed.) on Slavs as an apolitical, turbulent, anarchic race (112, 341) in the late nineteenth and early twentieth centuries. In his earlier work Jacobson had also shown that for East Europeans in general the war against the Philippines provided them with the means to whiten themselves through the domination of the Asiatic races (*Special Sorrows* 181–216).
11. In the last paragraph of the novel, Jim reflects back on the night of his and Ántonia's arrival in the countryside while sitting on the same road of arrival decades later. He muses, "I had the sense of coming home to myself, and of having found out what a little circle man's experience is" (210). See Barbara Bair for an interpretation of the religious and mythical metaphors of cyclicality (102–104).
12. For the very brief overview below of turn-of-the-century nativism in the United States, I relied on John Higham's *Strangers in the Land.*
13. In "Anti-Imperial Americanism," Michaels controversially argues that the inward-looking nativist movements were opposed to the imperialist ambitions of the United States; he suggests that nativist and the imperialist efforts are divorced in turn-of-the-century America. John Higham also mentions that there were "nativistic fears of racial pollution from subject peoples or from the new immigration," fears that imperialists dismissed (109).
14. See the third chapter of Morris Janowitz's *The Reconstruction of Patriotism: Education for Civic Consciousness* for one account of the zeal for "acculturation" and nationalism in the public school system between 1890 and 1940.
15. See, for example, Lawrence Fuchs's argument in *American Kaleidoscope* that Americanization and the conservation of immigrant cultures were fully compatible.
16. "This rage for newness and conventionality is one of the things which I deplore in the present-day Nebraska," she told an interviewer. Tearing down a beautiful old house to build an ugly new one and have it "furnished in correct taste" was abominable (*Willa Cather In Person* 46). Beauty was "everywhere," but it had to be appreciated: "Take the cottonwood, for example, the most beautiful tree on the plains. The people of Paris go crazy about them. . . . But the people of Red Cloud and Hastings chop them down."
17. See Stuart Hall's "Notes on Deconstructing 'the Popular'" and Janice Radway for critiques of the distinction between "folk" and "mass" in her discussion of the readership of romance novels. See also, for example, Jesús Martín-Barbero's chapter on folklore and popular culture for a historical discussion and Néstor García Canclini for "folk" and indigenous art and authenticity.
18. Walter Benn Michaels most provocatively positions Willa Cather as a nativist author in his much-discussed *Our America: Nativism, Modernism, and Pluralism*

(1995), in which he argues for a profound imbrication of political nativism and modernist U.S. literature. Nativism, according to Michaels, is not simply a background to modernism; the two coincide and echo one another in a myriad of ways. He reads Cather's later novels, especially *The Professor's House* and *A Lost Lady*, in the nativist register and concludes that Cather, like William Carlos Williams and many other modernists, valorizes racial purity and forges an idea of "America" as an exclusionary family based on likeness and incest. While I do not agree with Michaels's larger conclusions about identity politics as essentialist and racist (along with U.S. modernism), the works by Cather that Michaels draws on do exhibit anti-Semitism (*The Professor's House*), an exoticizing identification with fantasized Indians, and a retreat from exogamy. Cather's earlier works, however, do not bespeak such genealogies; perhaps that is why Michaels does not refer to them.

19. See the collection *Willa Cather and Her Critics*, edited by James Schroeter for these and other essays. That the charge that Cather was divorced from reality and "experience," was tinged with masculinist disdain was proved most pointedly by (who else?) Ernest Hemingway, who wrote to Edmund Wilson in 1923, after Cather had received the Pulitzer Prize for *One of Ours*: "E. E. Cummings' *Enormous Room* was the best book published last year that I read. Somebody told me it was a flop. Then look at *One of Ours*. Prize, big sale, people taking it seriously. You were in the war weren't you? Wasn't that last scene in the lines wonderful? Do you know where it came from? The battle scene in *Birth of a Nation*. I identified episode after episode. Catherized. Poor woman she had to get war experience somewhere" (in Lee, 167). See Sharon O'Brien's "Becoming Noncanonical: The Case Against Willa Cather," whose subtitle echoes the heading of Granville Hicks's essay, for an analysis of the gendered basis of the author's reception.

4. "CUANDO LLEGUEMOS / WHEN WE ARRIVE": THE SMALL TOWN AND THE POETICS OF CHICANA/O PLACE (PAGES 121–154)

1. For an important treatment of this groundbreaking novel, see Ramón Saldívar.
2. The literary locus of the urban barrio, not a subject of this chapter, is also important to Chicana/o literary history. See Villa for a tremendously helpful and original study.
3. For Cooper Alarcón, Aztlán is "a monolithic narrative, into which all Chicanos were to write themselves, regardless of intracultural differences" (Cooper Alarcón, "The Aztec Palimpsest" 39). The anachronicity of the symbol left many indifferent, argue Angie Chabram and Rosa Linda Fregoso: "[A]n ahistorical 'Aztec' identity [fell] on the deaf ears of an urban community versed in the rhythms of disco, conjunto music, and boleros" (206). Many scholars have provided more complex analyses of Mesoamerican cultures than the romanticized, indigenist vision conjured by the Movement. Marxist critics deplored the culturalist emphasis and the absence of class analysis; legendary labor leader César Chávez himself reacted to the fantasy of a borderless world, as he sought to check immigration to protect workers' jobs (Andouard-Labarthe 81). Feminists have had a highly ambivalent relationship to "El Plan"; some six hundred gathered in 1971 to address issues of the

"nation" ignored by the Plan, which the women nevertheless recognized. The document they produced, *Chicanas Speak Out*, never became part of the Chicano archives (Pratt, "Yo Soy" 861). Gloria Anzaldúa, Cherríe Moraga, and many others have taken issue with the Plan and Chicano nationalism in general, for its masculinist, heterosexist focus.

4. Some say the claim of Aztlán as rightful ancestral land can be challenged: John Chávez writes, "Both Indians and Chicanos see themselves as indigenous to and dispossessed of their homelands, which in the Southwest means they claim the same territory" (3). What is more, suggests Daniel Cooper Alarcón, it is entirely possible for African Americans and Asian Americans (as the first group via the Bering Strait) to lay claims to the very same lands as well (59).
5. In Brito's *El diablo en Téjas*, death and decay reign in the transborder towns of Presidio and Ojinaga where the two communities are connected by a bridge that the narrator calls "the devil's work." The bridge, contrary to its spirit, serves to separate rather than connect the once-united spaces, as it is divisive outsiders who have imposed its construction. In a vision more disheartening than Portillo Trambley's critique, the devil is a playful but malicious figure that constantly plays nasty tricks on a Chicana/o people under the Anglo yoke, and there is no respite from oppression, poverty, and humiliation. As Charles Tatum points out in his introduction to the bilingual edition of the novel, there is "no counterbalancing presence of a benevolent God" (12). Similarly, in Méndez's *Peregrinos de Aztlán*, the border region is for the migrant workers of Indian descent a landscape of poverty, suffering and exploitation, in profound contrast to the epic Indian past: "Del sur iban, a la inversa de sus antepasados, en una peregrinación sin sacerdotes ni profetas, arrastrando una historia sin ningún mérito para el que llegara a contarla, por lo vulgar y repetido de su tragedia" (64). In her introduction to the border narratives of Tijuana author Federico Campbell, Debra Castillo points out that some Chicano writers, among them Miguel Méndez, have deprecated border culture as an inauthentic formation that is merely an expression of U.S. oppression ("Borderlining" 11). Thus, the contemporary migrancy of the Mexican is a travesty of the "original" journey southward from Aztlán. Transnationality, in these narratives, is not a means of productive multiplicity but forced travel through spaces of suffering and pain. Unlike in the later formulations of the border by Anzaldúa, Gómez-Peña, or Hicks, the borderlands are not generative; they are crushing and disastrous.
6. El Paso's struggles against ASARCO, now a subsidiary Mexican conglomerate, continues to this day as the company has been consistently trying to reopen smelters in that polluted city, despite protests.
7. The border that creates differences, synthesizable or not, also collapses them. On the U.S. side, citizens can be treated like migrants: Cheech Marin's 1987 film *Born in East L. A.* is a bittersweet rendering of this citizenship in flux, in which the Chicano protagonist finds himself in the middle of an immigration raid, and despite the fact that he is a U.S. citizen who speaks English only, he is presumed Mexican and bussed "back" to Tijuana. In other repetition scenarios, such as the one in "Woman Hollering Creek," migrants often fail to find radical "difference" in their experiences of life on both sides, which are equally harsh. These works are not nec-

essarily about ahistorical repetitions. But, they do underline the crossborder persistence of gender and class divisions and their spatial expression.

5. THE POETICS OF *AQUÍ:* BARRIOCENTRISM IN PUERTO RICAN DIASPORA LITERATURE FROM MEAN STREETS TO NEO-NOIR (PAGES 155–195)

1. On Puerto Rico's status, see Burnett and Marshall, eds., *Foreign in a Domestic Sense.*
2. See Arlene Dávila's *Barrio Dreams* for an extensive treatment of the recent transformation of East Harlem. On the history of the barrio, see, for example, the work of Virginia Sánchez Korrol and Luis Aponte-Parés.
3. Marta Sánchez points out that despite Thomas's attempts at exploding racial binarization, the text was not considered Puerto Rican until the 1980s: "By enlisting differences of language, religion, and history [Puerto Rican studies scholars] reframed Thomas's text as black *and* white, something more than black *or* white" (44).
4. For important commentary on gender politics and the treatment of homosexuality and of Puerto Rican and white women, see Marta Sánchez, Lisa Sánchez González, Arnaldo Cruz-Malavé ("What"), Robert Reid-Pharr, and Michael Hames-García.
5. Michael Hames-García provides a full-length treatment of prisons and homosexuality in Thomas's work.
6. For a treatment of the intersections of noir, representations of ghettos, African American authors, and other left-wing writers, see Paula Rabinowitz's *Black and White and Noir.* On African American film, protest writing, and noir, see Manthia Diawara's "Noir by Noirs."
7. Thomas's title is taken, of course, from Raymond Chandler, who made the phrase immortal in his description of the figure of the detective, a decent, brave man confronting evils: "Down these mean streets a man must go who is not himself mean, who is neither tarnished nor afraid" (18).
8. See Jane Hill on language in public space. Hill argues, "White public space is constructed through (1) intense monitoring of the speech of racialized populations such as Chicanos and Latinos and African Americans for signs of linguistic disorder and (2) the invisibility of almost identical signs in the speech of Whites, where language mixing, required for the expression of a highly valued type of colloquial persona, takes several forms" (680).
9. Dismissing diaspora as a merely nostalgic conception, Yasemin Soysal has argued that diaspora is "the extension of the nation-state model" and implies a congruence between "territory, culture, and national identity" (3). There is little evidence for this; in fact, much of what we know about diasporas is that they spill out of national territories. As I indicated in the introduction (note 8), in fact there is an overromanticizing of such mobilities—literal and metaphorical—as "transgressions" of national territories.

WORKS CITED

Abernethy, Arthur T. *The Jew: A Negro. Being a Study of the Jewish Ancestry from an Impartial Standpoint.* Moravian Falls, N.C.: Dixie Publishing, 1910.

Acuña, Rodolfo. *Occupied America: A History of Chicanos.* 2nd ed. New York: Harper and Row, 1981.

———. "The Theoretical Subject(s) of *This Bridge Called My Back* and Anglo-American Feminism." In *Making Face / Making Soul / Haciendo Caras: Creative and Critical Perspectives by Women of Color,* edited by Gloria Anzaldúa, 356–369. San Francisco, Calif.: Aunt Lute, 1990.

Addams, Jane. *Twenty Years at Hull House, with Autobiographical Notes.* 1910. New York: Signet, 1981.

Alba, D. R., J. R. Logan, and B. J. Stults. "The Changing Neighborhood Contexts of the Immigrant Metropolis." *Social Forces* 79, no. 2 (2000): 587–621.

Algarín, Miguel, and Miguel Piñero, eds. *Nuyorican Poetry: An Anthology of Puerto Rican Words and Feelings.* New York: Morrow, 1979.

Amin, Ash. "Regions Unbound: Towards a New Politics of Place." *Geografiska Annaler* 86, B.1 (2004): 33–44.

Anaya, Rudolfo A. *Bless Me, Ultima.* Berkeley: Quinto Sol, 1972.

———. *Heart of Aztlán.* Berkeley: Editorial Justa, 1976.

———. "The Writer's Landscape: Epiphany in Landscape." *Latin American Literary Review* 10 (1977): 99–102.

Anaya, Rudolfo A., and Francisco Lomelí, eds. *Aztlán: Essays on the Chicano Homeland.* Albuquerque: University of New Mexico Press, 1989.

Andouard-Labarthe, Elyette. "The Vicissitudes of Aztlán." *Confluencia* (1990): 79–84.

Andrews, Malcolm. "The Metropolitan Picturesque." In *The Politics of the Picturesque: Literature, Landscape, and Aesthetics Since 1770,* edited by Stephen Copley and Peter Garside, 282–298. Cambridge: Cambridge University Press, 1994.

Anzaldúa, Gloria. *Borderlands / La Frontera: The New Mestiza.* San Francisco, Calif.: Aunt Lute, 1987.

Aponte-Parés, Luis. "Lessons from *El Barrio*—The East Harlem Real Great Society / Urban Planning Studio: A Puerto Rican Chapter in the Urban Fight for Self-Determination. *New Political Science* 20, no. 4 (1998): 399–420.

———. "What's Yellow and White and Has Land All Around It? Appropriating Place in Puerto Rican *Barrios*." In *The Latino Studies Reader: Culture, Economy, and Society*, edited by Antonia Darder and Rodolfo D. Torres, 271–280. Malden, Mass.: Blackwell, 1998.

Apter, Emily S. "Theorizing Francophonie." *Comparative Literature Studies* 42, no. 4 (2005): 297–311.

Arnold, Martin. "Many Hispanics, Scant Marketing." *New York Times*, 21 March 2002, E3.

Arrizón, Alicia. "Mythical Performativity: Relocating Aztlán in Chicana Feminist Cultural Productions." *Theatre Journal* 52, no. 1 (2000): 23–49.

Arteaga, Alfred. *Chicano Poetics: Heterotexts and Hybridities*. New York: Cambridge University Press, 1997.

Axel, Brian Keith. "The Diasporic Imaginary." *Public Culture* 14, no. 2 (2002): 411–428.

Bachelard, Gaston. *The Poetics of Space*. Translated by Maria Jolas. Boston: Beacon, 1969.

Bair, Barbara. "*My Ántonia* in American Studies: History, Landscape, and Memory." In *Approaches to Teaching Cather's My Antonia*, edited by Susan J. Rosowski, 100–106. New York: Modern Language Association of America, 1989.

Bakhtin, Mikhail. *The Dialogic Imagination. Four Essays by M. M. Bakhtin*. Edited by Michael Holquist. Austin: University of Texas Press, 1981.

Barrera, Mario. *Race and Class in the Southwest: a Theory of Racial Inequality*. Notre Dame, Ind.: University of Notre Dame Press, 1979.

Barrera Herrera, Eduardo. "Apropiación y tutelaje de la frontera norte." *Puentelibre* 4 (1995): 13–17.

Bartkowski, Frances. *Travelers, Immigrants, Inmates: Essays in Estrangement*. Minneapolis: University of Minnesota Press, 1995.

Basch, Linda, Nina Glick Schiller, and Cristina Szanton Blanc. *Nations Unbound: Transnational Project, Postcolonial Predicaments, and Deterritorialized Nation-States*. Langhorne, Pa: Gordon and Breach, 1994.

Bauman, Zygmunt. *Modernity and the Holocaust*. Ithaca, N.Y.: Cornell University Press, 1989.

Bederman, Gail. *Manliness and Civilization: A Cultural History of Gender and Race in the United States*. Chicago: University of Chicago Press, 1995.

Bender, Daniel. "Reform, the Savage Immigrant, and the Survival of the Unfit." *Journal of Social History* 42, no. 1 (2008): 5–29.

Blair, Sara. "Cultural Geography and the Place of the Literary." *American Literary History* 10 (1998): 544–567.

Blauner, Robert. *Racial Oppression in America*. New York: Harper, 1972.

Bonazzi, Tiziano. "Frederick Jackson Turner's Frontier Thesis and the Self-Consciousness of America." *Journal of American Studies* 27 (1993): 149–172.

Boorstin, Daniel. *The Americans: The National Experience*. New York: Random House, 1965.

Born in East L.A. Directed by Cheech Marin. 1986. Universal Studios.

Bourne, Randolph. *The Radical Will: Randolph Bourne, Selected Writings, 1911–1918*.

With a preface by Christopher Lasch. Selected and introduced by Olaf Hansen. New York: Urizen Books, 1977.

Boyarin, Jonathan. *Thinking in Jewish*. Chicago: University of Chicago Press, 1996.

Boyarin, Jonathan, and Daniel Boyarin. "Diaspora: Generational Ground of Jewish Identity." *Critical Inquiry* 19, no. 4 (1993): 693–725.

———. *Powers of Diaspora: Two Essays on the Relevance of Jewish Culture*. Minneapolis: University of Minnesota Press, 2002.

Brady, Mary Pat. *Extinct Lands, Temporal Geographies: Chicana Literature and the Urgency of Space*. Durham, N.C.: Duke University Press, 2003.

Brah, Avtar. *Cartographies of Diaspora: Contesting Identities*. New York: Routledge, 1996.

Braidotti, Rosi. *Nomadic Subjects: Embodiment and Sexual Difference in Contemporary Feminist Theory*. New York: Columbia University Press, 1994.

Brito, Aristeo. *El diablo en Texas / The Devil in Texas*. 1976. Translated by David William Foster. Tempe, Ariz.: Editorial Bilingüe / Bilingual Press, 1990.

Brodhead, Richard H. "Literature and Culture, 1865–1910." In *The Columbia Literary History of the United States*, edited by Emory Elliott, 467–481. New York: Columbia University Press, 1988.

———. "The Reading of Regions." In *Cultures of Letters: Scenes of Reading and Writing in Nineteenth-Century America*, 107–141. Chicago: University of Chicago Press, 1993.

Bruce-Novoa. *Chicano Authors: Inquiry by Interview*. Austin: University of Texas Press, 1980.

———. "Dialogical Strategies, Monological Goals: Chicano Literature." In *An Other Tongue: Nation and Ethnicity in the Linguistic Borderlands*, edited by Alfred Arteaga, 225–245. Durham, N.C.: Duke University Press, 1994.

Brückner, Martin. The Geographic Revolution in Early America: The Geographic Revolution in Early America. Chapel Hill: University of North Carolina Press, 2006.

Buell, Lawrence. "The Timeliness of Place: Response to the Presidential Address." American Quarterly 58 (2006): 17–22.

Buff, Rachel. *Immigration and the Political Economy of Home: West Indian Brooklyn and American Indian Minneapolis, 1945–1992*. Berkeley and Los Angeles: University of California Press, 2001.

Burnett, Christina Duffy, and Burke Marshall, eds. *Foreign in a Domestic Sense: Puerto Rico, American Expansionism, and the Constitution*. Durham, N.C.: Duke University Press, 2001.

Butler, Judith. *Bodies That Matter: On the Discursive Limits of Sex*. New York: Routledge, 1993.

Butler, Kim D. "Defining Diaspora, Refining a Discourse." *Diaspora: A Journal of Transnational Studies* 10, no. 2 (2001): 189–219.

Butor, Michel. "Travel Writing." Translated by John Powers and K. Lisket. *Mosaic* 8 (1974): 1–16.

Cabán, Pedro. "Subjects and Immigrants in the Progressive Era." *Discourse* 23, no. 3 (2001): 24–51.

Cahan, Abraham. "The Russian Jew in America." *Atlantic Monthly* 82 (July 1898): 263–287.

———. *Yekl & The Imported Bridegroom and Other Stories of The New York Ghetto.* 1896 and 1898 New York: Dover, 1970.

Calderón, Héctor, and José David Saldívar, eds. *Criticism in the Borderlands: Studies in Chicano Literature, Culture, and Ideology*. Durham, N.C.: Duke University Press, 1991.

Campbell, Dana. "Repudiating the Age of the Carved Cherry-Stones: The Naturalists' Reaction Against Women's Local Color Fiction." Ph.D. diss., University of Kansas, 1990.

Carden, Mary Paniccia. "Creative Fertility and the National Romance in Willa Cather's *O Pioneers!* and *My Ántonia*." *Modern Fiction Studies* 45, no. 2 (1999): 275–302.

Carlin, Deborah. *Cather, Canon and the Politics of Reading*. Amherst: University of Massachusetts Press, 1992.

Carson, Mina Julia. *Settlement Folk: Social Thought and the American Settlement Movement, 1885–1930*. Chicago: University of Chicago Press, 1990.

Carter, Sean. "The Geopolitics of Diaspora." *Area* 37, no. 1 (2005): 54–63.

Casey, Edward S. *The Fate of Place: A Philosophical History.* Berkeley and Los Angeles: University of California Press, 1997.

Castillo, Ana. *So Far From God*. New York: Plume, 1994.

Castillo, Debra A. "Borderliners: Federico Campbell and Ana Castillo." In *Feminist Explorations of Literary Space*, edited by Margaret Higgonet and Joan Templeton, 147–170. Amherst: University of Massachusetts Press, 1994.

———. "Borderlining: An Introduction." In *Tijuana: Stories on the Border*, by Federico Campbell. Translated and introduced by Debra A. Castillo. Berkeley and Los Angeles: University of California Press, 1995.

———. *Talking Back: Toward a Latin American Feminist Literary Criticism*. Ithaca, N.Y.: Cornell University Press, 1992.

Cather, Willa. "My First Novels (There Were Two)." In *Willa Cather on Writing: Critical Studies on Writing as an Art*, 89–98. Lincoln: University of Nebraska Press, 1920.

———. *The Kingdom of Art: Willa Cather's First Principles and Critical Statements, 1893–1896*. Edited by Bernice Slote. Lincoln: University of Nebraska Press, 1966.

———. *My Ántonia*. Boston: Houghton Mifflin, 1918.

———. *O Pioneers!*. 1913. New York: Penguin, 1989.

———. *Willa Cather in Person: Interviews, Speeches, and Letters.* Edited by L. Bren Bohlke. Lincoln: University of Nebraska Press, 1986.

Chabram, Angie, and Rosa Linda Fregoso. "Chicana/o Cultural Representations: Reframing Alternative Critical Discourses." *Cultural Studies* 4 (1990): 203–212.

Chabram-Dernersesian, Angie. "Latina/o: Another Site of Struggle, Another Site of Accountability." In *Critical Latin American and Latino Studies*, edited by Juan Poblete, 105–120. Minneapolis: University of Minnesota Press, 2003.

Chambers, Iain. *Migrancy, Culture, Identity*. London: Routledge, 1994.

Chametzky, Jules. *From the Ghetto: The Fiction of Abraham Cahan*. Amherst: University of Massachusetts Press, 1977.

Chandler, Raymond. "The Simple Art of Murder." 1944. In *The Simple Art of Murder*. New York: Vintage, 1988.
Chávez, Denise. "Space Is a Solid." In *The Last of the Menu Girls*, 95–136. Houston, Texas: Arte Público, 1987.
Chávez, John R. *The Lost Land: The Chicano Image of the Southwest*. Albuquerque: University of New Mexico Press, 1984.
Chávez, Linda. *Out of the Barrio: Towards a New Politics of Hispanic Assimilation*. New York: Basic, 1992.
Cheah, Pheng. "Given Culture: Rethinking Cosmopolitical Freedom in Transnationalism." In *Cosmopolitics: Thinking and Feeling Beyond the Nation*, edited by Pheng Cheah and Bruce Robbins, 290–328. Minneapolis: University of Minnesota Press, 1998.
Chilton, Paul. *Security Metaphors: Cold War Discourse from Containment to Common House*. New York: Peter Lang, 1996.
Chopin, Kate. *The Awakening*. 1899. Edited by Margaret Culley. New York: Norton, 1975.
Chow, Rey. "The Old/New Question of Comparison in Literary Studies: A Post-European Perspective." *ELH* 72, no. 2 (2004): 289–311.
Cisneros, Sandra. "Woman Hollering Creek." In *Woman Hollering Creek and Other Stories*, 43–56. New York: Vintage, 1991.
"City of Seguín." www.ci.seguin.tx.us/general/ history.htm, (accessed 14 April 2007).
Clifford, James. "Diasporas." *Cultural Anthropology* 9 (1994): 302–338.
———. "Traveling Cultures." In *Cultural Studies*, edited by Lawrence Grossberg, Cary Nelson, and Paula Treichler, 96–116. New York: Routledge, 1992.
Cohen, Robin. "Diasporas and the Nation-State: From Victims to Challengers." *International Affairs* 72 (1996): 507–520.
Colón, Jesús. *A Puerto Rican in New York and Other Sketches*. New York: Mainstream, 1961.
Connolly, William E. *The Ethos of Pluralization*. Minneapolis: University of Minnesota Press, 1995.
Connor, Walker. "Beyond Reason: The Nature of the Ethnonational Bond." In *Ethnicity*, edited by John Hutchinson and Anthony D. Smith, 69–75. New York: Oxford University Press, 1996.
Cooper Alarcón, Daniel. *The Aztec Palimpsest: Mexico in the Modern Imagination*. Tucson: University of Arizona Press, 1997.
———. "The Aztec Palimpsest: Toward a New Understanding of Aztlán, Cultural Identity and History." *Aztlán: A Journal of Chicano Studies* 19 (1988–90): 33–68.
Copley, Stephen, and Peter Garside, eds. *The Politics of the Picturesque: Literature, Landscape and Aesthetics since 1770*. New York: Cambridge University Press, 1994.
Cosgrove, Denis, and Stephen Daniels, eds. *The Iconography of Landscape: Essays on the Symbolic Representation, Design and Use of Past Environments*. Cambridge: Cambridge University Press, 1988.
Crawford, Rachel. "English Georgic and British Nationhood." *ELH* 65, no. 1 (1998): 123–158.
Cruz-Malavé, Armando. "Colonial Figures in Motion: Globalization and Translocal-

ity in Contemporary Puerto Rican Literature in the United States." *Centro Journal* 14, no. 2 (2002): 5–25.

———. "Teaching Puerto Rican Authors: Identity and Modernization in Nuyorican Texts." *ADE Bulletin* 91 (1988): 45–51. http://www.mla.org/ade/bulletin/no91/091039 .htm (accessed 9 September 2004).

———. "'What a Tangled Web': Masculinity, Abjection, and the Foundations of Puerto Rican Literature in the United States." *Differences: A Journal of Feminist Cultural Studies* 8, no. 1 (1996): 132–151.

Cunningham, Hilary, and Josiah McC. Heyman. "Introduction: Mobilities and Enclosures at Borders." In *Identities: Global Studies in Culture and Power* 11 (2004): 289–302.

Dainotto, Roberto Maria. *Place in Literature: Regions, Cultures, Communities.* Ithaca, N.Y.: Cornell University Press, 2000.

Dallal, Jenine. "American Imperialism UnManifest: Emerson's 'Inquest' and Cultural Regeneration." *American Literature* 73, no. 1 (2001): 47–83.

Davies, Richard. *Main Street Blues: The Decline of Small-Town America.* Columbus: Ohio State University Press, 1998.

Dávila, Arlene. *Barrio Dreams: Puerto Ricans, Latinos, and the Neoliberal City.* Berkeley and Los Angeles: University of California Press, 2004.

———."Dreams of Place: Housing, Gentrification, and the Marketing of Space in El Barrio." *Centro Journal* 15, no. 1 (2003): 112–138.

de Certeau, Michel. *The Practice of Everyday Life.* Translated by Steven Rendall. Berkeley and Los Angeles: University of California Press, 1984.

De la Campa, Román. "On New American Subjects and Intellectual Models." *Nepantla: Views from South* 4, no. 2 (2003): 235–243.

Deleuze, Gilles, and Félix Guattari. *A Thousand Plateaus: Capitalism and Schizophrenia.* Translated and with a foreword by Brian Massumi. Minneapolis: University of Minnestoa Press, 1987.

Deloria, Vine, and C. Lytle. *American Indians, American Justice.* Austin: University of Texas Press, 1983.

Dewey, John. "Americanism and Localism." *The Dial* 68 (1920): 684–688.

Diawara, Manthia. "Noir by Noirs: Toward a New Realism in Black Cinema." In *Shades of Noir: A Reader*, ed. Joan Copjec, 261–278. New York: Verso, 1993.

Diner, Hasia. *Lower East Side Memories: A Jewish Place in America.* Princeton, N.J.: Princeton University Press, 2000.

Diner, Hasia, Jeffrey Shandler, and Beth S. Wenger. "Introduction: Remembering the Lower East Side, a Conversation." In *Remembering the Lower East Side: American Jewish Reflections,* edited by Hasia Diner, Jeffrey Shandler, and Beth S. Wenger, 1–9. Bloomington: Indiana University Press, 2000.

———, eds. *Remembering the Lower East Side: American Jewish Reflections.* Bloomington: Indiana University Press, 2000.

Dirlik, Arif. "Bringing History Back In: Of Diasporas, Hybridities, Places, and Histories." In *Beyond Dichotomies: Histories, Identities, Cultures, and the Challenge of Globalization*, edited by Elisabeth Mudimbe-Boyi , 93–127. Albany: State University of New York Press, 2002.

———. "Place-Based Imagination: Globalism and the Politics of Place." In *Places and Politics in an Age of Globalization*, edited by Roxann Prazniak and Arif Dirlik, 15–52. Lanham, Md.: Rowman and Littlefield, 2001.

Doyle, Jacqueline. "Haunting the Borderlands: La Llorona in Sandra Cisneros's 'Woman Hollering Creek.'" *Frontiers* 16 (1996): 53–70.

Dubey, Madhu. "Postmodern Geographies of the U.S. South." *Nepantla: Views from South* 3, no. 2 (2002): 351–371.

Dussel, Enrique. *The Invention of the Americas: Eclipse of "the Other" and the Myth Of Modernity*. New York: Continuum, 1995.

Dyck, Reginald. "Frontier Violence in the Garden of America." In *Desert, Garden, Margin, Range: Literature on the American Frontier*, edited by Eric Hayne, 55–69. New York: Twayne, 1992.

Escobar, Arturo. "Culture Sits in Places: Reflections on Globalism and Subaltern Strategies of Localization." *Political Geography* 20, no. 2 (2001): 139–174.

Edwards, Brent Hayes. *The Practice of Diaspora:Literature,Translation, and the Rise of Black Internationalism*. Cambridge, Mass.: Harvard University Press, 2003.

———. "El Plan Espiritual de Aztlán." In *Aztlán: Essays on the Chicano Homeland*, edited by Rudolfo A. Anaya and Francisco Lomelí, 1–5. Albuquerque: University of New Mexico Press, 1989.

Elizondo, Sergio. "ABC: Aztlán, the Borderlands, and Chicago." In *Missions in Conflict: Essays on U.S.-Mexican Relations and Chicano Culture*, edited by Renate von Bardeleben, 13–23. Tübingen: Gunter Narr, 1986.

Ellison, Ralph. "Harlem Is Nowhere." In *Shadow and Act*, 294–302. New York: Random House, 1964.

Estévez, Sandra María. "Here." In *Latino Boom: An Anthology of Latino Literature*, edited by John S. Christie and José B. Gonzalez, 362–363. New York: Pearson/Longman, 2005.

Ettin, Andrew V. *Literature and the Pastoral*. New Haven: Yale University Press, 1984.

Evans, Brad. "Howellsian Chic: The Local Color of Cosmopolitanism." *ELH* 71, no. 3 (2004) 775–812.

Falcón, Angelo. "De'tras Pa'lante: The Future of the History of Puerto Ricans in New York City." January 2001. Institute for Puerto Rican Policy. Puerto Rican Legal and Education Fund. http: prldef.org/lib/Policy_Library.htm (accessed 30 April 2005).

Falcón, Rafael. *La enmigración a Nueva York en la novela puertorriqueña*. Valencia: Ediciones Albatros Hispanófila, 1983.

Fanon, Frantz. *The Wretched of the Earth*. Translated by Constance Farrington. New York: Grove, 1968.

Fetterley, Judith. "*My Ántonia*, Jim Burden and the Dilemma of the Lesbian Writer." In *Gender Studies: New Directions in Feminist Criticism*, edited by Judith Spector, 43–59. Bowling Green: Bowling Green State University Popular Press, 1986.

———, and Marjorie Pryse. *Writing Out of Place: Regionalism, Women, and American Literary Culture*. Champaign: University of Illinois Press, 2003.

Fischer, Mike. "Pastoralism and Its Discontents: Willa Cather and the Burden of Imperialism." *Mosaic* 23 (Winter 1990): 31–44.

Fisher, Philip. *Hard Facts: Setting and Form in the American Novel*. New York: Oxford University Press, 1985.

Fisher Fishkin, Shelley. "Crossroads of Cultures: The Transnational Turn in American Studies—Presidential Address to the American Studies Association, November 12, 2004." *American Quarterly* 57, no. 1 (2005): 17–57.

Fiol-Matta, Liza. "Beyond Survival: A Politics/Poetics of Puerto Rican Consciousness." In *Telling To Live: Latina Feminist Testimonios*, edited by the Latina Feminist Group, 148–155. Durham, N.C.: Duke University Press, 2001.

Flores, Juan. *Divided Borders: Essays on Puerto Rican Identity*. Houston, Texas: Arte Público, 1993.

———. *From Bomba to Hip-Hop: Puerto Rican Culture and Latino Identity*. New York: Columbia University Press, 2000.

———."Puerto Rican Literature: Stages and Perspectives." *ADE Bulletin* 91 (1988): 39–44. Http://www.mla.org/ade/bulletin/n091/091039.htm. (accessed 9 September 2004).

Flores, Richard R. "Memory-Place, Meaning, and the Alamo." *American Literary History* 10 (1998): 428–445.

Foner, Nancy. "What's New About Transnationalism? New York Immigrants Today and at the Turn of the Century." *Diaspora* 6, no. 3 (1997): 355–376.

Fonrobert, Charlotte Elisheva, and Vered Shemtov. "Introduction: Jewish Conceptions and Practices of Space." *Jewish Social Studies* 11, no. 3 (2005): 1–8.

Foote, Stephanie. *Regional Fictions: Culture and Identity in Nineteenth-Century American Literature*. Madison: University of Wisconsin Press, 2001.

Foucault, Michel. *The Birth of the Clinic: An Archaeology of Medical Perception*. Translated by A. M. Sheridan Smith. New York: Pantheon Books, 1973.

———. *Discipline and Punish: The Birth of the Prison*. New York: Vintage, 1977.

———. "The Eye of Power." With Jean-Pierre Baron and Michelle Perrot. In *Power / Knowledge: Selected Interviews and Other Writings, 1972–1977*, 146–165. New York: Pantheon, 1980.

———. *The History of Sexuality. Volume 1: An Introduction*. Trans. Robert Hurley. New York: Vintage, 1990.

———. "Of Other Spaces." *Diacritics* 16 (1986): 22–28.

———. "Questions on Geography." In *Power / Knowledge: Selected Interviews and Other Writings, 1972–1977*, 63–77. New York: Pantheon, 1980.

———. "Two Lectures." In *Power / Knowledge: Selected Interviews and Other Writings, 1972–1977*, 78–107. New York: Pantheon, 1980.

Fox, Claire. "Site-Specificity, Art, and the U.S.-Mexico Frontier." *Social Text* 41 (1994): 61–82.

Franco, Dean J. *Ethnic American Literature: Comparing Chicano, Jewish, and African American Writing*. Charlottesville: University of Virginia Press, 2006.

Freedman, Jonathan. *Klezmer America: Jewishness, Ethnicity, Modernity*. New York: Columbia University Press, 2008.

Fregoso, Rosa Linda. *Mexicana Encounters: The Making of Social Identities on the Borderlands*. Berkeley and Los Angeles: University of California Press, 2003.

Friedman, Paula. "Fiction in Brief: Ordinary Lives Twist, Turn in 'Bodega.'" *Atlanta Journal and Constitution*, 16 April 2000, L12.
Fuchs, Lawrence H. *The American Kaleidoscope: Race, Ethnicity, and the Civic Culture*. Middletown, Conn.: Wesleyan University Press, 1990.
García Canclini, Néstor. *Hybrid Cultures: Strategies for Entering and Leaving Modernity*. Trans. Christopher L. Chiappari and Silvia L. López. Minneapolis: University of Minnesota Press, 1995.
Garland, Hamlin. "Local Color in Art." 1894. In *Crumbling Idols: Twelve Essays on Art Dealing Chiefly with Literature, Painting, and the Drama*, edited by Jane Johnson, 49–55. Cambridge, Mass.: Harvard University Press, 1960.
———. "The Local Novel." In *Crumbling Idols: Twelve Essays on Art Dealing Chiefly with Literature, Painting, and the Drama*, edited by Jane Johnson, 59–65. Cambridge, Mass.: Harvard University Press, 1960.
———. *Main-Travelled Roads*. 1891. New York: Harper, 1899.
Geertz, Clifford. *Local Knowledge: Further Essays in Interpretive Anthropology*. New York: Basic Books, 1983.
Gelfant, Blanche. "Self-Reflexivity in *My Ántonia*." In *Approaches to Teaching Cather's My Ántonia*, edited by Susan J. Rosowski, 126–133. New York: Modern Language Association of America, 1989.
Genette, Gerard. *Paratexts: Thresholds of Interpretation*. Translated by Jane E. Lewin. Cambridge: Cambridge University Press, 1997.
Gilman, Sander. *The Jew's Body*. New York: Routledge, 1991.
Gilroy, Paul. *The Black Atlantic: Modernity and Double Consciousness*. Cambridge, Mass.: Harvard University Press, 1993.
———. "Diaspora." *Paragraph* 17, no. 1 (1994): 207–212.
Goldberg, David Theo. *Racist Culture: Philosophy and the Politics of Meaning*. Malden, Mass.: Blackwell, 1993.
Gómez-Peña, Guillermo. *The New World Border: Prophecies, Poems, and Loqueras for the End of the Century*. San Francisco, Calif.: City Lights, 1996.
———. *Warrior for Gringostroika: Essays, Performance Texts, and Poetry*. St. Paul, Minn.: Graywolf, 1993.
González, Gilbert G., and Raul A. Fernández. *A Century of Chicano History: Empire, Nations, and Migration*. New York: Routledge, 2003.
Gopinath, Gayatri. *Impossible Desires: Queer Diaspora and South Asian Public Cultures*. Durham, N.C.: Duke University Press, 2005.
Gordon, Milton. *Assimilation in American Life: The Role of Race, Religion and National Origins*. New York: Oxford University Press, 1964.
Gossett, Thomas F. *Race: The History of an Idea in America*. 1963. New York: Oxford University Press, 1997.
Griswold, Richard del Castillo, and Arnaldo De León. *North to Aztlán: A History of Mexican-Americans in the United States*. New York: Twayne, 1996.
Grosfoguel, Ramón. "The Epistemic Decolonial Turn: Beyond Political-Economy Paradigms." *Cultural Studies* 21, nos. 2–3 (2007): 211–223.
Grosfoguel, Ramón, and Chloe K. Georas. "'Coloniality of Power' and Racial Dy-

namics: Notes Toward a Reinterpretation of Latino Caribbeans in New York City." *Identities* 7, no. 1 (2000): 85–125.

Grosfoguel, Ramón, Nelson Maldonado-Torres, and José David Saldívar. "Latin@s and the Euro-American Menace." In *Latin@s in the World-System: Decolonization Struggles in the Twenty-First Century U.S. Empire*, edited by Ramon Grosfoguel, Nelson Maldonado-Torres, and Jose David Saldívar, 3–23. Boulder, Colo.: Paradigm, 2005.

Gupta, Akhil, and James Ferguson. "Beyond Culture: Space, Identity, and the Politics of Difference." *Cultural Anthropology* 7 (1992): 6–23.

Gutiérrez, David G. "Significant to Whom? Mexican Americans and the History of the American West." *Western Historical Quarterly* 24, no. 4 (1993): 519–539.

Gutiérrez-Jones, Carl. "Desiring Borders." *diacritics* 25, no. 1 (March 1995): 99–112.

———. "Humor, Literacy and Chicano Culture." *Comparative Literature Studies* 40, no. 2 (2003): 112–126.

———. *Rethinking the Borderlands: Between Chicano Culture and Legal Discourse.* Berkeley and Los Angeles: University of California Press, 1995.

Gutiérrez, Ramón. "Internal Colonialism: An American Theory of Race," *Du Bois Review* 1, no. 2 (2004): 281–295.

Haenni, Sabine. "Visual and Theatrical Culture, Tenement Fiction, and the Immigrant Subject in Abraham Cahan's *Yekl*." *American Literature* 71, no. 3 (1999): 493–527.

Halbwachs, Maurice. *The Collective Memory*. Translated by Francis J. Ditter, Jr., and Vida Y. Ditter. New York: Harper, 1980.

Hall, Stuart. "Cultural Identity and Diaspora." In *Identity: Community, Culture, Difference*, edited by Jonathan Rutherford, 222–237. London: Lawrence and Wishart, 1990.

———. "The Local and the Global: Globalization and Ethnicity." In *Culture, Globalization, and the World-System: Contemporary Conditions for the Representation of Identity*, edited by Anthony D. King, 19–39. Binghamton, N.Y.: Department of Art and Art History, State University of New York at Binghamton, 1991.

———. "Notes on Deconstructing the Popular." In *People's History and Socialist Theory*, edited by Raphael Samuel, 227–240. London: Routledge and Kegan Paul, 1981.

Hames-García, Michael. *Fugitive Thought: Prison Movements, Race, and the Meaning of Justice*. Minneapolis: University of Minnesota Press, 2004.

Halttunen, Karen. "Groundwork: American Studies in Place—Presidential Address to the American Studies Association, November 4, 2005." *American Quarterly* 58, no. 1 (2006): 1–15.

Handley, William R. *Marriage, Violence, and the Nation in the American Literary West.* Cambridge: Cambridge University Press, 2002.

Harap, Louis. *The Image of the Jew in American Literature: From Early Republic to Mass Immigration*. Philadelphia: Jewish Publication Society, 1975.

Harlow, Barbara. *Resistance Literature*. New York: Methuen, 1987.

Harshav, Benjamin. *Language in Time of Revolution*. Berkeley and Los Angeles: University of California Press, 1993.

Hart, John Mason. *Empire and Revolution: The Americans in Mexico Since the Civil War*. Berkeley and Los Angeles: University of California Press, 2002.

Harvey, David. *The Condition of Postmodernity: An Enquiry into the Origins of Cultural Change*. Oxford: Blackwell, 1989.

Heidegger, Martin. "Building/Dwelling/Thinking." In *Basic Writings*, 319–340. New York: Harper and Row, 1977.

Hernández, Carmen Dolores. *Puerto Rican Voices in English: Interviews with Writers*. Westport, Conn.: Praeger, 1997.

Hester Street. Directed by Joan Micklin Silver. Midwest Film Productions, 1974.

Hicks, Emily. *Border Writing: The Multidimensional Text*. Minneapolis: University of Minnesota Press, 1991.

Hicks, Granville. "The Case Against Willa Cather." *English Journal* 22, no. 9 (November 1933): 703–710. Reprinted in *Willa Cather and Her Critics*, edited by James Schroeter, 139–147. Ithaca, New York: Cornell University Press, 1967.

Higham, John. *Send These to Me: Jews and Other Immigrants in Urban America*. New York: Atheneum, 1975.

———. *Strangers in the Land: Patterns of American Nativism, 1860–1925*. New York: Atheneum, 1971.

Hill, Jane. "Language, Race, and White Public Space." *American Anthropologist* 100, no. 3 (1998): 680–689.

Hirsch, Marianne. "Projected Memory: Holocaust Photographs in Personal and Public Fantasy." In *Acts of Memory: Cultural Recall in the Present*, edited by Mieke Bal, Jonathan Crewe, and Leo Spitzer, 3–23. Hanover, N.H.: Dartmouth College / University Press of New England, 1999.

Hobsbawm, Eric. *Nations and Nationalism Since 1780: Programme, Myth, Reality*. New York: Cambridge University Press, 1992.

Hofstadter, Richard. *The Age of Reform: From Bryan to F.D.R.* New York: Random House, 1955.

Horsman, Reginald. *Race and Manifest Destiny: The Origins of American Racial Anglo-Saxonism*. Cambridge, Mass: Harvard University Press, 1981.

Howard, June. "Unraveling Regions, Unsettling Periods: Sarah Orne Jewett and American Literary History." *American Literature* 68 (1996): 365–384.

Howe, Irving. *World of Our Fathers*. New York: Simon and Schuster, 1976.

Howells, William Dean. *Criticism and Fiction and Other Essays*. New York: New York University Press, 1959.

———."New York Low Life in Fiction." *World* 1896. Partially reprinted in *American Jewish Historical Quarterly* 52 (1962): 51–52.

Hu-DeHart, Evelyn. "Concluding Commentary: On Migration, Diasporas, and Transnationalism in Asian American History." *Journal of Asian American Studies* 8, no. 3 (2005): 309–312.

Hsu, Hsuan L. "Literature and Regional Production." *American Literary History* 17, no. 1 (2005): 36–69.

Irving, Katrina. "Displacing Homosexuality: The Use of Ethnicity in Willa Cather's *My Ántonia*." *Modern Fiction Studies* 36 (1990): 91–102.

Islas, Arturo. *The Rain God: A Desert Tale*. New York: Avon, 1984.

Jacobs, Jane. *The Death and Life of Great American Cities*. 1972. New York: Random House, 2002.

Jacobson, David. *Place and Belonging in America*. Baltimore, Md.: Johns Hopkins University Press, 2002.

Jacobson, Matthew Frye. *Barbarian Virtues: The United States Encounters Foreign Peoples at Home and Abroad, 1876–1917*. New York: Hill and Wang, 2000.

———. *Special Sorrows: The Diasporic Imagination of Irish, Polish, and Jewish Immigrants in the United States*. Cambridge, Mass.: Harvard University Press, 1995.

———. *Whiteness of a Different Color: European Immigrants and the Alchemy of Race*. Cambridge, Mass.: Harvard University Press, 1998.

Jaher, Frederick C., ed. *The Age of Industrialism in America: Essays in Social Structures and Cultural Values*. New York: Free Press, 1968.

James, Henry. *The American Scene*. 1907. New York, Penguin, 1994.

———. *"The Question of Our Speech" and "The Lesson of Balzac": Two Lectures*. 1905. New York: Haskell House, 1972.

Janowitz, Morris. *The Reconstruction of Patriotism: Education for Civic Consciousness*. Chicago: University of Chicago Press, 1983.

Jewett, Sarah Orne. *The Country of Pointed Firs and Other Stories*. 1896. New York: Norton, 1982.

Johnson, Rhonda. "Book Capsule Review: *Bodega Dreams*. *EW.COM*. 3 May 2000. Http://www.ew.com/ew/article/0,,64671,00.html (accessed 20 November 2007).

Jones, Gavin. *Strange Talk: The Politics of Dialect Literature in Gilded Age America*. Berkeley and Los Angeles: University of California Press, 1999.

Jones, Howard Mumford. *The Age of Energy: Varieties of American Experience, 1865–1915*. New York: Viking, 1971.

———. *O Strange New World: American Culture: The Formative Years*. 1952. New York: Viking, 1967.

Kallen, Horace M. *Culture and Democracy in the United States*. New York: Boni and Liveright, 1924.

———. "Democracy *versus* the Melting Pot: A Study of American Nationality." *The Nation* (18 and 25 February 1915): 190–194 and 217–220.

Kammen, Michael. *Mystic Chords of Memory: The Transformation of Tradition In American Culture*. New York: Knopf, 1991.

Kaplan, Amy. "Homeland Insecurities: Reflections on Language and Space." *Radical History Review* 85 (2003): 82–93.

———. "Left Alone with America." In *Cultures of U.S. Imperialism*, edited by Amy Kaplan and Donald Pease, 3–21. Durham, N.C.: Duke University Press, 1993.

———. "Nation, Region, and Empire." *Columbia History of the American Novel: New Views*, edited by Emory Elliott, 240–266. New York: Columbia University Press, 1991.

Kaplan, Caren. *Questions of Travel: Postmodern Discourses of Displacement*. Durham, N.C.: Duke University Press, 1996.

Katrak, Ketu H. "South Asian American Literature." In *An Interethnic Companion to*

Asian American Literature, edited by King Kok Cheung, 192–218. New York: Cambridge University Press, 1997.

Kaup, Monika. "Reterritorializing the Border in Chicano/a Fiction." *Amerikastudien* 39 (1994): 579–596.

Kern, Stephen. *The Culture of Time and Space, 1880–1918*. Cambridge, Mass.: Harvard University Press, 1983.

Klein, Norman. *The History of Forgetting: Los Angeles and the Erasure of Memory.* New York: Verso, 1998.

Klor de Alva, J. Jorge. "Aztlán." In *Dictionary of Mexican American History*, edited by Matt S. Meier and Feliciano Rivera. Westport, Conn.: Greenwood, 1981.

Kolodny, Annette. *The Land before Her: Fantasy and Experience of the American Frontiers, 1630–1860*. Chapel Hill: University of North Carolina Press, 1984.

Kowalewski, Michael. Introduction to *Reading the West: New Essays on the Literature of the American West*, edited by Michael Kowalewski, 1–20. New York: Cambridge University Press, 1996.

———. "Writing in Place: The New American Regionalism." *American Literary History* 6 (1994): 171–183.

Kugelmass, Jack. "Turfing the Slum." In *Remembering the Lower East Side: American Jewish Reflections*, edited by Hasia Dinar, Jeffrey Shandler, and Beth S. Wegner, 179–211. Bloomington: Indiana University Press, 2000.

Láo-Montes, Augustín. "Niuyol: Urban Regime, Latino Social Movements, Ideologies of Latinidad." In *Mambo Montage: The Latinization of New York*, edited byAugustín Láo-Montes and Arlene Dávila, 118–157. New York: Columbia University Press, 2001.

Larsen, Neil. Foreword to *Border Writing: The Multidimensional Text*, by D. Emily Hicks, xi–xxiii. Minneapolis: University of Minnesota Press, 1991.

Lavie, Smadar, and Ted Swedenburg. Introduction to *Displacement, Diaspora, and Geographies of Identity*, edited by Smadar Lavie and Ted Swedenburg, 1–25. Durham, N.C.: Duke University Press, 1996.

Laviera, Tato. *AmeRícan*. Houston, Texas: Arte Público, 1985.

———. *La Carreta Made a U-Turn*. Houston, Texas: Arte Público. 1992.

Lawrence, D. H. *Studies in Classic American Literature*. 1923. London: Penguin, 1971.

Leach, William. *Country of Exiles: The Destruction of Place in American Life*. New York: Vintage, 1999.

Leal, Luis. "In Search of Aztlán." Translated by Gladys Leal. In *Aztlán: Essays on the Chicano Homeland*, edited by Rudolfo A. Anaya and Francisco Lomelf, 6–13. Albuquerque: University of New Mexico Press, 1989.

Lears, T. J. Jackson. *No Place of Grace: Antimodernism and the Transformation of American Culture, 1880–1920*. New York: Pantheon, 1981.

Lee, Hermione. *Willa Cather: Double Lives*. New York: Pantheon, 1989.

Lefebvre, Henri. *The Production of Space*. 1974. Translated by Donald Nicholson-Smith. Oxford: Blackwell, 1991.

Levine, Etan. "The Jews in Time and Space." In *Diaspora: Exile and the Jewish Condition*, edited by Etan Levine, 1–11. New York: Jason Aronson, 1983.

Lewis, Earl. "To Turn on a Pivot: Writing African Americans into a History of Overlapping Diasporas." *American Historical Review* 100, no. 3 (1995): 765–787.

Lewis, Oscar. *La Vida: A Puerto Rican Family in the Culture of Poverty—San Juan and New York*. New York: Random House, 1966.

Lewis, R. W. B. *The American Adam: Innocence, Tragedy, and Tradition in the Nineteenth Century*. Chicago: University of Chicago Press, 1955.

Limerick, Patricia. "The Adventures of the Frontier in the Twentieth Century." In *The Frontier in American Culture: Essays by Richard White and Patricia Nelson Limerick*, edited by James Grossman, 67–102. Berkeley and Los Angeles: University of California Press, 1994.

Limón, José E. *Mexican Ballads, Chicano Poems: History and Influence in Mexican-American Social Poetry*. Berkeley and Los Angeles: University of California Press, 1992.

Lindemann, Marilee. *Willa Cather: Queering America*. New York: Columbia University Press, 1999.

Liu, Alan. "Local Transcendence: Cultural Criticism, Postmodernism, and the Romanticism of Detail." *Representations* 32 (1990): 75–113.

Luebke, Friedrich. "Regionalism and the Great Plains: Problems of Concept and Method." *Western Historical Quarterly* 15 (1984): 19–38.

Lutz, Tom. *American Nervousness, 1903: An Anecdotal History*. Ithaca, N.Y.: Cornell University Press, 1991.

———. *Cosmopolitan Vistas: American Regionalism and Literary Value*. Ithaca, N.Y.: Cornell University Press, 2004.

Lyotard, Jean-François. *The Postmodern Condition: A Report on Knowledge*. Translated by Geoffrey Bennington and Brian Massumi. Minneapolis: University of Minnesota Press, 1984.

Mann, Arthur. *The One and the Many: Reflections on the American Identity*. Chicago: University of Chicago Press, 1979.

Marable, Manning. "The Problematics of Ethnic Studies." In *Color-Line to Borderlands: The Matrix of American Ethnic Studies*, edited by Johanella E. Butler, 42–64. Seattle: University of Washington Press, 2001.

Marcus, Sharon. "Same Difference? Transnationalism, Comparative Literature, and Victorian Studies." *Victorian Studies* 45, no. 4 (2003): 677–686.

Mariposa [María Teresa Fernández], "Ode to the DiaspoRican." *Centro: Journal of the Center for Puerto Rican Studies* 12, no. 1 (2000): 66.

Martin, Richard. *Mean Streets and Raging Bulls: The Legacy of Film Noir in Contemporary American Cinema*. Lanham, Md: Scarecrow, 1999.

Martin, Wendy. "'Remembering the Jungle': Josephine Baker and Modernist Parody." In *Prehistories of the Future: The Primitivist Project and the Culture of Modernim*, edited by Elazar Barkan and Ronald Bush, 310–325. Stanford, Calif.: Stanford University Press, 1995.

Martín-Barbero, Jesús. *Communication, Culture, and Hegemony: From the Media to Mediations*. Translated by Elizabeth Fox and Robert A. White. With an introduction by Philip Schlesinger. Newbury Park, Calif.: Sage, 1993.

Marx, Leo. *The Machine in the Garden: Technology and the Pastoral Ideal in America.* New York: Oxford University Press, 1964.
Massey, Doreen. "Geographies of Responsibility." *Geografiska Annaler* 86, no. 1 (2004): 5–18.
———. "A Global Sense of Place." In her *Space, Place, and Gender*, 146–156. London: Polity Press, 1994.
———. "A Place Called Home?" *New Formations* 17 (1992): 3–15.
Massey, Douglas. "Ethnic Residential Segregation: A Theoretical Synthesis and Empirical Review." *Sociology and Social Research* 69 (1985): 315–350.
Massey, Douglas A., and Nancy A. Denton. *American Apartheid: Segregation and the Making of the American Underclass.* Cambridge, Mass.: Harvard University Press, 1993.
Mazlish, Bruce. *Civilization and Its Contents.* Stanford: Stanford University Press, 2004.
McBride, Paul. *Culture Clash: Immigrants and Reformers, 1880–1920.* San Francisco, Calif.: Rand, 1975.
McKenna, Teresa. *Migrant Song: Politics and Process in Contemporary Chicano Literature.* Austin: University of Texas Press, 1997.
Mendoza, Louis. "The Border Between Us: Contact Zone or Battle Zone?" *Modern Fiction Studies* 40, no.1 (1994): 120–139.
Michaels, Walter Benn. "Anti-Imperial Americanism." In *Cultures of United States Imperialism*, edited by Amy Kaplan and Donald E. Pease, 365–391. Durham, N.C.: Duke University Press, 1993.
———. *Our America: Nativism, Modernism, and Pluralism.* Durham, N.C.: Duke University Press, 1995.
Michasiw, Kim Ian. "Nine Revisionist Theses on the Picturesque." *Representations* 38 (1992): 76–100.
Mignolo, Walter. *Local Histories, Global Designs: Coloniality, Subaltern Knowledges, and Border Thinking.* Princeton, N.J.: Princeton University Press, 2000.
———, and Madina Tlostanova. "The Logic of Coloniality and the Limits of Postcoloniality." In *The Postcolonial and the Global: Connections, Conflicts, Complicities*, edited by John Hawley and Revathi Krishnaswamy, 109–123. Minneapolis: University of Minnesota Press, 2007.
Mora, Pat. *Borders.* Houston, Texas: Arte Público, 1986.
Moraga, Cherríe. *The Last Generation: Prose and Poetry.* Boston: South End, 1993.
Morales, Rosario, and Aurora Levins Morales. *Getting Home Alive.* Boston: South End, 1984.
Morrison, Toni. "City Limits, Village Values: Concepts of the Neighborhood in Black Fiction." In *Literature and the Urban Experience: Essays on the City and Literature*, edited by Michael C. Jaye and Ann Chalmers Watts, 35–43. New Brunswick, N.J.: Rutgers University Press, 1981.
Mumford, Lewis. *Technics and Civilization.* 1934. New York: Harvest/HBJ, 1963.
Muñoz, Carlos. *Youth, Identity and Power.* New York: Verso, 1989.
Murphy, John J. "A Comprehensive View of Willa Cather's *O Pioneers!*" In *Critical Es-*

says on Willa Cather, edited by John J. Murphy, 113–127. Boston: G. K. Hall, 1984.

Naficy, Hamid. *An Accented Cinema: Exilic and Diasporic Filmmaking*. Princeton, N.J.: Princeton University Press, 2001.

Nancy, Jean-Luc. "Cut Throat Sun." In *An Other Tongue: Nation and Ethnicity in the Linguistic Borderlands*, edited by Alfred Arteaga, 113–124. Durham, N.C.: Duke University Press, 1994.

Naremore, James. *More Than Night: Film Noir in Its Contexts*. Berkeley and Los Angeles: University of California Press, 1998.

Nash, Roderick. *Wilderness and the American Mind*. New Haven, Conn.: Yale University Press, 1973.

Natter, Wolfgang, and John Paul Jones III. "Signposts Toward a Poststructuralist Geography." In *Postmodern Contentions: Epochs, Politics, Space*, edited by John Paul Jones III, Wolfgang Natter, and Theodore Schatzki, 165–204. New York: Guilford Press, 1993.

Navarro, Mireya. "Puerto Rican Presence Wanes in New York" ("Falling Back: A Special Report" series). *New York Times*, 28 February 2000, 1 and B7.

Nealon, Christopher. "Affect-Genealogy: Feeling and Affiliation in Willa Cather." *American Literature* 69 (1997): 5–37.

Negrón-Muntaner, Frances. "Feeling Pretty: West Side Story and Puerto Rican Identity Discourses." *Social Text* 18, no. 2 (2000): 83–106.

Nettels, Elsa. *Language, Race, and Social Class in Howells's America*. Lexington: University Press of Kentucky, 1988.

Nora, Pierre. *Les lieux de mémoire*. Paris: Gallimard, 1984.

Nordau, Max. "Jewry of Muscle." 1903. In *The Jew in the Modern World: A Documentary History*, edited by Paul R. Mendes-Flohr and Jehuda Reinharz, 434–435. New York: Oxford University Press, 1980.

Noriega, Jorge. "American Indian Education in the United States: Indoctrination for Subordination to Colonialism." In *The State of Native America: Genocide, Colonization, and Resistance. Boston*, edited by M. Annette Jaimes, 371–402. Boston: South End Press, 1972.

O'Brien, Sharon. "Becoming Noncanonical: The Case Against Willa Cather." In *Reading in America: Literature and Social History*, edited by Cathy N. Davidson, 240–258. Baltimore, Md.: Johns Hopkins University Press, 1989.

———. *Willa Cather: The Emerging Voice*. New York: Oxford University Press, 1987.

Olguín, B. V. "Sangre Mexicana / Corazón Americano: Identity, Ambiguity, and Critique in Mexican-American War Narratives." *American Literary History* 14, no. 1 (2002): 83–114.

Pease, Donald. "US Imperialism: Global Dominance without Colonies." In *A Companion to Postcolonial Studies*, edited by Henry Schwartz and Sangeeta Ray, 203–220. Malden, Mass.: Blackwell, 2000.

Peña, Devon, and Laura Pulido. "Environmentalism and Positionality: The Early Pesticide Campaign of the United Farm Workers' Organizing Committee, 1965–1971." *Race, Gender, and Class* 6, no. 1 (1998): 33–50.

Pérez, Emma. *Decolonial Imaginary: Writing Chicanas Into History*. Bloomington: Indiana University Press, 1999.

Pérez-Torres, Rafael. *Movements in Chicano Poetry: Against Myths, Against Margins*. New York: Cambridge University Press, 1995.

———. "Refiguring Aztlán." *Aztlán: A Journal of Chicano Studies* 22 (1997): 15–41.

Petry, Ann. *The Street*. 1946. Boston: Houghton Mifflin, 1991.

Philadelphia, Desa. "Moving Up." *Time* (27 March 2000). Http://www.time.com/time/magazine/article/0,9171,996458,00.html (accessed 28 November 2007).

Pietri, Pedro. *Puerto Rican Obituary*. New York: Monthly Review, 1973.

Pile, Stephen, and David Keith. *Place and the Politics of Identity*. New York: Routledge, 1993.

Piñero, Miguel. *La Bodega Sold Dreams*. Houston, Texas: Arte Público, 1980.

Porter, Carolyn. "'What We Know That We Don't Know': Remapping American Literary Studies." *American Literary History* 6 (1994): 466–526.

Portillo Trambley, Estela. *The Day of Swallows. Contemporary Chicano Theater*, edited by Roberto J. Garza. Notre Dame: University of Notre Dame Press, 1976.

———. "Rain of Scorpions." 1975. In *Rain of Scorpions and Other Stories*, 111–169. Rev. ed. Tempe, Ariz.: Bilingual Press, 1993.

———. *Trini*. Binghamton, N.Y.: Bilingual Press / Editorial Bilingüe, 1986.

Prashad, Vijay. "Ethnic Studies Inside Out." *Journal of Asian American Studies* 9, no. 2 (2006): 157–176.

———. *Everybody Was Kung-Fu Fighting: Afro-Asian Connections and the Myth of Cultural Purity*. Boston: Beacon, 2001.

———. *The Karma of Brown Folk*. Minneapolis: University of Minnesota Press, 2000.

Pratt, Mary Louise. *Imperial Eyes: Travel Writing and Transculturation*. New York: Routledge, 1992.

———. "Yo Soy La Malinche: Chicana Writers and the Poetics of Ethnonationalism." *Callalloo* 16 (1993): 859–873.

Probyn, Elspeth. "Travels in the Postmodern: Making Sense of the Local." In *Feminism / Postmodernism*, edited by Linda J. Nicholson, 176–189. New York: Routledge, 1990.

Quijano, Aníbal. "Coloniality of Power, Eurocentrism, Latin America." *Nepantla: Views from South* 1, no. 3 (2000): 533–580.

Quiñonez, Ernesto. *Bodega Dreams*. New York: Vintage, 2000.

Rabinowitz, Paula. *Black and White and Noir: America's Pulp Modernism*. New York: Columbia University Press, 2002.

Radway, Janice."What's in a Name? Presidential Address to the American Studies Association, 20 November, 1998." *American Quarterly* 51 (1999): 1–31.

Ramazani, Jahan. "The Wound of History: Walcott's *Omeros* and the Postcolonial Poetics of Affliction." *PMLA* 112 (1997): 405–417.

Rebolledo, Tey Diana. "Narrative Strategies of Resistance in Hispana Writing." *Journal Of Narrative Technique* 20 (1990): 134–146.

———. "Tradition and Mythology: Signatures of Landscape in Chicana Literature." In *The Desert Is No Lady: Southwestern Landscapes in Women's Writing and Art*, edited by Vera Norwood and Janice Monk, 96–124. New Haven, Conn.: Yale University Press, 1987.

Reed, Ishmael. "The American Literary Scene as a White Settler's Fortress." In *The Art of Literary Publishing: Editors on their Craft,* edited by Bill Henderson, 100–106. New York: Pushcart, 1980.

Reid-Pharr, Robert F. "Tearing the Goat's Flesh: Homosexuality, Abjection and the Production of a Late Twentieth-Century Black Masculinity." *Studies in the Novel* 28, no. 3 (1996): 372–394.

Reynolds, Guy. *Willa Cather in Context: Progress, Race, Empire.* New York: St. Martin's, 1996.

Riis, Jacob A. *How the Other Half Lives: Studies Among the Tenements in New York.* 1890. New York: Hill and Wang, 1957.

Rischlin, Moses. "Toward the Onomastics of the Great New York Ghetto: How the Lower East Side Got Its Name." In *Remembering the Lower East Side: American Jewish Reflections,* edited by Hasia Diner, Jeffrey Shandler, and Beth S. Wenger, 13–27. Bloomington: Indiana University Press, 2000.

Rivera, Tomás. *. . . y no se lo tragó la tierra.* 1971. Houston, Texas: Arte Público, 1987.

Robins, Kevin. "Prisoners of the City: Whatever Could a Postmodern City Be?" In *Space and Place: Theories of Identity and Location,* edited by Erica Carter, James Donald, and Judith Squires, 303–330. London: Lawrence and Wishart, 1993.

Robinson, Sidney K. *Inquiry into the Picturesque.* Chicago: University of Chicago Press, 1991.

Rock, Howard B., and Deborah Dash Moore. *Cityscapes: A History of New York in Images.* With the assistance of David Lobenstine. New York: Columbia University Press, 2001.

Rodríguez, Ana Patricia. "Refugees of the South: Central Americans in the U.S. Latino Imaginary." *American Literary History* 73, no. 2 (2001): 387–412.

Roediger, David R. "Whiteness and Ethnicity in the History of 'White Ethnics' in the United States." In his *Towards the Abolition of Whiteness: Essays on Race, Politics, and Working Class History,* 181–198. New York: Verso, 1994.

Rogin, Michael. "Liberal Society and the Indian Question." In *Politics and Society* 1 (1971). Reprinted in *Ronald Reagan, the Movie, and Other Episodes in Political Demonology,* 134–168. Berkeley and Los Angeles: University of California Press, 1987.

Rölvaag, Oleg. *Giants in the Earth.* New York: Harper and Row, 1929.

Romero, Mary. "The Death of Smeltertown: A Case Study of Lead Poisoning in a Chicano Community." In *The Chicano Struggles: Analyses of Past and Present Efforts,* edited by John García, Juan García, and Teresa Cordova, 26–41. Binghamton, N.Y.: Bilingual Press, 1984. Reprinted in *Chicano Studies: Survey and Analysis,* edited by Dennis Bixler-Marquez, Carlos F. Ortega, Rosalina Solorzano Torres, and Lorenzo LaFarelle, 115–122. Dubuque, Iowa: Kendall/Hunt Publishing, 1997.

Rosaldo, Renato. "Imperialist Nostalgia." *Representations* 26 (1989): 107–122.

———. "Politics, Patriarchs, and Laughter." *Cultural Critique* 6 (1987): 65–86.

Rose, Gillian. *Feminism and Geography: The Limits of Geographical Knowledge.* Minneapolis: University of Minnesota Press, 1993.

Rose, Jacqueline. *States of Fantasy*. Oxford: Clarendon, 1996.

Rosowski, Susan. *The Voyage Perilous: Willa Cather's Romanticism*. Lincoln: University of Nebraska Press, 1986.

Ross, Edward A. *The Old World in the New: The Signification of Past and Present Immigration to the American People*. New York: Century, 1914.

Rotella, Carlo. *October Cities: The Redevelopment of Urban Literature*. Berkeley and Los Angeles: University of California Press, 1998.

Roth, Henry. *Call It Sleep*. With an introduction by Alfred Kazin and a foreword by Hana Wirth-Nesher. New York: Picador, 2005.

Rouse, Roger. "Mexican Migration and the Social Space of Postmodernism." *Diaspora* 1 (1991): 8–23.

Royce, Josiah. *Race Questions, Provincialism, and Other American Problems*. New York: Macmillan, 1908.

Rubin, Louis D., introd. *I'll Take My Stand: The South and the Agrarian Tradition, by Twelve Southerners*. 1930. With biographical essays by Virginia Peck. Baton Rouge: Louisiana State University Press, 1997.

Ryan, Melissa. "The Enclosure of America: Civilization and Confinement in Willa Cather's *O Pioneers!*" *American Literature* 75, no. 2 (2003): 275–303.

Safran, William. "Diasporas in Modern Societies: Myths of Homeland and Return." *Diaspora* 1, no. 1 (1991): 83–99.

Saldívar, José David. "Américo Paredes and Decolonization." In *Cultures of United States Imperialism*, edited by Amy Kaplan and Donald Pease, 292–311. Durham, N.C.: Duke University Press, 1993.

———. *Border Matters: Remapping American Cultural Studies*. Berkeley and Los Angeles: University of California Press, 1997.

———. *The Dialectics of Our America: Genealogy, Cultural Critique, and Literary History*. Durham, N.C.: Duke University Press, 1991.

———. "Unsettling Race, Coloniality, and Caste: Anzaldúa's *Borderlands / La Frontera*, Martínez's *Parrot in the Oven* and Roy's *The God of Small Things*." *Cultural Studies* 21, no. 2–3 (2007): 339–367.

Saldívar, Ramón. *Chicano Narrative: The Dialectics of Difference*. Madison: University of Wisconsin Press, 1990.

Saldívar-Hull, Sonia. *Feminism on the Border: Chicana Gender Politics and Literature*. Berkeley and Los Angeles: University of California Press, 2000.

Sánchez, Marta E. *"Shakin' Up" Race and Gender: Intercultural Connections in Puerto Rican, African American, and Chicano Narratives and Culture*. Austin: University of Texas Press, 2005.

Sánchez González, Lisa. *Boricua Literature: A Literary History of the Puerto Rican Diaspora*. New York: New York University Press, 2001.

Sánchez Korrol, Virginia. *From Colonia to Community: A History of Puerto Ricans in New York*. Berkeley and Los Angeles: University of California Press, 1995.

Sanders, Ronald. *The Downtown Jews: Portraits of an Immigrant Generation*. New York: New American Library, 1977.

———. "Puerto Rican Identity Up in the Air: Air Migration, Its Cultural Representations, and Me 'Cruzando El Charco.'" In *Puerto Rican Jam: Rethinking Colonial-*

ism and Nationalism, edited by Frances Negrón-Muntaner and Ramón Grosfoguel, 189–208. Minneapolis: University of Minnesota Press, 1997.

Sandoval-Sánchez, Alberto. "*West Side Story*: A Puerto Rican Reading of 'America.'" *Jump Cut* 39 (1994): 59–66.

Sante, Luc. *Low Life: Lures and Snares of Old New York*. New York: Vintage, 1992.

Saragoza, Alex M. "Recent Chicano Historiography: An Interpretive Essay." *Aztlán: A Journal of Chicano Studies* 19 (1988–90): 1–52.

Schivelbusch, Wolfgang. *The Railway Journey: The Industrialization of Time and Space in the 19th Century*. Berkeley and Los Angeles: University of California Press, 1986.

Schroeter, James, ed. *Willa Cather and Her Critics*. Ithaca, N.Y.: Cornell University Press, 1967.

Schulten, Susan. *The Geographical Imagination in America, 1880–1950*. Chicago: University of Chicago Press, 2001.

Sedgwick, Eve Kosofsky. "Across Genders, Across Sexualities: Willa Cather and Others." *South Atlantic Quarterly* 88 (1989): 53–72.

Seguín, Juan Nepomuceno. *A Revolution Remembered: The Memoirs and Selected Correspondence of Juan N. Seguín*. Edited by Jesús de la Tela. Austin, Texas: State House, 1991.

Seigel, Micol. "Beyond Compare: Comparative Method After the Transnational Turn." *Radical History Review* 91 (2005): 62–90.

Sennett, Richard. "Something in the City: The Spectre of Uselessness and the Search for a Place in the World." *Times Literary Supplement*, 22 September 1995, 13–14.

Seyhan, Azade. *Writing Outside the Nation*. Princeton, N.J.: Princeton University Press, 2000.

Shankar, Lavina Dhingra and Rajini Srikanth, eds. *A Part, Yet Apart : South Asians in Asian America*. Philadelphia : Temple University Press, 1998.

Sheehan, Bernard W. *Seeds of Extinction: Jeffersonian Philanthropy and the American Indian*. New York: Norton, 1973.

Singh, Amritjit, and Peter Schmidt. "On the Borders Between U.S. Studies and Postcolonial Theory." In *Postcolonial Theory and the United States: Race, Ethnicity, and Literature*, edited by Amritjit Singh and Peter Schmidt, 3–69. Jackson: University Press of Mississippi, 2000.

Singh, Nikhil Pal. "Culture/Wars: Recoding Empire in an Age of Democracy." *American Quarterly* 50, no. 3 (1998): 471–522.

Slotkin, Richard. *Gunfighter Nation: The Myth of the Frontier in Twentieth-Century America*. New York: Atheneum, 1992.

Smith, Anthony D. *National Identity*. London: Penguin, 1991.

Smith, Henry Nash. *Virgin Land: The American West as Symbol and Myth*. New York: Vintage, 1950.

Snipps, Matthew C. "The Changing Political and Economic Status of the American Indians: From Captive Nations to Internal Colonies." *American Journal of Economics and Sociology* 45, no. 2 (1986): 145–157.

Soja, Edward J. *Postmodern Geographies: The Reassertion of Space in Critical Social Theory*. New York: Verso, 1989.

———. *Thirdspace: Journeys to Los Angeles and other Real-and-Imagined Places*. Cambridge, Mass.: Blackwell, 1996.

Sollors, Werner. *Beyond Ethnicity: Consent and Descent in American Culture*. New York: Oxford University Press, 1986.

Sorkin, Michael. "Introduction: Traffic in Democracy." In *Giving Ground: The Politics of Propinquity*, edited by Joan Copjec and Michael Sorkin, 1–15. New York: Verso, 1999.

Soysal, Yasemin Nuhoglu. "Citizenship and Identity: Living in Diasporas in Postwar Europe?" *Ethnic and Racial Studies* 23, no. 1 (2000): 1–15.

Spencer, Benjamin T. "Regionalism in American Literature." In *Regionalism in America*, edited by Merrill Jensen, 219–260. Madison: University of Wisconsin Press, 1965.

Spivak, Gayatri. *Death of a Discipline*. New York: Columbia University Press, 2003.

Stegner, Wallace. *The American Novel: From James Fenimore Cooper to William Faulkner*. New York: Basic, 1955.

Steinberg, Sybil. "Forecasts: Fiction. " *Publishers Weekly*, 17 January 2000, 42.

Stouck, David. "*My Ántonia* as Pastoral." In *Approaches to Teaching Willa Cather's My Ántonia*, edited by Susan J. Rosowski, 53–57. New York: Modern Language Association of America, 1989.

Sundquist, Eric, ed. and introd. *The Marrow of Tradition*. By Charles W. Chestnutt. New York: Penguin Books, 1993.

Swift, John N. "Willa Cather's *My Ántonia* and the Politics of Modernist Classicism." In *Narratives of Nostalgia, Gender and Nationalism*, edited by Jean Pickering and Suzanne Kehde, 107–120. New York: New York University Press, 1997.

Takaki, Ronald. *A Different Mirror: A History of Multicultural America*. Boston: Little, Brown, 1993.

Tatum, Charles. "Introduction: Stasis and Change Along the Rio Grande: Aristeo Brito's *The Devil in Texas*" 1976. In *El diablo en Texas / The Devil in Texas*, translated by David William Foster, 1–19. Tempe, Ariz.: Bilingual Press, 1990.

Thernstrom Stephen, ed. *The Harvard Encyclopedia of American Ethnic Groups*. Cambridge, Mass.: Harvard University Press, 1980.

Thomas, Piri. *Down These Mean Streets*. 1967. New York: Vintage, 1997.

Thrift, Nigel. *Spatial Formations*. London: Sage, 1996.

Tibbetts, John C. "The Small Town." In *The Columbia Companion to American History*, edited by Peter C. Rollins, 457–461. New York: Columbia University Press, 2004.

Tichi, Cecelia. "Women Writers and the New Woman." In *Columbia Literary History of the United States*, edited by Emory Elliot, 589–606. New York: Columbia University Press.

Tiryakian, Edward. "Dialectics of Modernity: Reenchantment and Dedifferentiation as Counterprocess." In *Social Change and Modernity*, edited by Hans Haverkamp and Neil Smelser, 79–90. Berkeley and Los Angeles: University of California Press, 1992.

Toffler, Alvin. *Future Shock*. New York: Random House, 1970.

Tölölyan, Khachig. "Rethinking Diaspora(s): Stateless Power in the Transnational Moment." *Diaspora* 5, no. 1 (1996): 3–36.

Torres, Arlene. "From Jíbara to Anthropologist: Puerto Rican Ethnography and The Politics of Representation." *Identities* 5, no. 1 (1998): 107–122.

Trachtenberg, Alan. "Experiments in Another Country: Stephen Crane's City Sketches." In *American Realism: New Essays*, edited by Eric Sundquist, 138–154. Baltimore, Md.: Johns Hopkins University Press, 1982.

———. *The Incorporation of America: Culture and Society in the Gilded Age*. New York: Hill and Wang, 1982.

Trilling, Lionel. *Sincerity and Authenticity: The Charles Eliot Norton Lectures, 1969–70*. Cambridge, Mass.: Harvard University Press, 1978.

Tuan, Yi-Fu. *Space and Place: The Perspective of Experience*. Minneapolis: University of Minnesota Press, 1977.

Turner, Frederick Jackson. *The Frontier in American History*. 1920. Tucson: University of Arizona Press, 1986.

Urcioli, Bonnie. *Exposing Prejudice: Puerto Rican Experiences of Language, Race, and Class*. Boulder, Colo.: Westview, 1996.

Valaskakis, Gail Guthrie. "Indian Country: Negotiating the Meaning of Land in Native America." In *Disciplinarity and Dissent in Cultural Studies*, edited by Cary Nelson and Dilip Parameshwar Gaonkar, 149–170. New York: Routledge, 1996.

Villa, Raúl Homero. *Barrio-Logos: Space and Place in Urban Chicano Literature and Culture*. Austin: University of Texas Press, 2000.

Vintage. "Author Q & A." Ernesto Quiñonez. Http://www.randomhouse.com/vintage/catalog/display.pperl?isbn=9780375705892&view=qa (accessed 5 July 2008).

Viramontes, Helena Maria. "Neighbors." In *The Moths and Other Stories*, 102–118. Houston, Texas: Arte Público, 1984.

———. *Under the Feet of Jesus*. New York: Dutton, 1995.

Von Hallberg, Robert. "Literature and History: Neat Fits." *Modernism / Modernity* 3 (1996): 115–120.

Wacquant, Loïc. "Ghetto." *International Encyclopedia of the Social and Behavioral Sciences*. Http://sociology.berkeley.edu/faculty/wacquant/wacquant_pdf/GHETTO-IESBS.pdf (accessed 25 April 2007).

Wald, Priscilla. *Constituting Americans: Cultural Anxiety and Narrative Form*. Durham, N.C.: Duke University Press, 1995.

Welty, Eudora. "Place in Fiction." 1977. In *The Eye of the Story: Selected Essays and Reviews*, 116–133. New York: Random House, 1977.

Wasserman, Susana. "Re-creating Recreations on the Lower East Side." In *Remembering the Lower East Side: American Jewish Reflections*, edited by Hasia Diner, Jeffrey Shandler, and Beth S. Wenger, 155–175. Bloomington: Indiana University Press, 2000.

Weisberg, David. "Coming of Age in Samoa and Nebraska." *Nepantla: Views from South* 2, no. 1 (2001): 139–172.

Whalen, Carmen Teresa. *From Puerto Rico to Philadelphia: Puerto Rican Workers and Postwar Economies*. Philadelphia: Temple University Press, 2001.

Wiebe, Robert H. *The Search for Order, 1877–1920*. New York: Hill and Wang, 1967.

Williams, Raymond. *The Country and the City*. London: Oxford University Press, 1973.

Williams, William Appleman. *Empire as a Way of Life. An Essay on the Causes and Character of America's Present Predicament, Along with a Few Thoughts About an Alternative*. New York: Oxford University Press, 1980.

Wilson, Rob. *American Sublime: The Genealogy of a Poetic Genre*. Madison: University of Wisconsin Press, 1991.

———. "Bloody Mary Meets Lois-Ann Yamanaka: Imagining Hawaiian Locality from *South Pacific* to Bamboo Ridge." *Public Culture* 8 (1995): 127–158.

Wirth-Nesher, Hana. "'Shpeaking Plain' and Writing Foreign: Abraham Cahan's *Yekl*." *Poetics Today* 22, no.1 (2001): 41–63.

Wolff, Janet. "The Invisible *Flâneuse*: Women and the Literature of Modernity." *Theory, Culture, and Society* 2 (1985): 37–46.

Wood, Ann Douglas. "The Literature of Impoverishment: The Women Local Colorists in America, 1865–1914." *Women's Studies* 1 (1972): 2–40.

Zagarell, Sandra A. "*Country*'s Portrayal of Community and the Exclusion of Difference." In *New Essays on The Country of Pointed Firs*, edited by June Howard, 39–60. New York: Cambridge University Press, 1994.

Zentella, Ana. *Growing Up Bilingual: Puerto Rican Children in New York*. Malden, Mass.: Blackwell, 1997.

———. "*José Can You See?* Latin@ Responses to Racist Discourse" In *Bilingual Games: Some Literary Investigations*, edited by Doris Sommer, 51–66. New York: Palgrave Macmillan, 2003.

Ziff, Larzer. *The American 1890s: Life and Times of a Lost Generation*. New York: Viking, 1966.

INDEX